CRITICAL THEORY

Critical Theory: The Key Concepts introduces over 300 widely used terms, categories and ideas drawing upon well-established approaches like New Historicism, postmodernism, psychoanalysis, Marxism, and narratology as well as many new critical theories of the last 20 years such as Actor-Network Theory, Global Studies, Critical Race Theory, and Speculative Realism. This book explains the key concepts at the heart of a wide range of influential theorists from Agamben to Žižek. Entries range from concise definitions to longer explanatory essays and include terms such as:

- Aesthetics
- Desire
- Dissensus
- Dromocracy
- Hegemony
- Ideology
- Intersectionality
- Late Capitalism
- Performativity
- Race
- Suture

Featuring cross-referencing throughout, a substantial bibliography and index, *Critical Theory: The Key Concepts* is an accessible and easy-to-use guide. This book is an invaluable introduction covering a wide range of subjects for anyone who is studying or has an interest in critical theory (past and present).

Dino Franco Felluga is Associate Professor of English at Purdue University. In addition to authoring and editing print books, he created the online Introductory Guide to Critical Theory and BRANCH: Britain, Representation and Nineteenth-Century History (branchcollective.org).

CRITICAL THEORY

The Key Concepts

Dino Franco Felluga

Routledge
Taylor & Francis Group

LONDON AND NEW YORK

First published 2015
by Routledge
2 Park Square, Milton Park, Abingdon, Oxon OX14 4RN

and by Routledge
711 Third Avenue, New York, NY 10017

Routledge is an imprint of the Taylor & Francis Group, an informa business

© 2015 Dino Franco Felluga

British Library Cataloguing in Publication Data
A catalogue record for this book is available from the British Library

Library of Congress Cataloging in Publication Data
Felluga, Dino Franco, 1966-
Critical theory : the key concepts / Dino Franco Felluga. -- First edition.
pages cm. -- (Routledge key guides)
1. Critical theory. 2. Criticism. I. Title.
B809.3.F44 2015
142--dc23
2014038955

ISBN: 978-0-415-69566-4 (hbk)
ISBN: 978-0-415-69565-7 (pbk)
ISBN: 978-1-315-71887-3 (ebk)

Typeset in Bembo
by Taylor & Francis Books
Printed by Ashford Colour Press Ltd.

CONTENTS

ACKNOWLEDGEMENTS

I have had the great honor of working with and being supported by a number of incredibly generous critical theorists who have taught and inspired me: as a graduate student at the University of California, Santa Barbara; as a postdoctoral fellow at Stanford University; and as a faculty member at Purdue University. All of the following theorists appear in the pages of this book. I would like particularly to thank Andrew Elfenbein, Regenia Gagnier, Barbara Gelpi, Paul Hernadi, Linda Hutcheon, Alan Liu, Jerome McGann, Elaine Showalter, Garrett Stewart, Herbert F. Tucker, and Hayden White for their guidance and encouragement through the various stages of my career. A number of people have also helped me through the writing of this particular book, including Emily Allen, Barbara Leckie, Maren Linett, Aparajita Sagar, Ryan Schneider, Marjorie Stone, and Marlene Tromp. In particular, I would like to thank two former PhD students of mine, Kenneth Crowell and Adam Watkins, who read through the entire manuscript and helped to keep me clear and honest throughout. About 200 words of my "Note on the Use of this Key Concepts Guide" is drawn from my article, "Theory, Late and Latest," published in *European Romantic Review* 18.2 (2007). A part of my definition of "simulacra" can be found in *"The Matrix*: Paradigm of Post-Modernism or Intellectual Poseur? (Part I)" in Glenn Yeffeth (ed.), 2003, *Taking the Red Pill: Science, Philosophy and Religion in The Matrix*, Dallas: BenBella Books. I thank Taylor & Francis and BenBella Books for permission to use that material here. I reserve my final acknowledgements for the many undergraduate and graduate students that I have taught, first at the University of California, Santa Barbara, where my *Guide to Theory* began as a photocopied hand-out, then at Purdue University, where a Center for Undergraduate Instructional Excellence fellowship in the College of Liberal Arts and an Indiana Higher Education Telecommunication System grant afforded me the time to create the online *Introductory Guide to Critical Theory*.

A NOTE ON THE USE OF THIS KEY CONCEPTS GUIDE

Upon reading of himself referred to as "the late Mark Twain," Twain famously quipped that "Rumors of my death have been greatly exaggerated." And so it is with theory, which, over the last few years, has been pronounced dead over and over again. The reason often given for this premature postmortem is that no new theoretical schools have emerged in the last decade or two with the same force that attended the rise of theories discussed in this book, including Marxism, cultural materialism, feminism, deconstruction, narratology, queer theory, new historicism, postmodernism, and various manifestations of psychoanalysis (Freudian, Lacanian, screen theory, etc.). What has characterized the theoretical work of the last decade is less a declaration of a particular school of thinking or critical methodology than a general implementation of many of the precepts and methods of critical theory in the examination and analysis of disparate cultural objects. Theory has become so much a part of the way critics understand culture and ideology that critics no longer feel the need to insist upon its life signs.

Terry Eagleton puts it well in his provocatively titled *After Theory* (2003): "If theory means a reasonably systematic reflection on our guiding assumptions, it remains as indispensable as ever. But we are living now in the aftermath of what one might call high theory, in an age which, having grown rich on the insights of thinkers like Althusser, Barthes and Derrida, has also in some ways moved beyond them" (2). Where we have moved to is often called Cultural Studies, a wide-ranging examination of various cultural phenomena that had been largely ignored because they were considered "low" or overly marginal: pop music, television, and film; the history of science (especially super-seded technologies or now discredited forms of medicine like phrenology, alchemy, and quackery); past understandings of sex and desire; or any number of ephemera (Byron's boots, Victorian wedding cakes, or early modern cartography, and so on).[1] One thing that theory has done for scholars is to free them from the exclusive exploration of literary texts or "high" historical documents, opening their sights outward to the entire social world.

High school and university classes have followed suit, so that a given survey of literature or history will now commonly include an examination of debates in the sciences, an exploration of penal structures, or an overview of changing sexual mores. Surveys of literature will often include an expanded canon of "great writers" that introduces a plethora of new voices (female, lower class, colonial, queer, populist, and so on) as literary study has changed in response to the insights of feminism, Marxism, postcolonial studies, queer theory, and cultural studies. These changes are informed by the various theories explicated in this book, though teachers will often refer to the various theoretical schools, terms, and proponents only in passing.

In other words, it is difficult for students not to be confronted by the ideas in this book at some point in their education. And yet, there are surprisingly few easily accessible sources to guide students who seek help with the often-difficult ideas being discussed in their courses or to explain to non-academics the concepts behind such disparate pop-cultural works as *The Matrix* trilogy, which is inspired by the theoretical work of Jean Baudrillard, or *Fight Club* and *Buffy: The Vampire Slayer*, which draw especially on Lacanian psychoanalysis and theories of gender and sex. The essay collections and introductions that have been published tend to be narrow in their interests and emphases, often concentrating on only one approach. Such collections are also often pitched at a level too difficult for students and non-academics to access easily.

In response to what I perceived as a lack of accessible guides to theory, I created my own, online *Guide to Critical Theory* (www.cla. purdue.edu/english/theory/). *Critical Theory: The Key Concepts* represents the most up-to-date version of any material found on the website (which makes up less than a fifth of this book and where one can still go for additional material). Almost every entry in the online *Guide to Critical Theory* has been updated or expanded in some way for this book. I have also tried here to represent how critical theory has developed over the last decade, with entries on such recent approaches as Actor-Network Theory, Cognitive Studies, Digital Humanities, Thing Theory, Ecocriticism, Global Studies, Cosmopolitanism, Critical Race Theory, and Speculative Realism, as well as concepts from the work of Giorgio Agamben, Alain Badiou, Pierre Bourdieu, Manuel DeLanda, Michael Hardt, Ernesto Laclau, Bruno Latour, Quentin Messailloux, Franco Moretti, Chantal Mouffe, Antonio Negri, Jacques

Rancière, Paul Virilio, and Slavoj Žižek. The website still offers me a space to respond to readers of this book and to include such additional material as lesson plans, sample applications of the theoretical concepts, and links to helpful websites.

The concepts discussed in this guide are often quite closely interrelated. When I mention a term that is included elsewhere in this Key Concepts book and that may require further explanation, I have highlighted it in bold; however, keep in mind that many words that are central to critical theory are sometimes used in their more traditional sense; in such cases I have not presented them in bold. For example, if I write that "ideology holds power over us," everyone can understand what is meant by "power" in that sentence; however, when a theorist uses "power," the scholar often expects that you understand the term in the sense articulated by critical theorists, especially Michel Foucault. In such cases, you will find "power" in bold.

Unlike other Routledge Key Concepts books, this one seeks to represent a variety of critical approaches, which means that a few terms discussed in this guide are particularly fraught, as they have been understood differently by different critical theorists. For these terms (for example, "ideology" or "history" or "gender" or "postmodernism"), you will find significantly longer entries that seek to untangle the different ways the concept has been understood over time by different schools of thought. Rather than provide a pat definition, then, I attempt here to explain the complexity of critical theory while seeking to be as clear and accessible as possible. Given the emphasis of this series on "key concepts," I have spent more time elaborating concepts than I have in providing in-depth overviews of the schools themselves. So, the entry on Frankfurt School asks you simply to read the Introduction where I discuss the school; I reserve explanation of the school's key concepts to entries on the concepts themselves. Throughout the book, I also try, when possible, to include quotations from the original theorists. I hope that this approach will embolden readers of this book to explore the original theoretical works themselves.

NOTE

1 My list alludes to various studies: Paul Youngquist's *Monstrosity* (2003), especially Chapter 7 ("Imperial Legs"); Emily Allen's "Culinary Exhibition: Victorian Wedding Cakes and Royal Spectacle" (2003); and Richard Helgerson's *Forms of Nationhood* (1992), especially Chapter 3 ("The Land Speaks").

INTRODUCTION

An archaeology of the Western subject

To comprehend what contemporary critical theory is attempting to do, one should consider the place of these ideas in a longer history of human thought. Indeed, critical theorists themselves tend to tell a story about the progression of human (particularly Western) thought that goes back to the beginnings of recorded history, to a time before what we now take for granted as "natural" became so, and that moment tends to be, for these critical theorists, ancient Greece and Rome, circa 1,000–400 BCE.[1] For example, Jean-François Lyotard and J.-L. Thébaud in *Just Gaming* (1985) go back to ancient pre-literate Greece to elucidate Lyotard's **postmodern** sense of justice; to theorize **feminist** and radical politics, Judith Butler in *Antigone's Claim* (2000) engages Sophocles' play, *Antigone*; to establish **deconstruction's** claims, Jacques Derrida (1981) returns to Plato; to understand the workings of the modern **nation-state**, Giorgio Agamben (1998, 2005) turns to ancient Greek and Roman culture; to make sense of **capitalism**, Karl Marx and Friedrich Engels (1932) theorize how society was structured when it relied on earlier **modes of production**; to establish his theory of **communicative action**, Jürgen Habermas contrasts modern rationality with the "mythological interpretation of the world" (1987: 45) characteristic of oral societies; to illustrate that biological notions of **race** are really **ideological**, theorists of **race** turn to earlier periods "to envisage a time before **race**, which in turn may assist in the struggle to build a future without racism" (H. Scott 2002: 181); to make sense of our contemporary understanding of **sexuality**, Michel Foucault (1990) looks backwards to ancient Greek society. The effort to understand what came before our current way of thinking allows theorists to put now **naturalized** forms of thought into historical context. As Pierre Bourdieu puts it, "there is no more potent tool for rupture than the reconstruction of genesis: by bringing back into view the conflicts and confrontations of the early beginnings and therefore all the discarded possibles, it retrieves the possibility that things could have been (and still could be) otherwise (1998: 40).

Foucault's entire career is driven by such a desire to bring back into view the conflicts and confrontations of the early beginnings and therefore all the discarded possibles, a methodology which he dubs **archaeology**. The ultimate goal of Foucault's methodology, which has been particularly influential on many of the theories discussed in this book, is to illustrate how any historical period is made up of disparate **discourses** (ways of knowing and structuring the world through language), which exist in a discontinuous relation to each other. In other words, these competing **discourses** can never be subsumed into a single all-encompassing concept or spirit of the age—though these **discourses** are shaped by the age in which they exist. Whereas historians have tended to understand historical change as a continuous **narrative**, Foucault argues that historical change occurs by way of rupture and discontinuity, a claim that is influenced by a **Marxist** and **neo-Marxist** understanding of **history**. The realization that our contemporary understanding of **narrative** structure is itself of recent invention (as explored, for example, by Hayden White) is just one example among many of how critical theory rethinks **naturalized** ideas by way of **archaeological** investigation.[2]

It is also impossible to make sense of our own period, which has been dubbed the **postmodern period** or **postmodernity** and is itself the subject of much theorizing, without understanding what came before. How can we understand the full force of that "post" without understanding not only the modern but also the premodern? We must keep in mind that one important aspect of **postmodern** theory is the effort to understand how technological innovations unique to the present (the computer, the Internet, television) are having transformative effects on human consciousness. As a result, **postmodern** critics often look backwards to the changes implemented by earlier technologies that we now take for granted— especially the written word, a tool that has become so **naturalized** that we tend not to think about it as a technology that affects our thought processes. By making sense of the transformative changes effected by earlier technologies, **postmodern** critics feel better able to recognize the transformative effects of more recent tools like the Internet.

This introduction therefore seeks to put in context the critical terms that are explained in the following pages and illustrates the ways that critical theory engages a rather long historical trajectory. I finish by defining critical theory and situating the rise of this way of thinking within a historical trajectory of its own.

PRE-LITERATE CULTURE

As I stated above, one way to understand the transformative but largely unnoticed changes effected by new technologies in the **postmodern** period is to think about the way the printed word changed our way of thinking about the world. That can then help us to think about the ways **postmodern** technologies (like the computer, the television, film, and mechanical image production) might be subtly but fundamentally changing our way of thinking about the world around us. An exercise I find useful when I introduce orality to students is to ask the question: "What is a tree?" as I did, for example, in a past class that started with Homer's *Odyssey*. As my students most ably responded on one particularly notable day, a tree is a plant with bark, branches, and leaves. A taxonomy of different examples was given (ash, oak, etc.), categorized by conifer and deciduous kinds. "Photosynthesis" and "oxygenation" were mentioned as important aspects of a tree's life cycle, and then different uses for trees were mentioned (paper, construction, shade, etc.). The class unanimously agreed with this definition. I then explained that studies of those oral cultures that still exist in the world have asked the same question of non-literate people.[3] Surprisingly, there too the response to the question was, for the most part, unanimous and yet completely different from our own: asked to explain what a tree is, the non-literate respondent will resist: "Why should I? Everyone knows what a tree is, they don't need me telling them" (Ong 1982: 53). If pushed, the non-literate respondent will often tie the definition to the human lifeworld, for example: "Well, a tree is like a man, whose arms reach up to heaven but whose roots are caught in hell." Why this radical difference in response?

The main reason we, in a literate culture, all unanimously agree with our definition is that we automatically turn to our communal literate source—the dictionary, which structures our experience of the world through the conventions of science and taxonomy (hence my class's use of such scientific language as "photosynthesis," "conifer," "deciduous," and "oxygenation," terms that clearly suggest that my students were drawn to language of a different register than quotidian oral speech). In an oral culture, there is no written source to which people can turn; there are instead oral stories and the world around us: "Oral cultures," writes Walter Ong, "tend to use concepts in situational, operational frames of reference that are minimally abstract in the sense that they remain close to the living human lifeworld" (1982: 49). As a result, oral society differs from our own in a number of fundamental ways. Looking at the difference between the present and pre-literate society is one of the ways that critical theorists seek to clarify how our own values—for example, our **empirical** faith in science, progress, and the direct connection between words and things—are contingent on historical change and therefore **ideologically** grounded. Consider, for example, the following basic concepts.

HISTORY

In an oral society, knowledge is based on what is relevant in the present: the stories that are told by rhapsodes change as social situations change.[4] The stories themselves are accreted versions of a story that has been told orally by countless rhapsodes, each changing elements of the story in the telling. For this reason, one can find clues of earlier times through story elements that persist even after Greek society was transformed by new technologies. In the *Odyssey*, for example, we can detect layers of archaeology (elements from the bronze age and iron age coexist, for example, as do eating habits from earlier stages in the development of Greek society). While some older elements persist, other story elements can change altogether according to the relevance of details to present-day listeners. A story about a king who had three sons can, over time, turn into a story about a king who had two sons if the third son's genealogical line never continued. Stories are determined far less by "facts" than by pragmatic concerns in the present— what will be most useful to listeners at the moment of telling. Oral narratives precede the demands for consistency and cause-and-effect logic that we are familiar with in, say, nineteenth-century novels. The very understanding of temporality was different. Narratives, including histories, tended to be episodic and repetitive or cyclical and had little compunction about mixing historical fact and literary fiction.

Critical theorists turn back to these earlier narratives to illustrate that contemporary beliefs in progress or historical "truth" are really social **ideologies** that can be challenged in favor of alternative models. Lyotard for example questions all **grand narratives** (like that of historical progress) in favor of what he terms *petits récits* or little stories. In *Metahistory*, Hayden White illustrates that **positivist** history is secretly structured by fictional, generic models. The mixing of fact and fiction—what Linda Hutcheon terms **historiographic metafiction**— has become an important aspect of **postmodern** creative work, from E. L. Doctorow's *Ragtime* to Oliver Stone's *JFK* or Steven Spielberg's *Schindler's List*. As Hutcheon puts it, it is the "very separation of the literary and the historical that is now being challenged in **postmodern** theory and art, and recent critical readings of both history and fiction have focused more on what the two modes of writing share than on how they differ" (1988: 105).

LAW

In an oral culture, without a book of rules to establish precedent, justice had to be determined by way of competing accounts and in a case-by-case manner. Examples in the *Odyssey* include the fact that Telemachus and the suitors in Book II must engage in a contest of storytelling in front of the elders of Ithaca in order to determine who is in the right; another example is how Helen and Meneláus engage in a storytelling contest of sorts in Book IV, with the prize being the very reputation of Helen. In such a society, a leader like Odysseus must have not only martial strength and skill but also a knowledge of common stories (that can be called on as we call on precedent) and also a certain amount of rhetorical guile (which is why Odysseus keeps getting placed in situations where he has no men, weapons, armor, or even clothes to aid him). Some critical theorists look back to this more **performative**, context-by-context justice of oral societies for an alternative model of justice to our own; in this effort, many theorists have questioned the tendency in our present-day society to see law and justice as synonymous, or the tendency to apply one set of laws to all groups. Lyotard in *Just Gaming* (1985) for example aligns the two phrases, "Let us be pagan" and "Let us be just" (19), arguing that pre-literate "pagan" societies are more just because they have no prescriptive system that determines what is just, an overarching system made possible by the permanence that writing affords (hence the "script" in prescriptive). "Paganism" for Lyotard is "a name, neither better nor worse than others, for the denomination of a situation in which one judges without criteria" (16).

AUTHORSHIP

In an oral society, there is no "**author**" in the modern sense, since stories are passed on for hundreds of years by many generations of rhapsodes. As a result, there is some question about who exactly "Homer" might have been, whether the authorship of both the *Iliad* and *Odyssey* can be attributed to this one figure, and whether the very idea of associating a single figure with these two tales is a mere fiction. Authorship and the ownership of original work are integrally connected to the establishment of literate culture (which allows you, for example, to keep records of original authorship). Copyright is only possible after you can *write copy*, you might say.

Critical theory tends to view the category of the author with suspicion, given how integral it has been for the establishment of **capitalist** culture and how much the original reasons for copyright (especially the protection of authorial creativity) have been perverted by multinational corporations intent on squelching the sort of creativity that resembles the communal or what we would now consider the plagiaristic methods of pre-literate and medieval "**authors**" like Homer or Chaucer. Examples in **postmodern** culture include open source software, hip hop, mash-ups, the Creative Commons movement, **historiographic metafiction**, and what Fredric Jameson terms **pastiche**.

SUBJECTIVITY

Our contemporary notion of a private self appears not to apply in the same way to earlier cultures. In an oral culture, **subjectivity** appears to be directed outward to others and to **performative** situations. Even classical architecture favors an atrium structure oriented to public spaces with no doors and little privacy. Public baths are popular. Some critics have characterized as "shame culture" this culture of public-oriented selves. In a shame culture, everything occurs, as it were, on the surface of things. Emotions are extreme and public because, as scholars have argued, people in this culture do not have our modern sense of **subjectivity** or of a private self. What therefore becomes important are questions of honor and shame, which is why, for example, Odysseus must immediately respond to the challenge of Euryalus during the Phaeacian games in Book VIII of the *Odyssey*. Questions of propriety and reputation become paramount, since in an oral society collective memory is only preserved through the stories that others tell about you.

Critical theorists look to this earlier model of **subjectivity** in order to argue that the at once **naturalized** and transcendent version of the **subject** that developed over the course of the nineteenth century is really an **ideological** construction that serves the interests of particular groups, especially the rising middle class. The emphasis in critical theory is on the historical conditions allowing for the establishment of a particular identity formation, as well as the alternative models of **subjectivity** that failed to become dominant in a given period. Foucault in defending queer identity for example goes backwards to ancient Greece in order to articulate an alternative model of subject formation, which he dubs "an aesthetics of existence" (1990: 2.10). Unlike the post-Christian emphasis on "codifications of conducts and the strict definition of what is permitted and what is forbidden"

(2.30), the early Greeks placed the accent, rather, "on the relationship with the self that enabled a person to keep from being carried away by the appetites and pleasures, ... to achieve a mode of being that could be defined by the full enjoyment of oneself, or the perfect supremacy of oneself over oneself" (2.31).

SEX

Of particular interest to theorists of **gender** and **sexuality** is the apparently greater acceptance of same-sex relations in ancient culture: between men, between men and boys, and between women. (This is not to suggest that the Greeks could not be exceptionally misogynistic, as the infamous passages against women in Hesiod's *Theogony* and Homer's *Odyssey* attest.) Foucault in his *The Use of Pleasure* looks back to this earlier culture in order to propose an alternative model for not only gay identity but also the modern **subject**. "Putting it schematically," Foucault explains, "we could say that classical antiquity's moral reflection concerning the pleasures was not directed towards a codification of acts, nor toward a **hermeneutics** of the **subject**, but toward a stylization of attitudes and an aesthetics of existence" (1990: 2.92). In other words, each individual had a greater say in their own personally stylized version of the self.[5] Another influential critic is Thomas Laqueur, who, in *Making Sex* (1990), explores how **sexuality** from the ancients through the Renaissance was structured quite differently than it was in the nineteenth century or is today. Specifically, he illustrates how science prior to the mid-eighteenth century tended to perceive men and women as versions of one sex, so to speak; women were seen, that is, as lesser men, with the clitoris and the uterus just reduced or inverted versions of the penis and scrotum. Such a one-sex model, as Laqueur terms it, meant that the differences between men and women were not clear (or even so important) in these early medical texts; both men and women were seen as parts (if unequal parts) of a larger cosmological order, as opposed to radically different and mutually exclusive creatures (the two-sex model). Laqueur insists that the difference in perception when it came to anatomy was not because of the stupidity of the pre-Renaissance observers but because of a different way of conceiving **sexuality**, just as our current perceptions about sex are being determined as much by political and epistemological structures as by "reality." Given such a historical record, Laqueur concludes that **sexuality** itself (rather than just gender) is something that is historically determined. As he puts it,

This book, then, is about the making not of **gender**, but of **sex**. I have no interest in denying the reality of **sex** or of sexual dimorphism as an evolutionary process. But I want to show on the basis of historical evidence that almost everything one wants to *say* about **sex**—however **sex** is understood—already has in it a claim about **gender**. **Sex**, in both the one-sex and the two-sex worlds, is situational; it is explicable only within the context of battles over **gender** and **power**. (1990: 11)

Laqueur thus places himself in the camp of a group of critics following in the wake of Foucault and **poststructuralism** who contest even the traditional **feminist** distinction between **nature** (one's bodily sex) and nurture (one's acquired **gender**). He argues, rather, that "Sometime in the eighteenth century, **sex** as we know it was invented" (149).

HUMAN RIGHTS

The concept of inalienable human rights, which is closely tied to the eighteenth-century understanding of the **subject**, is a construction of Enlightenment thinking. In previous cultures, by contrast, punishment is severe and, ideally, public, in order to illustrate the power and superiority of the punishing authority, e.g., Odysseus' extremely violent and brutal punishment of his unfaithful slaves and of the suitors seeking Penelope's hand. And yet, there is no sense that Odysseus has any "right" to be a leader. He remains a leader only so long as his power of might and his power of words enable him to stay in power. Were he to be defeated and enslaved, the best he could then do is to become a worthy slave (which is why so much time is spent with the worthy slave Eumáios in Books XIV to XVI). There is also no sense that there is any moral wrong in enslaving, raping, or decimating one's defeated enemies.

We tend to look back at the brutality of earlier penal systems and congratulate ourselves for having reformed our systems in such a way as to make such brutal violence no longer acceptable. That reform occurred because of the principles of the Enlightenment laid out below. Inspired first by Frankfurt School theorists such as Max Horkheimer and Theodor Adorno—who argued in *Dialectic of Enlightenment* that the Enlightenment did not enter mankind "into a truly human condition" but rather sank us "into a new kind of barbarism" (1944: xi)—and influenced subsequently by Michel Foucault's work on medicine (*Birth of the Clinic* [1975]), sexuality (*History of Sexuality* [1990]), psychiatry (*Madness and Civilization* [1965]), and penal reform (*Discipline and*

Punish [1977a]), critical theorists tend to question the extent to which Enlightenment principles really are as liberating as they seem at first blush. In particular, they question how the promise of inalienable rights developed alongside an ever-increasing emphasis on the regulation of the "normal." One is no longer subject to cruel and unusual punishment, be it in the prison or the insane asylum; instead, one is subject to experts seeking to rehabilitate us towards some conception of the normal. As Foucault puts it, "The judges of normality are present everywhere. We are in the society of the teacher-judge, the doctor-judge, the educator-judge, the 'social-worker'-judge; it is on them that the universal reign of the normative is based; and each individual, wherever he may find himself, subjects to it his body, his gestures, his behaviour, his aptitudes, his achievements" (1977a: 304). In the extreme, such an insistence on an increasingly medicalized version of normal **subjectivity** serves to suppress the rights of those groups deemed abnormal. Critics often keep Nazi Germany in mind because the judicial and legislative structures of Weimer society were established on Enlightenment principles yet those principles did not succeed in preventing the Holocaust from occurring. Foucault also illustrates how what replaces the old system of punishment, what he terms our current **carceral** system, is much more invasive, aided as it is by new mechanisms for the surveillance of people (from the nineteenth-century invention of the census to the computer-assisted information technology of today).

MONEY

As one of my students, Stacey Morgan, brilliantly put it in the class that I mentioned earlier, in pre-literate society "you could not buy more than you already have." Money, production, consumption, and labor could not be understood as abstract quantities that could be bought and sold on the open market (as they are through stocks, bonds, loans, and interest accretion in a transnational economy of limitless investment and speculation). Instead you paid the individual craftsman directly through barter and, thus, through a direct valuation of that laborer's particular product. As my student Meg Young-Spillers put it, in response, you are by force closer to the "materiality" of the individual's labor. Meg thus used the very terminology employed by Marx in the nineteenth century to critique **capitalist** culture.

Marx explains that in a barter society the objects exchanged are tied closely both to the **use value** of the objects (their immediate usefulness) and to the real, material **labor** expended to produce the object.

In **capitalism**, that concrete **labor** tends to get translated into an abstract quantity that can then stand as an **equivalent-form** that one can use to determine the exchangeability of all sorts of products. In this way, "concrete labour ... becomes the expression of abstract human labor" (1867: 150). We thus begin to move towards a "**universal equivalent**": a single abstract measure by which one can facilitate the exchange of categorically different items on the market. By accepting **money** as the **universal equivalent**, **capitalism** eventually manages to exploit the laborer upon whom all value ultimately inheres, according to Marx. That is, **money** tends to hide the real value behind any monetary exchange: **labor**. According to Marx, the more **labor** it takes to produce a product, the greater its value. Marx therefore concludes that "As **exchange-values**, all **commodities** are merely definite quantities of congealed **labour-time**" (1867: 130). However, what happens in a **capitalist** society is that people tend to believe that power and value really inhere in the **money-form** rather than in the **labor** that actually produces goods and services, leading to what Marx terms "**commodity fetishism**." To provide an alternative to such a system, Marx often looks backwards to **feudal** and primitive society for communal models of production.

THE EARLY MODERN TO THE ENLIGHTENMENT AND BEYOND

In addition to exploring the ancient past for differences from our current way of thinking, critical theory is interested in how what we take for granted as "truth" was, in fact, constructed over the last 400 years or so. Indeed, I have already given a few examples in the sections preceding this one. The Renaissance (sometimes termed the "early modern" because of its importance to our current way of thinking) is an important moment in this investigation. The Renaissance was a time of questioning and scientific discovery or re-discovery (acceptance of a Copernican vs. a Ptolemaic universe; advances in the natural sciences; questioning of the literal truth of the Bible; the first European universities) and a time of political revolution, particularly Oliver Cromwell's Republic in England; ideas circulating, if not implemented, during Cromwell's Republic included the extension of suffrage, freedom of religion, freedom of the press, and a social contract between rulers and ruled. The Renaissance Republics of Venice and Florence, which were so influential culturally on the rest of Europe in the period, were two other important experiments in the privileging of the state and the market over the church and hereditary monarchy.

Some of these changes can be attributed to a new "humanist" way of understanding; that is, various movements in the period put increasing emphasis on "the human" as distinct from the divine in understanding the world and ourselves, which impacts such disparate areas as politics, literature, science, and art. Art is a good example as it makes visible this shift; suddenly in the Renaissance, in a departure from Medieval and Byzantine art, painters moved increasingly away from religious subjects in order to represent individual people (the portrait), the human body (nudes), and simple material objects (the still life). Even the new technique of "perspective," where the art work is represented as if from the perspective of a single viewer, thus reproducing the three-dimensional view of a single human observer (what we now take for granted as representational art), takes us away from the religious symbolism of earlier artwork in order to put new emphasis on a given individual and what that individual sees.

This is not to say that religion lacked importance in the period, though changes in thinking about the human subject affected religion too. One important shift explored by critical theorists is the movement from ancient "shame culture" into a monotheistic belief system and the "guilt culture" it helped to instantiate. A helpful text to think through this transition is John Milton's Renaissance work, *Paradise Lost*, which tends to relegate the values of an oral, polytheistic shame culture to Satan and his cohort. The real epic battle here occurs instead internally as Eve must struggle against temptation. In a guilt culture, unlike in a shame culture, identity suddenly becomes "vertical," existing on a deep scale of internal struggle (think, for example, of the Freudian super-ego– ego–id model of human subjectivity). In short, the private self is invented, such that Milton can write, "The mind is its own place, and in itself/ Can make a Heav'n of Hell, a Hell of Heav'n" (1674: 1.254–55). In this post-Christian culture, we are all always already guilty, thanks to original sin, which Milton puts at the center of his monotheistic epic vision. By this same logic, we are also all, to some extent, equal (no one deserves to throw the first stone): slavery, warfare for mere material gain, misogyny, and rape must, by this logic, be seen as morally corrupt. At least, that is the logical extension of this shift, which would eventually reach its apogée in Enlightenment philosophy and then the legal and penal reforms of the nineteenth century. Every person according to this way of thinking, no matter how lowly, possesses certain inalienable rights that must never be denied.

One can see earlier manifestations of this transition in the movement from the Old Testament's "jealous God," Jahweh, to the sacrificing Christ of the New Testament. Indeed, the New Testament at various points must actively rewrite those passages in the Old Testament more evocative of the older shame culture, for example the following lines from Leviticus, Chapter 24:19–21:

19. And if a man cause a blemish in his neighbour; as he hath done, so shall it be done to him; 20. Breach for breach, eye for eye, tooth for tooth: as he hath caused a blemish in a man, so shall it be done to him again. 21. And he that killeth a beast, he shall restore it: and he that killeth a man, he shall be put to death.

Compare these to Matthew, Chapter 5:38–45:

38. Ye have heard that it hath been said, An eye for an eye, and a tooth for a tooth: 39. But I say unto you, That ye resist not evil: but whosoever shall smite thee on thy right cheek, turn to him the other also ... 43. Ye have heard that it hath been said, Thou shalt love thy neighbour, and hate thine enemy. 44. But I say unto you, Love your enemies, bless them that curse you, do good to them that hate you, and pray for them which despitefully use you, and persecute you; 45. That ye may be the children of your Father which is in heaven: for he maketh his sun to rise on the evil and on the good, and sendeth rain on the just and on the unjust.

This transition into a monotheistic belief system and the Renaissance shift to humanistic ways of thinking are both aided by the movement into literate culture but even more so by the movement to print culture, which was introduced in the Renaissance. (The transition is sometimes referred to as the Gutenberg revolution, after Johann Gutenberg, who is credited with the invention of the printing press or, more properly, movable type.) When one can write down and then print scripture, as Gutenberg did, the Bible becomes something that achieves the effect of permanence, therefore leading to the belief that one should not change it or even represent it (as the Puritan iconoclasts, for example, believed). The writing down of scripture and then its publication in the vernacular, however, also brings religion to the individual reader. As a result, the Puritans also opposed the hierarchical organization of Roman Catholicism, particularly the episcopacy (bishops), since they argued that each individual has the ability to access the word of God directly through the written word without the aid of such intermediaries.

Foucault reads in such disparate cultural shifts the very creation of the modern **nation-state**. In "The Subject and Power" (1982), for example, he argues that the church's form of "pastoral **power**" served to "spread new power relations throughout the ancient world" (214). Although "ecclesiastical institutionalization ... has ceased or at least lost its vitality since the eighteenth century," the function of pastoral **power** "has spread and multiplied outside the ecclesiastical institution" (214), adopted as it was by the emergent **nation-state**, particularly pastoral **power**'s emphasis on the sins and salvation of an individual's inner mind and soul. According to Foucault, "We have to promote new forms of **subjectivity** through the refusal of this kind of individuality which has been imposed on us for several centuries" (216).

The Enlightenment of the eighteenth century largely solidified the shifts that began to be felt in the Renaissance, putting ever more emphasis on human reason's ability to discover the truth of the world. On the one hand, Enlightenment philosophers and scientists posited a world of stable, unchanging truths achieved through reason and science. The human subject is perfectible and knowable; hierarchies, if based on reason (which is eternal), should not be contested. On the other hand, the continuing emphasis placed on the reasoning human **subject** as the center of this worldview ultimately led to the revolutions of the period, most notably the American Revolution of 1775 and the French Revolution of 1789, both of which were guided to a significant extent by Enlightenment philosophy.

The reforms of the nineteenth century in turn instantiated many of the shifts that began in the early modern period: prison reform rejected spectacular punishment in favor of the rehabilitation of the delinquent or abnormal **subject**; democracy shifted power from the aristocracy to the bourgeoisie; the modern **nation-state** came into existence; the industrial revolution reorganized society by the logic of maximum efficiency; the rise of literacy solidified for the masses the impact of Gutenberg's print revolution; government-financed public education and the expansion of the university system ensured the "enlightenment" of all people, regardless of class; the modern medical professions increasingly gained supremacy in codifying and proscribing the "normal" human **subject**.

THE RISE OF CRITICAL THEORY

The rise of critical theory can be traced to these changes of the late eighteenth and nineteenth centuries. Two figures from this time are important to mention as early influences on the concept of "critical" theory. However much Immanuel Kant's notion of the "transcendental subject" may itself be critiqued by critical theory, it is also true that in his works, *The Critique of Pure Reason* (1781), *The Critique of Practical*

Reason (1788), and *The Critique of Judgement* (1790), Kant established "critique" as an activity practiced by the autonomous, rational **subject**, who, untrammeled by the rules of authority, must seek to dispel all myths and unsubstantiated beliefs through the rigorous implementation of reason. What distinguishes critical theory from this autonomous **subject** is the insistence that all such critique must also be politically engaged. Marx was an important figure in recasting critique along these lines. Indeed, the first volume of Marx's magisterial work, *Capital* (1867), had as its subtitle "A Critique of Political Economy" and sought, like Kant's philosophical work, to dispel all ideological obfuscations, though in this case the goal was explicitly to change society through revolution. By showing **proletarian** workers how bourgeois **ideology** alienates and exploits them, Marx believed that he could effect an international communist revolution.

The term "critical theory" was actually dubbed by Max Horkheimer in his 1937 essay "Traditional and Critical Theory" (Horkheimer 1972). A **neo-Marxist**, Horkheimer and the Frankfurt School to which he belonged sought to rethink Marx's theories in light of the fact that the revolutions Marx predicted did not, in fact, occur. As with Marx, critical theory for Horkheimer seeks always to fight **ideological** mystification, class oppression, and **hegemony** with the goal of changing society for the better. Such a critical attitude, for Horkheimer, "is suspicious of the very categories of better, useful, appropriate, productive, and valuable, as these are understood in the present order, and refuses to take them as nonscientific presuppositions about which one can do nothing" (1972: 207). This critical stance questions one of the principles of bourgeois thought, the very idea of autonomous **subjectivity** that was developed from the Renaissance to the present and that Kant helped to theorize: "Bourgeois thought," according to Horkheimer, "is essentially abstract, and its principle is an individuality which inflatedly believes itself to be the ground of the world or even to be the world without qualification, an individuality separated off from events" (210). Horkheimer began his work in Germany, from which he fled after the rise of Nazism. Not surprisingly, he was also concerned with the contrary attitude whereby the **subject** is read as "the unproblematic expression of an already constituted society; an example would be a nationalist **ideology**" (210). Critical thinking seeks to counter both of these stances: "Critical thinking is the function neither of the isolated individual nor of a sum-total of individuals" (210–11). It seeks instead always to question all aspects of the current system of society, to be "critical of the present" (218), with the goal of instantiating new social forms, a "better reality" (217), a "society without injustices"

(221). It must also be prepared to critique idealistic tendencies in its own thinking: the theoretician "exercises an aggressive critique not only against the conscious defenders of the status quo but also against distracting, conformist, or utopian tendencies within his own household" (216). Unlike the "detached" figure of the ivory-tower "liberalist intelligentsia" (224), the critical theorist is, then, politically engaged while never being what Horkheimer terms "deeply rooted" in one **ideological** stance, as in totalitarian propaganda (223–24).

It is no coincidence that Horkheimer articulates his notion of critical theory at the time of Nazi Germany and the Holocaust. That period in Germany marks a significant moment in world history (and for critical theory) precisely because Weimar Germany, which directly preceded the rise of Nazism, had all the hallmarks of modern society and differed little from the countries that eventually formed the Allied Powers: democracy, a justice system, widespread literacy, religion, a revered university system, libraries, technological advances, scientific advances, **capitalism**, and high culture of all stripes. Yet none of that protected the country from descending into the barbarism of the Holocaust. That fact has led many critical theorists to question everything associated with progress, truth, civilization, science, and so on.

As practiced today, critical theory often adopts a political stance on the present, with the goal of forming a more just society, even when far removed from the **Marxist** roots of Horkheimer's thinking. Judith Butler for example adopts the notion of "**radical democracy**" in making sense of her struggle to defend queer identity; such critical theory sees itself as engaged in a project of "permanent political contest" (1993: 222), as she puts it. However, "critical theory" as a methodology has also developed beyond, while still very much influenced by, the Frankfurt School's emphasis on social transformation and has become a general term for the theoretical analysis of **culture** at large, thus bringing under its umbrella a tradition of thinking that extends from the **structuralists** of the modern period to the **deconstructionist** and **postmodern** theorists of the last 50 years. In this sort of critical theory, the aim is not so narrowly specific social change through the analysis of **class** antagonism than it is the examination of the larger linguistic and **ideological** structures by which we make sense of, while thus ideologically constructing, the world around us.

NOTES

1 Note that postcolonial theorists sometimes question critical theory's Eurocentric tendencies (see **Postcolonial Studies**).

2 For Hayden White's examination of narrative structure through the ages, see, in particular, Chapter One of *The Content of the Form* (1987), "The Value of Narrativity in the Representation of Reality." See also his work, *Metahistory* (1973).

3 For an overview, see Walter J. Ong (1982), pp. 49–57.

4 **Postcolonial Studies** might question the Eurocentrism of critical theory's tendency to concentrate on ancient Greek oral culture; postcolonial theorists can make a similar maneuver by turning to oral forms from other traditions, as does Spivak in analyzing the representation of rumor in work by the **Subaltern** Studies group (1988b: 21–26).

5 Note that I have throughout the manuscript adopted the grammatically incorrect "their" to follow the singular "each," thus conforming to the advice of **LGBTQ** theory, which suggests that we not delimit **sexual** identity to "his" or "her," which would be "grammatically" correct in this instance.

LIST OF KEY CONCEPTS

CRITICAL THEORY

The Key Concepts

ABJECT (ABJECTION)

In psychoanalysis, "abjection" is our reaction (horror, vomit) to a threatened breakdown in meaning caused by the loss of the distinction between **subject** and **object** or between self and **other**. The primary example is the corpse (which traumatically reminds us of our own materiality, thus making us feel like an **object** rather than a **subject**); however, other items can elicit the same reaction: an open wound, shit, sewage, even a particularly immoral crime (e.g., Auschwitz). The Lacanian feminist, Julia Kristeva, theorizes the concept in her influential work, *The Powers of Horror: An Essay on Abjection*. Kristeva posits that abjection is something that we must experience in our psychosexual development before entering into **the mirror stage**. On the level of archaic memory (what we superseded when we entered civilization), Kristeva refers to the primitive effort to separate ourselves from the animal: "by way of abjection, primitive societies have marked out a precise area of their culture in order to remove it from the threatening world of animals or animalism" (Kristeva 1982: 12–13). On the level of our individual psychosexual development, the abject marks the moment when we separated ourselves from the mother, when we began to recognize a boundary between "me" and **other**, between "me" and "(m)other." According to Kristeva, the abject is necessary since it teaches us how to set up boundaries, for example between self and other or between human and animal. Kristeva argues that the abject marks our movement out of what she terms the maternal **chora**.

More specifically, Kristeva associates the abject with the eruption of the **Real** into our lives. In particular, she associates such a response with our rejection of death's insistent materiality. Our reaction to such abject material makes us feel in immediate bodily ways what is essentially a pre-lingual response (something we went through as a child before we entered into language and the conventions of society). Kristeva therefore is quite careful to differentiate *knowledge* of death or the *meaning* of death (both of which can exist within the **symbolic order**) from the traumatic experience of being confronted with the sort of materiality that *shows you* your own death:

> A wound with blood and pus, or the sickly, acrid smell of sweat, of decay, does not *signify* death. In the presence of signified death—a flat encephalograph, for instance—I would understand, react, or accept. No, as in true theater, without makeup or masks, refuse and corpses *show me* what I permanently thrust aside

3

in order to live. These body fluids, this defilement, this shit are what life withstands, hardly and with difficulty, on the part of death. There, I am at the border of my condition as a living being. (Kristeva 1982: 3)

The corpse especially exemplifies Kristeva's concept since it literalizes the breakdown of the distinction between **subject** and **object** that is crucial for the establishment of identity and for our entrance into the **symbolic order**. What we are confronted with when we experience the trauma of seeing a human corpse (particularly the corpse of a friend or family member) is our own eventual death made palpably real. As Kristeva puts it, "The corpse, seen without God and outside of science, is the utmost of abjection. It is death infecting life. Abject" (Kristeva 1982: 4).

The abject must also be distinguished from **desire** (which is tied up with the meaning-structures of the **symbolic order**). It is associated, rather, with both fear and *jouissance*. In phobia, Kristeva reads the trace of a pre-linguistic confrontation with the abject, a moment that precedes the recognition of any actual object of fear: "The phobic object shows up at the place of non-objectal states of **drive** and assumes all the mishaps of **drive** as disappointed desires or as desires diverted from their objects" (Kristeva 1982: 35). The object of fear is, in other words, a **substitute formation** for the **subject**'s abject relation to **drive**. The fear of, say, heights really stands in the place of a much more primal fear: the fear caused by the breakdown of any distinction between subject and object, of any distinction between ourselves and the world of dead material objects. Kristeva also associates the abject with *jouissance*: "One does not know it, one does not desire it, one joys in it [*on en jouit*]. Violently and painfully. A passion" (1982: 9). This statement appears paradoxical, but what Kristeva means by such statements is that we are, despite everything, continually and repetitively drawn to the abject (much as we are repeatedly drawn to trauma in Freud's understanding of **repetition compulsion**). To experience the abject in literature carries with it a certain pleasure but one that is quite different from the dynamics of desire. Kristeva associates this aesthetic experience of the abject, rather, with poetic catharsis (the release and purification of strong emotion caused by art, as theorized by Aristotle). For Kristeva, poetic purification through catharsis is, in fact, "an impure process that protects from the abject only by dint of being immersed in it" (1982: 28).

The abject for Kristeva is, therefore, closely tied both to religion and to art, which she sees as two ways of purifying the abject: "The various means of *purifying* the abject—the various catharses—make up the history of religions, and end up with that catharsis par excellence called art, both on the far and near side of religion" (Kristeva 1982: 17). According to Kristeva, the best modern literature (Dostoevsky, Proust, Artaud, Céline, Kafka, etc.) explores the place of the abject, a place where boundaries begin to break down, where we are confronted with an archaic space before such linguistic binaries as self/ **other** or **subject/object**. The transcendent or **sublime**, for Kristeva, is really our effort to cover over the breakdowns (and subsequent reassertion of boundaries) associated with the abject; and literature is the privileged space for both the **sublime** and the abject: "On close inspection, all literature is probably a version of the apocalypse that seems to me rooted, no matter what its sociohistorical conditions might be, on the fragile border (borderline cases) where identities (**subject/object**, etc.) do not exist or only barely so—double, fuzzy, heterogeneous, animal, metamorphosed, altered, abject" (1982: 207). According to Kristeva, literature explores the way that language is structured over a **lack**, a want. She privileges poetry, in particular, because of poetry's willingness to play with grammar, metaphor, and meaning, thus laying bare the fact that language is at once arbitrary and limned with the abject fear of loss. See, in particular, her work, *Revolution in Poetic Language* (1984).

See also: **psychosexual development**.

Further reading: Kristeva 1982, 1984.

ACTOR-NETWORK THEORY (ANT)

This school of thought brings together a number of theorists who contest the common understanding of the terms, "social" and "society." Actor-network theorists question the tendency of traditional sociologists to see "society" as a stable, definable substrate for various aspects of modern existence: they argue instead that "the social is not a type of thing either visible or to be postulated" (Latour 2005: 8). According to Bruno Latour, an influential proponent of ANT, the traditional sense of the "social" is particularly unhelpful when dealing with moments of crisis or change, when "things accelerate, innovations proliferate, and entities are multiplied": "This is when a relativistic solution has to be devised in order to remain able to move between frames of reference and to regain some sort of commensurability between traces coming from frames traveling at very different speeds and acceleration" (2005:

12). Indeed, one method of ANT is to explore those moments when habitual ways of understanding the world are challenged, thus revealing the complex interactions between heterogeneous things (e.g., innovations, breakdowns, even counter-factual histories that imagine other ways that things might fit together). John Law, another important proponent of ANT, therefore concentrates particularly on mess in his book, *After Method: Mess in Social Science Research* (2004). That is, traditional social and natural science research tends to deal with things in the world that can "be made clear and definite": "Income distributions, global CO_2 emissions, the boundaries of nation states, and terms of trade, these are the kinds of provisionally stable realities that social and natural science deal with more or less effectively" (Law 2004: 2). What social and natural science cannot handle—or "mess up" in their desire to impose "simple clear descriptions"—are "mess, confusion and relative disorder" (2). Complex systems that refuse to conform to scientific methods are another favorite area of investigation for ANT theorists, as in the collection *Complexities* (2002), edited by John Law and Annemarie Mol.

For ANT theorists, a part of their method is to resist any pre-determined assumptions about what makes up the social: "Society is no more 'roughly' made of 'individuals,' of 'cultures,' of 'nation states' than Africa is 'roughly' a circle, France a hexagon or Cornwall a triangle" (Latour 2005: 24), explains Latour, for example. As he goes on, "Be prepared to cast off agency, structure, psyche, time, and space along with every other philosophical and anthropological category, no matter how deeply rooted in common sense they may appear to be" (24–25). ANT theorists prefer, then, to replace society with "collective" and to trace the associations that bring "actors" or "actants" (rather than subjects or individuals) together into what are termed "aggregates" or "**assemblages**." (Actors are actants that have been given some sort of figuration, some sort of **discursive** or figurative identity.) According to ANT, "*any thing* that does modify a state of affairs by making a difference is an actor—or, if it has no figuration yet, an actant" (Latour 2005: 71). Actors or actants can, then, include material objects ("*any thing*"), and, indeed, one goal of ANT is to understand better the effect of technological innovations on how the social is determined: "ANT is not the empty claim that objects do things 'instead' of human actors: it simply says that no science of the social can even begin if the question of who and what participates in the action is not first of all thoroughly explored, even though it might mean letting elements in which, for lack of a better term, we would call *non-humans*" (Latour 2005: 72). The "network" of Actor-Network

Theory refers, then, to the host of heterogeneous actants coming together (assembling) to form an always-provisional reality through actions that cause determinable changes—hence the ANT slogan, "'There is no in-formation, only trans-formation'" (Latour 2005: 149). Instead of viewing the world from some commanding **panopticon**, the ANT scholar examines how actants affect each other at the most local level of influence, what Latour terms the "oligopticon": "whenever anyone speaks of a 'system,' a 'global feature,' a 'structure,' a 'society,' an 'empire,' a 'world economy,' an 'organization,' the first ANT reflex should be to ask: 'In which building? In which bureau? Through which corridor is it accessible? Which colleagues has it been read to? How has it been compiled?'" (Latour 2005: 183). At the same time, each such local act is shot through with heterogeneous influences that come from other times and other places, which is what makes them uncertain "**mediators**." ANT terms actants who are not fully in control of their actions "**mediators**," which are contrasted to what are termed "**intermediaries**" (with stable cause-and-effect relationships). ANT scholars seek always to multiply the number of **mediators** they study because such mediators are truer to the ways actants act and are acted upon: "So, an actor-network is what is made to act by a large star-shaped web of **mediators** flowing in and out of it" (Latour 2005: 217). Ultimately, then, ANT scholars resist both the global and the local: "No place dominates enough to be global and no place is self-contained enough to be local" (Latour 2005: 204). There are many methods out there for "building formats, standards, and metrologies" (Latour 2005: 249) but such efforts at order and consensus are only ever provisionally employed to stabilize an ever-shifting background of what is not known.

Reality is provisional because groups are seen as constantly in the process of making and defining themselves through such efforts at standardization: "For ANT, if you stop making and remaking groups, you stop having groups" (Latour 2005: 35), which is to say that groups and "actors" are **performative**, in a way similar to how Judith Butler understands this term. As Latour explains, "the object of a **performative** definition vanishes when it is no longer performed" (Latour 2005: 37). ANT therefore concerns itself with the ever-repeated **performative** *acts* that bring a reality into being, often by excluding other acts or actants that are, in turn, defined as illegitimate by a given set of actants. Any act is itself always an uncertain and unstable one, according to ACT: "Action is not done under the full control of consciousness; action should rather be felt as a node, a knot, and a conglomerate of many surprising sets of agencies that have to be slowly disentangled" (Latour 2005: 44). This insight applies to the very discipline of science as traditionally conducted; that is, traditional scientific methods tend to create a particular version of reality through what amounts to **performative** acts. As John Law puts it, "Method is not ... a more or less successful set of procedures for reporting on a given reality. Rather it is **performative**. It helps to produce realities" (Law 2004: 143).

See also: **blackboxing, quasi-objects and quasi-subjects, things and Thing Theory**.

Further reading: Latour 1993, 1999, 2005; Law 2004; Law and Mol 2002.

AESTHETICS (THE AESTHETIC)

Aesthetics is a branch of philosophy that concerns itself with the understanding of art, beauty, and taste. Raymond Williams begins his *Keywords* with a definition of the term and helpfully traces its use to eighteenth-century German sources, particularly Alexander Baumgarten (1714–62), who first used the term, in Latin form, for his *Aesthetica*: "Baumgarten defined beauty as phenomenal perfection, and the importance of this, in thinking about art, was that it placed a predominant stress on apprehension through the *senses*" (Williams 1983: 31). The danger with Baumgarten's way of thinking about aesthetics is that it can lead to the critique that aesthetic judgment is purely subjective. Immanuel Kant (1724–1804) responded to that critique by instead arguing, in his *Critique of Judgement* (1790), that one must distinguish between "a judgement on the beautiful which is tinged with the slightest interest" and "the pure disinterested delight which appears in the judgement of taste" (Kant 1790: 477). Kant therefore defines taste as "the faculty of estimating an object or a mode of representation by means of a delight or aversion *apart from any interest*. The object of such a delight is called beautiful" (479) and can be understood as an object of *universal* delight following the logic of what Kant terms "common sense": "we assume a common sense as the necessary condition of the universal communicability of knowledge, which is presupposed in every logic and every principle of knowledge that is not one of scepticism" (492). According to Kant, aesthetic judgment may be subjective but it is subjective in the same way for everyone since we share the same faculties, and, so, one can make *a priori* judgments about taste, that is, judgments that proceed from theoretical deduction rather than from experience. As Kant writes, we are "justified in presupposing that the same subjective conditions of judgement which we find in ourselves are universally present in every man, and further that we have rightly subsumed the given object under these conditions" (517).

An influential list of German critical thinkers follow Kant's lead in thinking about aesthetics as a significant aspect of philosophy, including Frederick Schiller, Friedrich Wilhelm Schelling, G. W. F. Hegel, Arthur Schopenhauer, Søren Kierkegaard, Friedrich Nietzsche, and Martin Heidegger. A useful engagement with each of these thinkers can be found in Terry Eagleton's *The Ideology of the Aesthetic* (1990), which itself seeks to engage with the concept, seeing aesthetics as an enabling and therefore, for Eagleton, suspect **ideology** for the emergent bourgeoisie of the nineteenth century, as well as something that is potentially revolutionary and can be used against dominant bourgeois, **capitalist ideology**. As he writes, "The emergence of the aesthetic as a theoretical category is closely bound up with the material process by which cultural production, at an early stage of bourgeois society, becomes 'autonomous'—autonomous, that is, of the various social functions which it has traditionally served" (8–9). That notion of autonomy allows art to be "conveniently sequestered from all other social practices, to become an isolated enclave within which the dominant social order can find an idealized refuge from its own actual values of competitiveness, exploitation and material possessiveness" and "provides the middle class with just the **ideological** model of subjectivity it requires for its material operations," that is, "a mode of being which is entirely self-regulating and self-determining" (9). However, "this concept of autonomy is radically double-edged: if on the one hand it provides a central constituent of bourgeois **ideology**, it also marks an emphasis on the self-determining nature of human powers and capacities which becomes, in the work of Karl Marx and others, the anthropological foundation of a revolutionary opposition to bourgeois utility" (9).

Eagleton thus encapsulates critical theory's wide-ranging engagement with aesthetics, with many critics attacking it almost instinctually as a tool of dominant bourgeois **ideology** while others seek to articulate the revolutionary potential of aesthetics as a principle. Those critical theorists who reject aesthetics as suspect argue that its concern with beauty tends to run counter to the politicization called for by much critical theory in the tradition of the **Frankfurt School** (see **Introduction**). Walter Benjamin, who was connected to the Frankfurt School, goes so far as to suggest that fascism is "the consummation of '*l'art pour l'art*'" (1968: 242), which is the aesthetic ideal arguing that art should exist only for itself, for its own beauty, without regard for political or worldly concerns. Benjamin reads in Fascism "the introduction of aesthetics into political life" (241) and argues that "Communism responds by politicizing art" (242). As Jerome McGann puts it in his highly influential *The Romantic Ideology* (1983b), any "'purely' stylistic, rhetorical, formal, or other specialized analyses" must always "find their *raison d'être* in the socio-historical ground" (3).

Despite such critiques, aesthetics has remained a persistent concern for many critical theorists, even among **Marxists** and the theorists of the Frankfurt School. **Marxist** critic Georg Lukács, for example, claimed that literature, especially the mimetic, realist literature of authors such as Sir Walter Scott, Honoré de Balzac, Leo Tolstoy, and Thomas Mann, succeeds in helping humans become self-conscious of themselves and the social totality of a given period: "if we are ever going to be able to understand the way in which reactionary ideas infiltrate our minds, and if we are ever going to achieve a critical distance from such prejudices, this can only be accomplished by hard work, by abandoning and transcending the limits of immediacy, by scrutinizing all subjective experiences and measuring them against social reality" (1977: 37), something that, according to Lukács, realist fiction best does for us.

Although some members of the **Frankfurt School** were critical of aesthetics, Theodor Adorno, one of its leaders, published an entire work titled *Aesthetic Theory* (1970) in which he explores the extent to which art can claim a certain autonomy from the real world. Adorno makes a case for "a materialistic-dialectical aesthetics" (3), one that recognizes how "The concept of art is located in a historically changing constellation of elements; it refuses definition" (2). Yet, Adorno also argues that "Only by virtue of separation from **empirical** reality ... , does the artwork achieve a heightened order of existence" (4). Art therefore has a "double character as both autonomous and *fait social*" (5).

Poststructuralist critics of the last 50 years have consistently taken aim at the precepts of aesthetic theory, or dismissed them out of hand. Isobel Armstrong, in *The Radical Aesthetic* (2000), begins by stating that "The most influential cultural and literary theorists of the last two decades, even when they come from constituencies and traditions inimical to each other, have agreed—and sometimes it is all that they have agreed on—that the category of the aesthetic, together with its foundational philosophers, Kant and Hegel, is up for **deconstruction**. **Marxists**, **cultural materialists**, **poststructuralists**, and **deconstructive psychoanalysts**, have converged in what has sometimes looked like a mission in cultural eugenics" (1). And yet, one can find theorists of the aesthetic even among this group. The **deconstructionist** critic, Jean-François Lyotard, often turns to Kant's *Critique of Judgement* to articulate some of his privileged concepts, particularly the **sublime**, engaging most consistently with, while also critiquing aspects of, Kant's aesthetic theory in *Lessons on the Analytic of the Sublime* (1994). Julia Kristeva, who Armstrong would likely include in the category of

deconstructive psychoanalyst, often saw in aesthetic works, especially poetry, a revolutionary relationship to the status quo. Indeed, her privileging of the **abject** in literature is not so different from Lyotard's privileging of the **sublime**.

Most recently, Jacques Rancière has devoted several influential books to his own reconceptualization of aesthetics. For Rancière, "aesthetics can be understood in a Kantian sense—re-examined perhaps by Foucault—as the system of *a priori* forms determining what presents itself to sense experience. It is a delimitation of spaces and times, of the visible and the invisible, of speech and noise, that simultaneously determines the place and the stakes of politics as a form of experience" (2004: 13). Rancière thus seeks to recast politics in terms of aesthetics, as opposed to the politicization of aesthetics called for by Benjamin, arguing that both politics and aesthetics follow the same principles; that is, politics, like aesthetics as Rancière defines it, "revolves around what is seen and what can be said about it, around who has the ability to see and the talent to speak, around the properties of spaces and the possibilities of time" (13). Both aesthetics and politics construct rules that determine what will be accepted as part of a communal way of speaking, doing, and making, "the sensible delimitation of what is common to the community, the forms of its visibility and of its organization" (18); by delimiting what is common, such rules also, by necessity, exclude other aspects of experience which remain invisible, outside what Rancière terms "the **distribution of the sensible**."

Rancière argues, however, that the understanding of aesthetics that developed in the nineteenth century can function as a liberatory model for politics because he reads this new "aesthetic regime of the arts" as inspiring a properly egalitarian model of human subjectivity.

In other words, Rancière argues that the "aesthetic regime of the arts" is an important moment in the development of world history and human consciousness. He contrasts it with two other regimes that preceded it: (1) an *ethical regime of images*; and (2) a *poetic or representative regime of the arts*. In the former, what matters, regarding images, is "the question of their origin (and consequently their truth content) and the question of their end or purpose, the uses they are put to and the effects they result in" (2004: 20). Plato's writing exemplifies this regime since there the question is one of determining the difference between "true arts, that is to say forms of knowledge based on the imitation of a model with precise ends, and artistic simulacra that imitate simple appearances" (21). According to Plato's *Republic*, artistic simulacra (poetry, in particular) should be excluded from the community, prohibited, because they lead us away from the truth. The *ethical regime of images* is countered by the *poetic or representative regime of the arts*, where "It is the *substance* of the poem, the fabrication of a plot arranging actions that represent the activities of men, which is the foremost issue, to the detriment of the *essence* of the image" (21). In the representative regime, which Rancière aligns especially with Aristotle's theory of mimesis, one evaluates not the ethical impact of an image but how well the arts, now broadly construed to represent the "fine arts," represent fictional worlds according to certain rules: "Poetry owes no explanation for the 'truth' of what it says," according to this regime, "because, in its very principle, it is not made up of images or statements, but fictions, that is to say arrangements between actions" (36). In this evaluation, one also creates a hierarchy of genres.

The *aesthetic regime of the arts*, which Ranciére identifies as coming into being around the nineteenth century (with earlier inklings in the work of Vico and Cervantes), rejects hierarchizing maneuvers by understanding aesthetics not as "a division within ways of doing and making" but as "a sensible mode of being specific to artistic products" (2004: 22). In this regime, we are talking about "art" as a particular way of being, freed "from any specific rule, from any hierarchy of the arts, subject matter, and genres" (23) and aligned with "the formation and education of a specific type of humanity" (24) that also rejects hierarchical relations and exclusions. This understanding of art as an aesthetic way of being in the world "blurred the dividing line that isolated art from the jurisdiction of statements or images, as well as the dividing line that separated the logic of facts from the logic of stories" (36). Rancière argues that "This revolution first took place in literature," particularly literature of the nineteenth century, when for the first time "an epoch and a society were deciphered through the features, clothes, or gestures of an ordinary individual (Balzac); the sewer revealed a civilization (Hugo); the daughter of a farmer and the daughter of a banker were caught in the equal force of style as an 'absolute manner of seeing things' (Flaubert)" (32). Such an aesthetic regime "shifts the focus from great names and events to the life of the anonymous; it finds symptoms of an epoch, a society, or a civilization in the minute details of ordinary life" (33). The aesthetic regime is an egalitarian regime because it rejects hierarchies of **class** or genre and also breaks down the very distinction between art and other activities because, in this regime, the everyday and mundane—rather than any notion of "high" **culture**— provide meaning. Rancière therefore argues that we should not be calling for the politicization of art, as did Benjamin; rather, it is aesthetics that is best positioned to effect political change: "It is up to the various forms of politics to appropriate, for their own proper use, the modes of presentation or the means of establishing explanatory sequences produced by artistic practices rather than the other way around" (65).

We can also see a return to aesthetics in the recent rise of New Formalism (see **New Criticism and New Formalism**), particularly in such works as Marc Redfield's *Phantom Formations: Aesthetic Ideology and the Bildungsroman* (1996), Armstrong's *The Radical Aesthetic* (2000), and Jonathan Loesberg's *A Return to Aesthetics* (2005). Regenia Gagnier also returns to aesthetics in her *The Insatiability of Human Wants: Economics and Aesthetics in Market Society* (2000) but by aligning it with economics, thus standing the **Marxist** dismissal of aesthetics on its head, arguing instead, like Rancière, that aesthetics "functions as aesthetic spaces have always functioned when they have meant something more than social **capital**: as a space of freedom" (232).

See also: **inaesthetic, literarity**.

Further reading: Adorno 1970; I. Armstrong 2000; Cooper 1992, 1997; T. Eagleton 1990; Gagnier 2000; Kant 1790; Kristeva 1982, 1984; G. L. Levine 1994; Loesberg 2005; Lukács 1977; Lyotard 1994; McGann 1983b; Rancière 2004, 2010; Redfield 1996; Williams 1983.

AGENCY (AGENT)

"Agency" is a term that would seem to be straightforward: the "ability or capacity to act or exert power; active working or operation; action; activity" (*OED*); however, the development of critical theory has greatly complicated the concept. On the one hand, the political activism of critical theory, in the tradition of the **Frankfurt School** (see **Introduction**), seeks to make the world a better place by giving agency to previously exploited and **marginalized** groups. **Identity politics** could be said to take as its major goal the giving of agency (political, economic, social, and cultural power) to groups that have been excluded from the **hegemonic** center of **power**. However, **poststructuralism**, one influential form of this critique of **hegemony**, questions society's acceptance of the "sovereign **subject**" as the originary cause and governing intentionality of any action. As Jean-Luc Nancy puts it in the "Introduction" to the provocatively titled *Who Comes After the Subject?*, the question of the book's title "bears upon the critique or **deconstruction** of interiority, of self-presence, of consciousness, of mastery, of the individual or collective property of an essence" (Nancy 1991: 4). **Poststructuralism** thus creates problems for an ideological critique that wishes to give agency to the **marginalized**. As Homi Bhabha phrases it in a chapter titled "The Postcolonial and the Postmodern: The Question of Agency," "Is it possible to conceive of historical agency in that disjunctive, indeterminate moment of **discourse** outside the sentence? Is the whole thing no more than a theoretical fantasy that reduces any form of political critique to a daydream?" (Bhabha 1994: 183).

The questioning of agency occurs on a number of fronts in critical theory. **Psychoanalysis** questions to what extent the **ego** is in control of all of its actions, both because of the eruption of **unconscious** impulses (e.g., the return of the repressed) and because the actions available to us are determined by others (for example, Jacques Lacan's "**big Other**": language and the shared conventions of society). Mikhail Bakhtin in his notions of **dialogism** and **heteroglossia** argues that the idea of a "monologic" authorial intention is a retroactive myth that works against the way selves actually construct themselves through the use of language, which always entails intersubjective dialogue: "The speaker is not the biblical Adam, dealing only with virgin and still unnamed objects, giving them names for the first time" (Bakhtin 1986: 93). **Poststructuralist** theorists argue that intentional action is really a retroactive myth that is in fact determined by language, as in Jean-François Lyotard's understanding of **phrase regimen, phrase universe, and genre of discourse** or of **language games**. **Marxist** and **Neo-Marxist** critics question to what extent individual agents are in control of their own actions or are mere dupes of **ideology** or the larger economic forces, the **base**, of a given society. **Poststructuralist feminists** like Judith Butler argue that when we act, we are not so much independent, self-willed agents as we are "actors" **performatively** repeating conventions, especially **gender** conventions, that in fact constitute us as agents only in the act of performance, which is to say that there is no pre-existing interiority or consciousness in the traditional sense that is determining and controlling those actions: "**gender** cannot be understood as a *role* which either expresses or disguises an interior 'self,' whether that 'self' is conceived as sexed or not. As performance which is performative, **gender** is an 'act,' broadly construed, which constructs the social fiction of its own psychological interiority" (1990b: 279). **Actor-Network Theory** builds on Gilles Deleuze and Félix Guattari's notion of machinic **assemblage** in order to reject conscious, human agency altogether in favor of actants and "actors," understood as anything that modifies an existing state of affairs, be that *thing* a human being or a machine.

See also: **author, interpellation, intersectionality, subject.**

ALIENATION

According to Karl Marx, "alienation" is the process whereby workers are made to feel foreign to the products of their own labor. The creation of a **commodity** need not lead to alienation and can, indeed, be highly satisfying: workers pour their subjectivity into an object and they can even gain enjoyment from the fact that another in turn gains enjoyment from their craft. In capitalism, workers are exploited insofar as they do not work to create a product that they then sell to a real person; instead, the **proletariat** works in order to live, in order to obtain the very means of life, which they can only achieve by selling their **labor** to a **capitalist** for a wage (as if their **labor** were itself a property that can be bought and sold). Workers are alienated from their product precisely because they no longer own that product, which now belongs to the **capitalist** who has purchased the proletariat's **labor-power** in exchange for exclusive ownership over the **proletariat**'s products and all profit accrued by the sale of those products.

ANAL-SADISTIC PHASE

The anal-sadistic phase is the second phase of early childhood **psychosexual development**, according to Sigmund Freud, when pleasure is oriented to the anal orifice and defecation (roughly 2–4 years of age). This phase is split between active and passive impulses: the impulse to mastery on the one hand, which can easily become cruelty and sadism; the impulse to **scopophilia** (love of gazing) and anal eroticism, on the other hand. According to Freud, the child's pleasure in defecation is connected to his or her pleasure in creating something of his or her own, a pleasure that for women is later transferred to child-bearing.

See also: **mirror stage**.

Further reading: Freud 1916–17; Laplanche and Pontalis 1973.

ANTAGONISM

In the work of Ernesto Laclau and Chantal Mouffe, "antagonism" refers to sites of potential revolution (of real conflict) that arise at those places where the **discursive** markers of a society fail. Laclau and Mouffe theorize the term as that which "escapes the possibility of being apprehended through language, since language only exists as an attempt to fix that which antagonism subverts" (1985: 125). For Laclau and Mouffe, everything is determined by language, everything is **discursive**: "every object is constituted as an object of **discourse**" (107). They do not deny that there are objects that "exist externally to thought," only that objects cannot "constitute themselves as objects outside any **discursive** condition of emergence" (108). The social, for Laclau and Mouffe, is nothing but a set of provisional *"nodal points which partially fix meaning"* (113), a process they term **articulation**: "The social *is* **articulation** insofar as 'society' is impossible" (114). Society is "impossible" insofar as there is no transcendent meaning that definitively fixes the concept beyond such discursive **"articulations."** "Antagonisms," by this thinking, "are not *internal* but *external* to society; or rather, they constitute the limits of society, the latter's impossibility of fully constituting itself" (125). In this way, "antagonism" functions in a way similar to Jacques Lacan's notion of the **Real**.

See also: **differend, radical democracy**.

APPARATUS

"Apparatus" is the English translation of a term that appears consistently throughout Michel Foucault's work, that is, *dispositif*. He uses it, as he puts it, to "pick out ... a thoroughly heterogeneous ensemble consisting of **discourses**, institutions, architectural forms, regulatory decisions, laws, administrative measures, scientific statements, philosophical, moral, and philanthropic propositions—in short, the said as much as the unsaid. Such are the elements of the apparatus." He goes on to state that "The apparatus itself is the system of relations that can be established between these elements" (1980: 194).

Giorgio Agamben takes the term from Foucault and redefines it as

> anything that has in some way the capacity to capture, orient, determine, intercept, model, control, or secure the gestures, behaviors, opinions, or **discourses** of living beings. Not only, therefore, prisons, madhouses, the **panopticon**, schools, confession, factories, **disciplines**, juridical measures, and so forth (whose connection with **power** is in a certain sense evident), but also the pen, writing, literature, philosophy, agriculture, cigarettes, navigation, computers, cellular telephones and—why not—language itself, which is perhaps the most ancient of apparatuses. (2009: 14)

According to Agamben, **subjects** result from "the relation and, so to speak, from the relentless fight between living beings and apparatuses" (2009: 14). Although humans have always used apparatuses, Agamben points out that "today there is not even a single instant in which the life of individuals is not modeled, contaminated, or controlled by some apparatus" (15). The use of apparatuses is also different now since many of today's apparatuses entail what Agamben terms a degree of "desubjectification," whereby the user is reduced in some way, e.g., to a number (the cell phone) or a passive consumer and statistic (film and television).

See also: **articulation**.

ARCHAEOLOGY (ARCHAEOLOGICAL)

Michel Foucault uses this term to characterize his approach to historical investigation, which he sees as opposed to any **history** that attempts to establish a "**grand narrative**" to explain the past's relation to the present. In *The Archaeology of Knowledge* (1972), Foucault rejects the traditional historian's tendency to read straightforward narratives of progress in the historical record: "For many years now," he writes, "historians have preferred to turn their attention to long periods, as if, beneath the shifts and changes of political events, they were trying to reveal the stable, almost indestructible system of checks and balances, the irreversible processes, the constant readjustments, the underlying tendencies that gather force, and are then suddenly reversed after centuries of continuity, the movements of accumulation and slow saturation, the great silent, motionless bases that traditional history has covered with a thick layer of events" (3). Foucault, by contrast, argues that one should seek to reconstitute not large "periods" or "centuries" but "phenomena of rupture, of discontinuity" (4). The problem, he argues, "is no longer one of tradition, of tracing a line, but one of division, of limits" (5). Instead of presenting a monolithic version of a given period, Foucault argues that we must illustrate how any given period reveals "several pasts, several forms of connexion, several hierarchies of importance, several networks of determination, several teleologies, for one and the same science, as its present undergoes change: thus historical descriptions are necessarily ordered by the present state of knowledge, they increase with every transformation and never cease, in turn, to break with themselves" (5).

Archaeology can be distinguished from traditional history in a number of ways:

(1) "Archaeology tries to define not the thoughts, representations, images, themes, preoccupations that are concealed or revealed in **discourses**; but those **discourses** themselves, those **discourses** as practices obeying certain rules" (138). Foucault does not examine historical documents in order to read in them "a sign of something else" (138), for example the "truth" or "spirit" of a given historical period. Rather, Foucault tries to make sense of how a period's very approach to key terms like "**history**," "oeuvre," or "**subjectivity**" affect that period's understanding of itself and its **history**.

(2) "Archaeology does not seek to rediscover the continuous, insensible transition that relates **discourses**, on a gentle slope, to what precedes them, surrounds them, or follows them" (139). Instead, Foucault wishes to understand how disparate **discourses** function by their own distinct sets of rules and strategies. Archaeology wishes to "show in what way the set of rules that [**discourses**] put into operation is irreducible to any other" (139). In other words, different **discourses** have a disjunctive or discontinuous relation to each other.

(3) Archaeology "does not try to grasp the moment in which the *œuvre* emerges on the anonymous horizon. It does not wish to rediscover the enigmatic point at which the individual and the social are inverted into one another. It is neither a psychology, nor a sociology, nor more generally an anthropology of creation" (139). Rather, archaeology examines how a single œuvre can be shot through with different "types of rules for **discursive** practices" (139). It treats "different rules for **discursive** practices" as distinct from each other, and therefore never subsumable into some all-encompassing concept (e.g., the "author" or the "spirit of the age"). In other words, Foucault examines the multiple sets of rules that impinge on our understanding of any work at a given moment in history.

(4) Finally, archaeology "does not claim to efface itself in the ambiguous modesty of a reading that would bring back, in all its purity, the distant, precarious, almost effaced light of the origin" (139–40). Archaeology does not seek to reconstitute the "truth" of history but how any period is made up of a series of **discourses**: "It is not a return to the innermost secret of the origin; it is the systematic description of a **discourse**-object" (140).

See also: **discipline**, **discourse**, **history**.

Further reading: T. J. Armstrong 1992; Foucault 1966, 1972.

ARCHE-WRITING

See **phonocentrism**

ARTICULATION (ARTICULATORY)

"Articulation" is a term that is used by Ernesto Laclau and Chantal Mouffe in their *Hegemony and Socialist Strategy* (1985) and by Bruno Latour in his **Actor-Network Theory**. For Laclau and Mouffe, "articulation" is "any practice establishing a relation among elements such that their identity is modified as a result of the articulatory practice" (1985: 105). The result is a "**discursive** formation," in the sense of **discourse** theorized by Michel Foucault. In theorizing the concept of "articulation," Laclau and Mouffe seek to avoid a traditional approach to **ideology** as tied to a **superstructure** that is dissociated from actual material institutions, rituals, and practices and that posits a unifying principle like **class**. "Articulation," by contrast, is a "**discursive** practice which does not have a plane of constitution prior to, or outside, the dispersion of the articulated elements" (109). For Laclau and Mouffe, "every object is constituted as an object of **discourse**," which is to say that, although objects certainly do "exist externally to thought," they cannot "constitute themselves as objects outside any **discursive** condition of emergence" (108). In this, Laclau and Mouffe distinguish between the reality we experience after our entrance into language and a Lacanian **Real** that must, by definition, remain outside "articulation," outside that which can be communicated. As they explain, "Synonymy, metonymy, metaphor are not forms of thought that add a second sense to a primary, constitutive literality of social relations; instead, they are part of the primary terrain itself in which the social is constituted" (110). "Articulation," then, refers to the ways that we fix meaning within a social arena where everything is **discursive**. "**Subjects**" in this way of thinking are never more than "'subject-positions' within a **discursive** structure" (115).

Bruno Latour and **Actor-Network Theory** seek to go beyond the subsequent reduction of everything to language; rather than say that "language [has] invaded the universal problematic" (1985: 112), as do Laclau and Mouffe, Latour attempts to illustrate the ways that the material world, our tools, and our actions are intimately interconnected. He wishes to present "an alternative to the model of statements that posits a world 'out there' which language tries to reach through a correspondence across the yawning gap separating the two" (1999: 141). He takes terms that are usually applied to language use by humans (e.g., "proposition" and "articulation") and applies them to **things** themselves: "I am attempting to redistribute the capacity of speech between humans and nonhumans" (141). The goal is to multiply the number of **things** that can be considered "actants," including nonhuman things, which is how Latour understands his term "proposition": "Propositions are not statement, or things, or any sort of intermediary between the two. They are, first of all, actants" (141). He explains further: "They are not positions, things, substances, or essences pertaining to a **nature** made up of mute objects facing a talkative human mind, but *occasions* given to different entities to enter into contact. These occasions for interaction allow the entities to modify their definitions over the course of an event" (141). "Articulation" refers to the "relation established between propositions," between these various actants, both human and nonhuman. So, he explains that "articulation is in no way limited to language and may be applied not only to words but also to gestures, papers, settings, instruments, sites, trials" (142). Latour argues that "Articulation between propositions goes much deeper than speech. We speak *because* the propositions of the world are themselves articulated, not the other way around. More exactly, *we are allowed to speak interestingly by what we allow to speak interestingly*" (144).

See also: **apparatus**.

ASSEMBLAGE AND ASSEMBLAGE THEORY

"Assemblage" is a term used by Gilles Deleuze and Félix Guattari to counter all claims to presence or center in favor of the many material ways that objects come together over time. As they explain in *A Thousand Plateaus* (1987), referring to the very book they are writing,

> In a book, as in all things, there are lines of articulation or segmentarity, strata and territories; but also lines of flight, movements of deterritorialization and destratification. Comparative rates of flow on these lines produce phenomena of relative slowness and viscosity, or, on the contrary, constitutes an *assemblage*. A book is an assemblage of this kind, and as such is unattributable. It is a multiplicity. (3–4)

Rather than refer to unitary, essential things (a tree, an individual), Deleuze and Guattari wish to think about the multiplicity of things coming together over time that constitutes any action. So, they argue, for example, "There are no individual statements, only statement-producing machinic assemblages" (1987: 36).

The term, "assemblage," has been taken up by Bruno Latour in his **Actor-Network Theory** and it has been developed into "assemblage theory" by Manuel DeLanda. DeLanda wishes to combat what he calls "the *organismic metaphor*" in social theory, which underscores "*relations of interiority*," the conception that "wholes possess an inextricable unity in which there is a strict reciprocal determination between parts" (2006: 9). In other words, such theories represent complex wholes, like societies, as if they were organisms: "as bodily organs work together for the organism as a whole, so the function of social institutions is to work in harmony for the benefit of society" (8). DeLanda instead draws on Deleuze to argue for a theory of assemblages, where wholes are "characterized by *relations of exteriority*": "These relations imply, first of all, that a component part of an assemblage may be detached from it and plugged into a different assemblage in which its interactions are different" (10). Rather than turn to organisms for a guiding metaphor, DeLanda explains, "Deleuze gravitates towards other kinds of biological illustrations, such as the symbiosis of plants and pollinating insects. In this case we have relations of exteriority between self-subsistent components—such as the wasp and the orchid—relations which may become obligatory in the course of coevolution" (11). DeLanda applies the same logic to organisms themselves, explaining: "Conceiving an organism as an assemblage implies that despite the tight integration between its component organs, the relations between them are not logically necessary but only contingently obligatory: a historical result of their close coevolution" (11–12). According to DeLanda, assemblage theory allows a social theorist to frame more effectively "the problem of the relationships between the micro- and macro-levels of social phenomena" (25).

DeLanda's goal is to avoid what he terms "taxonomic essentialism"; such essentialism "starts with finished products (different chemical or biological species), discovers through logical analysis the enduring properties that characterize those products, and then makes these sets of properties into a defining essence (or a set of necessary and sufficient conditions to belong to a natural kind)" (2006: 28). Assemblage theory avoids such reification and essentialism by focusing "on the historical processes that produce those products, with the term 'historical' referring to cosmological and evolutionary history in addition to human history" (28). As a result, "The identity of any assemblage at any level of scale is always the product of a process (territorialization and, in some cases, coding) and it is always precarious, since other processes (deterritorialization and decoding) can destabilize it" (28). In other words, DeLanda rejects rigid classification in favor of the historically variable ways whereby assemblages at both the micro- and macro-level come together through centripetal forces (what DeLanda, following Deleuze and Guattari, terms territorialization, coding, universal singularities, and diagrams) while being continually destabilized by centrifugal forces (deterritorialization, decoding, "lines of flight").

Further reading: DeLanda 2006; Deleuze and Guattari 1983, 1987; Latour 2005.

AURA

Walter Benjamin popularized this term in his influential essay, "The Work of Art in the Age of Mechanical Reproduction" (1936 [1968]). He argues that, although "[i]n principle a work of art has always been reproducible … , [m]echanical reproduction of a work of art … represents something new" (1968: 218). According to Benjamin, "that which withers in the age of mechanical reproduction is the aura of the work of art" (221), which is to say the "presence of the original" (220), or its "uniqueness" (223), a function that has its roots, according to Benjamin, in the anthropological **fetish**. The underlying cause of this loss of aura is the "increasing significance of the masses in contemporary life" and, particularly, "the desire of contemporary masses to bring things 'closer' spatially and humanly, which is just as ardent as their bent toward overcoming the uniqueness of every reality by accepting its reproduction" (223). Although this tendency began with the "mechanical reproduction of writing" (218–19), Benjamin notes, it reached a new stage with the introduction of photography and then film. The result is that "the total function of art is reversed": "Instead of being based on ritual, it begins to be based on another practice—politics" (224), because art objects are thus brought ever closer to the lives of actual people. Benjamin concludes by stating that fascism is an example of a movement that makes use of this change by aestheticizing politics, as in the Futurist art movement's statement that "'War is beautiful'" (241). According to Benjamin, "Communism responds by politicizing art" (242).

See also: **aesthetics, simulacra and simulation**.

AUTHOR

Like **agency**, "author" would seem to be a term that is self-explanatory: "The writer of a book or other work; a person whose occupation is writing books" (*OED*); however, just as critical theory has made us question to what extent we are in fact **agents** in control of—the authors of—our own actions, so too has it problematized the notion of "author." For one, critical theory often points out that what we now take for granted as "authorship" is, in fact, a recent creation in human history, something that first sees its emergence only after we move from oral to literate culture and that does not fully come into existence until after the introduction of mechanical print in the Renaissance (see **Introduction**).

Sometimes inspired by modernist literature that eschews authorship in favor of a notion of **textuality** or the found object or the unconscious (Stéphane Mallarmé, Marcel Duchamp's "readymades," the automatic writing of the Surrealists, respectively), critical theory questions any simplistic understanding of intentional authorship, sometimes calling, in fact, for "The Death of the Author," as Roland Barthes puts it in his famous essay of that name. According to Barthes, the notion of the author seeks "to impose a limit" on a given **text**, "to furnish it with a final signified, to close the writing," an imposition that benefits the critic: "Such a conception suits criticism very well, the latter then allotting itself the important task of discovering the Author (or its hypostases: society, history, psyché, liberty) beneath the work: when the Author has been found, the **text** is 'explained'—victory to the critic" (Barthes 1977: 147). Barthes counters with a structuralist understanding of the **text**, which he explores most fully in his work *S/Z* (1974). As he puts it in "The Death of the Author," "We know now that a **text** is not a line of words releasing a single 'theological' meaning (the 'message' of the Author-God) but a multi-dimensional space in which a variety of writings, none of them original, blend and clash. The **text** is a tissue of quotations drawn from the innumerable centres of culture" (1977: 146). Barthes believes that, by releasing us from the grip of the Author, we open up the true space of meaning-production: the reader, "that *someone* who holds together in a single field all the traces by which the written **text** is constituted" (Barthes 1977: 148). As he puts it in the last sentence of the essay, "the birth of the reader must be at the cost of the death of the Author" (148). **Hermeneutics**, **New Criticism**, and **Reader-Response Theory** could all be said similarly to challenge the privileging of a given author's intentions (what the **New Critics** W. K. Wimsatt and Monroe Beardsley termed the "Intentional Fallacy") in favor of a reader's or critic's interpretation of a given work.

Michel Foucault in his essay "What is an Author?" (1977b) followed Barthes's move by stating that "we should reexamine the empty space left by the author's disappearance; we should attentively observe, along its gaps and fault lines, its new demarcation, and the reapportionment of this void" (139). Rather than speak of an author,

Foucault suggests that we should instead speak of an "author-function," that is, the way the concept of authorship is "tied to the legal and institutional systems that circumscribe, determine, and articulate the realm of **discourses**" (145).

Other critical theorists rethink authorship in terms of other concepts. Gilles Deleuze and Félix Guattari speak instead of **assemblages**, arguing that a book is really made up of "lines of flight, movements of deterritorialization and destratification" and, so, "as such is unattributable. It is a multiplicity" (1987: 3–4), an approach that is further explored by **Assemblage Theory** and **Actor-Network Theory**. Avital Ronell in the opening "User's Manual" for *The Telephone Book* (1989) offers herself as switchboard rather than as author: "Our problem was how to maintain an open switchboard, one that disrupts a normally functioning text equipped with proper shock absorbers." Indeed, she seeks to achieve a **"schizophrenic"** effect by playing with typography and the normal presentation of text, as did **deconstructionist** Jacques Derrida in his *Glas* (1986), where his "text induces by agglutinating rather than demonstrating, by coupling and decoupling, gluing and ungluing ... rather than by exhibiting the continuous, and analogical, instructive, suffocating necessity of **discursive** rhetoric" (75). Jane Gallop in the *Deaths of the Author* (2011) builds on Barthes's essay to postulate the death of the author in terms of **queer theory**'s notion of **queer temporality**. Finally, the **Digital Humanities** rethinks authorship in favor of models inspired by social networking, cyberspace **intertextuality**, and the database, as in Franco Moretti's concept of **distant reading** or Jerome McGann's **deformance**.

See also: **Body without Organs**, **subject**.

Further reading: Barthes 1977; Derrida 1986; Foucault 1977b; Gallop 2011; Wimsatt 1954.

AUTOETHNOGRAPHY

See **contact zone and transculturation**

BARE LIFE AND *HOMO SACER*

These terms are important ones in the critical writings of Giorgio Agamben, who builds on the work of Michel Foucault to interrogate the distinction between natural life and politics. Agamben points out in

Homo Sacer: Sovereign Power and Bare Life (1998) that the ancient Greeks had two, quite distinct, terms to describe life: "*zoē*, which expressed the simple fact of living common to all living beings (animals, men, or gods), and *bios*, which indicated the form or way of living proper to an individual or a group" (1). Because of this distinction, simple existence (*zoē*) and all the political issues tied to *bios* appeared to be completely separate. Agamben points out that for Foucault what marks the move into the modern period is "the entry of *zoē* into the sphere of the *polis*—the politicization of bare life as such" (4). See **bio-politics** and **bio-power** for Foucault's ideas along these lines. Agamben argues, however, that, in fact, as soon as you set up the idea of "bare life" as an exception, as that which is outside of politics and outside the rule of law, you enter into a situation where that exclusion is the very foundation for our very understanding of politics: "*it can even be said that the production of a **biopolitical** body is the original activity of sovereign power*" (1998: 6). In this way, bare life is tied to Agamben's understanding of the **state of exception**: "[a]t once excluding bare life from and capturing it within the political order, the state of exception actually constituted, in its very separateness, the hidden foundation on which the entire political system rested" (9).

To explain how this is so, Agamben gives the example of *homo sacer* in ancient Roman law. For Agamben, bare life is "the life of *homo sacer* (sacred man), who *may be killed and yet not sacrificed*" (1998: 8). Agamben gets his example of this ancient law from Pompeius Festus in his treatise *On the Significance of Words*: "'The sacred man is the one whom the people have judged on account of a crime. It is not permitted to sacrifice this man, yet he who kills him will not be condemned for homicide'" (71). Agamben explains that such a figure "takes the form of a double exception, both from the *ius humanum* and from the *ius divinum*, both from the sphere of the profane and from that of the religious" (82). That is, the figure is outside of penal, judicial law (you can kill him with impunity) and also outside of divine law (he may not be put to death by religious sacrifice). Agamben argues that *homo sacer* is thus structurally analogous to sovereign power (the king's right to put someone to death with impunity) and the **state of exception**: "*The sovereign sphere is the sphere in which it is permitted to kill without committing homicide and without celebrating a sacrifice, and sacred life—that is, life that may be killed but not sacrificed—is the life that has been captured in this sphere*" (83). Or, as he says a little later, "the sovereign and *homo sacer* present two symmetrical figures that have the same structure and are correlative: the sovereign is the one with respect to whom all men are potentially *homines sacri*, and *homo sacer* is the one with respect to whom all men act as sovereigns" (84). As a perfect "state of exception," then, *homo sacer* and bare life are "[n]either political *bios* nor natural *zoē*"; "sacred life" or "bare life" is, rather, "the zone of indistinction in which *zoē* and *bios* constitute each other in including and excluding each other" (90).

Agamben's goal, as in his writings on the **state of exception**, is to make sense of how state power was so easily abused in the modern period, leading to various genocides, including the Holocaust. According to Agamben, the very logic of sovereign power, which is constituted with regard to the **state of exception**, opens the system to abuse. He agrees with Foucault, who argues that **bio-power** designates "what brought life and its mechanisms into the realm of explicit calculation" (1990: 1.143), including politics (hence, "bio-politics"). Agamben states that "[o]nly because politics in our age had been entirely transformed into **bio-politics** was it possible for politics to be constituted as totalitarian politics to a degree hitherto unknown" (1998: 120); however, Agamben argues that the problem was always already a part of the system of governance and can be traced back to the figure of *homo sacer*, which he aligns with sovereign power. The Jew under Nazi Germany is, for him, a perfect case in point of how the logic of *homo sacer* has the capacity to infect statehood: "The Jew living under Nazism is the privileged negative referent of the new **bio-political** sovereignty and is, as such, a flagrant case of a *homo sacer* in the sense of a life that may be killed but not sacrificed" (114). For Agamben, Nazism and its policies are not an aberrant exception but a result of the **bio-political** foundation of all states: "only because biological life and its needs had become the *politically* decisive fact is it possible to understand the otherwise incomprehensible rapidity with which twentieth-century parliamentary democracies were able to turn into totalitarian states and with which this century's totalitarian states were able to be converted, almost without interruption, into parliamentary democracies" (122). In other words, Agamben reads the concentration camp not "as a historical fact and an anomaly belonging to the past (even if still verifiable) but in some way as the hidden matrix and *nomos* [i.e., usage, custom, law] of the political space in which we are living" (166).

Agamben's fear is that, as the state of exception (as in martial law) is invoked with ever more frequency by today's states, the logic of the *homo sacer* is increasingly being applied to all citizens: "If today there is no longer any one clear figure of the sacred man, it is perhaps because we are all virtually *homines sacri*" (1998: 115). Or, as Agamben states a little later, "Bare life is no longer confined to a particular place or a definite category. It now dwells in the biological body of every living being" (140). The reason for this is that, although "life and politics" may have been "originally divided" between *zoē* and *bios*, they became "linked together by means of the no-man's-land of the **state of exception** that is inhabited by bare life" (148). And "[w]hen life and politics ... begin to become one, all life becomes sacred" (in a sense analogous to *homo sacer*) "and all politics becomes the exception" (148).

Further reading: Agamben 1998, 2005, 2011; de la Durantaye 2009; Lechte and Newman 2013.

BASE AND SUPERSTRUCTURE

These terms are important ones in **Marxist** criticism and are used by Karl Marx in his own writings to distinguish between an economic base, what Marx saw as the determining foundation of a given society, and the legal, political and even ideological structures that are developed because of that underlying base, what he terms the superstructure. According to Marx, it is the economic base of a society that determines the very consciousness of men in a given epoch. As he puts it in his Preface to *A Contribution to the Critique of Political Economy* (1859), "It is not the consciousness of men that determines their being, but, on the contrary, their social being that determines their consciousness" (Marx and Engels 1962: 1.363). In the "Eighteenth Brumaire of Louis Napoleon" (1852), Marx aligns the superstructure with "distinct and peculiarly formed sentiments, illusions, modes of thought and views of life" (Marx and Engles 1962: 1.272). Whereas an individual "may imagine that they [sic] form the real motives and the starting-point of his activity" (1.272), the superstructure is in fact shaped out of a class's "material foundations and out of the corresponding social relations" (1.272), which Marx sees as the economic base or foundation of existence.

Revolution happens, according to Marx, when the base's **relations of production**, the structural mechanisms in place to help men produce things, are perceived not as enabling but constraining. The suggestion appears to be that only with a change in the economic base will the superstructure (laws, politics, and even consciousness) effectively change: "With the change of the economic foundation the entire immense superstructure is more or less rapidly transformed" (Marx and Engels 1962: 1.363). According to Marx, one must always distinguish between the structural mechanisms and relations that form the economic base of a society and all the ideological work that makes up the superstructure, particularly when one is discussing revolutionary transformations: "In considering such transformations a distinction should always be made between the material transformation of the economic conditions of production, which can be determined with the precision of natural science, and the legal, political, religious, aesthetic or philosophic—in short, ideological forms in which men become conscious of this conflict and fight it out" (1.363).

So-called "vulgar **Marxists**" adopted the terms base and super-structure in pursuing arguments about a society's economic foundation, whereby **ideology** (including **aesthetic** and cultural production) is seen as a mere reflection of economic conditions; however, many neo-**Marxists** have pointed out the complexities and uncertainties in the definition of the terms when examined in Marx's original writing. For example, at other times, Marx suggests that art can achieve a "semi-autonomous" status at odds with the economic base: "In the case of the arts, it is well known that certain periods of their flowering are *out of all proportion to* the general development of society, hence also to the material foundation, the skeletal structure as it were, of its organization" (1973: 110; my italics). Neo-**Marxists** have also had to contend with the fact that proletarian revolution did not occur in the way Marx predicted. The result has been a complex understanding among neo-**Marxists** of the relations among economic conditions, hegemonic political or legal forms, aesthetic forms, and ideology. See especially **ideology**, **history**, **aesthetics** and **Ideological State Apparatuses**.

BEING AND EVENT

These are two terms that are central to the philosophy of Alain Badiou and are articulated in his work, *Being and Event* (2005a). Badiou sets himself against the **poststructuralist** theories of the 1980s (his book was first published in French in 1988) by making the case for truth in philosophical thinking. According to Badiou, "A truth is solely con-stituted by rupturing with the order which supports it, never as an effect of that order" (xii); that is, one can never determine a truth from the mere facts of historical unfolding (e.g., market capitalism's victory over planned Communist economies in the 1980s). Badiou uses the term "event" to designate a rupture that opens up truths, for example, the rupture that can happen after a scientific breakthrough (Badiou sometimes gives Galileo as just such an example). Badiou also recasts the notion of the **subject**, based on his understanding of truth. According to Badiou, a **subject** "is nothing other than an active fidelity to the event of truth," which "means that a subject is a mili-tant of truth" (xiii). This militant of truth is found especially in four distinct conditions, or what Badiou terms "generic procedures": politics ("the political militant working for the emancipation of humanity in its entirety" [xiii]); art (see "**Inaesthetic**"); science (in its effort always to "open up a new theoretical field" [xiii]); and love. According to Badiou, the "being of truth" is "generic" insofar as it proves "itself an exception to any pre-constituted predicate of the situation in which that truth is deployed"; that is, "although it is situated in a world, a truth does not retain anything expressible from that situation. A truth concerns everyone inasmuch as it is a multiplicity that no particular predicate can circumscribe. The infinite work of a truth is thus that of a 'generic procedure.'" By this logic, "to be a Subject (and not a simple individual animal) is to be a local active dimension of such a procedure" (xiii). And Badiou argues that there are only four generic procedures: "Therefore, *stricto sensu*, there is no **subject** save the artistic, amorous, scientific, or political" (17). Each of these four generic procedures allows us to move beyond the particularities, beliefs, and constraints of the moment to discern something that goes beyond what can presently be thought, and it is that movement that connects us to that which, in fact, ties us all together, "the common-being, the multiple-essence" (17): "What happens in art, in science, in true (rare) politics, and in love (if it exists), is the coming to light of an indiscernible of the times, which, as such, is neither a known or recognized multiple, nor an ineffable singularity, but that which detains in its multiple-being all the common traits of the collective in question: in this sense, it is the truth of the collective being" (17). This is not to say that a subject can ever claim to have the truth, since that truth is compromised and delimited the moment you articulate it and thus tie it to a specific situation:

> Grasped in its being, the subject is solely the finitude of the generic procedure, the local effects of an eventual fidelity. What it "produces" is the truth itself, an indiscernible part of the situation, but the infinity of this truth transcends it. It is abusive to say that truth is a subjective production. A **subject** is much rather *taken up* in fidelity to the event, and *suspended* from truth; from which it is forever separated by chance. (2005a: 406)

Badiou often turns to mathematics to articulate his various concepts, particularly Georg Cantor's set theory and its understanding of "the infinity of pure multiples," as well as the mathematical theories of Kurt Friedrich Gödel and Paul Cohen, and, indeed, he goes so far as to argue that "insofar as being, qua being, is nothing other than pure multiplicity, it is legitimate to say that ontology, the science of the being qua being, is nothing other than mathematics itself" (2005a:

xiii). The discipline of philosophy finds itself in a strange position in Badiou's philosophy since it is, by definition, separated from each of the four conditions (politics, art, science, love). It can also not directly address ontology since "ontology = mathematics" (13); only mathematicians can do that. Badiou therefore assigns "philosophy to the thinkable articulation of two **discourses** (and practices) which *are not it*: mathematics, science of being, and the intervening doctrines of the event" (13). Philosophy is at best a meta-ontology, just as its engagement with politics is at best "**metapolitical**."

See also: **paradigm shift**.

Further reading: Badiou 2001, 2005a, 2005b, 2005c, 2009a, 2009b, 2011; Hallward 2003; Žižek 2008.

BETWEEN THE TWO DEATHS

"Between the two deaths" is the space of pure **death drive** without **desire**, between symbolic death and actual death. Jacques Lacan associates this space with an unconditional, insistent demand, like the ghost of Hamlet's father demanding he be revenged. In pop culture, this position is often taken up by the living dead (ghosts, vampires, zombies, etc.), by, as Slavoj Žižek puts it, "the fantasy of a person who does not want to stay dead but returns again and again to pose a threat to the living" (1991b: 22).

BINARY OPPOSITION (BINARISM)

Binary oppositions become important for critical theory in the wake of structuralist linguistics and anthropology. When one accepts Ferdinand de Saussure's contention that linguistic signs are arbitrary, that they come to mean not because of any intrinsic qualities but because of a system of differences, then binary opposition is revealed as one of the primary mechanisms by which signs come to mean something in the act of reading or interpretation. The structural anthropologist Claude Lévi-Strauss builds on this insight, for example, to establish through overarching structural oppositions the unconscious attitudes of a given society:

> Once we have defined these differential structures, there is nothing absurd about inquiring whether they belong strictly to the sphere considered or whether they may be encountered (often in transformed fashion) in other spheres of the same society or in different societies. And, if we find these structures to be

common to several spheres, we have the right to conclude that we have reached a significant knowledge of the unconscious attitudes of the society or societies under consideration. (1963: 87)

Algirdas Julien Greimas applies this same logic to all aspects of human experience expressed through language, which is most everything, and illustrates in his notion of the semiotic or **Greimassian square** that any word entails an implicit binary opposition ("white" can be understand only in contradistinction to "black," for example) and that such binaries actually entail up to ten terms that work out the implicit binaries of any given word. In this, he builds on Saussure's argument that "A particular word is like the center of a constellation; it is the point of convergence of an indefinite number of co-ordinated terms" (Saussure 1916: 126). See **Greimassian square**.

Poststructuralism builds on such structuralist insights, particularly Saussure's two principles for the linguistic sign: (1) that it is arbitrary, determined by convention and the oppositional differences between signs; and (2) that it can, therefore, only establish meaning over a temporal span. See **signifier and signified**. Jacques Derrida combines these two principles in his concept of *différance* (both to differ and to defer) in order to question all binary oppositions that, inevitably, seek to privilege one side against an opposing side (including Saussure's own privileging of spoken speech over writing): "Always differing and deferring, the **trace** is never as it is in the presentation of itself. It erases itself in presenting itself, muffles itself in resonating, like the *a* writing itself, inscribing its pyramid in *différance*" (1982: 23). In other words, any effort to posit the essence of something (being, *telos*, presence) is, in fact, always caught up in the differences and deferrals of meaning-production in language (it "erases itself in presenting itself"), which Derrida's neologism of *différance* not only represents but also enacts.

Feminism, **LGBTQ studies**, **queer theory**, disability studies and **postcolonial studies** have all benefited from Derrida's deconstruction of binary oppositions and each questions society's tendency to establish a privileged presence against which the **Other** of a binary opposition is defined (male/female, heterosexual/homosexual, able/disabled, Occident/Orient).

See also: **epistemology of the closet, semiotics**.

Further reading: Derrida 1976, 1978, 1982; Greimas 1976b; Lévis-Strauss 1963; Saussure 1916.

BIO-POLITICS AND BIO-POWER

These concepts are important ones in the late writings of Michel Foucault. According to Foucault, sovereign power, which is to say, the power of the king or his representatives, used to concern itself with "the right to decide life and death" (1990: 1.135) or, perhaps more specifically, the "right of seizure: of things, time, bodies, and ultimately life itself" (1.136). However, Foucault argues, "[s]ince the classical age the West has undergone a very profound transformation of these mechanisms of **power**" (1.136): "The old power of death that symbolized sovereign power was now carefully supplanted by the administration of bodies and the calculated management of life" (1.139–40). Whereas before, sovereign power only concerned itself with forms of seizure, it now concerns itself with life itself, particularly its definition and proper maintenance. According to Foucault, this new concern is precisely why, however paradoxically, the modern period has seen so many massacres and holocausts: "If genocide is indeed the dream of modern powers, this is not because of a recent return of the ancient right to kill; it is because **power** is situated and exercised at the level of life, the species, the race, and the large-scale phenomena of population" (1.137). According to Foucault, this helps to explain why capital punishment has gradually disappeared as an acceptable punishment whereas ever larger numbers of people have been killed in wars and genocides: "As soon as power gave itself the function of administering life, its reason for being and the logic of its exercise—and not the awakening of humanitarian feelings—made it more and more difficult to apply the death penalty" (1.138). By contrast, one could legitimize massive death in order to defend a particular way of living.

The important first step in this process is the increasing attention paid to an individual's body, followed by an increasing emphasis "on the species body, the body imbued with the mechanics of life and serving as the basis of the biological processes" (1990: 1.139). The supervision of these two poles—the individual body and the species body—"was effected through an entire series of interventions and *regulatory controls: a bio-politics of the population*. The **disciplines** of the body and the regulations of the population constituted the two poles around which the organization of **power** over life was deployed" (1.139). The result, starting with the eighteenth century, was "an era of 'bio-power,'" leading to "an explosion of numerous and diverse techniques for achieving the subjugation of bodies and the control of populations" (1.140). As a result, life itself, which for Aristotle was understood as separate from politics, suddenly became political.

Bio-power designates, then, "what brought life and its mechanisms into the realm of explicit calculation," including politics (hence, "bio-politics"), "and made knowledge-**power** an agent of transformation of human life" (1990: 1.143). The result "of this development of bio-power was the growing importance assumed by the action of the norm" (what is normal as opposed to what is defined as perverse), which requires "continuous regulatory and corrective mechanisms" that "qualify, measure, appraise, and hierarchize" both the individual body and the species body (1.144). Sex was particularly significant in this development, according to Foucault, since it linked the individual body and the species body; it "was at the pivot of the two axes," the life of the body and the life of the species, "along which developed the entire political technology of life" (1.145). This new concern with sex gave "rise to infinitesimal surveillances, permanent controls, extremely meticulous orderings of space, indeterminate medical or psychological examinations, to an entire micro-**power** concerned with the body. But it gave rise as well to comprehensive measures, statistical assessments, and interventions aimed at the entire social body or at groups taken as a whole" (1.145–46). Foucault's turn to the body as an area of critical investigation inspired a number of theorists that followed him. As Terry Eagleton puts it, referencing Foucault's influence on critical theory, "A recovery of the importance of the body has been one of the most precious achievements of recent radical thought" (1990: 7).

See also: **bare life and *homo sacer*.**

BLACKBOXING

This is a term used by Bruno Latour and **Actor-Network Theory** to describe one of the ways we tend to hide from ourselves the full network of "actants" (rather than "subjects" or "individuals") that are actually involved in any action, including nonhuman actants (machines, tools, etc). A good example of blackboxing is what occurs when we are confronted with an efficient machine: "When a machine runs efficiently, ... one need focus only on its inputs and outputs and not on its internal complexity. Thus, paradoxically, the more science and technology succeed, the more opaque and obscure they become" (Latour 1999: 304). Latour sometimes uses the term "punctualisation" to indicate the operation whereby a complex system, full of what Latour terms **mediators**, is turned into an abstract, simplified whole in the moment of operation (for example, when we drive a car), after which we no longer think about the actual complexity of the action and of what makes it possible. As long as the machine works, we do not think about the host of nonhuman actants that make up the device. In *Pandora's Hope* (1999), Latour offers the example of an overhead projector:

> Take, for instance, an overhead projector. It is a point in a sequence of action (in a lecture, say), a silent and mute **intermediary**, taken for granted, completely determined by its function. Now suppose the projector breaks down. The crisis reminds us of the projector's existence. As the repairmen swarm around it, adjusting this lens, tightening that bulb, we remember that the projector is made of several parts, each with its role and function and its relatively independent goals. Whereas a moment before the projector scarcely existed, now even its parts have individual existence, each its own "black box." In an instant our "projector" grew from being composed of zero parts to one to many. (183)

Actor-Network Theory is particularly interested in moments when devices break down since they then reveal the true complexity of our interaction with machines, which is normally hidden from us.

See also: **mediators and intermediaries, quasi-objects and quasi-subjects, things and Thing Theory**.

Further reading: Latour 1999, 2005; Law 2004; Law and Mol 2002.

BODY WITHOUT ORGANS

"Body without Organs" or BwO is a phrase used by Gilles Deleuze and Félix Guattari in their work, *A Thousand Plateaus* (1987), to designate any **assemblage** that is not unified in a single individual or **object** but that is understood in its multiple connections to other things over time; Deleuze and Guattari therefore explain that the Body without Organs "is not at all a notion or a concept but a practice, a set of practices" (150–51). The point is not to target "organs" themselves but the understanding of an "organism" as an ordered and stable hierarchy, where the organs are subordinate to a controlling body or mind, the "organic organization of the organs" (158):

> We come to the gradual realization that the BwO is not at all the opposite of the organs. The organs are not its enemies. The enemy

is the organism. The BwO is opposed not to the organs but to that organization of the organs called the organism. (158)

Deleuze and Guattari are interested in moving beyond the traditional emphasis on the **subject**'s stable relation to the objective world in favor of a model where "multiplicities" are constantly in the process of not only forming stable reference points (what they term the "territorialization" or "stratification" of "**assemblages**") but also exploding outward because of centrifugal forces (what they term "deterritorialization" or "lines of flight"). Instead of a stable organism, the Body without Organs refers to "the unformed, unorganized, nonstratified, or destratified body and all its flows" (43). Instead of stable objects in space, the BwO seeks out "intensities," which Deleuze and Guattari align with **desire**, particularly **desires** that are deemed by dominant society as **perverse**: "There is **desire** whenever there is the constitution of a BwO under one relation or another" (165).

Deleuze and Guattari are careful to state, however, that the Body without Organs is not simply the rejection of "stratification": "Staying stratified—organized, signified, subjected—is not the worst that can happen; the worst that can happen is if you throw the strata into demented or suicidal collapse, which brings them back down on us heavier than ever" (161). Instead, they wish to work counter to the "stratification" of the organism but without ending in death or catastrophe (161). As they explain,

> You have to keep enough of the organism for it to reform each dawn; and you have to keep small supplies of significance and subjectification, if only to turn them against their own systems when the circumstances demand it, when things, persons, even situations, force you to; and you have to keep small rations of **subjectivity** in sufficient quantity to enable you to respond to the dominant reality. Mimic the strata. You don't reach the BwO, and its plane of consistency, by wildly destratifying. (160)

See also: **schizoanalysis, rhizome.**

Further reading: DeLanda 2006; Deleuze and Guattari 1983, 1987.

BRICOLAGE (BRICOLEUR)

This term is borrowed from Claude Lévi-Strauss by Jacques Derrida to characterize his critical method; the term is now most closely associated with **deconstruction**. As Derrida explains, "[t]he *bricoleur*, says Lévi-Strauss, is someone who uses 'the means at hand,' that is, the instruments he finds at his disposition around him, those which are already there" (1978: 285). Rather than believe that one can make sense of everything (for example by establishing some origin or presence, what Derrida terms a "**transcendental signified**"), the *bricoleur* merely "plays" with the material found in a given cultural heritage, thus refusing to follow the path of totalization. According to Derrida, *bricolage* entails the acceptance of "a new status of **discourse**," that is, the "abandonment of all reference to a *center*, to a *subject*, to a privileged *reference*, to an origin, or to an absolute *archia*" (286). Rather than nostalgically mourn the loss of this center, *bricolage* is a form of "Nietzschean *affirmation*, that is the joyous affirmation of the play of the world and of the innocence of becoming, the affirmation of a world of signs without fault, without truth, and without origin which is offered to an active interpretation. *This affirmation then determines the noncenter otherwise than as loss of the center*" (292).

See also: **supplement**.

CAMP

"Camp" is a sensibility that revels in artifice, stylization, theatricalization, irony, playfulness, and exaggeration rather than content, as Susan Sontag famously defined the term in her short essay, "Notes on 'Camp'" (1964). According to Sontag, "Camp sensibility is disengaged, depoliticized—or at least apolitical" (277); however, some **postmodernists**, **feminists**, and **queer** theorists have explored the ways that camp (for example, the drag show) can trouble the belief that **gender** is "**natural**" or inherent, and can therefore work against **heteronormativity**. As Sontag argues, "Not all homosexuals have Camp taste. But homosexuals, by and large, constitute the vanguard—and the most articulate audience—of Camp" (290). By exaggerating sexual characteristics and personality mannerisms, such **queer**-inflected camp could be said to contend that all behavior is really **performative**. Camp is also tied to **postmodernism**. As Sontag puts it, "Camp sees everything in quotation marks. It's not a lamp, but a 'lamp'; not a woman, but a 'woman'" (280). In this way, the term resembles Linda Hutcheon's very similar understanding of **parody**, which Hutcheon offers as one of the major characteristics of **postmodern** art. Camp's relationship to **kitsch** is a close one; camp could be said to be a self-conscious **kitsch**. As Sontag writes, "Many examples of Camp are things which, from a 'serious' point of view, are either bad art or **kitsch**," though she also acknowledges that "some art which can be approached as Camp … merits the most serious admiration and study" (278). Sontag also distinguishes between "pure camp," which amounts to a **kitsch** that takes itself so seriously that we can now see it as hilarious (in other words, the camp sensibility is on the side of the audience not the author of the work), and "Camp which knows itself to be Camp ('camping')" (282) and is, therefore, already making fun of itself.

Further reading: Eco 2007; Hutcheon 1989; Meyer 1994; Sontag 1964.

CAPITAL AND CAPITALISM

According to Karl Marx, human society's entrance into capitalism occurred because of a transformation in the understanding of **exchange value** and of **labor**. In a barter society, goods are exchanged in a way that directly relates one item to another by consideration of the "specific useful and concrete **labour**" used to produce the object (1867: 150). The objects exchanged are tied closely both to the **use value** of the objects (their immediate usefulness) and to the real, material **labor** expended to produce the object. In capitalism, that concrete **labor** tends to get translated into an abstract quantity that can then stand as an **equivalent form** that one can use to determine the exchangeability of all sorts of products. In this way, "concrete labour … becomes the expression of abstract human labour" (150). The differences between different kinds of **labor** and different sorts of **use value** no longer matter: one begins to think of **labor** as an abstract, undifferentiated quantity that one can exchange for analogous abstract quantities of **labor** "congealed" in other products: the **labor** that creates value "is now explicitly presented as **labour** which counts as the equal of every other sort of human **labour**, whatever natural form it may possess, hence whether it is **objectified** in a coat, in corn, in iron, or in gold" (155). As Marx goes on, "The linen, by virtue of the form of value, no longer stands in a social relation with merely one other kind of **commodity**, but with the whole world of **commodities** as well" (155). We thus begin to move towards a "**universal equivalent**": a single abstract measure by which one can facilitate the exchange of categorically different items on the market. A similar transformation occurs in the value of the given product. In the exchange of goods on the capitalist market, **exchange value** rather than **use value** dominates. As Marx explains, **exchange value** must always be distinguished from **use value**, because "the exchange relation of

commodities is characterized precisely by its abstraction from their **use-values**" (127). By abstracting value into **exchange value**, the stage is set for the eventual dominance of first gold and then paper and then virtual money as the **universal equivalent** of capitalist society.

By accepting **money** as the **universal equivalent**, capitalism eventually manages to exploit the laborer upon whom all value ultimately inheres, according to Marx. That is, **money** tends to hide the real equivalent behind any monetary exchange: **labor**. The more labor it takes to produce a product, the greater its value. Marx therefore concludes that "As exchange-values, all **commodities** are merely definite quantities of congealed **labour-time**" (1867: 130). However, what happens in a capitalist society is that people tend to believe that power and value really inhere in the **money-form** rather in the **labor** that actually produces goods and services, leading to what Marx terms "**commodity fetishism**."

Money in turn allows for the accumulation of capital. In commodity exchange, one exchanges a **commodity** for **money**, which one then exchanges for some other **commodity**. One sells in order to buy something else of use to the consumer; Marx writes this formula as C-M-C (or Commodity-Money-Commodity). **Money** allows this formula to be transformed, however: now one can buy in order to sell (at a higher price) or M-C-M, which becomes for Marx the general formula for capital. In this second formula, "the circulation of **money** as **capital** is an end in itself, for the valorization of value takes place only within this constantly renewed movement. The movement of **capital** is therefore limitless" (1867: 253). The aim of the capitalist thus becomes "the unceasing movement of profit-making" (254). Indeed, the formula is reduced even further in the case of **usury**, when one loans money in return for the same money with interest, or M-M. A similar process occurs on the stock market: money making yet more money without the purchase of a tangible commodity.

But once again, what is forgotten in this process is the **labor-power** upon which the whole system of profit relies, according to Marx: the purchasing of a person's **labor-power** in exchange for full ownership of the product thus produced.

See also: **cultural capital**, **late capitalism**.

Further reading: Bottomore 1985; Foley 1986; Giddens 1973; Mandel 1972; K. Marx 1867, 1973; Marx and Engels 1932.

CARCERAL

See **panoptic, panopticon, and carceral**

CARNIVALESQUE

This term was popularized by Mikhail Bakhtin in his book, *Rabelais and His World* (1984b). The book was influential because it helped literary critics to reassess the value and to make sense of those literary works that had previously been considered too "low" for serious study, the comic tradition that Bakhtin saw as best exemplified in the work of François Rabelais, a sixteenth-century French author. According to Bakhtin, "No dogma, no authoritarianism, no narrow-minded seriousness can coexist with Rabelaisian images; these images are opposed to all that is finished and polished, to all pomposity, to every ready-made solution in the sphere of thought and world outlook" (3). Bakhtin reads this rejection of orthodoxy as an affirmation of the natural and bodily, "grotesque" world that he sees as persisting in a folk tradition that throughout history marked its rejection of dominant ideologies in moments of carnival. In contrast to the "classic" canon, the grotesque or carnivalesque canon underscores becoming and growth, the cyclical temporality of death and rebirth, universal equality, **dialogism**, and "the festive liberation of laughter and body" (89). Some critics have questioned Bakhtin's unapologetic celebration of carnival, particularly when the carnivalesque is proscribed in time and space (as it is in those carnivals that precede the advent of Lent). As Umberto Eco for example explains, "One must know to what degree certain behaviors are forbidden, and must feel the majesty of the forbidding norm, to appreciate their transgression. Without a valid law to break, carnival is impossible." Eco therefore argues that "comedy and carnival are not instances of real transgression: on the contrary, they represent paramount examples of law reinforcement. They remind us of the existence of the rule" (1984: 6).

Note that Henry Louis Gates in *The Signifying Monkey* (1988) illustrates that this carnivalesque tradition, as well as a tradition of **parody** and double-voicedness, has existed in the non-European African and Carribean tradition for centuries, thus completely separate from Bakhtin's exclusively Eurocentric understanding of the carnivalesque.

See also: **polyphony**.

Further reading: Bakhtin 1981, 1984b; Castle 1986; Eco 1984; Stallybrass and White 1986.

CASTRATION AND CASTRATION COMPLEX

The "castration complex" is the early childhood fear of castration that Sigmund Freud and Jacques Lacan both saw as an integral part of our **psychosexual development**. The castration complex is closely associated with the **Oedipus complex**, according to Freud: "the reaction to the threats against the child aimed at putting a stop to his early sexual activities and attributed to his father" (1953–74: 15.208). The young child with primitive desires, in coming face to face with the laws and conventions of society (including the prohibitions against incest and murder), will tend to align prohibition with **castration**. This alignment is reinforced by parents if they warn against, for example, masturbation by saying that the child will in some way be punished bodily, e.g., by going blind. Lacan builds on this Freudian concept in defining the Law or **Name-of-the-Father** (see **psychosexual development**).

Further reading: Freud 1916–17; Lacan 1968; Laplanche and Pontalis 1973; Žižek 1991b.

CATHEXIS (CATHEXES, TO CATHECT)

"Cathexis" is the **libido**'s charge of energy. Sigmund Freud often described the functioning of psychosexual energies in mechanical terms, influenced perhaps by the dominance of the steam engine at the end of the nineteenth century. He often described the **libido** as the producer of energies that, if blocked, required release in other ways. If an individual is frustrated in his or her desires, Freud often represented that frustration as a blockage of energies that would then build up and require release in other ways: for example, by way of **regression** and the "re-cathecting" of former positions (i.e., **fixation** at the **oral** or **anal** phase and the enjoyment of former sexual objects ["**object**-cathexes"], including auto-eroticism). When the **ego** blocks such efforts to discharge one's cathexis by way of **regression**, i.e., when the **ego** wishes to **repress** such desires, Freud uses the term "anti-cathexis" or countercharge. Like a steam engine, the **libido**'s cathexis then builds up until it finds alternative outlets, which can lead to **sublimation** or to the formation of sometimes disabling **symptoms**.

CHORA

According to the psychoanalytical thinker, Julia Kristeva, "chora" refers to our bodily **drives** (both life **drives** and **death drives**) before our entrance into language; she applies the term "semiotic" to chora in order to distinguish it from the Lacanian **symbolic**, arguing that it represents a pre-lingual order of the body, that it "logically and chronologically precedes the establishment of the symbolic and its **subject**" (1984: 41). The chora therefore also "precedes evidence, verisimilitude, spatiality, and temporality" (26); it is the "non-expressive totality formed by the drives and their stases in a motility that is as full of movement as it is regulated" (25). We are closest to it in the earliest stage in our **psychosexual development** (0–6 months). In this pre-lingual stage of development, the child is dominated by a chaotic mix of perceptions, feelings, and needs. The child does not distinguish its own self from that of its mother or even the world surrounding its self. Rather, it spends its time taking into itself everything that is experienced as pleasurable without any acknowledgement of boundaries. This is the stage, then, when an individual is closest to the pure materiality of existence, or what Lacan terms "the **Real**" (see **psychosexual development**).

This is not to say that the chora does not have any kind of organization; it follows, rather, the pre-lingual rhythms of Freud's **oral** and **anal** stages of **psychosexual development**: "The **oral** and **anal** drives, both of which are oriented and structured around the mother's body, dominate this sensorimotor organization" (1984: 27); at the same time, the chora includes a certain degree of what Kristeva terms "negativity" since it is often oriented to "destruction, aggressivity, and death" (28), as with the **death drive**. Kristeva therefore argues that "the semiotic *chora* is no more than the place where the subject is both generated and negated, the place where his unity succumbs before the processes of charges and stases that produce him" (28).

According to Kristeva, our entrance into language dissociates us to some extent from the chora of our infancy, though language also continually must negotiate the bodily fact of the chora: "Our **discourse**—all **discourse**—moves with and against the *chora* in the sense that it simultaneously depends upon and refuses it" (1984: 26). Although our adoption of language may have to some extent dissevered us from the chora, the "semiotic rhythm within language" (29) can still be found in literature, especially poetry: "Indifferent to language, enigmatic and feminine, this space underlying the written is rhythmic, unfettered, irreducible to its intelligible verbal translation; it is musical, anterior to judgment, but restrained by a single guarantee: syntax" (29).

See also: *écriture féminine*, **genotext and phenotext**.

CHRONOTOPE

Mikhail Bakhtin theorizes the "chronotope" as "the intrinsic connectedness of temporal and spatial relationships that are artistically expressed in literature" (1981: 84); he uses the term primarily to define generic distinctions and to understand the development of generic forms over time, particularly the development of the novel from earlier narrative forms like "the so-called 'Greek' or 'Sophist' novels written between the second and sixth centuries A.D." (86) or the "Rabelaisian novel" (85) of the sixteenth century. Literally "time-space," the chronotope helps Bakhtin to illustrate how the "*adventure-time*" (87) of earlier narrative forms amounts to an "empty time" that "leaves no traces anywhere, no indications of its passing" (91) and "an abstract expanse of space" (99) without local particularity. Bakhtin examines the development of various narrative forms over time to illustrate how temporality and spatiality become increasingly particularized as we move towards the nineteenth century and the rise of the novel: "the chronotope, functioning as the primary means for materializing time in space, emerges as a center for concretizing representation, as a force giving body to the entire novel" (250). This concretization of time and space is particularly visible in spaces that are caught up in temporal change, what Bakhtin terms "chronotopes," for example road intersections, thresholds, parlors and salons. By the nineteenth century, through the use of such chronotopes, "[t]he epoch becomes not only graphically visible (space), but narratively visible (time)" (247).

See also: **dialogism, speech genre**.

Further reading: Bakhtin 1981, 1986; Ferris 1991.

CLASS

It is important to keep in mind that the contemporary meaning of "class"—"A division or stratum of society consisting of people at the same economic level or having the same social status" (*OED*)—is, in fact, of rather recent invention. This sense of the term does not become common until the end of the eighteenth century and through the nineteenth century, precisely the period that saw a change in the way different classes of people interact and are defined. Before then, "estate," "degree," "rank," and "order" were commonly used instead. For Raymond Williams, who was one of the initiators of both **Cultural Materialism** and **Cultural Studies**, the semantic change is an important indicator of shifts in society at large, one he explores especially in *Culture and Society* (1958). As he puts it in his *Keywords*, "Development of class in its modern social sense, with relatively fixed names for particular classes (lower class, middle class, upper class, working class and so on), belongs essentially to the period between 1770 and 1840, which is also the period of the Industrial Revolution and its decisive reorganization of society" (1983: 61).

This fact has not kept Karl Marx and the **Marxist** theory he inspired from examining class struggle throughout history; indeed, Marx and Engels begin their *Manifesto of the Communist Party* with the famous opening, "The history of all hitherto existing society is the history of class struggles" (1848: 419). Throughout society, according to Marx and Engels, "we find almost everywhere a complicated arrangement of society into various orders, a manifold gradation of social rank" but always some relationship of "oppressor and oppressed" (419). **Cultural Materialism** and much **Marxist** criticism, following Williams's and Marx's lead, examine cultural and socio-political elements from the past to determine the ways that any cultural product or social formation is inextricably tied to class consciousness and class relations.

The nineteenth century, however, marked a change in the notion of class, according to Marx and Engels:

> Our epoch, the epoch of the bourgeoisie, possesses ... this distinctive feature: it has simplified the class antagonisms. Society as a whole is more and more splitting up into two great hostile camps, into two great classes directly facing each other—bourgeoisie and proletariat. (1848: 419–20)

After this point, the **relations of production** that characterize **capitalism** change class relations because now the **proletariat** has no control over the **means of production** and must sell their labor as an abstract quantity now translated into the **universal equivalent** of **money**. This situation allows the **bourgeoisie** to own the products of proletarian **labor** and to create **surplus value**, to sell those products at a profit, thus exploiting the lower classes while legitimating that exploitation through **ideological** obfuscation and **commodity fetishism**. Marx believed that if the **proletariat** could be shown the truth of the situation, they would be able to reject this **ideological** mystification (this **false consciousness**) and start a communist revolution.

That revolution did not occur in the way Marx predicted, which forced many **neo-Marxists** to rethink the notion of class. Apparently, it was not sufficient to point out to the **proletariat** that they are being exploited by a system where capitalists owned all the **means of production** and thus reaped profits through **surplus value**. Indeed, one of the abiding concerns of Antonio Gramsci in his theorization of **hegemony** was how the lower classes could act in ways that ran counter to their own best interests. In fact, Marx himself raises the issue of "class consciousness" and how it can be difficult to get a class to become conscious of their common interests. As Williams points out, class in Marx is "sometimes an economic category, including all who are objectively in that economic situation" and sometimes "a formation in which, for historical reasons, consciousness of this situation and the organization to deal with it have developed" (1983: 68). That is, sometimes "class" is an objective description—a class "in itself," as Marx would say—and sometimes an active, subjective choice ("workers of the world, unite!"), a class "for itself." Both senses can be found in Marx's and Friedrich Engels's *German Ideology*:

> The separate individuals form a class only insofar as they have to carry on a common battle against another class; otherwise they are on hostile terms with each other as competitors. On the other hand, the class in its turn achieves an independent existence over against the individuals, so that the latter find their conditions of existence predestined, and hence have their position in life and their personal development assigned to them by their class. (1932: 68).

In the "Eighteenth Brumaire of Louis Napoleon" (1852) Marx continues this distinction but underscores class *consciousness* as more important than class as objective economic description:

> In so far as millions of families live under economic conditions of existence that separate their mode of life, their interests and their culture from those of the other classes, and put them in hostile opposition to the latter, they form a class. In so far as there is merely a local interconnection among these small-holding peasants, and the identity of their interests begets no community, no national bond and no political organisation among them, they do not form a class. They are consequently incapable of enforcing their class interests in their own name, whether through a parliament or through a convention. (Marx and Engels 1962: 1.334)

Max Weber influentially pursued the difficulty of establishing class consciousness by suggesting that the situation is, in fact, more complex. Weber defines power as "the chance of a person or a group to enforce their own will even against the resistance of others involved, through a communal action by the *Gemeinschaft* [community]" (1921: 137). According to Weber, the distribution of power occurs not only in terms of classes (economic power) but also in terms of status (social honor, prestige) and political party (the legal order), each of which is distinct. As Weber points out, "the concept of 'class interest' is an ambiguous one, especially as an **empirical** concept. ... As a result of this ambiguity, the direction in which the individual worker pursues his interests may vary greatly, even if the class situation and other circumstances remain the same" (140). The ability to come together to effect political change is just as much affected by status groups— which are quite distinct from class and has led, for example, to the situation of threatened status groups forming "alliances with the prole-tariat against the 'bourgeoisie'" (142)—as it is by political parties. For political parties, communal action is "always directed towards a tacti-cally chosen goal" (148) that need not be economic: "In individual cases, parties can represent interests determined by 'class situations' or the situation of the 'Stände,' and thus recruit their followers accordingly. But they neither have to be pure 'class' parties nor pure 'Stände-related' parties; and mostly it is only partly the case, and often not at all" (149). Ernesto Laclau and Chantal Mouffe (1985) develop this idea into their own understanding of **hegemony**, which they define in contra-distinction to Gramsci's understanding of the term; they wish, in their understanding of **radical democracy**, to bring together people across disparate identity formations in support of a common good that is not necessarily reducible to class. See also **articulation**.

Pierre Bourdieu also builds on Max Weber's theories and has influentially critiqued what he sees as the overly simplified movement in Marx from "class-on-paper to the 'real' class" (1998: 11). According to Bourdieu, "The construction of a theory of the social space presupposes a series of breaks with **Marxist** theory" (1991: 229). One can under-stand class only if one examines the ways class gets instantiated in practice, Bourdieu explains: "The 'real' class, if it has ever 'really' existed, is nothing but the realized class, that is, the mobilized class, a result of the *struggle of classifications*, which is a properly symbolic (and political) struggle to impose a vision of the social world, or, better, a way to construct that world, in perception and in reality, and to construct classes in accordance with which this social world can be divided" (1998: 11). By the logic of Bourdieu's examination of **cultural, social, and symbolic capital**, "Social class is not defined by a property (not even the most determinate one, such as the volume and composition of capital) nor by a collection of properties (of sex, age, social origin, ethnic origin—proportion of blacks and whites, for example, or natives and immigrants—income, education level etc.), nor even by a chain of properties strung out from a fundamental property (position in the relations of production) in a relation of cause and effect, conditioner and conditioned; but by the structure of relations between all the pertinent properties which gives its specific value to each of them and to the effects they exert on practices" (1984: 106). Such practices become entrenched by our adoption of unconscious manners of action and response that Bourdieu terms **habitus**. There is, Bourdieu argues, a "class **habitus**" (1977: 85): "the **habitus** could be considered as a subjective but not individual system of internalized structures, schemes of perception, conception, and action common to all members of the same group or class and constituting the precondition for all objectification and apperception" (86). This term is closely aligned with Bourdieu's other term, **doxa**, those ideological (and therefore arbitrary) beliefs that a given group takes for granted as the **nature** of things. Class struggle, according to Bourdieu, therefore often proceeds on this symbolic level: "The dominated classes have an interest in pushing back the limits of *doxa* and exposing the arbitrariness of the taken for granted; the dominant classes have an interest in defending the integrity of **doxa** or, short of this, of establishing in its place the necessarily imperfect substitute, *orthodoxy*" (Bourdieu 1977: 169). Sometimes, Bourdieu goes so far as to state that "Social classes do not exist. ... What exists is a social space, a space of differences" (1998: 12). Bourdieu prefers instead to use the term **field** to describe this global social space of endlessly reproduced, performed differences.

Further reading: Ahmad 1992; Bourdieu 1977, 1984, 1991, 1998; Giddens 1973; Giddens and Held 1982; Laclau and Mouffe 1985; K. Marx 1867, 1973; Marx and Engels 1848, 1932; Weber 1921; Williams 1958, 1983.

COGNITIVE MAP

Throughout his career, Fredric Jameson has argued for **utopic** representation as a way to drive political activism in the present and to make sense of the complexities of the **postmodern** period. The concept of **utopia** also informs his concept of the "cognitive map," which he uses to counter the **poststructuralist** critique of **grand narratives**, including the **Marxist** grand narrative of proletarian, international revolution. For Jameson, "without a conception of the social totality (and the possibility of transforming a whole social system), no properly socialist politics is possible" (1988: 355). Indeed, Jameson sees the **postmodern** and **poststructuralist** critique of all totalizing, **uto-pian** maneuvers as a **symptom** of the current world system: "our dis-satisfaction with the concept of totality is not a thought in its own right but rather a significant **symptom**, a function of the increasing difficul-ties in thinking of such a set of interrelationships in a complicated society" (356).

The problem is that our ability to imagine a social totality has been challenged by the historical development of **capitalism**. According to Jameson, over the course of the nineteenth century, the fact of imperialism and the establishment of a world market meant that any one person's lived experience in a particular place (say, London) no longer coincided with the truth of how the world functioned, either politically or economically. Once one enters this "stage of imperialism," the "truth of that limited daily experience of London lies, rather, in India or Jamaica or Hong Kong; it is bound up with the whole colonial system of the British Empire that deter-mines the very quality of the individual's subjective life. Yet those structural coordinates are no longer accessible to immediate lived experience and are often not even conceptualizable for most people" (1988: 349). That situation gets even further exacerbated in post-modern **late capitalism**, "a moment in which not merely the older city but even the **nation-state** itself has ceased to play a central functional and formal role in a process that has in a new quantum leap of **capital** prodigiously expanded beyond them, leaving them behind as ruined and archaic remains of earlier stages in the develop-ment of this **mode of production**" (350). See **Global Studies**. Jameson's argument is that the problems of **late capitalism** are exacerbated by a situation where we are not able to imagine a target for our critique. Now that "nation" is no longer operative as the driving force of economics, what we need is a new "cognitive map" that can help us to make sense of the complex, transnational system that is **late capitalism**. Jameson builds on the work of Kevin Lynch, who, in his *Image of the City* (1960), examines the ways that actual denizens of a city construct their surrounding spaces mentally: "Lynch suggests that urban alienation is directly proportional to the mental unmapability of local cityscapes" (Jameson 1988: 353). Jameson argues that "the incapacity to map socially is as crippling to political experience as the analogous incapacity to map spatially is for urban experience" and that, therefore, "an aesthetic of cognitive mapping in this sense is an integral part of any socialist political project" (353). He uses Lynch's book emblematically, "since the mental map of city space explored by Lynch can be extrapolated to that mental map of the social and global totality we all carry around in our heads in variously garbled forms" (353).

Further reading: Jameson 1988, 1991; Lynch 1960.

COGNITIVE STUDIES

As the name suggests, Cognitive Studies uses advances in Cognitive Science—an interdisciplinary approach to cognition that draws from linguistics, neuroscience, psychology, artificial intelligence, philosophy, and anthropology—in its approaches to culture and literature. Like Cognitive Science, Cognitive Studies is interdisciplinary and highly varied in its perspectives and areas of investigation. Even so, Cognitive Studies maintains an overarching critical effort: to understand the relationship between the evolved human brain and culture. Thus, the central question for Cognitive Studies is, as Ellen Spolsky puts it in the Preface to *The Work of Fiction: Cognition, Culture, and Complexity* (2004), which she edits with Alan Richardson,

> how does the evolved architecture that grounds human cognitive processing, especially as it manifests itself in the universality of storytelling and the production of visual art, interact with the apparently open-ended set of cultural and historical contexts in which humans find themselves, so as to produce the variety of social constructions that are historically distinctive, yet also often translatable across the boundaries of time and place? (viii)

As the question suggests, Cognitive Studies is indebted to **Cultural Studies** and **New Historicism**, which created a critical environment fertile for the study of cognitive engagement with specific cultural realities, even if the critical forerunners of **Cultural Studies** "occluded," as Spolsky argues, the kind of question that Cognitive Studies works to answer (viii). Lisa Zunshine (2010: 6–7) revises Spolsky's sense of occlusion, instead arguing that the cognitive turn has simply been "dormant" in **Cultural Studies** for the last 40 years, citing as example Raymond Williams's long discussion of the brain and culture in *The Long Revolution* (1961). As Williams, one of the earliest proponents of **Cultural Materialism** and **Cultural Studies**, writes in that book, "The evolution of the human brain, and then the particular interpretation carried by particular cultures, give us certain 'rules' or 'models,' without which no human being can 'see' in the ordinary sense at all" (18).

One can identify four general areas of investigation that constitute Cognitive Studies at this time. The first is sometimes termed Cognitive Linguistics or Cognitive Rhetoric. Given the linguistic turn in critical theory after Ferdinand de Saussure (see **signifier and signified**), it is no surprise that the linguistic basis for understanding cognition impels the work of many cognitive theorists. George Lakoff and Mark Johnson's *Metaphors We Live By* (1980) has proven particularly influential on this score. Rather than prioritize syntax and grammar, as in traditional linguistics (see *lanque* **and** *parole*), Lakoff and Johnson highlight the semantic value of metaphoric phrasing, which they believe undergirds human cognition: "Our ordinary conceptual system, in terms of which we think and act, is fundamentally metaphorical in nature" (3). The usual or generic metaphors—spatial, embodied, social—are part of a limited number of metaphors that not only reappear consistently in human languages but also shape human cognition and thus how people experience the world. In *Reading Minds* (1991), Mark Turner builds on Lakoff and Johnson, offering "a design for research that might be called 'cognitive rhetoric'" (viii) in order to understand the relation between human cognition (which is necessarily reliant on language) and our embodied experience within a human environment. In his following work, *The Literary Mind* (1996), Turner moves from metaphor in particular to its fundamental process of "blending," the manner in which two mental states, when combined, yield a third, blended state. Such blending occurs, Turner argues, in the use of metaphors; in the projection of concepts onto spatial constructs to create new ideas; and in **narrative**.

A second area of investigation in Cognitive Studies, one that shares the interests and terminology of Cognitive Linguistics, is Cognitive **Narratology**. David Herman, a key figure in Cognitive **Narratology**, defines this sub-field as "the nexus between narrative and mind" and analyzes the use of **discursive** formations in ways comparable to cognitive linguists. In "Scripts, Sequences, and Stories" (1997), Herman uses terminology from cognitive psychology and artificial intelligence to understand how culturally defined conceptual "scripts" and "schemas" shape how readers engage narrative texts. Another approach is offered by Patrick Colm Hogan's exploration of narrative universals in *The Mind and Its Stories* (2003). Building on Cognitive Linguistics, Hogan works to isolate narrative patterns and elements that cross cultural boundaries, showing how they coincide with universals of emotion supported by the evolved human brain.

A third particularly influential area of investigation is Theory of Mind, which Paula Leverage and colleagues (2011) define as "mind reading, empathy, creative imagination of another's perspective: in short, it is simultaneously a highly sophisticated ability, and a very basic necessity for human communication" (1). Critics like Lisa Zunshine bring "the recent findings of cognitive psychologists into literary studies" in order to show how Theory of Mind can help us to understand imaginative works, how "behavior in terms of the underlying states of mind—or *mind-reading* ability—can furnish us with a series of surprising insights into our interaction with literary texts" (2006: 4).

One can identify a fourth strand of Cognitive Studies that engages with the insights of **poststructuralism** and **New Historicism**. Ellen Spolsky's *Gaps in Nature: Literary Interpretation and the Modular Mind* (1993) is an influential example. Spolsky identifies her work, in part, as an effort to reconcile the insights of **poststructuralism** with the materialist approaches of **Marxists** and **New Historicists**. As she puts it, "While research in many areas of the humanities and social sciences is concerned ... with understanding the **power** of **culture** to structure and constrain, it is worthwhile at the same time to investigate the role of biological materialism as co-legislator of human life and under-standing." Referring at once to **Cultural Studies** and **deconstruction**, Spolsky argues that "The inevitable slippage we have come to acknowl-edge between words and the world has at least an analogue, and pre-sumably also a source, in the workings of the human brain" (3). Mary Thomas Crane in *Shakespeare's Brain* (2000) concurs: "The cognitive emphasis on the embodiment of thought offers the possibility of a more radical materialism than does current **Marxist** theory, since it attempts to explore the literally material origins of the self" (17).

Further reading: Crane 2000; Herman 1997; Hogan 2003; Lakoff and Johnson 1980; Leverage *et al.* 2011; Pinker 1997; Spolsky 1993; Spolsky and Richardson 2004; M. Turner 1991, 1996; Zunshine 2006, 2010.

COMING COMMUNITY

See **cosmopolitanism**

COMMODIFICATION

"Commodification" is the subordination of both private and public realms to the logic of **capitalism**. In this logic, such things as friendship, knowledge, time, etc. are understood only in terms of their monetary value. In this way, they are no longer treated as things with intrinsic worth but as **commodities**. (They are valued, that is, only extrinsically in terms of **money**, in terms of a **universal equivalent**.) By this logic, a factory worker can be reconceptualized not as a human being with specific needs that, as humans, we are obliged to provide but as a mere wage debit in a businessman's ledger.

See also: **commodity fetishism**.

COMMODITY

According to Karl Marx, a commodity is an "external object, a thing which through its qualities satisfies human needs of whatever kind" (1867: 125) and is then exchanged for something else. When Marx speaks of commodities, he is particularly concerned with the "physical properties of the commodity" (126), which he associates closely with the **use value** of an object. However, **use value** does not automatically lead to a commodity: "He who satisfies his own need with the product of his own labour admittedly creates use-values, but not commodities. In order to produce the latter, he must not only produce **use-values**, but **use-values** for others, social **use-values**" (131). Commodities, therefore, "possess a double form, i.e. natural form and value form" (138). (See **use value and exchange value**.) The actual physical body of the commodity is made up of: (1) the material provided by nature (e.g., linen, gold, etc.); and (2) the labor expended to create it (see 1867: 133). Note that a commodity can refer to tangible things as well as more ephemeral products (e.g., a lecture). What matters is that something be exchanged for the thing.

See also: **capital and capitalism, commodification, commodity fetishism**.

COMMODITY FETISHISM

"Commodity fetishism" is the tendency to attribute to commodities (including money) a power that really inheres only in the labor expended to create commodities. Karl Marx turns to fetishism to make sense of the apparently magical quality of the **commodity**: "A **commodity** appears at first sight an extremely obvious, trivial thing. But its analysis brings out that it is a very strange thing, abounding in metaphysical subtleties and theological niceties" (1867: 163). Fetishism in anthropology refers to the primitive belief that godly powers can inhere in inanimate things (e.g., in totems). Marx borrows this concept to make sense of what he terms "commodity fetishism." As Marx explains, the commodity remains simple as long as it is tied to its **use value**. When a piece of wood is turned into a table through human labor, its **use value** is clear and, as product, the table remains tied to its material use; however, as soon as the table "emerges as a **commodity**, it changes into a thing which transcends sensuousness" (163). The connection to the actual hands of the laborer is severed as soon as the table is connected to **money** as the **universal equivalent** for exchange. People in a **capitalist** society thus begin to treat commodities as if value inhered in the objects themselves, rather than in the amount of real **labor** expended to produce the object. As Marx explains, "The mysterious character of the **commodity**-form consists therefore simply in the fact that the **commodity** reflects the social characteristics of men's own labour as objective characteristics of the products of labour themselves, as the socio-natural properties of these things" (164–65). What is, in fact, a social relation between people (between capitalists and exploited laborers) instead assumes "the fantastic form of a relation between things" (165).

This situation occurs because in a **capitalist** society the real producers of **commodities** remain largely invisible. We only approach their products "through the relations which the act of exchange establishes between the products" (Marx 1867: 165). We access the products of the **proletariat** through the exchange of **money** with those institutions that glean profit from the **labor** of the proletariat. Since we only ever relate to those products through the exchange of **money**, we forget the "secret hidden under the apparent movements in the relative values of **commodities**" (168); that is, **labor**: "It is ... precisely this finished form of the world of commodities—the **money form**—which conceals the social character of private **labour** and the social relations between the individual workers, by making those relations appear as relations between material objects, instead of revealing them plainly" (168–69). In **capitalist** society, gold and then paper money become "the direct incarnation of all human labour" (187), much as in primitive societies the totem becomes the direct incarnation of god-head. Through this process, "Men are henceforth related to each other in their social process of **production** in a purely atomistic way; they become **alienated** because their own relations of **production** assume a material shape which is independent of their control and their conscious individual action" (187). Although value ultimately accrues because of human **labor**, people in a **capitalist** system are led to believe that they are not in control of the market forces that appear to exist independently of any individual person.

The situation differed in **feudal society**: In such a society, "we find everyone dependent—serfs and lords, vassals and suzerains, laymen and clerics." Because "relations of personal dependence form the given social foundation, there is no need for labour and its products to assume a fantastic form different from their reality. They take the shape, in the transactions of society, of services in kind and payments in kind" (Marx 1867: 170). Transactions in **feudal society** involve the particularity of **labor** rather than the abstract **universal equivalent** necessary for **commodity** production. Marx therefore concludes that "Whatever we may think … of the different roles in which men confront each other in such a society, the social relations between individuals in the performance of their **labour** appear at all events as their own personal relations, and are not disguised as social relations between things, between the products of **labour**" (170).

COMMUNICATIVE ACTION

Jürgen Habermas argues that, against contemporary developments that threaten to destroy a **public sphere** of rational debate and critique, we must reconstruct a space where private human beings can debate in a public forum governed by rationality and oriented towards the promise of argumentatively achieved consensus. In this, Habermas sets himself against the **postmodern** suspicion of Enlightenment reason and **postmodern** theory's tendency to argue for **incommensurability** between **subject** positions (see, for example, **differend** and **dissensus**). Habermas argues, by contrast, that whenever "we engage in moral argument," we rely on the "intuitive knowledge" that "valid norms must be capable in principle of meeting with the rationally motivated approval of everyone affected under conditions that neutralize all motives except that of cooperatively seeking the truth" (1987: 1.19). He defines communicative action as

> The interaction of at least two subjects capable of speech and action who establish interpersonal relations (whether by verbal or by extraverbal means). The actors seek to reach an understanding about the action situation and their plans of action in order to coordinate their actions by way of agreement. (1987: 1.86)

Language in this understanding of communicative action must be understood not as a tool to achieve what one wishes (what Habermas terms a "**teleological** model") nor as a conveyer of pre-approved cultural values (the "normative model") nor as a reflection of personal expression (the "dramaturgical model") but rather "as a medium of uncurtailed communication whereby speakers and hearers, out of the context of their preinterpreted **lifeworld**, refer simultaneously to things in the objective, social, and subjective worlds in order to negotiate common definitions of the situation" (1987: 1.95). These three "worlds" are understood as follows: "(1) The objective world (as the totality of all entities about which true statements are possible); (2) The social world (as the totality of all legitimately regulated interpersonal relations); and (3) The subjective world (as the totality of the experiences of the speaker to which he has privileged access)" (1.100). Communicative action always has recourse to issues of validity, thanks to the universal background of language and culture for all communication that Habermas terms the human **lifeworld**: "The concept of communicative action presupposes language as the medium for a kind of reaching understanding, in the course of which participants, through relating to a world, reciprocally raise validity claims that can be accepted or contested" (1.99). Those validity claims include at least the following three:

(1) That the statement made is true (or that the existential pre-suppositions of the propositional content mentioned are in fact satisfied);
(2) That the speech act is right with respect to the existing normative context (or that the normative context that it is supposed to satisfy is itself legitimate); and
(3) That the manifest intention of the speaker is meant as it is expressed. (1987: 1.99)

According to Habermas, we are here talking about "universal validity" for his concept of rationality (1987: 1.138), based on the universality of language and culture, which form a common "cultural stock of knowledge that is 'always already' familiar" (2.125): "this is an attempt at rationally reconstructing universal rules and necessary presuppositions of speech actions oriented to reaching understanding" (1.138).

See also: **communicative reason**, **discourse ethics**.

Further reading: Habermas 1987, 1991, 1993, 1999.

COMMUNICATIVE REASON OR RATIONALITY

The notion of communicative reason (or rationality) supports Jürgen Habermas's theory of **communicative action**. In short, communication and even an ethical relationship to others are not possible without some understanding of the universality of reason or rationality, which is, in turn, best posited, according to Habermas, in terms of communication. As Habermas explains, "If we assume that the human species maintains itself through the socially coordinated activities of its members and that this coordination has to be established through communication—and in certain central spheres through communication aimed at reaching agreement—then the reproduction of the species *also* requires satisfying the conditions of a rationality that is inherent in communicative action" (1987: 1.397). Habermas thus seeks to counter the relativism and **incommensurability** posited by much critical theory (see, for example, **differend** and **dissensus**).

See also: **discourse ethics**, **public sphere**.

Further reading: Habermas 1987, 1991, 1993, 1999.

COMPRADOR

This term (Portuguese for "buyer") was, formerly, "the name of a native servant employed by Europeans, in India and the East, to purchase necessaries and keep the household accounts: a house-steward" (*OED*); also, "Now, in China, the name of the principal native servant, employed in European establishments, and especially in houses of business, both as head of the staff of native employés, and as intermediary between the house and its native customers" (*OED*). **Marxists** use the term to refer to **bourgeois** members of a local economy who serve the interests of foreign monopolies, a function that continues in global, **late capitalist** society (hence the use of the term also in **Global Studies**). Postcolonial theorists often use the term in a broader sense to include all elements of a local culture that are supported by the continuation of and legitimization of colonial power, including academics and artists. As Gayatri Chakravorty Spivak explains, combining all three approaches, "it is in the 'interest' of **capital** to preserve the comprador theater in a state of relatively primitive labor legislation and environmental regulation" (1987: 166–67).

COMPULSORY HETEROSEXUALITY AND HETEROCENTRICITY

In her article, "Compulsory Heterosexuality and Lesbian Existence" (1980), Adrienne Rich critiques **feminism**'s almost exclusive concentration on **gender** and the **binary opposition**, male/female, since that approach privileges heterosexuality as the model for identity, thus marginalizing alternative **sexualities** such as "lesbian existence." As she puts it, the article "was written in part to challenge the erasure of lesbian existence from so much of scholarly **feminist** literature, an erasure which I felt (and feel) to be not just anti-lesbian, but anti-**feminist** in its consequences" (23). Rich also uses the term "hetero-centricity" to describe a situation where meaning is understood always in relation to the dominant, **hegemonic** center of heterosexuality, just as **feminists** critiqued in the notion of "**phallogocentrism**" the privileging of **patriarchy** in society at large, and before them Jacques Derrida critiqued in his term "**logocentrism**" the privileging of any privileged center to stop the **semiotic** play of language or *différance*. As Rich argues, "The lie of compulsory female heterosexuality today afflicts not just **feminist** scholarship, but every profession, every reference work, every curriculum, every organizing attempt, every relationship or conversation over which it hovers" (63).

See also: **LGBTQ Studies, queer theory**.

Further reading: Eskridge 1999.

CONDENSATION

Condensation is one of the methods by which the **repressed** returns in hidden ways. For example, in dreams multiple dream-thoughts are often combined and amalgamated into a single element of the manifest dream (e.g., symbols). According to Sigmund Freud, every situation in a dream seems to be put together out of two or more impressions or experiences. One need only think about how people and places tend to meld into composite figures in our dreams. The same sort of condensation can occur in **symptom**-formation. The other method whereby the repressed hides itself is **displacement**.

Further reading: Freud 1900, 1916–17, 1932; K. Silverman 1983.

CONTACT ZONE AND TRANSCULTURATION

Mary Louise Pratt theorizes this concept, which has been subse-quently taken up by **postcolonial** critics. As Pratt explains, "I use this term to refer to social spaces where cultures meet, clash, and grapple with each other, often in contexts of highly asymmetrical relations of power, such as colonialism, slavery, or their aftermaths as they are lived out in many parts of the world today" (1991: 34). She examines, for example, instances where indigenous populations seek to represent themselves by commandeering and repurposing elements of the colonizer's **discourse**. She names this activity "autoethnography." She explains that by "autoethnographic **text**,"

> I mean a **text** in which people undertake to describe themselves in ways that engage with representations others have made of them. Thus if ethnographic **texts** are those in which European metropolitan subjects represent to themselves their others (usually their conquered others), autoethnographic **texts** are representations that the so-defined others construct *in response to* or in dialogue with those **texts**. (1991: 35)

Autoethnographic **texts** are exemplary products of contact zones. As they are "often addressed to both metropolitan audiences and the speaker's own community," their political valences are complex (sometimes accommodating of the colonizer's discourse, sometimes critical) and their "reception is thus highly indeterminate" (1991: 35).

Pratt develops this idea into the concept of "transculturation" in her book *Imperial Eyes* (1992). In addition to the ways that subordinated groups adopt and re-invent material from the dominating group, the term addresses those instances where the creations of the subordinated group then affect the dominant group:

> While the imperial metropolis tends to understand itself as determining the periphery (in the emanating glow of the civilizing mission or the cash flow of development), it habitually blinds itself to the ways in which the periphery determines the metropolis, beginning perhaps with the latter's obsessive need to present and represent its peripheries and its others continually to itself. (6)

We thus see contact zones working in both directions: culture translates or transfers to the **marginalized** colonial space and also back to the supposedly inviolable center, hence "transculturation."

See also: **binary opposition, liminal and liminality, hybridity, mimicry**.

Further reading: Pratt 1991, 1992.

CONTAINMENT

Whereas Marx-inspired **Cultural Materialists** tend to examine sites of subversion in literature, **New Historicists** tend to concern themselves with forces of containment and the ways **hegemonic** forces consolidate the status quo. **New Historicists** look at moments of rupture to examine how forces of rebellion are still able to be co-opted by the powers that be (e.g., how Public Enemy's message in "Fight the Power" is compromised and even nullified by the group's participation in the corporate music industry).

See also: **carnivalesque, differend, dissensus, distribution of the sensible, doxa, habitus, Matrix of Domination**.

CONTEXT

Marxists, Cultural Materialists, New Historicists, and **Cultural Studies** theorists reject the **New Critical** precept that **texts** are autonomous units that should be examined without bringing in what **New Critics** termed the "intentional fallacy" (i.e., biographical criticism) or the "historical fallacy." Many theorists of the last two decades, by contrast, argue that **texts** are always intimately connected to their historical and social context, especially perhaps when **texts** attempt to repress that context. To put it another (**psychoanalytical**) way, **history** serves as the repressed **unconscious** of literature, as **Marxist** Fredric Jameson for example argues in the *Political Unconscious* (1981) or **New Historicist** Alan Liu argues in *Wordsworth: The Sense of History* (1989b).

CORRELATIONISM

"Correlationism" is a term used in **speculative realism** to describe the dominant belief in philosophy after Immanuel Kant (1724–1804) that one cannot access the "thing-in-itself," the objective world separate from our subjective understanding of that world. As Quentin Meillassoux explains, "By 'correlation' we mean the idea according to which we only ever have access to the correlation between thinking and being, and never to either term considered apart from the other" (2008: 5). According to Meillassoux, "it becomes possible to say that every philosophy which disavows naïve realism has become a variant of correlationism" (5), including not only **phenomenology** but also Jürgen Habermas's theories of **communicative action**, Lacanian **psychoanalysis**'s disjunction between reality and the **Real**, or **poststructuralism**'s insistence on language's role in determining our understanding of reality. As Meillassoux continues,

"Thus, one could say that up until Kant, one of the principle [sic] problems of philosophy was to think substance, while ever since Kant, it has consisted in trying to think the correlation" (6), be that correlation understood in terms of **subjectivity** or understanding/consciousness or language. Even when one is discussing a reality that pre-existed the arrival of human beings, what Meillassoux terms "ancestral statements," a correlationist always insists on tying that supposed "reality" to an inter-subjective relation between **subjects** and their objects of study: "It is the intersubjectivity of the ancestral statement—the fact that it should by right be verifiable by any member of the scientific community—that guarantees its objectivity, and hence its 'truth'" (15), not the properties of the thing in itself outside of our observation and discussion of that thing. **Speculative realism** wishes to re-establish the primary qualities of objects, especially their mathematical properties (e.g., length, width, movement, depth, figure, size), outside of any relation to the human **subject**, hence the use of the term "realism" in **speculative realism**. The goal, as Meillassoux puts it, is "*to get out of ourselves*, to grasp the in-itself, to know what is whether we are or not" (27).

COSMOPOLITANISM

Although one can point even earlier to the Egyptian, Anhnaton (1526 BCE), who "asserted that all human beings have moral duties to one another beyond their immediate communal spheres" (Brown and Held 2010: 3), the term "cosmopolitan" has its roots in ancient Greece where Diogenes of Sinope (c. 404 BCE–323 BCE) declared himself a cosmopolitan—from the Greek (κοσμοπολίτης) for "citizen of the world." Diogenes' cosmopolitanism then influenced the philosophy of the Stoics (early third century BCE) and many others afterwards, eventually undergirding the principles of the Enlightenment that precipitated the American and French Revolutions and their promulgation of the principle of the "rights of man." The cosmopolitan principle is most influentially developed by Immanuel Kant in his essay *Toward Perpetual Peace* (1795), where he posits a "cosmopolitan right, to the extent that individuals and states, who are related externally by the mutual exertion of influence on each other, are to be regarded as citizens of a universal state of humankind (*ius cosmopoliticum*)" (73). Kant also posits the principle of "universal hospitality," which he articulates as "the right of a stranger not to be treated in a hostile manner by another upon his arrival on the other's territory" (82).

These concepts of cosmopolitanism and hospitality have been developed in critical theory that seeks to establish an ethical principle for our relation with each other, for example in **poststructuralist** Jacques Derrida's theories of friendship and hospitality in *Politics of Friendship* (1997) and *Of Hospitality* (2000); Emmanuel Levinas's theorization of our obligation to the face of the **Other** (in *Totality and Infinity* [1991], *Entre nous: On Thinking-of-the-Other* [1998], and *Humanism of the Other* [2003]); Jürgen Habermas's positing of a principle of **communicative action** and **discourse ethics**; or Giorgio Agamben's notion of *The Coming Community* (1993) where, in the new global system, persons are seen as "whatever singularities" who "form a community without affirming an identity" such that "humans co-belong without any representable condition of belonging (87).

Cosmopolitanism has gained increasing force as a theoretical movement since the rise of **Global Studies** in the 1990s and 2000s, offering an ethico-political grounding for thinking about our obligation to others in the new global order. As Garrett Wallace Brown and David Held put it in the introduction to their *Cosmopolitanism Reader* (2010), which begins with four essays on Kant, "In the most basic form, cosmopolitanism maintains that there are moral obligations owed to all human beings based solely on our humanity alone, without reference to race, gender, nationality, ethnicity, culture, religion, political affiliation, state citizenship, or other communal particularities" (1). This is not to say that cosmopolitanism does not have its critics; David Harvey for example fears that cosmopolitanism, which he argues promulgates the principles of Western middle-class liberalism, could well be "nothing other than an ethical and humanitarian mask for **hegemonic** neoliberal practices of class domination and financial and militaristic imperialism" (2009: 84). Despite such critiques—and others have raised similar questions (e.g., Brennan 2001, Mouffe 2005, Pollock *et al.* 2000)—a number of critics have proceeded cautiously to posit a principle of cross-cultural and cross-national cosmopolitanism that works at a variety of levels: ethical, legal, cultural, political and environmental. As Kwame Anthony Appiah puts it, "The challenge ... is to take minds and hearts formed over long millennia of living in local troops and equip them with ideas and institutions that will allow us to live together as the global tribe we have become" (2014: 405).

Further reading: Agamben 1993; A. Anderson 2001; Appiah 2014; Archibugi 2003; Breckenridge *et al.* 2002; Brennan 2001; Brown and Held 2010; Cheah and Robbins 1998; Derrida 1997, 2000; Gunn 2013; Habermas 1987, 1991, 1993, 1999; Harvey 2009; Kant 1795; Levinas 1991; 1998, 2003; Mouffe 2005; Pollock *et al.* 2000; Robbins 1999, 2012.

COUNTER-HEGEMONY

See **hegemony**

CRITICAL DISCOURSE ANALYSIS

See **discourse**

CRITICAL LEGAL STUDIES

See **Critical Race Theory**

CRITICAL RACE THEORY

This critical school developed out of and largely superseded Critical Legal Studies (CLS). CLS, which was an active school of critical theory in the 1970s and 1980s, applied **poststructuralist** and **Marxist** strategies to critique legal institutions, questioning the extent to which one can separate law and politics while illustrating the ways that the legal system is designed to support the dominant class at the expense of **marginalized**, **subaltern** groups. Although Critical Race Theory (CRT) started as an offshoot of CLS, it has largely eclipsed that school of thought and has become the dominant way of approaching such legal questions. Its main area of investigation is, as Cornel West puts it, "the historical centrality and complicity of law in upholding white supremacy (and concomitant hierarchies of gender, class, and sexual orientation)" (1995: xii). In the tradition of critical theory (see the **Introduction**), its practitioners are also committed to fight oppression and to change society for the better; however, CRT is careful to distinguish its goals from those of liberal civil rights scholarship and activism. Although it takes inspiration from earlier civil rights agitation, the practitioners of CRT "take racial power to be at stake across the social plane—not merely in the places where people of color are concentrated but also in the institutions where their position is normalized and given legitimation" (Crenshaw *et al.* 1995: xxii). Critiquing the liberal view that law is separate from politics because of its purported adherence to neutral and apolitical rational debate, CRT argues that the problem lies with the way law itself is conceived. The goal, then, is not just to change the law, as in the civil rights movement, but also to uncover "how law was a constitutive element of **race** itself: in other words, how law *constructed* **race**" (xxv). At the same time, CRT questions the tendency of some **deconstructionist** and **postmodern** CLS scholars to dismiss **race** altogether because, these CLS scholars argue, the very concept of **race** entails an overly essentialist view of subjectivity (e.g., biological, inherent, immutable); this is a CLS position that CRT scholars "have come to call 'vulgar anti-essentialism'" (xxvi). As the editors of *Critical Race Theory: The Key Writings* explain,

> It was obvious to many of us that although race was … socially constructed (the idea of biological race is "false"), race was nonetheless "real" in the sense that there is a material dimension and weight to the experience of being "raced" in American society, a materiality that in significant ways has been produced and sustained by law. Thus, we understood our project as an effort to construct a race-conscious and at the same time anti-essentialist account of the processes by which law participates in "race-ing" American society. (Crenshaw *et al.* 1995: xxvi)

Critical Race Theory therefore adopts a rather complex approach to issues of **race**, as evidenced in key concepts that it shares with Black Feminist thought (see **feminism**), including the **Matrix of Domination, intersectionality**, and **whiteness as property**. For example, rather than see racism as an aberrant, now no longer common act that directly targets minorities by denying them their rights, CRT scholars examine what they term "micro-aggressions," those common, quotidian, minor acts that serve to mark a racial minority as inferior (repetition of racial clichés, body language, even simply the avoidance of someone's gaze). "White privilege" functions in much the same way: "reserving favors, smiles, kindness, the best stories, one's most charming side, and invitations to real intimacy for one's own kind or class" (Delgado and Stefancic 2001: 25). Racism, according to CRT, "is ordinary, not aberrational—'normal science,' the usual way society does business, the common, everyday experience of most people of color in this country" (7). A legal notion of equality that is "color-blind," purporting to provide the same opportunities to everyone regardless of race, gender, sexual orientation, and so on, only addresses "the most blatant forms of discrimination, such as mortgage redlining or the refusal to hire a black Ph.D. rather than a white high school dropout, that do stand out and attract our attention" (7). According to CRT, the liberal doctrine of "color-blind" equality (e.g., the principle of meritocracy, which is used to reject affirmative-action rules) in fact serves to legitimate all the other forms of oppression and marginalization that constitute the daily experience of **subaltern** racial, gender, and sexual identity. The law's support of color-blind equality thus keeps dominant identity groups from having to address the real, everyday injustices or even the systemic mechanisms (e.g., standardized tests, police profiling, legal precedence) that deny **subaltern** groups power, status, respect, and wealth. One way that CRT scholars seek to reveal daily, common forms of racism is through "legal storytelling," the recounting of personal anecdotes that illustrate the inherent racism of our society and culture, or through alternative histories that retell the history of civil rights legislation from the less triumphalist and always suspicious perspective of subaltern identities, as in Howard Zinn's *A People's History of the United States* (1999) or Derrick A. Bell Jr.'s recounting of the real (and secret) governmental impetus behind *Brown v. Board of Education*.

Although sometimes included under the umbrella of Critical Race Theory, a few other movements have grown out of CRT, including Critical Race Feminism (CRF), Latino Critical Race Studies (LatCrit), Asian American Critical Race Studies (AsianCrit), and American Indian Critical Race Studies (TribalCrit).

See also: **contact zone and transculturation, mimicry, postcolonial studies**.

Further reading: Bell 1973, 1980; Collins 2000; Crenshaw 1991; Crenshaw *et al.* 1995; Delgado and Stefancic 2001; Zinn 1999.

CRITICAL THEORY

See **Introduction**

CULTURAL CAPITAL, SOCIAL CAPITAL, AND SYMBOLIC CAPITAL

According to Pierre Bourdieu, "**capital**" inheres in more things than simply economic processes of exchange. Following Karl Marx, Bourdieu defines **capital** as "accumulated labor ... which, when appropriated on a private, i.e., exclusive basis by agents or groups of agents, enables them to appropriate social energy in the form of reified and living labor" (1986: 280). That is, value really inheres in **labor** but in **capitalism** a situation is created where **labor** is translated into an exchangeable unit that can be bought and sold, which leads to the exploitation of the proletariat in favor of a bourgeoisie that controls all the **means of production**. According to Bourdieu, however, capital exists in other forms as well: "It is in fact impossible to account for the structure and functioning of the social world unless one reintroduces **capital** in all its forms and not solely in the one form recognized by economic theory" (280). Bourdieu argues that **capital** in fact presents itself

> in three fundamental guises: as economic capital, which is immediately and directly convertible into money and may be institutionalized in the form of property rights; as cultural capital, which is convertible, on certain conditions, into economic capital and may be institutionalized in the form of educational qualifications; and as social capital, made up of social obligations ("connections"), which is convertible, in certain conditions, into economic capital and may be institutionalized in the form of a title of nobility. (Bourdieu 1986: 281)

Cultural capital in turn exists in three distinct forms: (1) in the embodied state, "in the form of long-lasting dispositions of the mind and body" (1986: 282), which corresponds to Bourdieu's notion of **habitus**; (2) in the objectified state, "in the form of cultural goods (pictures, books, dictionaries, instruments, machines, etc.)" (282); and (3) in the institutionalized state, for example clubs, universities, and various organized groups. For Bourdieu, cultural capital refers to all the techniques of "taste" and "upbringing" that guarantee success for children born into the dominant classes, especially "the domestic transmission of cultural capital" (282). Each family in the dominant class invests cultural capital in their children and further supports them by also transferring social capital to them, that is, "all the institutions which are designed to favor legitimate exchanges and exclude illegitimate ones by producing occasions (rallies, cruises, hunts, parties, receptions, etc.), places (smart neighborhoods, select schools, clubs, etc.), or practices (smart sports, parlor games, cultural ceremonies, etc.) which bring together, in a seemingly fortuitous way, individuals as homogeneous as possible in all the pertinent respects in terms of the existence and persistence of the group" (287).

The term "symbolic capital" encompasses all the other forms of capital and simply means any *represented* form of capital: "capital—in whatever form—insofar as it is represented, i.e., apprehended symbolically, in a relationship of knowledge or, more precisely, of misrecognition and recognition" (1986: 289). Symbolic capital is, according to Bourdieu, "any property (any form of capital whether physical, economic, cultural or social) when it is perceived by social agents endowed with categories of perception which cause them to know it and to recognize it, to give it value" (1998: 47).

John Guillory influentially extends Bourdieu's cultural capital argument to the field of critical theory itself, the rise of which he sees as aligned with a larger devaluation of the cultural capital of literature in society at large: "The moment of theory is determined, then, by a certain defunctioning of the literary curriculum, a crisis in the market value of its cultural capital occasioned by the emergence of a professional-managerial class which no longer requires the (primarily literary) **cultural capital** of the old bourgeoisie" (1993: xii).

See also: **ideology**.

Further reading: Bourdieu 1984, 1986, 1992, 1998; Guillory 1993.

CULTURAL MATERIALISM

See **New Historicism and Cultural Materialism**

CULTURAL STUDIES

See **culture**

CULTURE

Various trends in critical theory have released critics to explore the place of cultural forms in the construction of human society and **subjectivity**: **Cultural Materialism**'s **Marxist** concern with how cultural forms reflect changes in the development of **capitalism**; **semiology**'s invitation to read all social sign systems for meaning; the breaking down of the distinction between "high" and "low" culture that distinguishes **postmodern** artists from their Modernist precursors. **Frankfurt School** theorists—many writing during the modernist period—tended to be critical of mass culture, with Walter Benjamin questioning the effects of film in his 1936 "Work of Art in the Age of Mechanical Reproduction" and Max Horkheimer and Theodor Adorno attacking the "**culture industry**" in their 1944 *Dialectic of Enlightenment*. Some more recent critical theorists are still quite dismissive of popular cultural forms, for example, Fredric Jameson's critique of **pastiche** or Jean Baudrillard's attacks against **kitsch** and its "aesthetics of **simulation**."

However, other critical theorists have sought to engage certain forms of popular culture directly. Take, for instance, Slavoj Žižek's **psychoanalytical** engagement with the films of Alfred Hitchcock and many others. Also exemplary are Linda Hutcheon's efforts to define a poetics of **postmodern** works that she applies to Terry Gilliam's *Brazil* as much as to the **historiographic metafiction** of novels like John Fowles's *The French Lieutenant's Woman* or E. L. Doctorow's *Ragtime*. As Žižek puts it in *Looking Awry: An Introduction to Jacques Lacan through Popular Culture* (1991b), "Lacanian theory serves" in his book "as an excuse for indulging in the idiotic enjoyment of popular culture" (viii). So it is with many of the critical theories that are used to engage with, **deconstruct**, or elucidate the products of popular mass entertainment, leading to the rather broad umbrella term, **Cultural Studies**. Other theoretical approaches follow Linda Hutcheon's lead in arguing that only certain popular works (especially those dubbed **postmodern**) manage to combat the **kitsch** of the majority of mass entertainment; "the increasing uniformization of mass culture is one of the totalizing forces that **postmodernism** exists to challenge" (1988: 6), Hutcheon argues.

Regardless of whether the critical theorist is taking popular culture seriously or dismissing it as a symptom of larger social changes, such theorists tend to read in cultural forms the signs of the times. Raymond Williams, who helped to establish both **Cultural Materialism** and **Cultural Studies**, argues that the modern definition of "culture" (along with the modern sense of "industry," "democracy," "class," and "art") comes into existence in the nineteenth century precisely to accommodate other larger changes in society at large. Such changes in meaning, "at this critical period, bear witness to a general change in our characteristic ways of thinking about our common life: about our social, political and economic institutions; about the purposes which these institutions are designed to embody; and about the relations to these institutions and purposes of our activities in learning, education and the arts" (1958: xiii). Culture, for Williams, functions as "a special kind of map by means of which" the changes in our "social, economic and political life ... can be explored" (xvii). The relationship of culture to society is not simply one of "reflection," however, where culture reacts to (reflects) larger structural changes in the economic **base**. As Williams concludes, "we are coming increasingly to realize that our vocabulary, the language we use to inquire into and negotiate our actions, is no secondary factor, but a practical and radical element in itself" (338).

In this, Williams could be said to follow the general "linguistic turn" of critical theory after the publication of Ferdinand de Saussure's *Course in General Linguistics* in 1916 (see **signifier and signified** and **semiotics**). If our very notion of reality is created by language, then one should be free, by this logic, to examine any **discursive** event for clues to how **ideology** undergirds our very **subjectivity**, as in the cultural **semiotics** of Roland Barthes (1972, 1977, 1983). Inspired by Williams and Barthes, then by Michel Foucault's approach to **discourse**, which seeks to establish the "**discourse**-formations" that structure our negotiation of knowledge and **power** in a given society at a given time, critics from different theoretical perspectives have extended the analysis of culture from "high" literature to the production of all **discourse**. The cultural anthropology of Clifford Geertz has been another influence on this approach to culture and society (see **thick description**). Sometimes placed under the broad umbrella of **Cultural Studies**, these approaches include **New Historicism**, **Discourse Analysis** and **Critical Discourse Analysis**, **Cultural Materialism**, **Semiotics**, and Media Studies in general. Cultural Studies in Britain was also influenced by the Centre for Contemporary Cultural Studies at the University of Birmingham, led by Stuart Hall, its director from 1968 to 1979 (see, especially, Hall *et al.* 1980).

Others pursue more fully Williams's notion of high "culture" (in the sense of being "cultured") as a means to demarcate "distinction" for certain classes of individuals in positions of power. Pierre Bourdieu's work has been particularly influential in this regard. As Bourdieu explains, "Taste classifies, and it classifies the classifier. Social subjects, classified by their classifications, distinguish themselves by the distinctions they make, between the beautiful and the ugly, the distinguished and the vulgar, in which their position in the objective classifications is expressed or betrayed" (1984: 6). See **cultural capital**, **doxa**, **habitus**, and **symbolic violence**.

Postcolonial theorist Homi Bhabha uses the term "culture" in a slightly different way in his influential book, *The Location of Culture* (1994); that is, as a guarantor of cultural difference. According to Bhabha, we must examine the many diverse ways that authoritarian notions like "**nation**" are **performed** in multiform, contradictory ways in the day-to-day experience of actual people. Culture, for Bhabha, is a particularly fruitful place to look for alternatives to the status quo. Bhabha argues that "Cultural difference marks the establishment of new forms of meaning, and strategies of identification, through processes of negotiation where no **discursive** authority can be established without revealing the difference of itself." For Bhabha, "the 'difference' of cultural knowledge ... is the enemy of the *implicit* generalization of knowledge or the implicit homogenization of experience" (1990a: 313). The heterogeneity of culture thus works against any effort to establish a single, dominant norm for society, according to Bhabha. Working from the British critical tradition of Cultural Studies at the Centre for Contemporary Cultural Studies at the University of Birmingham, Dick Hebdige earlier made a similar argument regarding what he terms "subcultures," "the expressive forms and rituals of those subordinate groups—the teddy boys and mods and rockers, the skinheads and the punks—who are alternately dismissed, denounced and canonized; treated at different times as threats to public order and as harmless buffoons" (1979: 2).

Further reading: Barthes 1972, 1977, 1983; Bhabha 1990b, 1994; Bourdieu 1984, 1992; Edgar and Sedgwick 2008; Guillory 1993; Hall *et al.* 1980; Hebdige 1979; Hutcheon 1988; Williams 1958, 1995; Žižek 1991b, 1992a, 1992b.

CULTURE INDUSTRY

Max Horkheimer and Theodor Adorno coin this term in their 1944 work *Dialectic of Enlightenment*. In that work, these **Frankfurt School** critics attack mass culture, arguing that it is largely in the control of capitalist monopolies. "Under monopoly all mass culture is identical" (1944: 121), they argue, so that "culture now impresses the same stamp on everything" (120) and "The whole world is made to pass through the filter of the culture industry" (126). Unlike the rebelliousness of the detail, which characterized "the period from Romanticism to Expressionism" (125), the culture industry "puts an end to this": "Though concerned exclusively with effects, it crushes their insubordination and makes them subserve the formula, which replaces the work" (126). The goal is to keep the consumer from any "independent thinking," which would be seen as "work" and not entertainment; amusement "is sought after as an escape from the mechanized work process, and to recruit strength in order to be able to cope with it again" (137); however, it becomes merely a form of mechanization in alternate form: "What happens at work, in the factory, or in the office can only be escaped from by approximation to it in one's leisure time" (137). Cultural production is thus put in the service of monopoly capitalism and the viewer is denied the ability to sustain thought in "the relentless rush of facts" that characterizes the sound film (127) or the uniform stylization of any number of cultural products from jazz (127–28) to Donald Duck cartoons (138). Instead, "The culture industry as a whole has molded men as a type unfailingly reproduced in every product" (127), a product that, in the end, is hardly distinguishable from mere advertising.

See also: **culture**.

CYBERPUNK

Cyberpunk is a subgenre of **dystopic** science fiction that imagines the future effects of computer technology. A neologism mashing together cybernetics and punk, cyberpunk tends to be set in a **dystopic** world of social breakdown and often includes plots tied to rebellion by way of hacking (hence the "punk"). Fredric Jameson in his work, *Postmodernism* (1991), sees William Gibson's cyberpunk fiction as exemplary of our current **postmodern, late capitalist** society because of its attempt to represent a massively powerful world order that one cannot easily grasp or combat, as in conspiracy theory: "conspiracy theory (and its garish narrative manifestations) must be seen as a degraded attempt—through the figuration of advanced technology—to think the impossible totality of the contemporary world system." As he goes on, "Such narratives, which first tried to find expression through the generic structure of the spy novel, have only recently crystallized in a new type of science fiction, called *cyberpunk*, which is fully as much an expression of transnational corporate realities as it is of global paranoia itself" (38).

CYBORG

Donna Harraway in her "A Cyborg Manifesto" (originally published in 1985) makes the argument that at the end of the twentieth century, "we are all ... theorized and fabricated hybrids of machine and organism; in short we are cyborgs. The cyborg is our ontology; it gives us our politics" (Harraway 1991: 150). She places her "cyborg myth" among other "**postmodern** strategies" (152), arguing that "[t]he cyborg is a kind of disassembled and reassembled, **postmodern** collective and personal self. This is the self **feminists** must code" (163). She adopts this myth because she believes that there are "great riches for **feminists** in explicitly embracing the possibilities inherent in the breakdown of clean distinctions between organism and machine and similar distinctions structuring the Western self" (174). In addition to the breakdown of distinctions between organism and machine, other **binary oppositions** that she troubles with her cyborg myth are "self/other, mind/body, **culture/nature**, male/female, civilized/primitive, reality/appearance, whole/part, agent/resource, maker/made, active/passive, right/wrong, truth/illusion, total/partial, God/man" (177). According to Harraway, **postmodern** "[h]igh-tech culture challenges these dualisms in intriguing ways" (177), opening up a **feminist** strategy that starts from a position of "irony" (180), "noise" (176), **"heteroglossia"** (181), **hybridity**, and fluidity. As she asks, "[w]hat kind of politics could embrace partial, contradictory, permanently unclosed constructions of personal and collective selves and still be faithful, effective—and, ironically, socialist-**feminist**?" (157).

See also: **digital humanities, subjectivity**.

DEATH DRIVE

The death drive is the bodily **instinct** to return to the state of quiescence that preceded our birth. The death drive, according to Sigmund Freud's later writings (*Beyond the Pleasure Principle* [1920], "The 'Uncanny'" [1919]), explains why humans are drawn to repeat painful or traumatic events (even though such repetition appears to contradict our instinct to seek pleasure). Through such a compulsion to repeat, the human subject attempts to "bind" the trauma, thus allowing the subject to return to a state of quiescence. When it comes to traumatic events, **repetition compulsion** is, therefore, not so much the **libido**'s efforts to expend its **cathexis** of sexual energy as it is an effort to come to grips with and to accept the fact of death. This was a difficult point for Freud to make sense of, since it would seem that both the **pleasure principle** and the **reality principle** would logically demand the forgetting of painful events, because both principles are ultimately committed to gratification. (The **reality principle** merely allows for some delay or a modicum of pain to ensure our gratification will happen in the face of real obstacles.) In dealing with patients suffering trauma from the ravages of the First World War, Freud felt the need to point to some principle that was far removed from sexuality. As a result, he wrote the influential work, *Beyond the Pleasure Principle* (1920), in which he begins to develop a system wherein the human psyche is driven by two major instinctual drives: (1) Eros or the sexual **instincts**, which he later saw as compatible with the self-preservative **instincts**; and (2) Thanatos or the death-**instinct**, a natural desire to "re-establish a state of things that was disturbed by the emergence of life" (1923: 709). In other words, whereas one part of the human psyche is seeking gratification, another part is geared to seek a return to the quiet of non-existence: the "death-**instinct**." This concept of the "death-**instinct**" or "death-drive" allowed Freud to make sense of the human tendency towards destruction, including sometimes self-destruction.

This tension between the death-instinct and the sexual instincts has been put into interesting use by the narratologist, Peter Brooks, who argues in *Reading for the Plot* (1985) that **narrative** structure employs a similar tension between the "irritation of plot" and the pull towards the quiescence of **narrative** closure.

See also: **transference**.

Further reading: P. Brooks 1985; Freud 1919, 1920, 1923; Laplanche and Pontalis 1973.

DECONSTRUCTION (DECONSTRUCTIONIST)

See **poststructuralism**

DEFORMANCE

See **reader, reading, and Reader-Response Criticism**

DESIRE

We can read a marked shift in the notion of "desire" as we move from Sigmund Freud to Jacques Lacan. For Freud, desire is tied to instinctive and biological motors that produce desire: **libido, pleasure principle**, stages of **psychosexual development**. Inspired as he was early in his career by neurology and zoology, Freud tended to tie desire to natural "**drives**" that could be said to have their source in the material body. Lacan reworked Freud's notion of desire by making it much more a function of language. According to Lacan, because of our reliance on language for entrance into the symbolic order, we are not in control of our own desires since those desires are themselves as separated from our actual bodily needs as the **phallus** is separated from any biological penis. For this reason, Lacan suggests that, whereas the zero form of sexuality for animals is copulation, the zero form of sexuality for humans is masturbation. The act of sex for humans is so much caught up in our fantasies (our idealized images of both ourselves and our sexual partners) that it is ultimately **narcissistic**. As Lacan puts it, "That's what love is. It's one's own ego that one loves in love, one's own ego made real on the imaginary level" (1991: 142).

Because we are working on the level of fantasy construction, it is quite easy for "love" to turn into disgust, for example when a lover is confronted with his love-**object**'s body in all its materiality (moles, pimples, excretions, etc.), the sorts of things that would have no effect on animal copulation. By entering into the **symbolic order** (with its laws, conventions, and images for perfection), we effectively divorce ourselves from the materiality of our bodily drives, which Lacan tends to distinguish with the term "**jouissance**." Through the Law (which we come to acknowledge by way of the **Oedipus complex**), the human **subject** effectively chooses **culture** over **nature** and the **Real**: "The primordial Law is therefore that which in regulating marriage ties superimposes the kingdom of **culture** on that of **nature** abandoned to the law of copulation" (1968: 40). That Law, for Lacan, is "identical to an order of Language" (40), specifically what he terms the **symbolic order** and it is supported by the symbolic fiction of the "**Name-of-the-Father**."

Desire, in other words, has little to do with material **sexuality** for Lacan; it is caught up, rather, in social structures and strictures, in the fantasy version of reality that forever dominated our lives after our entrance into language. For this reason, Lacan writes that "the unconscious is the discourse of the **Other**." Even our unconscious desires are, in other words, organized by the linguistic system that Lacan terms the **symbolic order** or "the big Other" (see **Other**). And, indeed, the command of the **super-ego**, according to Lacan, is not "obey!" but "enjoy!" In constructing our fantasy-version of reality, we establish coordinates for our desire; we situate both ourselves and our **object** of desire (what Lacan terms the *objet petit a*), as well as the relation between. As Slavoj Žižek puts it, "*through fantasy, we learn how to desire*" (1991b: 6). Our desires therefore necessarily rely on **lack**, since fantasy, by definition, does not correspond to anything in the **Real**. (The "**Real**," Lacan therefore argues, is impossible—we cannot access it after our entrance into language.) This Lacanian understanding of desire has been particularly influential on theories about film; see **screen theory**, **scopophilia**, and **suture**.

Gilles Deleuze and Félix Guattari in *Anti-Oedipus* (1983) contest this understanding of desire, arguing instead:

> Desire does not lack anything; it does not lack its object. It is, rather, the *subject* that is missing in desire, or desire that lacks a fixed **subject**; there is no fixed **subject** unless there is **repression**. ... The objective being of desire is the **Real** in and of itself. (126–27)

In rejecting the notion of a stable organism and exploring instead the many ways that "desiring machines" (rather than centripetal subjects) interact with other machines through fluid "**assemblages**," Deleuze and Guattari counter the subjectivity of Freudian and Lacanian psychoanalysis with the exploded notion of a "**body without organs**," a body that is completely oriented towards and defined by outside forces and interactions. Rather than distinguish between fantasy production and material reality, they argue that "Desiring-machines are not fantasy-machines or dream-machines, which supposedly can be distinguished from technical and social machines. Rather, fantasies are secondary expressions, deriving from the identical nature of the two sorts of machines in any given set of circumstances" (30).

Deleuze and Guattari also completely overturn the priority given to "need" over "desire" in Lacanian and Freudian psychoanalysis, arguing instead that "Desire is not bolstered by needs, but rather the contrary; needs are derived from desire: they are the counterproducts within the real that desire produces" (27). The organs of the subject do not serve as the motors of the human (**libido**, **drive**); instead, the subject is constructed through its relation to the external world. According to this formulation, "The **real** is not impossible; on the contrary, within the **real** everything is possible, everything becomes possible" (27). It is only the fictional construct of the **subject** that seeks to curtail desire and close off the **Real**. Deleuze and Guattari therefore seek to overturn the Freudian notion of the subject in favor of a **body without organs**.

Certain feminist critics have also rejected the Freudian and Lacanian models for desire, particularly the tendency in those theories to align women with passivity or **lack** when it comes to desire (see **phallo-centrism**). As Luce Irigaray argues in *This Sex which Is Not One* (1985b), "About woman and her pleasure, this view of the sexual relation has nothing to say. Her lot is that of '**lack**,' 'atrophy' (of the sexual organ), and 'penis envy,' the penis being the only sexual organ of recognized value" (23). As a result, "woman's desire has doubtless been submerged by the logic that has dominated the West since the time of the Greeks" (25). Irigaray therefore establishes an alternative model for female pleasure, one based on the particularities of female anatomy. As she writes, unlike men, "Woman 'touches herself' all the time, and moreover no one can forbid her to do so, for her genitals are formed of two lips in continuous contact. Thus, within herself, she is already two—but not divisible into one(s)—that caress each other" (24). Irigaray thus seeks to establish an alternative model for female desire, one that gets away from the goal-driven logic of Freud's **pleasure principle** or Lacan's "**object**-cause" of **desire**.

Female desire, by contrast, "really involves a different economy more than anything else, one that upsets the linearity of a project, undermines the goal-object of a desire, diffuses the polarization toward a single pleasure, disconcerts fidelity to a single **discourse**" (1985b: 29–30). Irigaray aligns female pleasure, rather, with fluidity, flux, mobility, nearness, touch, multiplicity, and process. As she writes,

> You remain in flux, never congealing or solidifying. What will make that current flow into words? It is multiple, devoid of causes, meanings, simple qualities. Yet it cannot be decomposed. These movements cannot be described as the passage from a beginning to an end. These rivers flow into no single, definitive sea. These streams are without fixed banks, this body without fixed boundaries. This unceasing mobility. (1985b: 215)

The principle is aligned in Irigaray and other feminist critics with a different understanding of writing, a feminine writing that is also fluid, mobile, and multiple (see *écriture féminine*). Hélène Cixous describes such writing as the rejection of "**phallocentric** representationalism" and the "multiplication of the effects of the inscription of desire, over all parts of my body and the other body" (1976: 314).

Further reading: Cixous 1976, 1986; Deleuze and Guattari 1983; Freud 1916–17, 1932; Irigaray 1985a, 1985b; Lacan 1968, 1977, 1991, 1998; Žižek 1991b, 1994.

DIALECTIC (DIALECTICS) AND DIALECTICAL MATERIALISM

The term "dialectic" has a long history that goes back to ancient Greece, where, in the original Greek (ἡ διαλεκτική), it meant the art of logical, reasoned debate. Both Plato (c. 424 BCE–c. 348 BCE) and Aristotle (384 BCE–322 BCE), however, distinguish dialectical thinking from "mere" rhetoric, which they associate with the Sophists, a group of teachers who were paid by politicians and the upper classes to teach the art of rhetoric and, in particular, the ability to persuade listeners through a variety of means (including the use of emotion and false logic). Plato argued that dialectical thinking, unlike Sophist rhetoric, taught the truth through principles of reason and logic. According to Plato, a true philosopher should not be paid to help the rich and famous but should only be concerned with reaching truth through the dialectical method. That method could lead to the following resolutions: (1) through debate, which involves the positing of theses and antitheses, one can arrive at the conclusion that a given hypothesis leads to a contradiction and is, therefore, not true (e.g., by pursuing the hypothesis to a logical but absurd consequence, as in *reductio ad absurdum*); or (2) one can move beyond an apparent disagreement (two contending opinions about a truth) by logically positing a third thesis that resolves the contradiction (a "sublation" or "synthesis").

Whereas Aristotle agrees in his *Topics* (c. 345 BCE) that dialectical thinking is superior to the Sophist's art of rhetoric, he sees the dialectic as inferior to true philosophy since dialectical thinking reasons "from opinions that are or seem to be reputable" (167), rather than from "true and primary" principles, and it is largely critical (in its search for contradiction), not a true form of understanding. Immanuel Kant (1724–1804) largely agrees with Aristotle's dismissal of dialectical thinking, arguing that "it was nothing else than a logic of illusion—a sophistical art for giving ignorance, nay, even intentional sophistries, the colouring of truth, in which the thoroughness of procedure which logic requires was imitated, and their topic employed to cloak the empty pretensions." As such, it "is quite unbecoming the dignity of philosophy" (1781: 37).

For critical theory, the dialectic is particularly influenced by Friedrich Hegel's nineteenth-century reworking of the concept, which was then retooled by Karl Marx and Friedrich Engels for what was later termed their method of "dialectical materialism" (as distinct from **historical materialism**). Dialectical materialism is commonly understood as the philosophy behind **Marxism**, **historical materialism** as the economic "science" behind **Marxism**.

In opposition to Kant, Hegel saw dialectics not as a way to uncover contradiction but as the secret logic of the universe. No thing in the universe exists by itself but is related to the whole through dialectical relations. Hegel himself rejected the tri-fold terms, "thesis," "antithesis," and "synthesis," which have become associated with his dialectical method, preferring other triadic terms, e.g., Abstract-Negative-Concrete. Heuristically, the more common terms are nonetheless useful in thinking about how the dialectic functions. In working out the relation between subject and object, which we can align with thesis and antithesis, Hegel for example argues that what matters is not the primacy of one or the other but their mediation, which can logically be resolved in a third thing, a synthesis: "neither one nor the other is only *immediately* present in sense-certainty, but each is at the same time *mediated*: I have this certainty *through* something else, viz. the thing; and it, similarly, is in sense-certainty *through* something else, viz. through the 'I'" (1807: 59). All subjects and objects are tied together by this process of thesis and antithesis: "the object is *in one and the same respect the opposite of itself: it is for itself, so far as it is for another, and it is for another, so far as it is for itself*" (76). That which synthesizes such an opposition only ever "sublates" it (the original German, "*Aufhebung*" means simultaneously "to lift up," "to cancel," "to suspend," "to preserve," and "to transcend")— that is, it both cancels it and preserves it in the new "synthesis," as in Hegel's notion of the "simple infinity" or "absolute Notion" that transcends the subject/object dialectic. This idealist maneuver, for Hegel, gets around the "*Unhappy Consciousness*" (126) that is only concerned with the inherent dialectical contradictions of existence and cannot move beyond that. Instead, Hegel posits an "absolute Spirit," which we can perceive in Nature "as its living immediate Becoming" (492), the "*free contingent happening*" (492) that enters the Spirit into Time and Space; and that we can perceive in History as "a succession in Time in which one Spirit relieved another of its charge" (492) in an eternal process of Becoming. That dialectical process of Becoming, a long sequence of World Spirits working towards the progressive betterment of man, is for Hegel eternal, such that the thesis/antithesis of Being/Nothingness is always logically sublated by Becoming.

Marx and Engels adopt Hegel's dialectical method but do so by first rejecting the idealistic elements of the philosophy in favor of a materialist understanding of history. As Marx puts it in a letter of 6 March 1868, "my method of development is not Hegelian, since I am a materialist and Hegel is an idealist. Hegel's dialectics is the basic form of all dialectics, but only *after* it has been stripped of its mystified form, and it is precisely this which distinguishes *my* method" (Bottomore *et al.* 1983: 123). Whereas Hegel saw Reason—through the Absolute Notion and the Absolute Spirit—as the driving force of History, Marx argues that dialectical development is determined by the dominant **modes of production**, which inevitably lead to the exploitation of a given group and subsequently a set of ideological contradictions caused by that class antagonism. To resolve those antagonisms, a new principle for the organization of the **modes of production** is established, usually through violent revolution, which sublates the previous antagonism but then in turn creates its own exploitations, antagonisms, and contradictions. Friedrich Engels, in *Anti-Dühring* (1878) and *Dialectics of Nature* (1883), goes so far as to argue that dialectics is the logic of not only human thought but also all **empirical** nature. **Marxists** will employ the dialectical method both to make sense of historical development (so-called dialectical materialism, which generally concerns itself with the economic "**base**" of society) and to make sense of developments in ideological concepts over time (the "**superstructure**").

Dialectics is defined slightly differently by each of the **Marxist** thinkers that followed Marx, as succinctly explained by Roy Bhaskar:

> Within Western **Marxism**, besides [Georg] Lukács's own dialectic of historical self-consciousness or subject-object dialectics, there are [Antonio] Gramsci's theory/practice, [Herbert] Marcuse's essence/ existence and [Lucio] Colletti's appearance/reality contradictions. ... In [Walter] Benjamin dialectic represents the discontinuous and catastrophic aspect of history; in [Ernst] Bloch it is conceived as objective fantasy; in [Jean-Paul] Sartre it is rooted in the intelligibility of the individual's own totalizing activity; in [Henri] Lefebvre it signifies the goal of de-alienated man. Among the more anti-Hegelian Western **Marxists** ... , the [Galvano] Della Volpean dialectic consists essentially in non-rigid, non-hypostatized thinking, while the [Louis] Althusserian dialectic stands for the complexity, pre-formation and overdetermination of wholes. Poised between the two camps, [Theodor] Adorno emphasizes, on the one hand, the immanence of all criticism and, on the other, non-identity thinking. (Bottomore *et al.* 1983: 128)

In this complicated tradition, one can see elements of the long history of dialectics, from Jürgen Habermas's Platonic affirmation of the power of reasonable, dialectical debate (see **communicative action, communicative reason, discourse ethics** and **public sphere**) to the more suspicious version of Theodor Adorno's "negative dialectics," which rejects the Hegelian principle that dialectical resolution will always lead to improvement on the world stage because—after the Holocaust ("All post-Auschwitz culture, including its urgent critique, is garbage" [Adorno 1966: 367])—all thought must by necessity pursue an extreme skepticism about itself. As Adorno writes, "The unity of world history which animates the philosopher to trace it as the path of the world spirit is the unity of terror rolling over mankind; it is the immediacy of antagonism" (341).

Further reading: Adorno 1966; Bottomore *et al.* 1983; Cornforth 1971; Engels 1878, 1883; Hegel 1807; Kolakowski 1978; Lefebvre 1968; Lukács 1968; Ollman 1993; Žižek 2012.

DIALOGIC (DIALOGISM)

Mikhail Bakhtin theorized dialogism in many of his writings as a way to make sense of the style of the novel. Unlike poetry, which tends, according to Bakhtin, to be monologic, underscoring "the unity of the language system and the unity (and uniqueness) of the poet's individuality as reflected in his language and speech" (1981: 264), the novel tends to be "**heteroglot**, multi-voiced, multi-styled" and even "multi-languaged" (265). Bakhtin believed this dialogism worked to counter the "cultural, national and political centralization of the verbal-ideological world in the higher official socio-ideological levels" (273), a task that is also accomplished by the dialogic genres of the **carnivalesque**. Bakhtin in fact theorizes that all language is at heart dialogical: "The living utterance, having taken meaning and shape at a particular historical moment in a socially specific environment, cannot fail to brush up against thousands of living dialogic threads, woven by socio-ideological consciousness around the given object of an utterance; it cannot fail to become an active participant in social dialogue" (276). Beyond the historical complexity of any utterance's **heteroglot** usage, "every word" is also "directed toward an *answer* and cannot escape the profound influence of the answering word it anticipates" (280). That includes not only the give-and-take of characters in dialogue but also the give-and-take with the reader that any writer cannot help but anticipate: "Every literary discourse more or less sharply senses its own listener, reader, critic, and reflects in itself their anticipated objections, evaluations, points of view" (1984a: 196).

See also: **polyphony**.

Further reading: Bakhtin 1981, 1984a, 1986; Holquist 1990.

DIEGESIS

"Diegesis" has two senses, depending on whether you are approaching the term from the perspective of ancient Greek mimetic theory or that of contemporary film theory. Both Plato in his *Republic* and Aristotle in his *Poetics* argue that narratives can be distinguished by whether they are presented to us in the voice of a narrator who tells us what happens in his or her own voice (what they term "diegesis") or whether the events are presented as if they are actually happening, without any narratorial mediation whatsoever, as in drama (what they term "mimesis"). In this tradition, Gérard Genette in *Narrative Discourse* (1980) and *Narrative Discourse Revisited* (1988) distinguishes among diegetic narratives (the primary story told); metadiegetic narratives (stories told by a character who is a part of the principal, diegetic narrative); and extradiegetic narratives (stories that frame the primary story and thus are outside it).

In film theory, the term diegesis has been used, rather, to designate a narrative's time-space continuum, to borrow a term from *Star Trek*; that is, the diegesis of a narrative is its entire created world, with all the rules that govern that particular fictional world. Any narrative includes a diegesis, whether you are reading science fiction, fantasy, mimetic realism, or psychological realism, though each genre constructs the rules of its fictional universe differently. What Samuel Taylor Coleridge coined the "suspension of disbelief" that we all perform upon entering into a fictional world entails an acceptance of a story's diegesis, the laws that govern its fictional time-space continuum. The *Star Trek* franchise is of interest for **narratology** because it has managed to create such a complex and multi-generational diegetic universe in which the narratives of all five television shows (TNG, DS9, STV, *Enterprise*, and the original *Star Trek*) as well as all the movies take place.

DIFFÉRANCE

"*Différance*" is a neologism proposed by Jacques Derrida, playing on the fact that *différer* in French means both to differ and to defer; the term thus captures the two essential elements of meaning-production: (1) we can make sense of words less through the things to which they refer than in their difference from other words in a signifying chain; that difference precedes any effort to stabilize a specific referent for the words we use. We can understand the meaning of "road," for example, only in terms of its difference from or relation to the meanings of "city," "nature," "space," and "time." (2) Because of this inherent instability of meaning-production, we must always defer meaning in the act of understanding a string of words. In hearing a sequence of words, we must wait for the various differences that establish the terms of what we hear; for example, are we talking about some specific road or is the word being used in some metaphorical sense? Meaning, not to mention all the metaphysical gambits that seek to stabilize meaning, including **subjectivity** or consciousness itself, is always an *ex post facto* operation that must first rely on the play of language, on *différance*. As Derrida writes, "the speaking or signifying **subject** could not be present to itself, as speaking or signifying, without the play of linguistic or semiological différance" (1982: 16).

Différance is pronounced exactly the same as the French word *différence* or difference, so that its significance can only be understood by looking at the written word: "it is read, or it is written, but it cannot be heard. It cannot be apprehended in speech" (1982: 3). Derrida thus seeks to counter the **phonocentrism** of past philosophy, which privileges the spoken word over writing because it is represented as having more presence, truth, being, or divinity. Derrida argues instead that there is an **arche-writing** that precedes speech insofar as speech, like writing, follows the same logic of difference and deferral by which meaning is constructed.

See also: **signifier and signified**, **trace**, **supplement**.

DIFFEREND

Jean-François Lyotard defines this term in the first sentence of his book of the same name: "As distinguished from a litigation, a differend [*différend*] would be a case of conflict, between (at least) two parties, that cannot be equitably resolved for lack of a rule of judgment applicable to both arguments" (1988a: xi). Lyotard's argument is that "a universal rule of judgment between heterogeous genres is lacking in general" (xi), which is to say that he is opposed to the application of a single set of rules to all things, particularly the application of the rules of one "**genre of discourse**" to a completely different "**genre of discourse**." He terms such an imposition "a **wrong**." He defines "a wrong" as "a damage [*dommage*] accompanied by the loss of the means to prove the damage" (5). Lyotard applies this concept to juridical law, stating: "I would like to call a *differend* [*différend*] the case where the plaintiff is divested of the means to argue and becomes for that reason a victim" (9). He ties this juridical understanding of the differend to his understanding of **genres of discourse** by explaining that "[a] case of differend between two parties takes place when the 'regulation' of the conflict that opposes them is done in the idiom of one of the parties while the wrong suffered by the other is not signified in that idiom" (9). One tries, that is, to impose the rules and goals of one **genre of discourse** onto another that is, by definition, structured by different rules and goals. A good example is the exploited laborer (in the **Marxist** sense): in a juridical system established around contract law, "the laborer or his or her representative has had to and will have to speak of his or her work as though it were the temporary cessation of a **commodity**, the 'service,' which he or she putatively owns" (9–10). The laborer is forced, in other words, to describe his damages in the **genres of discourse** that legitimize the goals of **capitalism**: "The tribunal thereby makes this regimen and/or this genre prevail over the others" (140). **Marxism**, however, questions the very presuppositions of contract law, so there is no way to discuss the **wrongs** perpetrated on the laborer (exploitation) within the current system of jurisprudence; what we have here, then, is a case of differend.

The only way to deal with a case of differend is to create new **genres of discourse** that will allow the victim to articulate wrong effectively. As Lyotard explains, "In the differend something 'asks' to be put into phrases, and suffers from the wrong of not being able to be put into phrases right away." Because of the resulting "feeling of pain which accompanies silence (and of pleasure which accompanies the invention of a new idiom)," human beings who experience a case of differend "recognize that what remains to be phrased exceeds what they can presently phrase, and that they must be allowed to institute idioms which do not yet exist" (1988a: 13). Lyotard turns to the **sublime** as the call to phrase what presently cannot be phrased. For Lyotard, then, there is a "multiplicity of justices" since each form of justice is "defined in relation to the rules specific to each **[language] game**." At the same time, however, "Justice here does not consist merely in the observance of the rules; as in all the games, it consists in working at the limits of what the rules permit, in order to invent new moves, perhaps new rules and therefore new games" (Lyotard and Thébaud 1985: 100), something that the **sublime** makes possible, according to Lyotard.

See also: **antagonism**, **dissensus**, **incommensurability**.

DIGITAL HUMANITIES

Like **Global Studies** (and sometimes connected to it because of the global nature of the digital revolution), the Digital Humanities is a fast-growing, multidisciplinary and transformative approach to scholarship that has affected a variety of disciplines. Although some critics have suggested that the field is more concerned with the functionality of tools and databases than with theory and knowledge, it has certainly inspired a huge amount of theoretical work that has questioned or recast such key concepts as **textuality** (Landow 1997, Ryan 1999, McGann 2001 and 2004, Loizeaux and Fraistat 2002); human **subjectivity** (Harraway 1991, Gaggi 1997, Hayles 1999); the relationship of **subject** and **object** (Hayles 2005); **narrative** (Murray 2000, Ryan 2001); **reading** and interpretation (McGann 2001, Ramsay 2011, Hayles 2012, Jockers 2013, Moretti 2013), **culture** (J. H. Miller 1992), embodiment (Hayles 1999, Hansen 2000) and knowledge (Liu 2004, Drucker 2009, Hayles 2012). In fact, what has particularly constituted its challenge to traditional scholarship has been its tendency to bring the practical aspects of software and hardware design front and center in thinking through our presuppositions about all aspects of how we "mediate" the things we record in media, including critical theory itself. This rethinking of the ways and means of our critical thinking has, in turn, been driven by the rapid and ineluctable nature of the digital revolution. As Franco Moretti puts it, "today, we can replicate in a few minutes investigations that took a giant like Leo Spitzer months and years of work. When it comes to phenomena of language and style, we can do things that previous generations could only dream of" (2013: 212). Moretti not only explores this new ability to data mine and visualize results from vast data sets through his Stanford Literary Lab but also theorizes what he posits as new ways of **reading** and doing criticism in the digital age—what he has influentially dubbed "**distant reading**."

Not surprisingly, the digital humanities has questioned various aspects of traditional university research, aiming often to change how traditional critical theory has in the past conducted its investigations. Unlike the weighty, philosophical manuscript of the great thinker, the work of the digital humanities often occurs in alternative (e.g., unfinished, collaborative, even ephemeral) forms that challenge traditional notions of **agency**, **authorship**, and argumentation (Twitter feeds; social networking software; folksonomy tagging and the semantic web; data mining; wikis, crowd-sourcing, open-source software, and other forms of massively collaborative creation, to name just a few). Changes in the tools we use, in other words, are driving the theory being proposed to understand those changes. Consider one example among many, Anne Burdick *et al.*'s rumination on the title of their collection, *Digital_Humanities* (2012):

> The underscore between the two words references the white space between them as a vital yoke and shifting **signifier**, one that presents the two concepts in a productive tension, without either becoming absorbed into the other. The underscore is not merely a graphical notation; rather, it is used deliberately as an over-determined marker of the critical nexus between "digital" and "humanities." It references the precarious, experimental, and undefined future of the humanities in a world fundamentally transformed by everything digital. Although we do not use the underscore throughout the text, it remains the subject of every page of this book. And while it may seem paradoxical to write a book

called *Digital_Humanities*, the very act demonstrates the continuities that link current practice to long-standing traditions. (ix-x)

In such critical theory, the very medium that presents the argument to the reader—white space, typographical notation and the uncertain relation between the digital and the codex book—becomes a part of the critical theory being developed, whether the argument is being made in a printed book or in some other form.

See also: **deformance**, **postmodernism and postmodern theory**, **postmodernity**.

Further reading: Bartscherer and Coover 2011; Burdick *et al.* 2012; Drucker 2009; Felluga 2006, 2013; Gaggi 1997; Gold 2012; Harraway 1991; Hayles 1999, 2005, 2012; Jockers 2013; Landow 1997; Liu 2004; Loizeaux and Fraistat 2002; McGann 2001, 2004, 2013; Moretti 2013; Murray 2000; Ramsay 2011; M.-L. Ryan 1999, 2001; Schreibman *et al.* 2004; Terras *et al.* 2013.

DISCIPLINE

Critical theorists who use the term "discipline" often use it in the sense articulated by Michel Foucault throughout his work. Foucault likes the term because it brings together two elements that he argues are central to our use of language: knowledge and power. That is, discipline refers both to the organization of knowledge into a set of rules and procedures (as in a discipline of study) and to the enforcement of a power dynamic that Foucault argues is always a part of that organization of knowledge (as in disciplining someone who breaks the rules). Foucault therefore defines disciplines in this way: "Disciplines constitute a system of control in the production of **discourse**, fixing its limits through the action of an identity taking the form of a permanent reactivation of the rules" (Foucault 1971: 155). In *Discipline and Punish* (1977a), Foucault makes the case that the nineteenth-century reorganization of society across disciplines that define the "normal" (medicine, psychology, and so on) and across specialized disciplines that organize knowledge (history, biology, ethnography, sociology, etc.) are part and parcel of a rethinking of the **subject** in terms of normality/abnormality and the mechanisms of rehabilitation and self-discipline that we see exemplified in nineteenth-century reforms to the prison system. According to Foucault, the logic of that prison reform eventually gets extended to the entire social system, which, he argues, is inherently **carceral** in its disciplinary mechanisms and in its understanding of the modern **subject**. As he puts it in that work, "If, after the age of 'inquisitorial' justice, we have entered the age of 'examinatory' justice, if, in an even more general way, the method of examination has been able to spread so widely throughout society, and to give rise in part to the sciences of man, one of the great instruments for this has been the multiplicity and close overlapping of the various mechanisms of incarceration" (1977a: 305). The result has been a general diffusion of the "power-knowledge" represented in nineteenth-century prison reform until "The judges of normality are present everywhere." As Foucault continues, "We are in the society of the teacher-judge, the doctor-judge, the educator-judge, the 'social-worker'-judge; it is on them that the universal reign of the normative is based; and each individual, wherever he may find himself, subjects to it his body, his gestures, his behaviour, his aptitudes, his achievements" (304).

Further reading: T. J. Armstrong 1992; Foucault 1971, 1977a.

DISCOURSE

"Discourse" is a term that has been used in so many different ways by different theorists that one must take care in its use. Originally meaning either any conversation between people or a more formal piece of writing (e.g., a treatise or a dissertation), it has achieved a more specialized meaning in various branches of critical theory. In **narratology**, it is contrasted with "story" to understand the basic building blocks of narrative and, as such, has a very prescribed and specific meaning that differs from its more common use in other theoretical work; see **story and discourse**.

According to Jacques Derrida, discourse marks the moment when we eschew the myth of a center that grounds the play of signification: "This was the moment when language invaded the universal problematic, the moment when, in the absence of a center or origin, everything became discourse—provided we can agree on this word—that is to say, a system in which the central signified, the original or **transcendental signified**, is never absolutely present outside a system of differences" (1978: 280). This sense of discourse is commensurate with the "linguistic turn" in critical theory that follows the publication of Ferdinand de Saussure's *Course in General Linguistics* in 1916, and refers to the "system of differences" by which any language is constructed according to a set of **semiotic** rules (see **signifier and signified**). This is the sense of "discourse" commonly used by critical theorists, though one should keep in mind that "discourse" is used by Saussure himself in the more delimited sense of words spoken or written in a sequence, which

Saussure aligns with *parole* and what he terms the **syntagmatic** relations of language.

Many theorists, however, use "discourse" in the sense established by Michel Foucault, who throughout his work examines the conjunction of knowledge and **power** in anyone's use of language in a given context. He too concerns himself with **semiotic** rules but makes his focus all rules and exclusions by which we determine what can be said in a given situation. In other words, rather than be concerned with discourse as a general linguistic "system of differences," Foucault explores the many "discourse-formations" that structure our negotiation of knowledge and **power** in a given society at a given time. Each discourse has its own specific history of emergence and entails a certain set of rules that govern what objects may be spoken of within the discourse, what rituals should accompany use of the discourse and which **subjects** have the right to speak within the discourse. As Foucault writes in "The Discourse on Language," "Religious discourse, juridical and therapeutic as well as, in some ways, political discourse are all barely dissociable from the functioning of ritual that determines the individual properties and agreed roles of the speakers" (1971: 156). "Discourse" may well have originally meant simply conversation or speech but Foucault argues that any speech is in fact shot through with various assumptions, rules, and principles of exclusion: "In appearance," he explains, "speech may well be of little account, but the prohibitions surrounding it soon reveal its links with desire and power" (149). For Foucault, then, discourse is "a violence that we do to things, or, at all events, as a practice we impose upon them" (158).

To understand the functioning and emergence of various discourses, Foucault seeks to examine at once (1) "the principles of ordering, exclusion and rarity in discourse" (1971: 162) that exist in any given time period; and (2) the processes by which new discursive formations come into being through a discontinuous process of emergence; see **history** and **archaeology** for an explanation of Foucault's methodology for understanding what he sometimes terms the "genealogical" emergence of various discourses over the course of history. His major works explore the way that a specific "discourse," a particular system of rules and exclusions, evolves and then is structured into a **discipline**, from the legal and juridical (*Discipline and Punish*) to the medical (*Birth of the Clinic*) and the psychological (*Madness and Civilization*). In each of these works, Foucault examines a general change in the understanding of discourse itself, where the emphasis moves from the event of speaking (enunciation), which was held as particularly important in pre-literate society, to the meaning or truth of what is said (the enunciated), which is held as most important in post-Enlightenment culture. This more general historical change in the understanding of discourse allowed individual disciplines, each with their own unique genealogy, to disavow the will to power that, according to Foucault, is in fact inextricably bound up in the post-Enlightenment "will to truth."

Foucault's approach to discourse has influenced a number of disparate critics who can be loosely brought together under the banner of "discourse analysis" or "discourse studies." Some of these theorists also build on the **poststructuralist** approach to discourse that one finds in Jacques Lacan, Roland Barthes, and Derrida. **Neo-Marxists** Ernesto Laclau and Chantal Mouffe bring together these theoretical touchstones in their version of discourse analysis, which they promoted through the graduate program in Ideology and Discourse Analysis they founded at the University of Essex (see especially **articulation** but also **antagonism**, **hegemony**, and **radical democracy**). Critical Discourse Analysis, which is supported by several journals including *Discourse Studies* and *Critical Discourse Studies*, examines language as a social practice in order to establish how language and power intersect. As Ruth Wodak puts it, Critical Discourse Analysis "considers institutional, political, gender and media discourses (in the broadest sense) which testify to more or less overt relations of struggle and conflict" (2001: 2). Reiner Keller has promoted his own version of Foucauldian discourse analysis in what he terms the Sociology of Knowledge Approach to Discourse, or SKAD. The emphasis here is on the social construction of reality with discourse understood as *"concrete and material"*: "This means that discourse appears as speech, **text**, discussion, visual image, use of symbols, which have to be performed by actors following social instructions and therefore discourses are a *real social practice*" (2011: 48–49). SKAD thus "follows Foucault and examines discourses as performative statement practices which constitute reality orders and also produce power effects in a conflict-ridden network of social actors, institutional *dispositifs*, and knowledge systems" (48). Friedrich Kittler is another influential discourse theorist who, in his book *Discourse Networks* (1990), builds on Foucault's suggestion that "[t]he frontiers of a book are never clear-cut"; a book is only ever a "node within a network" (Foucault 1972: 23). To establish the "network" that governs a given period's organization of knowledge, Kittler examines, in particular, the actual machines that facilitate the production of discourse (the pen, the typewriter, the computer), "the network of technologies and institutions that allow a given culture to select, store, and process relevant data" (Kittler 1990: 369).

Jürgen Habermas, in conscious contradistinction to Foucault and the examples of discourse analysis listed above, understands discourse as the shared linguistic background and critical procedures that make possible dialogue at all. Without an agreed-upon set of universal protocols for conducting argumentation and communication, there can be no ethical relationship to others, Habermas argues. According to Habermas, then, "Discourse generalizes, abstracts, and stretches the presuppositions of context-bound **communicative actions** by extending their range to include competent subjects beyond the provincial limits of their own particular form of life" (1991: 202). See **discourse ethics** and **communicative action**.

See also: **communicative reason, power**.

Further reading: T. J. Armstrong 1992; Dreyfus and Rabinow 1983; Foucault 1971, 1975, 1977a, 1980, 1991a; Habermas 1987, 1991, 1993; Jaworski and Coupland 1999; Kittler 1990; Wodak 2001.

DISCOURSE ANALYSIS OR DISCOURSE STUDIES

See **discourse**

DISCOURSE ETHICS

Building on the work of Karl-Otto Apel, Jürgen Habermas theorizes this concept to explain his method of "grounding moral norms in communication" (1991: 195) and, more specifically, in the "universal presuppositions of argumentation" (1993: 9). According to Habermas, and against the suspicion of universality characteristic of other critical theorists, "Every morality revolves around equality of respect, solidarity, and the common good" (1991: 201) because we all share a common linguistic and cultural ground (the **lifeworld**) that makes possible communication and the promise of consensus through argumentation: "the meaning of the basic principle of morality can be explicated in terms of the content of the unavoidable presuppositions of an argumentative practice that can be pursued only in common with others" (1993: 1). One can claim universality for morality only because we can ground that universality on **discourse** itself, the shared linguistic background of all communication. Regarding the potential critique that "my moral principle is ... just a reflection of the prejudices of adult, white, well-educated, Western males of today" (1991: 197):

> the thesis that discourse ethics puts forth ... is that anyone who seriously undertakes to participate in argumentation implicitly accepts by that very undertaking general pragmatic presuppositions that have a normative content. The moral principle can then be derived from the content of these presuppositions of argumentation if one knows at least what it means to justify a norm of action. (1991: 197–98)

In other words, language itself ensures the universality of morality, achieved through what Habermas terms **communicative action**: "Linguistically and behaviorally competent subjects are constituted as individuals by growing into an intersubjectively shared **lifeworld**, and the **lifeworld** of a language community is reproduced in turn through the **communicative action** of its members" (1991: 199). **Discourse**, in this model, ensures the universality of moral claims: "There is only one reason why discourse ethics, which presumes to derive the substance of a universalistic morality from the general presuppositions of argumentation, is a promising strategy: discourse or argumentation is a more exacting type of communication, going beyond any particular form of life" (202).

See also: **communicative reason**, **public sphere**.

Further reading: Habermas 1987, 1991, 1993, 1999.

DISPLACEMENT

Displacement is one of the methods by which the **repressed** returns in hidden ways, according to Sigmund Freud. For example, in dreams the affect (emotions) associated with threatening impulses is often transferred elsewhere (displaced), so that, for example, apparently trivial elements in the manifest dream seem to cause extraordinary distress while "what was the essence of the dream-thoughts finds only passing and indistinct representation in the dream" (Freud 1953–74: 22.21). On "manifest dream" and "dream-thoughts," see **repression**. For Freud, "Displacement is the principal means used in the *dream-distortion* to which the dream-thoughts must submit under the influence of the censorship" (22.21). The same sort of displacement can occur in **symptom**-formation. The other method whereby the repressed hides itself is **condensation**.

DISPOSITIF

See **apparatus**

DISSENSUS

This concept, popularized for critical theory by Jacques Rancière, refers to a process whereby an excluded group seeks to create a fissure in what Rancière terms the **distribution of the sensible**, a given society's established framework for seeing, thinking, and acting. Dissensus is closely tied to Jean-François Lyotard's theorization of **phrase regimens**, **language games**, **differend** and **wrong**; indeed, Lyotard uses the term himself in *Peregrinations* (1988b): "The network formed by all these **phrases**, for which no common code exists" necessarily resists consensus. "It seems to me," he continues, "that the only consensus we ought to be worrying about is one that would encourage this heterogeneity or 'dissensus'" (44). For Rancière, genuine political *or* artistic activity (he aligns the two as inextricable) results in dissensus. The goal of dissensus is to make visible that which remains excluded (invisible, unsayable) in a given regime. Dissensus therefore, by definition, acts outside of any extant juridical procedures. According to Rancière, the best exemplification of the role of the police is not the **interpellation** of Louis Althusser's "Hey, you there!" but, rather, "Move along! There's nothing to see here!" As Rancière explains,

> The police is that which says that here, on this street, there's nothing to see and so nothing to do but move along. It asserts that the space for circulating is nothing but the space of circulation. Politics, by contrast, consists in transforming this space of "moving-along," of circulation, into a space for the appearance of a **subject**: the people, the workers, the citizens. It consists in refiguring space, that is, in what is to be done, to be seen and to be named in it. It is the instituting of a dispute over the **distribution of the sensible**. (2010: 37)

This "political" act is what Rancière terms dissensus, though Rancière understands "politics" in a very specific, even idiosyncratic sense: "Dissensus is not a confrontation between interests or opinions. It is the demonstration (*manifestation*) of a gap in the sensible itself" (2010: 38). Rancière offers his notion of dissensus in opposition to Jürgen Habermas's model of **communicative action**, which, he argues, is not viable as it will always leave out groups of people who have been excluded from a given society's **distribution of the sensible**. J. Hillis Miller adopts the concept of dissensus in *Black Holes* (1999) to imagine the future of the university as a "culture of dissensus made up of persons with irreconcilable values and goals" (171).

DISTANT READING

See **reader, reading and Reader-Response Criticism**

DISTRIBUTION OF THE SENSIBLE

The "distribution of the sensible" (*le partage du sensible*, sometimes translated as the partition of the sensible) is a phrase proposed by Jacques Rancière to describe the ways we make certain things visible and others invisible or unsayable through the communal establishment of rules and presuppositions. This distribution in turn affects what can be made, thought, said, and done. A given distribution of the sensible will tend to be established by excluding other actions, thoughts, and statements that then remain invisible or unsayable. Rancière has identified three different distributions of the sensible with regard to the history of the arts: the ethical regime of images, the representative regime of art, and the **aesthetic** regime of art.

See also: **aesthetics, dissensus, doxa, field, habitus, metapolitics, wrong**.

Further reading: Rancière 1999, 2004, 2010.

DIVISION OF LABOR

In **Marxism**, the "division of labor" refers to the way that different tasks are apportioned to different people in a given society. According to Karl Marx and Friedrich Engels, "How far the productive forces of a nation are developed is shown most manifestly by the degree to which the division of labour has been carried" (1932: 43). Human progress has led to various developments in the division of labor: first the "separation of industrial and commercial from agricultural labour, and hence to the separation of *town* and *country* and to the conflict of their interests" (43). The "various stages of development in the division of labour are just so many different forms of ownership" (43). Marx and Engels outline those stages as: (1) the tribal form, which is really "a further extension of the natural division of labour existing in the family" (44); (2) primitive communism: "the ancient communal and State ownership which proceeds especially from the union of several tribes into a *city* by agreement or by conquest" (44), during which time the concept of private property begins to develop; (3) **feudal** or estate property; and (4) **capitalism**.

DOMINANT, RESIDUAL, AND EMERGENT

These terms are theorized by Raymond Williams, who is an important early influence on **cultural materialism**. Following the dictates of **historical materialism**, he refuses to tell **history** from the perspective of the victors, of the dominant class in any given time period. His goal, rather, is to find moments of crisis and **antagonism** in the past in order to tell the story of marginalized and oppressed groups. He proposes that any given time period's dominant or **hegemonic** group must continually struggle to maintain dominance: **hegemony** "does not just passively exist as a form of dominance. It has continually to be renewed, recreated, defended, and modified. It is also continually resisted, limited, altered, challenged by pressures not at all its own" (1977: 112). In addition to exploring the concepts of "counter-hegemony" and "alternative hegemony" (113) to represent this unending conflict, Williams proposes that we must also explore "residual" and "emergent" elements in a given society.

As Williams explains,

> The residual, by definition, has been effectively formed in the past, but it is still active in the cultural process, not only and often not at all as an element of the past, but as an effective element of the present. Thus certain experiences, meanings, and values which cannot be expressed or substantially verified in terms of the dominant culture, are nevertheless lived and practiced on the basis of the residue—cultural as well as social—of some previous social and cultural institution or formation. (1977: 122)

Unlike an "archaic" element that "is wholly recognized as an element of the past" (1977: 122), the residual is an element of the past that is still viable in the present and can "have an alternative or even oppositional relation to the dominant culture" (122). Williams offers as example "the idea of rural community." The idea is "predominantly residual" but it is also "in some limited respects alternative or oppositional to urban industrial capitalism, though for the most part it is incorporated, as idealization or fantasy, or as an exotic—residential or escape—leisure function of the dominant order itself" (122). Although the dominant culture continually works to incorporate residual elements as a part of its **hegemonic** ideology, the residual can be called on to "represent areas of human experience, aspiration, and achievement which the dominant culture neglects, undervalues, opposes, represses, or even cannot recognize" (123–24).

By "emergent," Williams means "that new meanings and values, new practices, new relationships and kinds of relationship are continually being created" (1977: 123). Of course, it can be difficult to distinguish between new elements that are merely novel (therefore evanescent) and those that presage a properly emergent formation that will effectively oppose the dominant culture. Even when one pinpoints a properly emergent formation, "the development [of the new element] is always uneven" (124). He gives as an example "the emergence of the working class as a **class**," which was "immediately evident (for example, in nineteenth-century England) in the cultural process" (124) but was highly uneven in its instantiation. Although this complex process of emergence "can still in part be described in **class** terms," there is "always other social being and consciousness which is neglected and excluded [in dominant culture]: alternative perceptions of others, in immediate relationships; new perceptions and practices of the material world. In practice these are different in quality from the developing and articulated interests of a rising **class**" (126). The main point Williams wishes to make, and he puts this in italics, is that "*no mode of production and therefore no dominant social order and therefore no dominant culture ever in reality includes or exhausts all human practice*" (125). The dominant culture may well have "effectively seized ... the ruling definition of the social"; however, for the historical materialist, "It is this seizure that has especially to be resisted. For there is always, though in varying degrees, practical consciousness, in specific relationships, specific skills, specific perceptions, that is unquestionably social and that a specifically dominant social order neglects, excludes, represses, or simply fails to recognize" (125).

See also: **doxa, habitus, ideology, radical democracy**.

DOXA (DOXIC)

Pierre Bourdieu uses the term "doxa" to designate those **ideological** (and, therefore, arbitrary) beliefs that are made to seem part of the natural order of things and that are therefore accepted without question. They are thus taken for granted, misrecognized as necessary when in fact they are the result of **ideological** choices. Bourdieu distinguishes doxa "from an orthodox or heterodox belief implying awareness and recognition of the possibility of different or antagonistic beliefs" (Bourdieu 1977: 164). Doxic belief, by contrast, reproduces "the social world by producing immediate adherence to the world, seen as self-evident and undisputed" (164). Bourdieu explains that "the stabler the objective structures and the more fully they reproduce themselves in the agents' dispositions, the greater the extent of the field of doxa," until "the established cosmological and political order is perceived not as arbitrary, i.e. as one possible order among others, but as a self-evident and **natural** order which goes without saying and therefore goes unquestioned" (165–66). To relate doxa to Bourdieu's other two privileged terms, **habitus** and **field**, one could say that **doxa** applies to the situation when **habitus** encounters a **field** of which it is the product; in such a situation, "it is like a 'fish in water': it does not feel the weight of the water, and it takes the world about itself for granted" (Bourdieu and Wacquant 1992: 127); however, it is only "because this world has produced me, because it has produced the categories of thought that I apply to it, that it appears to me as self-evident" (128).

See also: **nature and naturalize**.

Further reading: Bourdieu 1977.

DREAM DISTORTION

See **repression**

DREAM THOUGHTS

See **repression**

DRIVES

Drives are instinctual (pre-lingual) bodily impulses or **instincts**, according to psychoanalysis. Sigmund Freud ultimately decided they could be reduced to two primary drives: (1) the life drives (both the **pleasure principle** and the **reality principle**); and (2) the **death drive**, which Freud saw as even more primal than the life drives.

DROMOCRACY AND DROMOLOGY

These terms were created by the theorist Paul Virilio, who argues that technologically achieved speed and movement over space, especially in support of war, are the dominant forces transforming social and political reality, especially since about 1789, the year of the French Revolution: "history," he writes in *Speed and Politics* (1977), "progresses at the speed of its weapons systems" (90). Virilio argues that speed has therefore replaced politics in various ways, hence his term **"dromocracy"** (*dromos* from the Greek: to race). In terms of class struggle, for example, the automobile succeeded in destroying the danger of mass uprising by revolutionizing how we approach space and time: "The stroke of genius will consist in doing away with the direct repression of riots, and the political **discourse** itself ... : the transportation capacity created by the mass production of automobiles (since 1914 with Ford) can become a social assault, a revolution sufficient and able to modify the citizen's way of life by transforming all the consumer's needs, by totally remodeling a territory that (need we be reminded of it?) at the beginning had no more than 400 kilometers of road" (1977: 50). Whereas the French Revolution of 1789 was a revolt "against the *constraint to immobility* symbolized by the ancient feudal serfdom" (53), the new system of control could be characterized as "an *obligation to mobility*," a "*dictatorship of movement*" (53). There is still the danger of mobilizing the new technology of speed into forms of rebellion, so Virilio argues that, at base, all efforts to control this technology (through speed limits and government regulation) is a kind of warfare performed by states to control the masses. Virilio argues in *Speed and Politics* that the movement whereby speed takes over politics gains traction with the British Empire's control of the seas in the nineteenth century, which allowed it to conceive of "[s]peed as a pure idea without content" (68); speed on the sea had no "content" insofar as ships can move in any direction at speed—no obstacles. That idea then gets translated to other forms of control and movement: "The right to the sea creates the right to the road of modern States, which through this become totalitarian States" (69). The armored tank of the First World War followed a similar logic, destroying space since the vehicles and their projectiles could follow any trajectory (like ships at sea); air war and then nuclear war increased the speed of such unbridled trajectories. After 1945 and the collapse of various totalitarian states, the same logic was applied to global economics and, after that, to the digital revolution. At each stage, what matters is speed and control, so Virilio argues that throughout what we are seeing is not the rise of democracy as dominant political reality but, rather, a science of speed and war: "In fact, there was no 'industrial revolution,' but only a 'dromocratic revolution'; there is no democracy, only dromocracy; there is no strategy, only dromology" (69). The result is a world dominated by what Virilio terms "total war": "Dromocratic intelligence is not exercised against a more or less determined military adversary, but as a permanent assault on the world, and through it, on human nature" (86). What matters, then, is no longer space but time, the *"war of time"* (155)—how quickly a weapon can penetrate, for example: "We have to face the facts," Virilio writes: "today, speed is war, the last war" (155).

Further reading: Virilio 1977, 1989, 2008, 2010

DYSTOPIA (DYSTOPIC)

A dystopia is an imagined universe (usually the future of our own world) in which a worst-case scenario is explored (the opposite of **utopia**). Dystopic stories have been especially influential on **postmodernism**, as writers and film-makers imagine the effects of various aspects of our current **postmodern** condition, for example, the world's take-over by machines (*The Terminator, The Matrix, Battlestar Galactica*); the social effects of the hyperreal (*Neuromancer*); a society completely run by media commercialism (*The Running Man, The Hunger Games*); the triumph of late capitalism (*Blade Runner*); bureaucratic control run amok (*Brazil, 1984*); and so on. A subgenre of dystopic fiction that has particularly influenced **postmodernism** is **cyberpunk**.

See also: **heterotopia**.

ECOCRITICISM (ECOCRITICAL)

As Cheryl Glotfelty has defined it in the introduction to the *The Ecocriticism Reader* (1996), edited by Glotfelty and Harold Fromm, ecocriticism is—to define it baldly—"the study of the relationship between literature and the physical environment," both of which are understood in cultural as well as ecological terms. Ecocriticism is, as she continues, "an earth-centered approach to literary studies" (xviii). While not recognized as a distinct critical movement until the late twentieth century, environmentally focused scholarship has been a part of **Cultural Studies** since the latter's inception, particularly in Romanticism and nineteenth-century American Studies, given the importance of those periods in the understanding of the environment (see **nature**). Scholars working in those sub-fields have explored such issues as regionalism, geographical frontiers, pastoral spaces, the country, **nature**, and landscape **aesthetics**.

Two significant and oft-cited precursors to the critical understanding of human and environment interrelations are Leo Marx's *The Machine in the Garden* (1964) and Raymond Williams's *The Country and the City* (1973). For both Marx and Williams, the pristine country provides a pastoral ideal at odds with the technological and urban realities of the human environment within the historical moment they study. In this sense, while neither of these authors refers to "ecology"—the "study of or concern for the effect of human activity on the environment" and "advocacy of restrictions on industrial and agricultural development as a political movement" (*OED*)—both go beyond a study of **Nature** as a culturally constructed representation toward a more complex understanding of interrelations between human organisms and their milieu.

The work of Marx and Williams helped shape ecocriticism, fostering a common feature of this theory: its political orientation. In the same "Introduction" where Glotfelty defines ecocriticism, she correlates its formation as a critical school with the "global environmental crisis" (xv)—and, indeed, ecocriticism has gained increasing traction and complexity within the larger field of **Global Studies**. In this regard, ecocriticism often focuses on a "green politics" and wields a conservationist ethos. This can be seen in two representational works from Romanticism and American studies, Jonathan Bate's *Romantic Ecology* (1991) and Lawrence Buell's *The Environmental Imagination* (1995). Bate focuses primarily on the politicized (rather than idyllic) pastoral of William Wordsworth (1770–1850), a version of **nature** that incorporates labor, economics, and a proto-conservationist understanding of **nature**'s value. His concern is particularly with an ecological understanding of **nature**: "A green reading of Wordsworth ... has strong historical force, for if one historicizes the idea of an ecological viewpoint—a respect for the earth and a scepticism as to the orthodoxy that economic growth and material production are the be-all and end-all of human society—one finds oneself squarely in the Romantic tradition" (9). Ultimately, Wordsworth, for Bate, teaches his audience how best to exist within their own environment. Buell, looking to Henry David Thoreau (1817–62), identifies a similar project: "If, as environmental philosophers contend, western metaphysics and ethics need revision before we can address today's environmental problems, then environmental crisis involves a crisis of the imagination the amelioration of which depends on finding better ways of imagining

nature and humanity's relation to it" (2). Much of the ecocriticism following Bate and Buell provides a comparable message: the exploration of proto-ecological views in Romantic and Transcendental writing might be just the thing to reframe our unproductive and even detrimental attitudes toward the natural environment.

Two significant trends have since altered the ecocritical landscape, resulting from self-aware reappraisals of what ecocriticism is and what it might accomplish. One such reappraisal can be found in Timothy Morton's *Ecology without Nature* (2007), where Morton argues "that the very idea of '**nature**' which so many hold dear will have to wither away in an 'ecological' state of human society. Strange as it may sound, the idea of **nature** is getting in the way of properly ecological forms of culture, philosophy, politics, and art" (1). Morton's questioning of **nature** is not necessarily new in itself, as the semantic value of this concept had been questioned by Williams and in more contemporary **New Historicism**; however, in Morton's application, the questioning of **Nature** allows for a more sophisticated, because less idealized, understanding of the relationships between persons and their environment.

The second trend is interconnected with the first: in rejecting an overly straightforward advocacy of **Nature**, scholars have adopted a more theoretically driven ecocriticism. Given its prior, activist tendencies, ecocriticism had often been seen as more **praxis** than theory, and Buell and Bate both position their criticism in opposition to the dominant theories of their critical moment: **poststructuralism** and **New Historicism**. The theoretical turn in ecocriticism is readily seen in the comparison of *The Ecocriticism Reader* (Glotfelty and Fromm 1996) and *Ecocritical Theory* (2011), edited by Axel Goodbody and Kate Rigby. More recent scholarship in this field has more clearly engaged with and developed from, for example, **Cultural Materialism, poststructuralism, phenomenology, Cognitive Studies, postcolonialism** and **feminism**. These incorporations have led to such hybrids as eco-feminism, eco-imperialism, eco-phenomenology, eco-**semiotics** and **postcolonial** ecocriticism; these new theoretical approaches to ecology also tend to engage the growing field of **Global Studies**.

Further reading: Bate 1991; Buell 1995; Glotfelty and Fromm 1996; Goodbody and Rigby 2011; L. Marx 1964; Morton 2007; Siewers 2014.

ECOLOGY

See **ecocriticism**

ÉCRITURE FÉMININE

Some feminist theorists have argued that language itself in the Western world tends to be structured in such a way as to privilege the masculine. One need only mention the principle by which we revert to the masculine to denote humans of both genders: "man," "mankind," "postman," etc. Some theorists go further, reworking the **deconstructionist** notion of **logocentrism** to argue that language's myth of a center, an origin, a transcendental **signified**, or a presence—aspects of language that are questioned by **deconstruction**—also tends to be gendered male. Feminist theorists therefore created the neologism "**phallocentrism**" or "**phallogocentrism**" to designate this tendency of masculine language to orient itself toward not only center and presence but also order, logic, hierarchy, stable meanings, rules, and **binary oppositions**. As Hélène Cixous for example writes,

> Nearly the entire history of writing is confounded with the history of reason, of which it is at once the effect, the support, and one of the privileged alibis. It has been one with the phallocentric tradition. It is indeed that same self-admiring, self-stimulating, self-congratulatory **phallocentrism**. (1976: 311)

Critics like Cixous have made a call, then, to articulate an alternative kind of writing that is more properly feminine, characterized by multiplicity and heterogeneity, flux, uncertainty, play, laughter, bodily sexuality, creativity, and the breaking of grammatical rules. The goal of the female writer, according to Cixous, is to "forge for herself the antilogos weapon" (1976: 312). Indeed, she argues that, as a result, "It is impossible to *define* a feminine practice of writing" because "this practice can never be theorized, enclosed, coded—which doesn't mean that it doesn't exist. But it will always surpass the **discourse** that regulates the **phallocentric** system; it does and will take place in areas other than those subordinated to philosophico-theoretical domination" (313). Such writing, according to Cixous, is instead bodily and subversive with regard to rules and codes: "Women must write through their bodies, they must invent the impregnable language that will wreck partitions, classes, and rhetorics, regulations and codes" (315). Poetry, because of its willingness to break syntactical rules, is often privileged: "only the poets," Cixous writes, "not the novelists, allies of representationalism" (311). Julia Kristeva similarly points to the revolutionary nature of poetry in her *Revolution in Poetic Language* (1984). As she writes, "Magic, shamanism, esoterism, the carnival, and 'incomprehensible' poetry all underscore the limits of socially useful **discourse** and attest to what it represses: the *process* that exceeds the **subject** and his communicative structures" (16).

See also: **carnivalesque, chora, genotext and phenotext**.

Further reading: Cixous 1976, 1986; M. Eagleton 1986; Kristeva 1984.

EGO

For Sigmund Freud, the ego is "the representative of the outer world to the **id**" (1923: 708). In other words, the ego represents and enforces the **reality principle** whereas the **id** is concerned only with the **pleasure principle**. Whereas the ego is oriented towards perceptions in the real world, the **id** is oriented towards internal **instincts**; whereas the ego is associated with reason and sanity, the **id** belongs to the passions. The ego, however, is never able fully to distinguish itself from the **id**, of which the ego is, in fact, a part, which is why in his pictorial representation of the mind Freud does not provide a hard separation between the ego and the **id**. The ego could also be said to be a defense against the **super-ego** and its ability to drive the individual subject towards inaction or suicide as a result of crippling guilt. Freud sometimes represents the ego as continually struggling to defend itself from three dangers or masters: "from the external world, from the **libido** of the **id**, and from the severity of the **super-ego**" (1923: 716).

EGO IDEAL

See **ideal ego and ego ideal**

EMERGENT

See **dominant, residual and emergent**

EMPIRE

Most people understand "empire" in the sense clarified by the *Oxford English Dictionary*: "An extensive territory under the control of a supreme ruler (typically an emperor) or an oligarchy, often consisting of an aggregate of many separate states or territories. In later use also: an extensive group of subject territories ultimately under the rule of a single sovereign state." This sense of the term informs the term, imperialism, "The principle or policy of empire; the advocacy of holding political dominion or control over dependent territories" (*OED*). Both "empire" and "imperialism," in this sense, are important terms for **Postcolonial Studies**, which seeks to make sense of the **national** and ethnic identity of previously subjugated peoples.

The term has, however, been redefined for **Global Studies** by Michael Hardt and Antonio Negri in their book, *Empire* (2000). Whereas "[t]he sovereignty of the **nation-state** was the cornerstone of the imperialisms that European powers constructed throughout the modern era," "Empire," for them, names a new form of sovereignty, "composed of a series of national and supranational organisms united under a single logic of rule" (xii). The new logic "is a *decentered* and *deterritorializing* apparatus of rule that progressively incorporates the entire global realm within its open, expanding frontiers" (xii). Although this new logic of rule is often associated with the United States, Hardt and Negri argue forcefully that "*The United States does not, and indeed no nation-state can today, form the center of an imperialist project.* Imperialism is over. No nation will be world leader in the way modern European nations were" (xiii–xiv). Instead, Hardt and Negri's theoretical concept has the following characteristics: (1) "The concept of Empire is characterized fundamentally by a lack of boundaries: Empire's rule has no limits" (xiv); (2) "Empire presents its rule not as a transitory moment in the movement of history, but as a regime with no temporal boundaries and in this sense outside of history or at the end of history" (xiv–xv); (3) "The object of its rule is social life in its entirety, and thus Empire presents the paradigmatic form of **biopower**" (xv); and (4) "although the practice of Empire is continually bathed in blood, the concept of Empire is always dedicated to peace—a perpetual and universal peace outside of history" (xv). Although Hardt and Negri are highly critical of Empire as it currently exists, their ultimate goal is to "invent new democratic forms and a new constituent power that will one day take us through and beyond Empire." As they explain, "The creative forces of the multitude that sustain Empire are also capable of autonomously constructing a counter-Empire, an alternative political organization of global flows and exchanges" (xv).

Further reading: Hardt and Negri 2000; Hobsbawm 2008; Mommsen 1980; Negri 2008a, 2008b.

EMPIRICISM (EMPIRICAL)

See **positivism and empiricism**

EPISTEMOLOGY OF THE CLOSET

Eve Kosofsky Sedgwick argues in *Epistemology of the Closet* (1990), a work that helped to establish **queer theory** as a critical school and set of critical practices, that "many of the major nodes of thought and knowledge in twentieth-century Western culture as a whole are structured—indeed, fractured—by a chronic, now endemic crisis of homo-heterosexual definition, indicatively male, dating from the end of the nineteenth century" (1). That is, rather than see homosexuality as only a **marginal** concern of a minority group, Sedgwick argues that dominant, **hegemonic**, **heteronormative ideology** relies on the homosexual to establish its very frame of reference—what it can *know* ("epistemology" is the science or theory of knowledge). As she states, "I am trying to make the strongest possible introductory case for a hypothesis about the centrality of this nominally **marginal**, conceptually intractable set of definitional issues to the important knowledges and understandings of twentieth-century Western culture as a whole" (2).

In this, she adopts a "**deconstructive**" (9) approach to issues of **binary opposition**. As she explains, in a way that also helps to explain the key concept of **binary opposition**, the analytic move

> is to demonstrate that categories presented in a culture as symmetrical **binary oppositions**—heterosexual/homosexual, in this case—actually subsist in a more unsettled and dynamic tacit relation according to which, first, term B is not symmetrical with but subordinated to term A; but, second, the ontologically valorized term A actually depends for its meaning on the simultaneous subsumption and exclusion of term B; hence, third, the question of priority between the supposed central and the supposed marginal category of each dyad is irresolvably unstable, an instability caused by the fact that term B is constituted as at once internal and external to term A. (9–10)

Her goal throughout her work is then to **deconstruct** the binary, to "move through a **deconstructive** description of the instability of the **binarism** itself, usually couched as the simultaneous interiority and exteriority of a **marginalized** to a normative term, toward an examination of the resulting definitional incoherence" (92).

Sedgwick dates the centrality of homosexual definition in Western culture to the end of the nineteenth century since that is when "homosexual" is first defined and named. After this point, "New, institutionalized taxonomic discourses—medical, legal, literary, psychological—centering on homo/heterosexual definition proliferated and crystallized with exceptional rapidity" (2). Taking Michel Foucault's theories about **bio-politics and bio-power** as "axiomatic" (3), Sedgwick develops a highly influential understanding of the central place of the homosexual in heterosexual **discourse**'s ongoing efforts to establish a series of binary oppositions where the first term (A) is given dominance over the subordinated B term: "masculine/feminine, majority/minority, innocence/initiation, **natural**/artificial, new/old, growth/decadence, urbane/provincial, health/illness, same/different, cognition/paranoia, art/**kitsch**, sincerity/sentimentality, and volun-tarity/addiction" (72). Sedgwick argues that the "suffusing stain of homo/heterosexual crisis" has been so pervasive "that to discuss any of these indices in any context, in the absence of an antihomophobic analysis, must perhaps be to perpetuate unknowingly compulsions implicit in each" (73), an argument that she also pursues in her notion of **homosocial** as distinct from (but also the obverse of) homosexual desire.

Sedgwick's approach has influenced later queer theorists who seek to establish the central structural significance of "queerness" to a Western culture obsessed about **sexuality** after the ascendance of **bio-politics and bio-power** in the governance of the **nation-state**'s citizens. Sometimes building on Sedgwick's mention of "queer time" (xi) in her work *Tendencies* (1994), such critics establish an alternative "**queer temporality**" that works at odds with the temporal, historical, and **narratological** structures of **compulsory heterosexuality**.

See also: **GLBTQ Studies**

EQUIVALENT FORM

According to Karl Marx, things can be exchanged on the market because they are always related to a third thing, abstract human **labor**, which functions as the equivalent form of the **commodity**. By having **money** serve as the **universal equivalent** in **capitalist** society, we forget the real **labor** of the worker that undergirds the production of goods and services, according to Marx. In the equiva-lent form, real private **labor** "takes the form of its opposite, namely labour in its directly social form" (1867: 151).

See also: **commodity fetishism**.

ETHNIC AND ETHNICITY

See **race and ethnicity**

EVENT

See **being and event**

EXCHANGE VALUE

See **use value and exchange value**

EXTRADIEGETIC

See **diegesis**

FACE OF THE OTHER

See **Other**

FACTIALITY

"Factiality" is a term used by Quentin Meillassoux and **Speculative Realism** to make the argument that things must be understood as existing in themselves outside of their relation to my own thought. "Facticity" for Meillassoux "designates our essential ignorance about either the contingency *or* the necessity of our world and its invariants" (2008: 54), that is, "the impossibility of establishing any ultimate ground for the existence of any being." "Factiality" describes "the speculative essence of *facticity*, viz., that the facticity of every thing cannot be thought as a fact" (79). It is, rather, an absolute that guarantees the existence of things outside of their relation to me but without determining what that existence might absolutely *be*. In other words, Meillassoux wishes to absolutize facticity itself: "we do not maintain that a determinate entity exists, but that it is absolutely necessary that every entity might not exist." As he goes on to explain, "This is indeed a speculative thesis, since we are thinking an absolute, but it is not metaphysical, since we are not thinking any *thing* any (entity) that would *be* absolute. The absolute is the absolute impossibility of a necessary being" (60).

FALSE CONSCIOUSNESS

See **ideology**

FATHER OF ENJOYMENT

See **super-ego**

FEMINISM (FEMINIST)

Feminism is both a critical school and a broad social movement that seeks to fight against the privileging of men and the mechanisms of **patriarchal** power in culture and society. As a critical theory, it has its roots in the logic of Enlightenment philosophy, which argued for the inalienable rights of all men and impelled both the American and French Revolutions (see **Introduction**). Most feminists acknowledge Mary Wollstonecraft (1759–97) as the first feminist writer. In her book, *A Vindication of the Rights of Woman* (1792), Wollstonecraft indeed applies the principles of the French Revolution to argue for a "REVOLUTION in female manners" (230). As Anne Mellor (2014) explains, "Grounded on the affirmation of universal human rights endorsed by such Enlightenment thinkers as Voltaire, Jean-Jacques Rousseau, and John Locke—the affirmation that underpinned both the American Revolution in 1776 and the French Revolution in 1789—Wollstonecraft argued that females are in all the most important aspects the same as males, possessing the same souls, the same mental capacities, and thus the same human rights." The so-called "first wave" of feminist writers pursued a similar "equality" or "liberal" feminist theory throughout the nineteenth and into the twentieth centuries, arguing for the equal rights and privileges of women in various arenas (the right to vote, legal rights, equal education, equal pay, and other rights fundamental to liberal ideals of selfhood).

A "second wave" of feminist writers can be identified as arising in the decades following the Second World War. While still committed to fighting oppression and inequality, these critical theorists looked more widely at various cultural and institutional mechanisms that privileged **patriarchal** culture, arguing that a truly liberated feminist thinking needed to fight against **binary oppositions** that privileged men and the characteristics attributed to men (reason, science, control, strength, writing) against a subordinated set of terms tied to women (feeling, family, hysteria, passivity, nature). These theorists critiqued such **binary oppositions** at the same time being able to find value in the subordinated terms of such binary oppositions. We even see feminist writers of this period theorizing a counter-tradition of feminine identity, as in Luce Irigaray's theorization of **desire**, Hélène Cixous's formulation of an *écriture féminine*, or Julia Kristeva's theorization of the **chora** and the **genotext**. Feminist writers, thinkers, and public figures were "recovered" during this period and made a part of the university curriculum; Women's Studies programs became an important part of most universities.

This period also saw the rise of many of the critical theories discussed in this book, which in turn influenced feminist writers who adopted and contributed to the new critical methodologies. Each of these approaches are still common in critical theory today: **Marxist** feminists examine the class and economic issues that impact women; **psychoanalytical** feminists (especially in the Lacanian and Kristevan traditions) examine the **objectification** of women before the **scopophylic** fantasies of the male **gaze** (see also **suture**); **postcolonial** feminists examine the plight of women in subjugated colonial holdings (see **subaltern**); **poststructuralist** feminists use **deconstructionist** techniques to dismantle **binary oppositions** and to "trouble" the distinction between **nature** and **culture**, between biological **sex** and **gender** conventions, illustrating how all aspects of "reality" are, in fact, **discursive, ideological,** and **performative**.

A "third wave" of feminism has been identified in thinkers of the last three decades who have critiqued the feminist investigation of the past for its almost exclusive focus on the relationships between men and women. Adrienne Rich for example argues that such an exclusive focus entails a **compulsory heterosexuality** that fails to take into account or even to acknowledge alternative **sexualities** (see also **epistemology of the closet, homosocial desire, LGBTQ Studies, queer temporality**, and **queer theory**). Other third-wave feminists fault past thinkers for not taking into consideration issues of **race** since women from certain racial groups are doubly disadvantaged in contemporary culture. This has led to the rise of Black Feminism, particularly **Critical Race Theory** (see **intersectionality, Matrix of Domination, whiteness as property**).

Further reading: Butler 1990a, 1990b, 1993; Cixous 1976, 1986; Collins 2000; Crenshaw *et al.* 1995; Cudd and Andreason 2005; M. Eagleton 1986; Gilbert and Gubar 1984; Irigaray 1985a, 1985b; James and Sharpley-Whiting 2000; Keohane, Rosaldo and Gelpi 1982; Kristeva 1980, 1984; Mellor 2014; Rich 1980; Saul 2003; Sedgwick 1985, 1990; Showalter 1985, 1989; Swarr and Nagar 2010; Wollstonecraft 1792.

FETISHISM

Fetishism is the **displacement** of desire and fantasy onto alternative objects or body parts (e.g., a foot fetish or a shoe fetish), in order to obviate a subject's confrontation with the **castration complex**. According to Sigmund Freud, fetishism is connected to the childhood belief that the mother has a penis: "the fetish is a substitute for the woman's (the mother's) penis that the little boy once believed in and—for reasons familiar to us—does not want to give up" (1953–74: 21.152–53). Freud came to realize in his essay on "Fetishism" (1928) that the fetishist is able *at one and the same time* to believe in his fantasy and to recognize that it is nothing but a fantasy, so that fetishism occupies a position between **neurosis** and **psychosis**. Freud originally distinguished between **neurosis** and **psychosis** in the following way: "the essential difference between **neurosis** and **psychosis** was that in the former the **ego**, in the serve of reality, suppresses a piece of the **id**, whereas in a **psychosis** it lets itself be induced by the **id** to detach itself from a piece of reality" (1953–74: 21.155). In analyzing a case of mourning, Freud is forced to rethink this distinction in his essay on fetishism: "In the analysis of two young men I learned that each ... had failed to take cognizance of the death of his beloved father ... and yet neither of them had developed a **psychosis**. Thus a piece of reality which was undoubtedly important had been disavowed by the **ego**, just as the unwelcome fact of women's castration is disavowed in fetishists" (21.155–56). The fact of recognizing the fantasy *as fantasy* in no way reduces its power over the individual. As Freud goes on, "It was only one current in their mental life that had not recognized their father's death; there was another current which took full account of that fact. The attitude which fitted in with the wish and the attitude which fitted in with reality existed side by side" (21.156). Similarly, the fetish is able to become the vehicle of both "the disavowal and the affirmation of the **castration**" (21.156). Octave Mannoni, in an influential essay (1969), phrased this paradoxical logic in this way: "*je sais bien, mais quand-même*" or "I know very well, but nevertheless." Slavoj Žižek (1991a) builds on this idea in theorizing the nature of **ideology**, which follows a similar contradictory logic. Julia Kristeva goes so far as to associate all language with fetishism:

It is perhaps unavoidable that, when a **subject** confronts the factitiousness of **object** relation, when he stands at the place of the want that founds it, the fetish becomes a life preserver, temporary and slippery, but nonetheless indispensable. But is not exactly language our ultimate and inseparable fetish? And language, precisely, is based on fetishist denial ("I know that, but just the same," "the sign is not the thing, but just the same," etc.) and defines us in our essence as speaking beings. (1982: 37)

Postcolonial theorist Homi Bhabha reads the "racial stereotype of colonial discourse in terms of fetishism" (1994: 74). Just as the young boy wishes to disavow his mother's difference from himself, fearing his own **castration**, the colonial "fetish or stereotype" about the subjugated **Other** "gives access to an 'identity' which is predicated as much on mastery and pleasure as it is on anxiety and defence, for it is a form of multiple and contradictory belief in its recognition of difference and disavowal of it" (75). Radical difference is "disavowed," in other words, "by the fixation on an object that masks that difference and restores an original presence" (74). As with the sexual fetish, that **imaginary** object, the "'fullness' of the stereotype," is, in fact, "always threatened by '**lack**'" (77).

See also: **commodity fetishism**.

Further reading: Apter and Pietz 1993; Bhabha 1994; Kristeva 1982; L. J. Kaplan 2006; Mannoni 1969; Žižek 1991a.

FEUDAL SOCIETY (FEUDALISM)

Feudalism is the stage of society that preceded capitalism, during which a small elite (the aristocracy) demanded recompense from a peasantry in exchange for military protection. As Karl Marx and Friedrich Engels explain, "Like tribal and communal ownership, it is based again on a community; but the directly producing **class** standing over against it is not, as in the case of the ancient community, the slaves, but the enserfed small peasantry" (1932: 45). In the city, the feudal structure manifested itself in trade guilds. The organization of both the country and the city "was determined by the restricted conditions of production—the small-scale and primitive cultivation of the land, and the craft type of industry" (46), which meant that there "was little **division of labour** in the heyday of feudalism" (46). Exploitation functioned differently during this stage than during the height of **capitalism**, according to

Marx and Engels, because each feudal peasant knew exactly what proportion of his **labor** had to be handed over to the aristocracy and the church; the rest was his or hers to use.

FIELD

Pierre Bourdieu uses the term, "field," to distinguish his form of socio-logical and anthropological analysis from the **Marxist** study of **class** struggle. On occasion, Bourdieu goes so far as to state that "Social **classes** do not exist," at least not in the sense theorized by Karl Marx. "What exists is a social space, a space of differences, in which classes exist in some sense in a state of virtuality, not as something given but as *something to be done*" (1998: 12). Bourdieu instead examines "the structure of the distribution of the forms of power or the kinds of **capital** which are effective in the social universe under consideration— and which vary according to the specific place and moment at hand" (32). As that structure of distribution "is not immutable" (32), Bourdieu describes "the global social space as a *field*, that is, both as a field of forces, whose necessity is imposed on agents who are engaged in it, and as a field of struggles within which agents confront each other, with differentiated means and ends according to their position in the structure of the field of forces, thus contributing to conserving or transforming its structure" (32).

According to Bourdieu, there are numerous fields in a given society, each with its own structures, forms of **cultural capital,** and internal struggles. He speaks for example of the economic field; the educational field; the field of **culture** (e.g., literature and the arts); the political field; and so on. All the various fields that constitute a given society are brought together in Bourdieu's concept of the "field of power," which he makes clear is "not a field like the others" and "should not be confused with the political field" (1998: 34). Bourdieu defines the field of power "as the space of play within which the holders of **capital** (of different species) struggle *in particular* for power over the state, that is, over the statist capital granting power over the different species of capital and over their reproduction (particularly through the school system)" (42). Although this was not always the case, contemporary society gives the **nation-state** the greatest determining say in the field of power, particularly through acts of both physical (military, police) and symbolic violence:

> The state is an X (to be determined) which successfully claims the monopoly of the legitimate use of physical and *symbolic* violence

over a definite territory and over the totality of the corresponding population. If the state is able to exert symbolic violence, it is because it incarnates itself simultaneously in objectivity, in the form of specific organizational structures and mechanisms, and in subjectivity, in the form of mental structures and categories of perception and thought. By realizing itself in social structures and in the mental structures adapted to them, the instituted institution makes us forget that it issues out of a long series of acts of *institution* (in the active sense) and hence has all the appearances of the *natural*. (Bourdieu 1998: 40)

To understand how the state controls the field of power and **naturalizes** our relationship to its **ideological** investments, one needs to understand the relationship among Bourdieu's privileged terms, **habitus**, field and **doxa**.

Field and **habitus** work together and are sometimes difficult to distinguish. Bourdieu explains that the "field structures the **habitus**, which is the product of the embodiment of the immanent necessity of a field," the "social made body" (Bourdieu and Wacquant 1992: 127). On the other hand, "**Habitus** contributes to constituting the field as a meaningful world, a world endowed with sense and value, in which it is worth investing one's energy" (127). As Bourdieu goes on to explain, "Social reality exists, so to speak, twice, in things and in minds, in fields and in **habitus**, outside and inside of agents" (127). Bourdieu's term **doxa** applies to the situation when **habitus** encounters a field of which it is the product, which makes the **subject-agent** feel as if that social reality is completely **natural**, self-evident. In such a situation, "the agent does what he or she 'has to do' without posing it explicitly as a goal, below the level of calculation and even consciousness, beneath **discourse** and representation" (128). Symbolic violence is the act whereby what are in fact arbitrary, **ideological** values are imposed on dominated groups, thus constituting their symbolic reality within a given field. As Bourdieu puts it, "Symbolic violence is the violence which extorts submission, which is not perceived as such, based on 'collective expectations' or socially inculcated beliefs" (1998: 103). Of course, in contemporary society, the state has the most power to effect this sort of symbolic violence: "the genesis of the state is inseparable from the process of unification of the different social, economic, cultural (or educational), and political fields which goes hand in hand with the progressive constitution of the state monopoly of legitimate physical and *symbolic* violence" (33).

See also: **cultural capital, social capital and symbolic capital**.

Further reading: Bourdieu 1984, 1991, 1992, 1993, 1996, 1998; Bourdieu and Wacquant 1992.

FIXATION

According to psychoanalysis, "fixation" refers to one's **desire** being tied to an **object** of desire connected to an earlier phase in one's **psycho-sexual development**, for example, a fixation on oral pleasure, which Sigmund Freud would see as "stuck" at the **oral phase** even though other aspects of one's development may have proceeded normally. As Freud explains, "I regard it as possible in the case of every particular sexual trend that some portions of it have stayed behind at earlier stages of its development, even though other portions may have reached their final goal" (1953–74: 16.340). This term is closely related to **regression**.

FORMALISM

See **structuralism**

FRANKFURT SCHOOL

See **Introduction**; also, **history** and **ideology**

GAZE

The Gaze in Jacques Lacan refers to the **uncanny** sense that the object of our eye's look or glance is somehow looking back at us, a feeling that affects us in the same way as **castration** anxiety (reminding us of the **lack** at the heart of the **symbolic order**). Lacan in fact complicated his position on the Gaze as he developed his theories. At first, gazing was important in his theories in relation to the **mirror stage**, where the **subject** appears to achieve a sense of mastery by seeing itself as **ideal ego**. By viewing itself in the mirror, the **subject** at the **mirror stage** begins its entrance into culture and language by establishing its own subjectivity through the fantasy image inside the mirror, an image that the **subject** can aspire towards throughout its life (a stable coherent version of the self that does not correspond to the chaotic **drives** of our actual material bodies). Once the subject enters the

symbolic order, that **narcissistic** ideal image is maintained in the **imaginary order**. That fantasy image of oneself can be filled in by others who we may want to emulate in our adult lives (role models, love objects, etc.), anyone that we set up as a mirror for ourselves in what is, ultimately, a **narcissistic** relationship.

In his later essays, Lacan complicates this understanding of the **narcissistic** view in the mirror by distinguishing between the eye's look and the Gaze. We may believe that we are in control of our eye's look; however, any feeling of **scopophilic** power is always undone by the fact that the materiality of existence (the **Real**) always exceeds and undercuts the meaning structures of the **symbolic order**. Lacan's favorite example for the Gaze is Hans Holbein's *The Ambassadors*. When you look at the painting, it at first gives you a sense that you are in control of your look; however, you then notice a blot at the bottom of the canvas, which you can only make out if you look at the painting from the side at an angle, from which point you begin to see that the blot is, in fact, a skull staring *back* at you. By having the object of our eye's look *look back at us*, we are reminded of our own **lack**, of the fact that the **symbolic order** is separated only by a fragile border from the materiality of the **Real**. The symbols of power and desire in Holbein's painting (wealth, art, science, ambition) are thus completely undercut. As Lacan puts it, the magical floating object "reflects our own nothingness, in the figure of the death's head" (Lacan 1981: 92).

Lacan then argues in "Of the Gaze as *Objet Petit a*" (1981) that there is an intimate relationship between the *objet petit a* (which coordinates our desire) and the Gaze (which threatens to undo all desire through the eruption of the **Real**). According to Lacan, at the heart of **desire** is a misrecognition of fullness where there is really nothing but a screen for our own **narcissistic** projections. It is that **lack** at the heart of **desire** that ensures we continue to desire; however, because the *objet petit a* (the **object** of our desire) is ultimately nothing but a screen for our own **narcissistic** projections, to come too close to it threatens to give us the experience precisely of the Lacanian Gaze, the realization that behind our **desire** is nothing but our **lack**: the materiality of the **Real** staring back at us. That **lack** at the heart of **desire** at once allows **desire** to persist and threatens continually to run us aground upon the underlying rock of the **Real**.

This concept has been particularly influential on a group of feminist film theorists who explore, on the one hand, how female objects of desire in traditional Hollywood film are reduced to passive screens for the projection of male **scopophilic** fantasies, and, on the other hand, how the male desire for the mastery of the look is, in fact, continually undercut by a certain **castration** at the heart of cinema: the blank space between the frames that, only in its *elision*, can create the *illusion* of cinematic "reality" (see **suture**). That blank space between the frames is analogous to the ever-threatening **Real** over which we project our **narcissistic** fantasy of "reality."

Further reading: Lacan 1977, 1981; Mulvey 1989; Salecl and Žižek 1996; K. Silverman 1983; Žižek 1989, 1991b.

GENDER AND SEX

It is widely held that while one's sex is determined by anatomy, the concept of "gender"—the traits that constitute masculinity and femininity—is largely, if not entirely, a cultural construct, effected by the omnipresent **patriarchal** biases of our civilization. The masculine in this fashion has been identified as active, dominating, adventurous, rational, creative; the feminine, by systematic opposition to such traits, as passive, acquiescent, timid, emotional, and conventional. Recent theorists of gender and sex have greatly complicated this **binary opposition**, however. It is impossible to characterize quickly the basic concepts employed by theorists of gender and sex, given the incredible diversity of this area of study. The effort to do so is complicated not only by the complexity of the concepts but also by the fact that such theorists employ the strategies of a wide range of critical schools in their analysis of gender and sex. As a result, sex and gender theorists can be divided into various sub-schools that bring together the insights of disparate approaches (e.g., materialist **feminists**, Foucauldian theorists of gender, **postmodern** and **post-structuralist** theorists of gender, **psychoanalytical feminists**, and **LGBTQ**—Lesbian, Gay, Bisexual, Transgender, and Queer or Questioning—theorists).

To make sense of the difference between gender and sex and the difficulty of easily distinguishing the two, many theorists of gender and sex consider the history of human **sexuality**, because, they argue, what many now take to be a product of **nature** in fact has a cultural history. As Thomas Laqueur for example explores in *Making Sex* (1990), sexuality from the ancients through the Renaissance was structured quite differently than it was in the nineteenth century or is today. Specifically, he illustrates how science prior to the mid-eighteenth century tended to perceive men and women as versions of one sex, so to speak; women were seen, that is, as lesser men, with the clitoris and the uterus but reduced or inverted versions of the penis and scrotum.

Such a one-sex model, as Laqueur terms it, meant that the differences between men and women were not clear (or even so important) in these early medical texts; both men and women were seen as parts (if unequal parts) of a larger cosmological order. Given such a historical record, Laqueur concludes that sexuality itself (rather than just gender) is something that is historically determined. As he puts it,

> I have no interest in denying the reality of sex or of sexual dimorphism as an evolutionary process. But I want to show on the basis of historical evidence that almost everything one wants to *say* about sex—however sex is understood—already has in it a claim about gender. Sex, in both the one-sex and the two-sex worlds, is situational; it is explicable only within the context of battles over gender and power. (11)

Laqueur thus places himself in the camp of a group of critics following in the wake of Michel Foucault and **poststructuralism** who contest even the traditional **feminist** distinction between **nature** (one's bodily sex) and nurture (one's acquired gender).

According to Foucault, it may well be that many of the sexual issues of Christian culture can be found in various pagan texts, including a fear of masturbation and of excessive sexual activity, a demand for self-restraint, a valuation of heterosexual monogamy, and a negative representation of homosexuality; however, what is lacking in earlier cultures is the pervasive, rigid, and enforced "codification" of sexual behavior that is common from approximately the eighteenth century on, a codification and enforcement that is made possible because of various new strategies of social control. These include: science and its principles of rational organization, the contemporary penal system, the medicalization of the **subject**'s private and public acts, and the interiorization of disciplinary rules. According to Foucault, "moral conceptions in Greek and Greco-Roman antiquity," by contrast, "were much more oriented toward practices of the self and the question of askesis than toward codifications of conducts and the strict definition of what is permitted and what is forbidden" (1990: 2.30). For this reason, according to Foucault, our very idea of sexuality does not exist in ancient Greece, at least not as a single, monolithic entity applicable to all (see **bio-politics and bio-power**).

By most scholarly accounts, the eighteenth century was a transitional period in understandings of gender and **sexuality**. It was during this period that the groundwork was laid for the "**naturalization**" of gender categories, which became especially important in the nineteenth century and which provided for the belief that gendered behavior was a matter of biology. Eighteenth-century medical science paved the way for a strictly binary system of gender by "discovering" the incommensurable differences between male and female bodies. As Laqueur puts it, "Sometime in the eighteenth century, sex as we know it was invented" (1990: 149). He continues:

> All the complex ways in which resemblances among bodies, and between bodies and the cosmos, [formerly] confirmed a hierarchical world order were reduced to a single plane: **nature**. In the world of reductionist explanation, what mattered was the flat, horizontal, immovable foundation of physical fact: sex. (151)

Under this new system of sexual dimorphism, women and men were taken to be one another's opposites in most things. Many of the truisms about gender behavior that contemporary theorists of gender and sex work to dismantle (e.g., "boys will be boys") date from this period.

After this point, it became important to regulate sexuality because it was now seen as "natural" or biologically determined, and a sign of the general health of the human species. So, for the first time, we see ever-increasing caveats in the period about masturbation, which, according to Samuel-Auguste-David Tissot (1728–97), one of the most influential doctors of the period, could lead to everything from gonorrhea to blindness to painful and shameful death. The new fears about masturbation (which hardly existed before the eighteenth century) set the stage for the nineteenth-century fascination with the disciplining of the private body and its desires. Much of the rhetoric directed at the Onanist (the common term in the period for a masturbator) would, indeed, later be redirected to the homosexual after the medicalization of homosexuality at the end of the nineteenth century.

The nineteenth century was dominated by the idea of **"natural"** gender distinctions and by a conception of normative sexuality that was centered largely on the middle-class family. There were, of course, many expressions and forms of *non*-normative (i.e., non-procreative, non-heterosexual) sexuality, but these fell under increasing scrutiny and discipline from a variety of institutions, including medicine and the law. The middle-class culture that came about in Britain and America as a result of urbanization, industrialization, and strong economic growth imagined itself as existing in two complementary but separate spheres: the public and the private. These spheres were roughly commensurate with the binary gender distinctions discussed above. The public sphere belonged to men: it was the sphere of business and money-making, of politics and empire building, of industry and struggle. The private sphere, on the other hand, was considered to be a feminine preserve: it was the space of the home and the hearth, of sympathy and nurture, of simple piety and childrearing.

The assumption of binary gender did not happen overnight, however, or occur without contestation. Some critics argue that eighteenth-century culture's emphasis on public display and ceremony meant that people accepted gender categories as **performative** rather than inherent or "**natural**," thus opening up spaces for the questioning of these categories. As Terry Castle has shown in *Masquerade and Civilization* (1986), for example, the enormously popular masquerades of the eighteenth century (huge costume parties in which revelers often dressed in transvestite disguise) demonstrated the fluidity and artificiality of gender categories. Of particular importance in this period is also the rise of Enlightenment values of equality, fraternity, and liberty, which many female thinkers argued needed to be applied to all humanity, including women, making the eighteenth century an important moment in the rise of **feminism** as well. It is no coincidence that the person many regard as the first feminist, Mary Wollstonecraft (1759–97), wrote her book, *A Vindication of the Rights of Woman* (1792), during this period.

The idea of **performativity** has been particularly influential on theorists of gender and sex, thanks especially to the influential work of Judith Butler. Butler throughout her work questions the belief that certain gendered behaviors are **natural**, illustrating the ways that one's learned performance of gendered behavior (what we commonly associate with femininity and masculinity) is an act of sorts, a performance, one that is imposed upon us by normative heterosexuality. Butler thus offers what she herself calls "a more radical use of the doctrine of constitution that takes the social **agent** as an *object* rather than the **subject** of constitutive acts" (1990b: 270). In other words, Butler questions the extent to which we can assume we can constitute ourselves; she wonders to what extent our acts are determined for us, rather, by our place within language and convention. She follows **postmodernist** and **poststructuralist** practice in using the term "**subject**" (rather than "individual" or "person") in order to underline the linguistic nature of our position within what Jacques Lacan terms the **symbolic order**, the system of signs and conventions that determines our perception of what we see as reality. Unlike theatrical acting, Butler argues that we cannot even assume a stable **subjectivity** that goes about performing various gender roles; rather, it is the very act of performing gender that constitutes who we are. Identity itself, for

Butler, is an illusion retroactively created by our performances: "In opposition to theatrical or **phenomenological** models which take the gendered self to be prior to its acts, I will understand constituting acts not only as constituting the identity of the actor, but as constituting that identity as a compelling illusion, an object of *belief*" (271). That belief (in stable identities and gender differences) is, in fact, compelled "by social sanction and taboo" (271), so that our belief in "**natural**" behavior is really the result of both subtle and blatant coercions. One effect of such coercions is also the creation of that which cannot be articulated, "a domain of unthinkable, **abject**, unlivable bodies" (1993: xi) that, through **abjection** by the "normal" **subject**, helps that **subject** to constitute itself. By underlining the artificial, proscribed, and **performative** nature of gender identity, Butler seeks to trouble the definition of gender, challenging the status quo in order to fight for the rights of those marginalized identities (especially gay and lesbian identity) that in our current culture tend to inhabit the domain of **abject** bodies.

Indeed, Butler argues that gender, as an objective natural thing, does not exist: "Gender reality is **performative** which means, quite simply, that it is real only to the extent that it is performed" (1990b: 278). Gender, according to Butler, is by no means tied to material bodily facts but is solely and completely a social construction, a fiction, one that, therefore, is open to change and contestation: "Because there is neither an 'essence' that gender expresses or externalizes nor an objective ideal to which gender aspires; because gender is not a fact, the various acts of gender creates [sic] the idea of gender, and without those acts, there would be no gender at all. Gender is, thus, a construction that regularly conceals its genesis" (273). That genesis is not corporeal but **performative**, so that the body becomes its gender only "through a series of acts which are renewed, revised, and consolidated through time" (274). By illustrating the artificial, conventional, and historical nature of gender construction, Butler attempts to critique the assumptions of normative heterosexuality: those punitive rules (social, familial, and legal) that force us to conform to **hegemonic**, hetero-sexual standards for identity, what Adrienne Rich terms **compulsory heterosexuality**.

Butler takes her formulations even further by questioning the very distinction between gender and sex. Before Butler, **feminists** reg-ularly made a distinction between bodily sex (the *corporeal* facts of our existence) and gender (the *social* conventions that determine the dif-ferences between masculinity and femininity). Such feminists accepted the fact that certain anatomical differences do exist between men and women but they pointed out how most of the conventions that determine the behaviors of men and women are, in fact, *social* gender constructions that have little or nothing to do with our corporeal sexes. According to traditional **feminists**, sex is a biological category; gender is a historical category. Butler questions that distinction by arguing that our "gender acts" affect us in such material, corporeal ways that even our perception of corporeal sexual differences are affected by social conventions. For Butler, sex is not "a bodily given on which the construct of gender is artificially imposed, but … a *cultural* norm which governs the materialization of bodies" (1993: 2–3; my italics). Sex, for Butler, "is an ideal construct which is forcibly materialized through time. It is not a simple fact or static condition of a body, but a process whereby regulatory norms materialize 'sex' and achieve this materialization through a forcible reiteration of those norms" (2). Butler here is influenced by the **postmodern** tendency to see our very conception of reality as determined by language, so that it is ultimately impossible even to think or articulate sex without imposing linguistic norms: "there is no reference to a pure body which is not at the same time a further formation of that body" (10). The very act of saying something about sex ends up imposing cultural or ideological norms, according to Butler. As she puts it, "'sex' becomes something like a fiction, perhaps a fantasy, retroactively installed at a prelinguistic site to which there is no direct access" (5). Nonetheless, that fiction is central to the establishment of **subjectivity** and human society, which is to say that, even so, it has material effects: "the 'I' neither precedes nor follows the process of this gendering, but emerges only within and as the matrix of gender relations themselves" (7). That linguistic construction is also not stable, working as it does by always re-establishing boundaries (and a zone of abjection) through the endlessly repeated performative acts that mark us as one sex or another. "Sex" is thus unveiled not only as an artificial norm but also a norm that is subject to change. Butler's project, then, is "to 'cite' the law in order to reiterate and coopt its power, to expose the heterosexual matrix and to displace the effect of its necessity" (15).

LGBTQ Studies has extended the analysis of sexuality to all sexual identities represented by that acronym: Lesbian, Gay, Bisexual, Transgender, and Queer or Questioning. Indeed, some theorists have questioned earlier **feminism**'s almost exclusive concentration on gender, specifically the male/female **binary opposition**, since that opposition still falls within the logic of **compulsory heterosexuality** and thus ignores or even actively **marginalizes** other sexual identities.

Further reading: Bem 1993; Butler 1990a, 1990b, 1993, 1997; Castle 1986; Foucault 1990; Jagger 2008; Laqueur 1990, 2003; Rich 1980; Sedgwick 2003.

GENITAL PHASE

Sigmund Freud tends to see this phase of **psychosexual development** as "normal" heterosexuality. According to Freud, heterosexual intercourse should be the goal of **psychosexual development** (a position that has since been questioned by **feminists** and **queer** theorists). At this point in "normal" development, Freud writes, "the subordination of all the component sexual instincts under the primacy of the genitals" is witnessed (1953–74: 16.328). In this way, the individual enters adulthood and ensures the survival of the species. For Freud, a desire for oral or anal pleasure constitutes a **fixation** on or a **regression** to an earlier stage in one's **psychosexual development**.

Further reading: Freud 1916–17, 1932; Laplanche and Pontalis 1973.

GENOTEXT AND PHENOTEXT

These are terms posited by psychoanalyst Julia Kristeva. Phenotext denotes "language that serves to communicate, which linguistics describes in terms of 'competence' and 'performance'. ... The phenotext is a structure ... ; it obeys rules of communication and presupposes a subject of enunciation and an addressee" (1984: 87); however, according to Kristeva, this traditional notion of how language functions obscures the fact that all language is, in fact, founded on an "underlying foundation" (87) that she terms the genotext. The genotext is closely aligned with Kristeva's notion of the **chora** and thus evocative of our earliest stage of **psychosexual development** when we were most closely tied to our life and death **drives**. "Designating the genotext in a text" therefore "requires pointing out the transfers of drive energy that can be detected in phonematic devices (such as the accumulation and repetition of phonemes or rhyme) and melodic devices (such as intonation or rhythm)" (86). In other words, the genotext refers to the physical, rhythmic nature of language outside of signification. Unlike the phenotext, the genotext "is a process; it moves through zones that have relative and transitory borders and constitutes a *path* that is not restricted to the two poles of univocal information between two full-fledged subjects" (87). Kristeva argues that art and especially poetry can return language to the genotext because of art's willingness to break lexical, syntactic, and semantic rules and to play with the sonic and rhythmic aspects of language.

GENRE OF DISCOURSE

See **phrase regimen, phrase universe, and genre of discourse**

GLBT: GAY, LESBIAN, BISEXUAL, AND TRANSGENDER

See **LGBTQ Studies**

GLOBALIZATION AND GLOBAL STUDIES

"Globalization"—unlike the term "international," which developed alongside the rise of the **nation-state** and imperialism at the end of the eighteenth century and through the nineteenth—refers specifically to the increasingly global nature of various aspects of our current **postmodern** period, including multinational capitalism (see **late capitalism**), the global communication network (the Internet, social media, mobile computing—see **Digital Humanities**), new global forms of military domination and resistance (drone strikes, cross-national coalitions and trade embargoes, terrorism) and the increasing realization that the major problems facing humanity in the future are cross-national (global warming, species extinction, pollution, radio-active fall-out, pandemics, water, food—see **ecocriticism**). Global Studies refers to a growing critical approach that examines various aspects of this new global system.

Although closely aligned with **Postcolonial Studies**, Global Studies has been seen by some critics (During 1998, 2000; Gikandi 2001; Krishnaswamy and Hawley 2008; Loomba *et al.* 2005; Nkrumah 1965; Wilson *et al.* 2010) as posing a challenge or offering a new direction to **Postcolonial Studies**, which in the 1980s and 1990s was particularly concerned with the **binary opposition** Occident/**Orientalism** and with the imperialism of the heyday of the **nation-state** (the nineteenth century through to the Second World War). Global Studies, by contrast, is influenced by the influential thesis that what we are seeing today—as, for example, Michael Hardt and Antonio Negri argue in *Empire* (2000)—is "the decline of **nation-states** as boundaries that mark and organize the divisions in global rule." As they go on, "The establishment of a global society of control that smooths over the striae of national boundaries goes hand in hand with the realization of the world market and the real subsumption of global society under **capital**" (332). See **empire**. Global Studies tends also to be more interdisciplinary, encompassing as it does the disciplines of sociology, geography, economics, political science, communications, English, history, earth sciences, computer science, technology, food science, hydrology, climate study, military science, and medicine, among others.

One can identify three strands of thinking in Global Studies: (1) celebrationists (see **cosmopolitanism**) who see in the new global order possibilities for the improvement of the human condition (from a greater appreciation of the global impact of local acts to improved material living conditions for the poor, Non-Governmental Organizations or NGOs and more effective populist movements advocating for positive change); (2) alarmists who see in the new global forms of dissemination and control the increasing dominance of the "First World" over the "Third World," an increasing homogenization of culture that privileges the values of **hegemonic** classes, countries, and ethnicities against **subaltern** groups and an exponentially accelerated destruction of the natural world; and (3) "critical globalism," which examines the processes of globalization in a measured way, recognizing both its dangers and opportunities. Critical globalist theorists recognize that globalization "has often perpetuated poverty, widened material inequalities, increased ecological degradation, sustained militarism, fragmented communities, marginalized subordinated groups, fed intolerance and deepened crises of democracy," but also acknowledge the positive effects, for example "trebling world per capita income since 1945, halving the proportion of the world living in abject poverty, increasing ecological consciousness, and possibly facilitating disarmament, while various subordinated groups have grasped opportunities for global organisation" (Scholte 1996: 53).

See also: **cognitive map, comprador, contact zone and transculturation, subaltern**.

Further reading: Berger and Huntington 2002; Bordo *et al.* 2003; During 1998, 2000; Gagnier 2010; Gikandi 2001; Hardt and Negri 2000; Hoogvelt 1997; Jameson 1991; Juergensmeyer 2014; Kofman and Youngs 2008; Krishnaswamy and Hawley 2008; Loomba *et al.* 2005; Mittelman 1996; Negri 2008a, 2008b; Nkrumah 1965; Scholte 1996; A. Scott 1997; Waters 1995; Wilson *et al.* 2010.

GOVERNMENT, GOVERNMENTALITY, AND GOVERNMENTAL RATIONALITY

When critical theorists refer to "government," they sometimes mean the sense of the term theorized by Michel Foucault in his later writings; Foucault also uses the terms "governmentality" and "governmental rationality" to designate what he saw as a new domain of research. Foucault turns to the concept of **"government"** in his later work in order to clarify how **power** functions:

> Basically **power** is less a confrontation between two adversaries or the linking of one to the other than a question of government. This word must be allowed the very broad meaning which it had in the sixteenth century. "Government" did not refer only to political structures or to the management of states; rather it designated the way in which the conduct of individuals or of groups might be directed: the government of children, of souls, of communities, of families, of the sick. It did not only cover the legitimately constituted forms of political or economic subjection, but also modes of action, more or less considered and calculated, which were destined to act upon the possibilities of action of other people. To govern, in this sense, is to structure the possible field of action of others. The relationship proper to **power** would not therefore be sought on the side of violence or of struggle, nor on that of voluntary linking (all of which can, at best, only be the instruments of **power**), but rather in the area of the singular mode of action, neither warlike nor juridical, which is government. (1982: 221)

Foucault thus turns from what can seem like a reified and monumental sense of **power** in his earlier work, *Discipline and Punish* (1977a), to an understanding of **power** that is always tied to the actions of individual people as delimited by the various **discourses** and **disciplines** of a given time period. As Foucault puts it in "Questions of Method," "To put the matter clearly: my problem is to see how men govern (themselves and others) by the production of truth (I repeat once again that by production of truth I mean not the production of true utterances, but the establishment of domains in which the practice of the true and false can be made at once ordered and pertinent)" (Foucault 1991b: 79).

The very notion of government also has a history, Foucault makes clear: "Government as a general problem seems to me to explode in the sixteenth century, posed by discussions of quite diverse questions," including "the government of oneself," the "government of souls and lives" as in "Catholic and Protestant pastoral doctrine," the "government of children," especially questions of pedagogy, and "the government of the state by the prince" (Foucault 1991c: 87). What begins to occur in the sixteenth century is the increasing alignment of three different kinds of government: "the art of self-government, connected with morality; the art of properly governing a family, which belongs to economy; and finally the science of ruling the state, which concerns politics" (91). What happens by the nineteenth century, aided especially by the population explosion and society's increasing reliance on statistics to make sense of that population, is the notion that family is "an element internal to population" and that it is "a fundamental instrument in its government" (99). Following the establishment of this historical trajectory, Foucault argues that by "governmentality" he means three specific things:

(1) The ensemble formed by the institutions, procedures, analyses and reflections, the calculations and tactics that allow the exercise of this very specific albeit complex form of **power**, which has as its target population, as its principal form of knowledge political economy, and as its essential technical means **apparatuses** of security.
(2) The tendency which, over a long period and throughout the West, has steadily led towards the pre-eminence over all other forms (sovereignty, discipline, etc.) of this type of power which may be termed government, resulting, on the one hand, in the formation of the whole series of specific governmental **apparatuses**, and, on the other, in the development of a whole complex of *savoirs* [forms of knowledge].
(3) The process, or rather the result of the process, through which the state of justice of the Middle Ages, transformed into the administrative state during the fifteenth and sixteenth centuries, gradually becomes "governmentalized" (Foucault 1991c: 102–3).

Although this work was left uncompleted at Foucault's death in 1984, it has been picked up and developed by a number of critics, including Peter Miller, Nikolas Rose, and Mitchell Dean. Foucault's examination of the relationship between government and earlier religious thinking is also explored by Giorgio Agamben in *The Kingdom and the Glory: For a Theological Genealogy of Economy and Government* (2011).

Further reading: Agamben 2011; T. J. Armstrong 1992; Burchell, Gordon and Miller 1991; Dean 1999; Foucault 1982, 1991c; Miller and Rose 2008; Rose 1999.

GRAND NARRATIVE

Critical theory tends to be suspicious of all "grand" narratives that seek to explain history in terms of a single overarching rubric, e.g., progress or the liberation of man. Indeed, Jean-François Lyotard argues that what characterizes the **postmodern** is precisely the rejection of all grand narratives in favor of what he terms *petits récits* or "little stories": "The grand narrative has lost its credibility, regardless of what mode of unification it uses, regardless of whether it is a speculative narrative or a narrative of emancipation" (1991: 37). Inspired to some extent by the **Marxist** desire to read history from the "bottom up," from the perspective of the underclass or oppressed minorities, critical theory tends to adopt alternative models for **history** instead, for example, uneven development; **antagonism**; disjuncture and rupture; **dominant, emergent, and residual**; or the Lacanian **Real**.

See also: **history**.

GREIMASSIAN SQUARE (SEMIOTIC SQUARE)

Algirdas Julien Greimas seeks in his writing to find the "deep structure" of all narrativity. He wishes to find behind any "manifestation of narrativity" a *"fundamental semantics and grammar"* (1976b: 65). Greimas is also interested in extending the relevance of **narratology** to all experience: "Our own concern ... has been to extend as much as possible the area of application of the analysis of narrative" (1976b: 63). Greimas therefore can be found applying his **narratological** models to phenomena that we might think fall outside of structural rules, for example passion (as he does in "On Anger: A Lexical Semantic Study" [1976a] or in *The Semiotics of Passions* [1993]). Greimas can do so because of a foundational precept of post-Saussurian **semiotics**: all language is arbitrary. There is no connection (other than convention) that links linguistic signs like writing or speaking to their referents. The sounds or written lines that make up the word "cat" have only an arbitrary, conventional connection to the actual cat that exists in the world (see **signifier and signified**). "Because of this," Greimas writes, "linguists became aware of the possibilities of a generalized **semiotic** theory that could account for all the forms and manifestations of signification" (1976b: 17). Anything that we as humans articulate in language (which is to say, pretty much everything) should therefore conform to structural rules: in this principle, we find the heart of Greimas's discipline, **semiotics** or the study of signification (which is to say, the study of the use of signs to refer to things). To put this another way, the connection between signification and the real world is completely arbitrary; however, signification is in itself not arbitrary because language tends to follow structural rules. Humans are therefore caught in a system of rules and deep structures that bear no relation to the real world. This disjunction between language and reality is, in fact, a central precept of contemporary theory, from Jacques Lacan's understanding of the **real** to Judith Butler's understanding of **performativity** to Jean Baudrillard's theorization of the **simulacrum**. Greimas's goal, by contrast, is purely **structuralist**: he wishes to find the deep structures by which all signification orders the world of perception.

Greimas's most influential model for making sense of the structural logic behind almost all things is the semiotic or Greimassian square. The semiotic square has proven to be an influential concept not only in **narrative** theory but also in the ideological criticism of Fredric Jameson, who uses the square as "a virtual map of conceptual closure, or better still, of the closure of **ideology** itself" (1976: xv). Greimas's schema is useful because it illustrates the full complexity of any given semantic term (seme). Greimas points out that any given seme entails its opposite or "contrary." "Life" for example is understood in relation to its contrary, "death." Rather than rest at this simple **binary opposition**, however, Greimas points out that the opposition, "life" and "death," suggests what Greimas terms a contradictory pair, that is, "not-life" and "not-death." We would therefore be left with the following semiotic square (Figure 1).

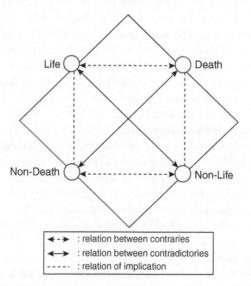

Figure 1 Sample Greimassian Square 1

As Jameson explains in the Foreword to Greimas's *On Meaning*, the "contradictory pair"—which in this example are taken up by "not-death" and "not-life"—"are the simple negatives of the two dominant terms, but include far more than either: thus 'nonwhite' includes more than 'black,' 'nonmale' more than 'female'" (1976b: xiv); in our example, not-life would include more than merely death and not-death more than life. Indeed, in a given narrative, alternative terms will often suggest themselves for the contradictory pair.

Almost any utterance therefore includes a hidden complexity of meaning. Indeed, we can infer in even a simple phrase like "the road is clear" an implied dominant binary, activity and quiescence. Were we reading a narrative where we find a post-apocalyptic world in which the last surviving humans are presented walking through a series of deserted streets in which they must fight the machines that have taken over, the contradictory seme not-activity might be taken up by machine parts or the abandoned city itself. Not-quiescence could conversely be taken up by human consciousness. Our semiotic square would therefore look something like Figure 2.

Such a semiotic square might in turn be tied to other dominant binary oppositions in the narrative, including quite possibly "life and death." As Greimas explains, "nothing permits us to assert that a **semiotic** manifestation is dependent on only one system at a time. And so far as it is dependent on several, its closure can be attributed to the interaction of the different systems that produce it" (1976b: 60). In other words, one can construct a series of, say, three semiotic squares that explore various levels of a story's manifested **diegesis**, each semiotic square related to the next.

Narratives will also tend to find figures that resolve the implied oppositions of a given semiotic square. The union of the dominant

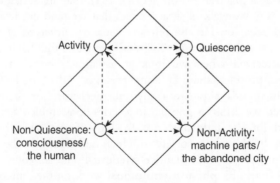

Figure 2 Sample Greimassian Square 2

binary (S), here "activity" and "quiescence," will often be reserved for the utopic solution for the problems of the work's **diegesis**, perhaps represented in the hero of the tale; in our hypothetical sci-fi narrative, perhaps the hero is able at the end of the story to reconstruct the pre-apocalyptic bourgeois lifestyle that saw the balance of work and leisure (or activity and quiescence) as the principle of human freedom. The resolution of the opposition, activity and the human, might be taken up in the story by, for example, a slave force; the resolution of the opposition, quiescence and machine parts, might be represented by the use of humans as batteries for the machine (as in the film *The Matrix*). Finally, the resolution of the combination not-quiescence and not-activity might be taken up by the central A.I. that runs the post-apocalyptic world (as in *Neuromancer*'s Wintermute), a figure that would also inhabit the contradictory space of both not-life and not-death. As Jameson continues, "The entire mechanism then is capable of generating at least ten conceivable positions out of a rudimentary **binary opposition** (which may originally have been no more than a single term, e.g., 'white,' which proves to be internally defined by a hidden opposition we articulate by promoting the concealed pole 'black' to visibility)" (1976: xiv–xv). In our hypothetical sci-fi narrative, the ten terms would be: activity, quiescence, non-activity, the aban-doned machine, non-quiescence, human consciousness, A.I., human slaves, human batteries, and the utopic hero.

HABITUS

This term has been popularized for critical theory by Pierre Bourdieu, who takes the concept from Marcel Mauss. Mauss uses the term to characterize those aspects of our daily lives, what he terms "collective and individual practical reason" (1979: 101), that are so natural to us (e.g., the way we walk or sit at a table) that we tend not to see them as learned behavior. He also refers to these as "*techniques of the body*" (104). Mauss points out that the "social nature of the 'habitus'" (101) is best perceived when we look at variations "between societies, educations, proprieties and fashions, prestiges" (101). As he explains, "The constant adaptation to a physical, mechanical or chemical aim (e.g., when we drink) is pursued in a series of assembled actions, and assembled for the individual not by himself alone but by all his education, by the whole society to which he belongs, in the place he occupies in it" (104–5). Maurice Merleau-Ponty explores a similar sense of habit in his **phenomenological** work on the "intentionality of the body." As he writes, "Bodily experience forces us to acknowledge an imposition of meaning which is not the work of a universal constituting consciousness" (2004: 124) and yet is meaningful in our bodily movements themselves.

Bourdieu builds on this earlier work to define habitus as all those actions that appear completely "natural" to an individual though they are the result, in fact, of entrenched social expectations. So, "practical evaluation of the likelihood of the success of a given action in a given situation brings into play a whole body of wisdom, sayings, commonplaces, ethical precepts ('that's not for the likes of us') and, at a deeper level, the unconscious principles of the *ethos* which, being the product of a learning process dominated by a determinate type of objective regularities, determines 'reasonable' and 'unreasonable' conduct for every agent subjected to those regularities" (1977: 77). These actions are not completely conscious; rather, "The schemes of thought and expression [each agent] has acquired are the basis for the *intentionless invention* of regulated improvisation" (79). As Bourdieu explains, "It is because subjects do not, strictly speaking, know what they are doing that what they do has more meaning than they know" (79). It is this sort of unconscious action that nonetheless instantiates **ideology** with each **performative** repetition that defines the habits: "The habitus is the universalizing mediation which causes an individual agent's practices, without either explicit reason or signifying intent, to be none the less 'sensible' and 'reasonable'" (79). Habitus is "transmitted in practice, in its practical state, without attaining the level of **discourse**" (87). It is, as Bourdieu puts it, "the social made body" (Bourdieu and Wacquant 1992: 127). For the relation of the habitus to social relations in general, see **field**.

See also: **ideology**, **doxa**.

Further reading: Bourdieu 1977, 1984, 1998; Bourdieu and Wacquant 1992; Mauss 1979; Merleau-Ponty 2004; Wacquant 2011.

HEGEMONY (HEGEMONIC)

Hegemony refers to the processes by which dominant culture maintains its dominant position: for example, the use of institutions to formalize power; the employment of a bureaucracy to make power seem abstract (and, therefore, not attached to any one individual); the inculcation of the populace in the ideals of the hegemonic group through education, advertising, publication, etc.; the mobilization of a police force as well as military personnel to subdue opposition. Antonio Gramsci extended the concept beyond the traditional concept of hegemony as "political rule or domination, especially in relations between states" (Williams 1977: 108) and redefined hegemony as "a complex interlocking of political, social, and cultural forces" (108), including alternative centers of power, which he sometimes terms "counter-hegemonies." This effort to find a more complex model for understanding political resistance is in large part a result of the fact that Karl Marx's promise of revolution and of the international unification of the **proletariat** did not occur as predicted (see **Marxism**). Gramsci therefore felt the need for a more complex understanding of how best to effect revolution. He underscores, in particular, "the importance of the 'cultural aspect'" in any "practical (collective) activity." As he goes on, "An historical act can only be performed by 'collective man,' and this presupposes the attainment of a 'cultural-social' unity through which a multiplicity of dispersed wills, with heterogeneous aims, are welded together with a single aim, on the basis of an equal and common conception of the world, both general and particular" (Gramsci 2000: 348). This attained unity goes to the heart of Gramsci's notion of "hegemony."

For Gramsci, this sort of hegemony applies just as much to the ruling group as it does to those groups seeking to form "counter-hegemonies." Regarding the ruling group, "hegemony" in this formulation points to the complex ways that a dominant group makes its **ideological** beliefs appear **natural** and necessary, thus convincing individuals to accept their own subjection. Raymond Williams, an important theorist of **Cultural Materialism** who was greatly influenced by Gramsci, explains:

> Hegemony is then not only the articulate upper level of "**ideology**," nor are its forms of control only those ordinarily seen as "manipulation" or "indoctrination." It is a whole body of practices and expectations, over the whole of living: our senses and assignments of energy, our shaping perceptions of ourselves and our world. It is a lived system of meanings and values—constitutive and constituting—which as they are experienced as practices appear as reciprocally confirming. It thus constitutes a sense of reality for most people in the society, a sense of absolute because experienced reality beyond which it is very difficult for most members of the society to move, in most areas of their lives. It is, that is to say, in the strongest sense a "**culture**," but a culture which has also to be seen as the lived dominance and subordination of particular classes. (1977: 110)

This understanding of hegemony influences a number of related concepts, for example Louis Althusser's understanding of **Ideological State**

Apparatuses as distinct from the State Apparatuses of the courts, the police, and the military; or Pierre Bourdieu's concept of the **habitus**.

The goal for critical theory, given its neo-Marxist roots in Max Horkheimer's desire to make the world better, to fight for the oppressed (see **praxis** and **Introduction**), is to find ways of combating this insidious, and to a large extent internalized, form of hegemony. Gramsci's understanding of hegemony is influential on this score as well, for Gramsci was ultimately interested in thinking through how a counter-hegemony might be formed that could contest the **dominant** group's hegemony and eventually establish what he termed a new "historical bloc." According to Gramsci, the only way to counter the pervasive nature of the dominant **class**'s cultural hegemony was not simply to attack it directly through military means (what Gramsci terms a "war of maneuver"). Premature military action would only lead to failure and a counter-revolution. Rather the ground for military action must first be prepared through the gradual consolidation of one's cultural influence (a "war of position"). This process requires an effective intellectual class who can convince ever larger swathes of a population to join a new collective will that can then bring into being a new hegemony. The process is one of continual **ideological** struggle, in other words. As Williams writes, hegemony "does not just passively exist as a form of dominance. It has continually to be renewed, recreated, defended, and modified. It is also continually resisted, limited, altered, challenged by pressures not at all its own" (1977: 112).

Ernesto Laclau and Chantal Mouffe build on Gramsci's theories in their influential work, *Hegemony and Socialist Strategy*; however, they reject Gramsci's emphasis on "fundamental **classes**" and Gramsci's "postulate that ... every social formation structures itself around a single hegemonic centre" (1985: 138). Instead of a model where one imagines one **class**-based emergent hegemony fighting a **class**-based dominant hegemony, they argue for "a plurality of political spaces" (137): "In a given social formation, there can be a variety of hegemonic nodal points" (139), which, they make clear, is not the same as proposing "either pluralism or the total diffusion of power within the social" (142). Laclau and Mouffe want, rather, to rethink how effective political change happens, thus moving beyond the "classic conception of socialism," which "supposed that the disappearance of private owner-ship of the **means of production** would set up a chain of effects which, over a whole historical epoch, would lead to the extinction of all forms of subordination. Today we know that this is not so" (178). Laclau and Mouffe adopt Gramsci's notion of "war of position" to think about how more effective change can happen:

The concept of a "war of position" implies precisely the *process* character of every radical transformation—the revolutionary act is, simply, an internal moment of this process. The multiplication of political spaces and the preventing of the concentration of power in one point are, then, preconditions of every truly democratic transformation of society. (178)

Laclau and Mouffe adopt the term **"radical democracy,"** arguing that "It is not in the abandonment of the democratic terrain but, on the contrary, in the extension of the field of democratic struggles to the whole of civil society and the state, that the possibility resides for a hegemonic strategy of the Left" (176).

See also: **doxa**.

Further reading: S. Hall 1986; Laclau and Mouffe 1985; Williams 1977.

HERMENEUTIC AND PROAIRETIC CODES

These terms come from the narratologist Roland Barthes who, in his work *S/Z* (1974), wishes to distinguish between the two forces that drive **narrative** and, thus by implication, our own desires to keep reading or viewing a story. The "hermeneutic" and "proairetic codes" are two ways of creating suspense in **narrative**, the first caused by unanswered questions, the second by the anticipation of an action's resolution. The hermeneutic code refers to those plot elements that raise questions on the part of the reader of a text or the viewer of a film. Indeed, we are not satisfied by a narrative unless all such "loose ends" are tied. A good example is the genre of the detective story. The entire narrative of such a story operates primarily by the hermeneutic code. We witness a murder and the rest of the narrative is devoted to determining the questions that are raised by the initial scene of violence. The proairetic code, on the other hand, refers to cause-and-effect actions—those plot events that simply lead to yet other actions. For example, a gunslinger draws his gun on an adversary and we wonder what the resolution of this action will be. We wait to see if he kills his opponent or is wounded himself. Suspense is thus created by action rather than by a reader's or a viewer's wish to have mysteries explained.

HERMENEUTICS

Hermeneutics is the theory of interpretation, particularly textual interpretation, although it can apply to other forms of interpretation.

As a theory, it has its roots in ancient Greece (in the work of Plato and Aristotle), then in Biblical exegesis (the interpretation of the Bible). Its significance for critical theory begins with the philosophical writings of Friedrich Schleiermacher (1768–1834) and William Dilthey (1833–1911), both of whom establish hermeneutics not as the interpretation of particular texts but as a general theory of linguistic meaning and human understanding. They seek to bridge the gap between universalist notions of linguistic understanding (e.g., grammar) and the individual, idiosyncratic, stylistic uses of language in any given instance by a particular individual. The ability to reconcile or bridge that difference constitutes the reason and justification for the humanities (as opposed to the natural sciences). In the modern period, Martin Heidegger (1889–1976) in his *Being and Time* (1927) developed hermeneutics into a general theory of knowledge and ontology, which he reconciled with **phenomenology**. According to Heidegger, understanding is quite simply a mode of being (what he terms *Dasein*), for our very existence in the world entails a pre-reflective understanding of the totality of the world, including intersubjectivity, a notion of existence that is captured by the **phenomenological** concept of **lifeworld**. For Heidegger, the "hermeneutic circle" refers to the constant relation between the totality of our **lifeworld** and our individual acts of interpretation. Hermeneutics thus becomes an issue of being in the world; in this sense, it later influenced existentialism, especially through the writing of Jean-Paul Sartre (1905–80). Hans-Georg Gadamer (1900–2002), Heidegger's student, later aimed in *Truth and Method* (1960) to reconcile Heidegger with the linguistic turn in philosophy (see **signifier and signified**). According to Gadamer, we are so reliant on language and on convention that it is impossible to approach any work of the past as it was understood by its original contemporaries. Interpretation entails, then, a constantly changing relation to the works and actions of the past since it must negotiate all past interpretations of a given work or historical fact—what Gadamer refers to as the "fusion of horizons," Gadamer's version of the "hermeneutic circle." That process of interpretation is, by definition, endless.

Hermeneutics has suffered to some extent at the hands of critical theory, which tends to question both the notion of a totality of experience in the **lifeworld** and the privileging of canonical tradition implied by Gadamer's fusion of horizons. The "hermeneutic circle" is thus replaced by what is often termed, following Paul Ricoeur in *Freud and Philosophy* (1970), a "hermeneutics of suspicion." However, hermeneutics persists in altered form in the work of such influential critics as Jürgen Habermas (who adopts the term **lifeworld** from

phenomenology while eschewing Gadamer's emphasis on tradition in favor of what he terms **communicative reason**—see **communicative action, discourse ethics,** and **public sphere**) and Paul Ricoeur (who reconciles hermeneutics with **phenomenology** in his own theory of the **subject**'s relation to the **Other**). Hermeneutics has also influenced **Reader-Response Criticism,** particularly through the work of Hans Robert Jauss.

Further reading: Gadamer 1960; Grondin 1994; Habermas 1987, 1991; Heidegger 1927; Ricoeur 1970, 1981; Thompson 1981.

HETEROGLOSSIA (HETEROGLOT)

According to Mikhail Bakhtin, "language is heteroglot from top to bottom" (1981: 291), which is to say that it is stratified into "expressive planes" (290). That stratification is generic ("oratorical, publicistic, newspaper and journalistic genres, the genres of low literature ... or, finally, the various genres of high literature" [1981: 288–89]); professional ("in the broad sense of 'professional': the language of the lawyer, the doctor, the businessman, the politician, the public education teacher and so forth" [1981: 289]); and social. All language is heteroglot in so far as "it represents the co-existence of socio-**ideological** contradictions between the present and the past, between differing epochs of the past, between different socio-**ideological** groups in the present, between tendencies, schools, circles and so forth, all given bodily form" in the linguistic conventions of different **ideological** purviews (291). Bakhtin questions traditional stylistic analysis because it tends to seek the underlying structures and rules behind language use and therefore remains largely blind to the heteroglot complexity of language as it is actually used in context. According to Bakhtin, comic forms from Menippean satire through the **carnivalesque** works of Rabelais to the nineteenth-century novel and the **polyphonic** novels of Fyodor Dostoevsky all share various degrees of "parodic stylization," whereby the dialects of other genres, professions, and social spheres are represented alongside the author's own voice: such work thus becomes "double-voiced," with the writing often slipping into the linguistic register of others. Bakhtin goes so far as to argue that "The novelist does not acknowledge any unitary, singular, naively (or conditionally) indisputable or sacrosanct language. Language is present to the novelist only as something stratified and heteroglot" (1981: 332).

See also: **dialogism.**

HETERONORMATIVITY (HETERONORMATIVE)

"Heteronormativity" refers to those punitive rules (social, familial, and legal) that force us to conform to **hegemonic**, heterosexual standards for identity. The term is a short version of "normative heterosexuality."

HETEROTOPIA

This concept is theorized in Michel Foucault's work, "Of Other Spaces" (1986). Unlike **utopias**, which do not actually exist in the world but rather "present society itself in a perfected form, or else society turned upside down" (24), heterotopias are "real places—places that do exist and that are formed in the very founding of society—which are something like counter-sites, a kind of effectively enacted **utopia** in which the real sites, all the other real sites that can be found within the culture, are simultaneously represented, contested, and inverted" (24). They tend to conform to two main categories: there are crisis heterotopias, which are common in "so-called primitive societies" (24); these "are privileged or sacred or forbidden places, reserved for individuals who are, in relation to society and to the human environment in which they live, in a state of crisis: adolescents, menstruating women, pregnant women, the elderly, etc." (24). Foucault argues that these heterotopias of crisis are disappearing today and "are being replaced ... by what we might call heterotopias of deviation: those in which individuals whose behavior is deviant in relation to the required mean or norm are placed" (25). Foucault offers a few principles that apply to heterotopias: (1) "there is probably not a single culture in the world that fails to constitute heterotopias" but they "obviously take quite varied forms" (24). (2) The function of a heterotopia can change over time, as for example has happened with cemeteries. (3) "The heterotopia is capable of juxtaposing in a single real place several spaces, several sites that are in themselves incompatible" (25), as on the theater stage or the cinema stage or the garden (which functions as a microcosm of the world). (4) "Heterotopias are most often linked to slices in time—which is to say that they open onto what might be termed, for the sake of symmetry, heterochronies" (26). For example, they may be tied to an "absolute break with ... traditional time" (26), as is the case with cemeteries, or with a "perpetual and indefinite accumulation of time in an immobile place" (26), as is the case with museums and libraries, or with "time in its most fleeting, transitory, precarious aspect, to time in the mode of the festival" (26). (5) "Heterotopias always presuppose a system of opening and closing that both isolates them and makes them penetrable" (26). The entry may be compulsory, as with a prison, or it may entail "rites and purifications" (26). (6) "The last trait of heterotopias is that they have a function in relation to all the space that remains" (27).

See also: **chronotope**.

HISTORICAL MATERIALISM

Although the two terms are certainly related, critics generally distinguish between "**dialectical materialism**," the philosophy of **Marxism** derived from Friedrich Hegel, and "historical materialism," which is understood as the economic science of **Marxism**. Friedrich Engels defines the methodology in the introduction to his *Socialism: Utopian and Scientific* (1892): historical materialism "designate[s] that view of the course of history, which seeks the ultimate cause and the great moving power of all important historic events in the economic development of society, in the changes in the **modes of production** and exchange, in the consequent division of society into distinct **classes**, and in the struggles of these **classes** against one another" (23). Both Engels and Karl Marx saw historical materialism as an **empirical** science that examines the material economic **base** of society, which Engels and Marx argue is the real foundation of society, from which all other things (politics, **ideology**, **culture**) follow: "The **mode of production** of material life conditions the social, political and intellectual life process in general" (Marx and Engels 1962: 1.363). All of Marx's writing after about 1844, especially *Capital* (1867), can be seen as implementing this method of historical investigation.

Some neo-**Marxist** critics argue that historical materialism actively works against traditional **history**, which, as Walter Benjamin for example argues, only tells the history of the victors. For this reason, Benjamin famously contends that "There is no document of civilization which is not at the same time a document of barbarism" (1968: 256). The job of the historical materialist is, then, "to brush **history** against the grain" (257), Benjamin argues. Rather than read the present as inevitable, as the result of a "sequence of events like the beads of a rosary" (263), the historical materialist examines the past as if about "to seize hold of a memory as it flashes up at a moment of danger" (255), an approach to the past and to the present that he later terms "*jetztzeit*," the "time of the now" (263). The threat that constitutes that moment of danger is "that of becoming a tool of the ruling class" (255).

Historical materialism influences a number of theories, including **Cultural Materialism, poststructuralism** (e.g., Jacques Derrida's *Specters of Marx* [1994]), **postcolonial studies, Critical Race Theory, feminism,** and **queer theory**.

Further reading: Althusser and Balibar 1970; Baudrillard 1975; Benjamin 1968; Engels 1892; Mandel 1972; Marx 1867, 1973; Marx and Engels 1932.

HISTORIOGRAPHIC METAFICTION

Linda Hutcheon uses this term in her work to distinguish a particular kind of **postmodern** work. As she explains in *A Poetics of Postmodernism* (1988), by historiographic metafiction "I mean those well-known and popular novels which are both intensely self-reflexive and yet paradoxically also lay claim to historical events and personages: *The French Lieutenant's Woman, Midnight's Children, Ragtime, Legs, G., Famous Last Words*" (5). In such work, a "theoretical self-awareness of history and fiction as human constructs (historio*graphic meta*fiction) is made the grounds for its rethinking and reworking of the forms and contents of the past" (5). In what Hutcheon sees as prototypical **postmodern** fashion, historigraphic metafiction does not outright reject the elements it critiques (e.g., referentiality, the **subject, grand narratives, ideology**) but rather "always works *within* conventions in order to subvert them" (5). For example, such work does not "deny the *existence* of the past" but rather questions "whether we can ever *know* that past other than through its **textualized** remains" (20), thus questioning the very distinction between fiction and **history**: "The problematizing of the nature of historical knowledge, in novels like this, points both to the need to separate and to the danger of separating fiction and **history** as narrative genres" (111). Such work is historical but also political and often employs the strategy of **parody** to achieve its effects. Historiographic metafiction also tends to "bridge the gap between élite and popular art" (20), often by ironically parodying both high and low art forms: "as typically **postmodernist** contradictory **texts**, novels like these parodically use and abuse the conventions of both popular and élite literature, and do so in such a way that they can actually *use* the invasive **culture industry** to challenge its own **commodification** processes from within" (20). Through such maneuvers and contradictions, such postmodern fiction "disturbs readers, forcing them to scrutinize their own values and beliefs, rather than pandering to or satisfying them" (45).

Further reading: Hutcheon 1988, 1989.

HISTORY

"History," like **"power"** or **"gender,"** is a concept that would seem to be straightforward but in fact has a complicated, contested meaning when used by critical theorists. History also has a history; in fact, what we now understand as history is really a rather recent development of the nineteenth century, as explained by Hayden White in his books, *Metahistory* (1973) and the *Content of the Form* (1987). In the former, White also illustrates the extent to which history as a discipline borrows from generic, narrative forms to make sense of the historical record, specifically "the archetypes of Romance, Comedy, Tragedy, and Satire" (1973: x). He therefore questions to what extent contemporary historical accounts are any better than the annals and chronicles of previous centuries: "Does the world really present itself to perception in the form of well-made stories, with central subjects, proper beginnings, middles, and ends, and a coherence that permits us to see 'the end' in the beginning? Or does it present itself more in the forms that the annals and chronicle suggest, either as mere sequence without beginning or end or as sequences of beginnings that only terminate and never conclude?" (1987: 24).

An important early influence on the reconceptualization of history is the neo-Marxist **Frankfurt School**. The **Frankfurt School** questioned traditional history because of its tendency (1) to tell the story of the past from the perspective of the victors; and (2) to order the past in a progressive narrative of cause and effect. In fact, **Frankfurt School** theorists went so far as to question Karl Marx's own **"grand narratives"** about historical progression and economic determinism. As Walter Benjamin explains,

> Historicism contents itself with establishing a causal connection between various moments in history. But no fact that is a cause is for that very reason historical. It became historical posthumously, as it were, through events that may be separated from it by thousands of years. A historian who takes this as his point of departure stops telling the sequence of events like the beads of a rosary. Instead, he grasps the constellation which his own era has formed with a definite earlier one. Thus he establishes a conception of the present as the "time of the now" which is shot through with chips of Messianic time. (1968: 263)

Rather than tell the story of the victors, the **"historical materialist,"** according to Benjamin, must "brush history against the grain" (1968:

257), for the true "depository of historical knowledge" is "Not man or men but the struggling, oppressed **class** itself" (260). The goal, then, is "to make the continuum of history explode" (261); one tells not the history of the victors but a history constantly in a "state of emergency" (257) where opposing forces and discourses are constantly struggling for dominance, potential revolution continually struggling against oppression and exploitation.

This version of history had a particularly strong influence on British **cultural materialists**, who took as their mission the analysis of how **hegemonic** forces in a culture seek to marginalize and disenfranchise the oppressed. As with Benjamin, the goal is to tell the story of marginalized groups (the **proletariat**, women, racial groups, homosexuals). Rather than examine history "from above" or from the perspective of the victors, the goal is to identify competing forces in a given time period. Raymond Williams, for example, influentially suggests that history should consider not only the **dominant**, **hegemonic** forces of a given time period but also the "**residual**" and "**emergent**" forces that can offer groups the possibility of a counter-hegemonic formation (see **dominant, residual and emergent**).

This distrust of traditional history can be found in the work of many critical theorists. Jean-François Lyotard, for example, characterizes **postmodernism** as the rejection of all histories "from above": "The **grand narrative** has lost its credibility, regardless of what mode of unification it uses" (1991: 37). Instead, all we have are *petits récits* or "little stories" tied not to an all-encompassing theory of legitimation but to an innumerable number of **language games** and **phrase regimens**.

Michel Foucault has been another important influence on critical theory's understanding of history. He adopts the term "**archaeology**" to designate his historical method, which he defines in distinction to both traditional history and the traditional history of ideas. He wishes to explore the system of rules governing our understanding of reality by turning to what he terms "**discourses**," which is to say that he approaches history structurally or synchronically (all the different formal rules existing at a given time in relation to each other) rather than diachronically (as a temporal or narrative progression). In so doing, he rejects any "**grand narrative**" that would purport to offer up the truth of the age or the cause-and-effect logic of the present's emergence. Rather, he reads the past as shot through with different, competing ways of interpreting the world. History, then, is not progressive but disjunctive, characterized by ruptures at moments when one **discourse** is (often violently) disrupted by an emergent one (see

discourse and **archaeology**). Foucault's approach to history has influenced a number of critical schools, including **New Historicism**, **Cultural Materialism**, **Postcolonial Studies**, **Critical Race Theory**, **Discourse Analysis**, and the theoretical work of Giorgio Agamben (see **apparatus**, as well as **bare life and *homo sacer***).

Not all critical theorists reject **grand narratives**, it should be pointed out. One important voice questioning the wholesale rejection of such overarching narratives is that of Fredric Jameson. He argues, for one, that you cannot tell the story of how we post-modernists overcame our desire for **grand narratives** without telling that story in grand narrative form (1991: xii). Indeed, Jameson tends to see the **postmodern** rejection of traditional history—in favor of **historiographic metafiction**—as symptomatic of the larger problems of **late capitalism** in our present moment. He also sees value in **utopian** narratives that imagine a **teleology** for one's actions in the present; how else, he asks, can we pursue effective change? Even Jameson, however, rejects a simple understanding of history, borrowing Jacques Lacan's notion of the **Real** to articulate his notion of history: he proposes, to be precise, "that history is *not* a **text**, not a **narrative**, master or otherwise, but that, as an absent cause, it is inaccessible to us except in textual form, and that our approach to it and to the **Real** itself necessarily passes through its prior **textualization**, its narrativization in the political unconscious" (1981: 35). History, then, functions like Lacan's **Real**—it cannot be represented directly but we can begin to read it in those **antagonisms** of any given moment that threaten to erupt into revolutionary change: "History is what hurts, it is what refuses **desire** and sets inexorable limits to individual as well as collective **praxis**. ... [T]his History can be apprehended only through its effects, and never directly as some reified force" (1981: 102).

Further reading: Attridge *et al.* 1987; Benjamin 1968; Foucault 1972, 1980; Jameson 1981, 1988, 1991; Lyotard 1991; White 1973, 1987, 1992; Williams 1977.

HOMO SACER

See **bare life and *homo sacer***

HOMOSEXUAL PANIC

See **homosocial desire**

HOMOSOCIAL DESIRE (HOMOSOCIALITY)

Eve Kosofsky Sedgwick, who helped to establish the methodologies of **queer theory**, makes the argument in *Between Men* (1985) that mid-eighteenth to mid-nineteenth-century **patriarchal** culture was structured around what she terms "homosocial desire." As she points out, the term "is a kind of oxymoron" (1); it is "a neologism, obviously formed by analogy with 'homosexual,' and just as obviously meant to be distinguished from 'homosexual'" (1). After all, "it is applied to such activities as 'male bonding,' which may, as in our society, be characterized by intense homophobia, fear and hatred of homosexuality" (1). Sedgwick illustrates, however, that in a basic structural way homosociality—the glue that holds together **patriarchal** culture through such pervasive male–male relations as friendship, mentorship, entitlement, and rivalry—relies on the threat of homosexuality not only to define itself but also to give an erotic charge to those avowedly heterosexual relations. As she writes, "To draw the 'homosocial' back into the orbit of **'desire**,' of the potentially erotic, then, is to hypothesize the potential unbrokenness of a continuum between homosocial and homosexual—a continuum whose visibility, for men, in our society, is radically disrupted" (1–2).

That continuum exists even in apparently heterosexual plotlines, particularly the pervasive plot device whereby two men compete for the same woman in an erotic love triangle. Sedgwick builds on *Deceit, Desire, and the Novel* (1965), where René Girard illustrates how, "in any erotic rivalry, the bond that links the two rivals is as intense and potent as the bond that links either of the rivals to the beloved" (Sedgwick 1985: 21). Indeed, the structure of the erotic triangle is ultimately misogynistic, Sedgwick argues, with women functioning "as exchangeable, perhaps symbolic, property for the primary purpose of cementing the bonds of men with men" (1985: 25–26). It is also homophobic since it is caught up in a system of **compulsory heterosexuality** whereby the relation between the men always entails "a structural residue of terrorist potential, of *blackmailability*, of Western maleness through the leverage of homophobia" (1985: 89), leading to what Sedgwick terms "homosexual panic." As she elaborates in *Epistemology of the Closet* (1990), "at least since the eighteenth century in England and America, the continuum of male homosocial bonds has been brutally structured by a secularized and psychologized homophobia, which has excluded certain shiftingly and more or less arbitrarily defined segments of the continuum from participating in the overarching male entitlement—in the complex web of male power over the production, reproduction, and exchange of goods, persons, and meanings" (185). That is, "Because the paths of male entitlement, especially in the nineteenth century, required certain intense male bonds that were not readily distinguishable from the most reprobated bonds, an endemic and ineradicable state of what I am calling male homosexual panic became the normal condition of male heterosexual entitlement" (185).

See also: **feminism, gender and sex, LGBTQ Studies, phallocentrism and phallogocentrism**.

Further reading: Krishnaswamy 1998; Sedgwick 1985, 1990, 1994, 2003.

HYBRIDITY

This term is particularly significant in **Postcolonial Theory**, as in the work of Homi Bhabha. The space of hybridity exists between what Bhabha terms "pedagogical" or authoritarian, totalizing **discourse** and the single individual's **performative** enunciation of **discourse**. Bhabha defines the term this way: "Hybridity is the perplexity of the living as it interrupts the representation of the fullness of life; it is an instance of iteration, in the minority **discourse**, of the time of the arbitrary sign—'the minus in the origin'—through which all forms of cultural meaning are open to translation because their enunciation resists totalization" (1990a: 314). Drawing on Jacques Derrida's notion of *différance*, Bhabha argues that "hybrid sites of meaning open up a cleavage in the language of culture which suggests that the similitude of the *symbol* as it plays across cultural sites must not obscure the fact that repetition of the *sign* is, in each specific social practice, both different and differential" (1990a: 314). In other words, unlike "cultural diversity"—and "liberal notions of multiculturalism, cultural exchange or the culture of humanity" (1994: 34)—the site of what Bhabha terms "cultural difference" makes us question the very foundation of meaning-production because at these "boundaries of cultures … meanings and values are (mis)read or signs are misappropriated." As he goes on, "Culture only emerges as a problem, or a problematic, at the point at which there is a loss of meaning in the contestation and articulation of everyday life, between classes, genders, races, nations" (1994: 34). The instability of such hybrid zones of contact ensures that totalitarian notions of empire or identity will always fail before the reality of heterogeneous, emergent, and contestatory minority **discourse**. See also the related concepts of **contact zone and transculturation**, **liminality** and **mimicry**.

Bruno Latour and **Actor–Network Theory** sometimes uses the term "hybrid" to discuss those instances where it is not easy to distinguish between **subjects** and **objects**. He terms such instances **quasi-objects and quasi-subjects**. See also **mediators and intermediaries**. Donna Harraway explores a similar concept in her theorization of the **cyborg**.

Further reading: Bhabha 1990a, 1994; Harraway 1991; Latour 1993.

HYSTERIA

"Hysteria" refers to the symptomatic return of **repressed** childhood sexual trauma—whether the result of real events or unresolved frustrations of sexual fantasy. The two main forms of hysteria are (1) conversion hysteria, in which the **symptoms** are manifested on the body (e.g., psychosomatic illness); and (2) anxiety hysteria, in which one feels excessive anxiety because of an external object (e.g., phobias). Feminists have questioned the concept because of the ways that women have been particularly tied to it over the history of psychology. Indeed, the very term is etymologically tied to "womb."

Further reading: Bronfen 1998; David-Ménard 1989; Didi-Huberman 2003; Showalter 1987, 1997.

ID

According to Sigmund Freud, the id is the great reservoir of the **libido**, from which the **ego** seeks to distinguish itself through various mechanisms of **repression**. Because of that **repression**, the id seeks alternative expression for those impulses that we consider evil or excessively sexual, impulses that we often felt as perfectly natural at an earlier or archaic stage and have since **repressed**. The id is governed by the **pleasure principle** and is oriented towards one's internal **instincts** and passions but, because of its antagonistic relationship to the **super-ego**, is "the dark, inaccessible part of our personality" (1953–74: 22.73). Freud also argues on occasion that the id represents the inheritance of the species, which is passed on to us at birth. Carl Jung developed this idea into his concept of a collective unconscious of the species that is inherited by each individual at birth and is informed by collective, impersonal, and universal archetypes.

Further reading: Freud 1923, 1932; Laplanche and Pontalis 1973.

IDEAL EGO AND EGO IDEAL

Although these two terms appear to be quite similar, Sigmund Freud did make a distinction between them. The ideal ego refers to the perfect **narcissism** that a given person enjoyed in childhood. The ego ideal, by contrast, is bound up with the rules of the **super-ego** and represents at once the ideal of perfection that the ego strives to emulate and a nostalgia for a necessarily lost **narcissism**. As Freud puts it, the **super-ego** is "the vehicle of the ego ideal by which the **ego** measures itself, which it emulates, and whose demand for ever greater perfection it strives to fulfill" (1953–74: 22.65). Given the intimate connection of the **super-ego** to the **Oedipus complex**, the ego ideal is likely "the precipitate of the old picture of the parents, the expression of admiration for the perfection which the child then attributed to them" (1953–74: 22.65). Jacques Lacan also makes a distinction between the "ideal ego" and the "ego ideal," the former of which he associates with the **imaginary order**, the latter of which he associates with the **symbolic order**. Lacan's "ideal ego" is the ideal of perfection that the ego strives to emulate; it first affected the subject when he saw himself in a mirror during the **mirror stage**, which occurs around 6–18 months of age (see **psychosexual development**). Seeing that image of oneself established a discord between the idealizing image in the mirror (bounded, whole, complete) and the chaotic reality of one's body between 6 and 18 months, thus setting up the logic of the **imaginary**'s fantasy construction that would dominate the subject's psychic life ever after. For Lacan, the "ego-ideal," by contrast, is when the subject looks at himself or herself as if from that ideal point; to look at oneself from that point of perfection is to see one's life as vain and useless. The effect, then, is to invert one's "normal" life, to see it as suddenly repulsive. Caught up as the ego ideal is with the **symbolic order**, one can characterize it as the **Name-of-the-Father**'s disapproval of the subject, a situation one cannot escape since the subject, by definition, can never fully meet the **symbolic order**'s expectations.

IDENTIFICATION

According to Sigmund Freud, identification is the process whereby one's **ego** seeks to emulate another. It is particularly important in overcoming the **Oedipus complex**: the young child deals with his primitive desires by identifying with his parents, imitating them to such an extent that, ultimately, he **introjects** the parental authority—and thus develops a **super-ego**. Identification is quite different from **object**-choice: "If a boy identifies himself with his father, he wants to *be like* his father; if he makes him the **object** of his choice, he wants to *have* him, to possess him" (Freud 1953–74: 22.63).

Further reading: Freud 1932; Laplanche and Pontalis 1973.

IDENTITY POLITICS

This is a term that has been applied to a number of movements, often placed under the umbrella of **Cultural Studies**, which seek to fight for the rights of oppressed groups, including **Critical Race Theory**, **Queer Theory**, **Feminism**, **Postcolonial Studies**, and **Marxism**. Markers of identity like **race**, **gender**, **sexuality**, and **class** are analyzed to fight against oppression and stereotyping. Although these theorists often build on a deconstructionist analysis of uneven **binary oppositions**, they tend to reject **poststructructuralism**'s problematizing of agency and power since the goal of these theoretical schools is to empower the traditionally excluded, **marginalized**, exploited, and downtrodden.

One criticism of this general approach is that it can contribute to an agonistic understanding of the social sphere, where each group is forever in conflict with others on the political stage. **Feminist** theorist Judith Butler for example turns to the notion of "**radical democracy**" to call for a situation of "permanent political contest" (Butler 1993: 222) on behalf of excluded groups. The logic of identity politics has also been questioned by Kimberlé Crenshaw, who argues that the emphasis on particular identity markers has kept critics from thinking through how multiple identity markers are often at play in oppression. As she writes, "Although racism and sexism readily intersect in the lives of real people, they seldom do in feminist and antiracist practices" (1991: 1242). She therefore turns to the concept of **intersectionality** to think about the common intersection of multiple identity markers in a given individual (e.g., black woman, queer black man, etc.).

IDEOLOGICAL STATE APPARATUSES (ISAs)

Louis Althusser complicates Karl Marx's understanding of the relation between **base and superstructure** by adding his concept of "Ideological State Apparatuses." Marx distinguished among various "levels" in a society: the infrastructure or economic **base** and the **superstructure**, which includes political and legal institutions (law, the police, the government) as well as **ideology** (religious, moral, legal, political, etc.). The **superstructure** has a relative autonomy with relation to the **base**; it relies on the economic **base** but can sometimes persist for a long period after major changes in the economic **base**. Althusser does not reject the Marxist model; however, he does want to explore the ways in which **ideology** is more pervasive and more "material" than previously acknowledged. As a result, he proposes to distinguish "Ideological State Apparatuses" (ISAs for short) from the repressive State Apparatus (SA for short). The State Apparatus includes "the Government, the Administration, the Army, the Police, the Courts, the Prisons, etc." (Althusser 2001: 96). These are the agencies that function "by violence," by at some point imposing punishment or privation in order to enforce power.

To distinguish ISAs from the SA, Althusser offers a number of examples:

- the religious ISA (the system of the different public and private "Schools");
- the family ISA;
- the legal ISA;
- the political ISA (the political system, including the different Parties);
- the trade union ISA;
- the communications ISA (press, radio, and television, etc.);
- the cultural ISA (literature, the arts, sports, etc.).

These ISAs, by contrast to the SA, are less centralized and more heterogeneous; they are also believed to access the private rather than the public realm of existence, although Althusser's goal here is to question the bourgeois distinction between private and public: "The distinction between the public and the private is a distinction internal to bourgeois law, and valid in the (subordinate) domains in which bourgeois law exercises its 'authority'" (2001: 97). The main thing that distinguishes the ISAs from the SAs is **ideology**: "the Repressive State Apparatus functions 'by violence,' whereas the Ideological State Apparatuses function 'by **ideology**'" (97). To be more precise, Althusser explains that the SA functions *predominantly* by violence or repression and only secondarily by **ideology**. Similarly the ISAs function predominantly by **ideology** but can include punishment or repression secondarily: "Schools and Churches use suitable methods of punishment, expulsion, selection, etc., to 'discipline' not only their shepherds, but also their flocks. The same is true of the Family. ... The same is true of the cultural IS Apparatus (censorship, among other things), etc." (2001: 98).

Although the ISAs appear to be quite disparate, they are unified by subscribing to a common **ideology** in the service of the ruling **class**; indeed, the ruling **class** must maintain a degree of control over the ISAs in order to ensure the stability of the repressive State Apparatus (the SA): "To my knowledge, *no class can hold State power over a long period without at the same time exercising its **hegemony** over and in the State Ideological Apparatuses*" (2001: 98). It is much harder for the ruling class to maintain control over the multiple, heterogeneous, and relatively autonomous ISAs (alternative perspectives can be voiced in each ISA), which is why there is a continual struggle for **hegemony** in this realm.

It is also worth mentioning that, according to Althusser, "what the bourgeoisie has installed as its number-one, i.e. as its dominant ideological State apparatus, is the educational apparatus, which has in fact replaced in its functions the previously dominant ideological State apparatus, the Church" (2001: 103–4). Through education, each mass of individuals that leaves the educational system at various junctures (the laborers who leave the system early, the petty bourgeoisie who leave after their B.A.s, and the leaders who complete further specialist training) enters the work force with the **ideology** necessary for the reproduction of the current system: "Each mass ejected en route is practically provided with the **ideology** which suits the role it has to fulfill in class society" (2001: 105). Other ISAs contribute to the replication of the dominant **ideology** but "no other ideological State apparatus has the obligatory (and not least, free) audience of the totality of the children in the **capitalist** social formation, eight hours a day for five or six days out of seven" (105). The very importance of this function is why schools are invested in hiding their true purpose through an obfuscating **ideology**: "an **ideology** which represents the School as a neutral environment purged of **ideology** (because it is ... lay), where teachers respectful of the 'conscience' and 'freedom' of the children who are entrusted to them (in complete confidence) by their 'parents' (who are free, too, i.e. the owners of their children) open up for them the path to the freedom, morality and responsibility of adults by their own example, by knowledge, litera-ture and their 'liberating' virtues" (105–6). So pervasive is this **ideology**, according to Althusser, that "those teachers who, in dreadful conditions, attempt to turn the few weapons they can find in the history and learning they 'teach' against the **ideology**, the system and the practices in which they are trapped ... are a kind of hero" (106).

See also: **cultural capital, social capital, and symbolic capital, doxa, habitus**.

IDEOLOGY (IDEOLOGICAL)

The critique of ideology is a major aspect of "critical theory," so it is not surprising that this term is a particularly fraught one, because it tends to be interpreted a little differently by each critical school. The understanding of how ideology works has also undergone various shifts over the last century and a half. The term emerges at the time of the French Revolution but the most important version of the term for critical theory is in the work of Karl Marx. Marx's understanding of ideology was complex and he himself tended to think about ideology in different ways as he developed his theories. His most straightforward statement about ideology appears in *The German Ideology* (1932), which he wrote with Friederich Engels. Ideology represents the "production of ideas, of conceptions, of consciousness," all that "men say, imagine, conceive," and includes such things as "politics, laws, morality, religion, metaphysics, etc." (47). Ideology functions as the **superstructure** of a civilization: the conventions and culture that make up the dominant ideas of a society. The "ruling ideas" of a given epoch are, however, those of the ruling **class**: "The ruling ideas are nothing more than the ideal expression of the dominant material relationships, the dominant material relationships grasped as ideas; hence of the relationships which make the one **class** the ruling one, therefore, the ideas of their dominance" (64). Since one goal of ideology is to legitimize those forces in a position of **hegemony**, it tends to obfuscate the violence and exploitation that often keep a disempowered group in its place (from slaves in **tribal society** to the peasantry in **feudal society** to the **proletariat** in **capitalist** society). The obfuscation necessarily leads to logical contradictions in the dominant ideology, which **Marxism** works to uncover by returning to the material conditions of a society: a society's **mode of production**.

In *The German Ideology* (1932), Marx and Engels offer up the possibility that one can address the real conditions of human existence, outside of ideological mystification:

> The premises from which we begin are not arbitrary ones, not dogmas, but real premises from which abstraction can only be made in the imagination. They are the real individuals, their activity and the material conditions under which they live, both those which they find already existing and those produced by their activity. These premises can thus be verified in a purely **empirical** way. (42)

Marx refers to the material conditions existing at a given time period as the **means of production**. Any given time period's ideology is most clearly revealed by uncovering the material conditions of production: the **means of production**, as well as the **relations of production** (the ways the society structures the relations between individuals, particularly through the **division of labor**), which together make up the **mode of production**: "life involves before everything else eating and drinking, a habitation, clothing and many other things. The first historical act is thus the production of the means to satisfy these needs, the production of material life itself" (48). For Marx, it is the materiality of human production that directly influences life: "Life is not determined by consciousness, but consciousness by life" (47). As Marx and Engel explain further in *The German Ideology* (1932),

> **Empirical** observation must in each separate instance bring out empirically, and without any mystification and speculation, the connection of the social and political structure with production. The social structure and the State are continually evolving out of the life-process of definite individuals, but of individuals, not as they may appear in their own or other people's imagination, but as they really are; i.e. as they operate, produce materially, and hence as they work under definite material limits, presuppositions and conditions independent of their will. (46–47)

This belief that one can directly access the real conditions of history (sometimes referred to as "reflection theory" or "vulgar Marxism") is questioned by neo-Marxists, particularly in the wake of Louis Althusser's Lacanian rethinking of ideology (see **Marxism**).

The **Frankfurt School** provided an important early rethinking of Marx's understanding of ideology, particularly in its practitioners' tendency to be highly skeptical of any claim to absolute truth. For **Frankfurt School** theorists like Max Horkheimer, Theodor Adorno, and Herbert Marcuse, critical theory sought, as best as it could, to step outside of dominant, **hegemonic** ways of understanding the world in order to critique all obfuscating ideologies with the goal of changing society for the better (see **Introduction**); they adopted Marx's **dialectical materialism** as method but with the understanding that critical theorists must always be prepared to question their own methodology too, particularly if the real world of **praxis** offered evidence that questioned the theory being used. This more skeptical version of **dialectical materialism** was developed into a theory of **negative dialectics** by Herbert Marcuse and Theodor Adorno.

Marx is, in fact, more complicated on this issue, since at times he suggests that some aspects of ideology (for example, literature) can have a semi-autonomous existence; that is, that such cultural products can exert an influence that is at odds with the dominant **mode of production**. Still, neo-Marxism does mark an important shift in thinking about this concept. Marx's version of ideology has been termed by some "false consciousness," a false understanding of the way the world in fact functions (for example, the suppression of the fact that the products we purchase on the open market are, in fact, the result of the exploitation of laborers). Althusser explains that for Marx "Ideology is ... thought as an imaginary construction whose status is exactly like the theoretical status of the dream among writers before Freud. For those writers, the dream was the purely imaginary, i.e. null, result of the 'day's residues'" (2001: 108). Althusser, by contrast, approximates ideology to Lacan's understanding of "reality," the world we construct around us after our entrance into the **symbolic order**. (Pierre Bourdieu's understanding of the **habitus** and **doxa** is another effort to illustrate how entrenched and unconscious are our ideological assumptions and predispositions.) For Althusser, as for Lacan, it is impossible to access the "**Real** conditions of existence" due to our reliance on language; however, through a rigorous "scientific" approach to society, economics, and history, we can come close to perceiving if not those "**Real** conditions" at least the ways that we are inscribed in ideology by complex processes of recognition and misrecognition. Althusser's understanding of ideology has in turn influenced a number of important Marxist thinkers, including Chantal Mouffe, Ernesto Laclau, Slavoj Žižek, and Fredric Jameson.

Althusser posits a series of hypotheses that he explores to clarify his understanding of ideology:

(1) "*Ideology represents the imaginary relationship of individuals to their real conditions of existence*" (2001: 109). The traditional way of thinking of ideology led Marxists to show how ideologies are false by pointing to the real world hidden by ideology (for example, the "real" economic **base** for ideology). According to Althusser, by contrast, ideology does not "reflect" the real world but "represents" the "**imaginary** relationship of individuals" to the real world; the thing ideology (mis)represents is itself already at one remove from the **real**. In this, Althusser follows the Lacanian understanding of the **imaginary order**, which is itself at one step removed from the Lacanian **Real**. In other words, we are always within ideology because of our reliance on language to

establish our "reality"; different ideologies are but different representations of our social and **imaginary** "reality," not a representation of the **Real** itself.

(2) *"Ideology has a material existence"* (2001: 112). Althusser contends that ideology has a material existence because "an ideology always exists in an **apparatus**, and its practice, or practices" (112). Ideology always manifests itself through actions, which are "inserted into practices" (114), for example, rituals, conventional behavior, and so on. Indeed, Althusser goes so far as to adopt Pascal's formula for belief: "Pascal says more or less: 'Kneel down, move your lips in prayer, and you will believe'" (114). It is our performance of our relation to others and to social institutions that continually instantiates us as **subjects**. Judith Butler's understanding of **performativity** could be said to be strongly influenced by this way of thinking about ideology.

(3) *"[A]ll ideology hails or interpellates concrete individuals as concrete subjects"* (2001: 115). According to Althusser, the main purpose of ideology is in " '*constituting*' *concrete individuals as* **subjects**" (116). So pervasive is ideology in its constitution of **subjects** that it forms our very reality and thus appears to us as "true" or "obvious." Althusser gives the example of the "hello" on a street: "the rituals of ideological recognition ... guarantee for us that we are indeed concrete, individual, distinguishable and (naturally) irreplaceable **subjects**" (117). Through "**interpellation**," individuals are turned into **subjects** (which are always ideological). Althusser's example is the hail from a police officer: "'Hey, you there!'": "Assuming that the theoretical scene I have imagined takes place in the street, the hailed individual will turn round. By this mere one-hundred-and-eighty-degree physical conversion, he becomes a *subject*" (118). The very fact that we do not recognize this interaction as ideological speaks to the power of ideology:

> what thus seems to take place outside ideology (to be precise, in the street), in reality takes place in ideology. ... That is why those who are in ideology believe themselves by definition outside ideology: one of the effects of ideology is the practical *denegation* of the ideological character of ideology by ideology: ideology never says, "I am ideological." (2001: 118)

(4) "[I]ndividuals are always-already **subjects**" (2001: 119). Although he presents his example of interpellation in a temporal form (I am interpellated and thus I become a **subject**, I enter ideology),

Althusser makes it clear that the "becoming-**subject**" happens even before we are born. "This proposition might seem paradoxical" (119), Althusser admits; nevertheless, "That an individual is always-already a **subject**, even before he is born, is ... the plain reality, accessible to everyone and not a paradox at all" (119). Even before the child is born, "it is certain in advance that it will bear its Father's Name, and will therefore have an identity and be irreplaceable. Before its birth, the child is therefore always-already a **subject**, appointed as a **subject** in and by the specific familial ideological configuration in which it is 'expected' once it has been conceived" (119). Althusser thus once again invokes Lacan's ideas, in this case Lacan's understanding of the "**Name-of-the-Father**."

Most subjects accept their ideological self-constitution as "reality" or "**nature**" and thus rarely run afoul of the repressive State Apparatus, which is designed to punish anyone who rejects the dominant ideology. **Hegemony** is thus reliant less on such repressive State apparatuses as the police than it is on those **Ideological State Apparatuses (ISAs)** by which ideology is inculcated in all **subjects**. As Althusser puts it, "the individual *is interpellated as a (free)* **subject** *in order that he shall submit freely to the commandments of the* **Subject***, i.e. in order that he shall (freely) accept his subjection*, i.e. in order that he shall make the gestures and actions of his subjection 'all by himself'" (2001: 123). Pierre Bourdieu examines a similar mechanism in his theorization of the concepts of **doxa**, **field**, **habitus**, and **cultural capital**.

Fredric Jameson's theories about ideology have influenced theories of ideology more recently. He is particularly influenced by Lacan and those post-Marxist theorists who have made use of Lacan's distinction between reality and "the **Real**" in order to understand ideology (Louis Althusser, Chantal Mouffe, and Ernesto Laclau). At one point, Jameson quotes Althusser's Lacanian definition of ideology: "the representation of the subject's **Imaginary** relationship to his or her **Real** conditions of existence" (1991: 51). Those "**Real** conditions of existence" remain, by definition, outside of language. History therefore functions for Jameson as an "absent cause," insofar as, in its totality, it remains inexpressible; however, it nonetheless does exist as that which drives real **antagonisms** in the present (for example, between social classes). We may not be able to get out of ideological contradiction altogether; however, Jameson asserts the importance of attempting, nonetheless, to acknowledge the real **antagonisms** that are, in fact, driving our fantasy constructions.

Jameson also makes it clear that there is not one ideological dominant in any period. In this, Jameson follows Raymond Williams's useful distinctions among "residual" ideological formations (ideologies that have been mostly superseded but still circulate in various ways); "emergent" ideological formations (new ideologies that are in the process of establishing their influence); and "dominant" ideological formations (those ideologies supported by what Althusser terms "**Ideological State Apparatuses**"; e.g., schools, government, the police, and the military). See **residual, emergent, and dominant**. Jameson insists on the value of such a model because "If we do not achieve some general sense of a cultural dominant, then we fall back into a view of present history as sheer heterogeneity, random difference, a coexistence of a host of distinct forces whose effectivity is undecidable" (1991: 6). By determining the ideological dominant of our age in his book, *Postmodernism* (1991), Jameson hopes to provide his readers with a "**cognitive map**" of the present, which then can make possible effective and beneficial political change.

Slavoj Žižek's theories about ideology (throughout his work but especially in *The Sublime Object of Ideology* [1989] and *Tarrying with the Negative* [1993]) have also been influential, particularly his explanation of why ideology is so difficult to dislodge even when you explain to a person the contradictions and problems in his or her way of thinking. Žižek uses Freud's concept of **fetishism** (as reworked by Octave Mannoni) to show how it's possible for a person to realize that an ideology is wrong yet still follow it. In the case of **fetishism**, the fetishist is able *at one and the same time* to believe in his fantasy and to recognize that it is nothing but a fantasy. And yet, the fact of recognizing the fantasy *as fantasy* in no way reduces its power over the individual. Octave Mannoni phrased this paradoxical logic in this way: "*je sais bien, mais quand-même*" or "I know very well, but nonetheless." Žižek builds on this idea in theorizing the nature of ideology, which follows a similar contradictory logic: *we may very well know*, for example, that paper **money** holds no special power over us and is really a way to alienate **commodities** from the **labor power** that truly gives any commodity its value, *but nonetheless* we act as if it has power over us in our daily use of that **money-form**. As Žižek puts it, "Cynical distance is just one way—one of many ways—to blind ourselves to the structuring power of ideological fantasy: even if we do not take things seriously, even if we keep an ironical distance, *we are still doing them*" (1989: 33).

Further reading: Althusser 2001; Eagleton 1991; Jameson 1988, 1991; G. L. Levine 1994; Marx and Engels 1932; McGann 1983b; Žižek 1989, 1993.

ILLOCUTIONARY ACT

See **speech act and Speech-Act Theory**

IMAGINARY ORDER

"Imaginary order" refers to the fundamental **narcissism** by which the human **subject** creates fantasy images of both himself and his ideal **object** of desire, according to Jacques Lacan. The imaginary order is closely tied to Lacan's theorization of the **mirror stage** and marks the movement of the subject from primal need to what Lacan terms "demand." As the connection to the **mirror stage** suggests, the "imaginary" is primarily **narcissistic** even though it sets the stage for the fantasies of **desire**. Whereas needs can be fulfilled, demands are, by definition, unsatisfiable; in other words, we are already making the movement into the sort of **lack** that, for Lacan, defines the human **subject**. Once a child begins to recognize that its body is separate from the world and its mother, it begins to feel anxiety, which is caused by a sense of something lost. The demand of the child, then, is to make the **other** a part of itself, as it seemed to be in the child's now lost state of **nature** (the neo-natal months). The child's demand is, therefore, impossible to realize and functions, ultimately, as a reminder of loss and **lack**. (The difference between "demand" and "desire," and thus between the imaginary and the **symbolic order**, is simply the acknowledgement of language, law, and community in the latter; the demand of the imaginary does not proceed beyond a dyadic relation between the self and the object one wants to make a part of oneself.) The mirror stage corresponds to this demand insofar as the child misrecognizes in its mirror image a stable, coherent, whole self, which, however, does not correspond to the real child (and is, therefore, impossible to realize). The image is a fantasy, one that the child sets up in order to compensate for its sense of **lack** or loss, what Lacan terms an "Ideal-I" or "**ideal ego**." That fantasy image of oneself can be filled in by others who we may want to emulate in our adult lives (role models, etc.), anyone that we set up as a mirror for ourselves in what is, ultimately, a **narcissistic** relationship. What must be remembered is that for Lacan this imaginary realm continues to exert its influence throughout the life of the adult and is not merely superseded in the child's movement into the **symbolic order**. Indeed, the imaginary and the symbolic are, according to Lacan, inextricably intertwined and work in tension with the **Real** (see **psychosexual development**).

See also: **scopophilia, suture**.

Further reading: Lacan 1977, 1991.

IMAGINED COMMUNITY

See **nation, nation-state and nationalism**

INAESTHETIC

This term is popularized by Alain Badiou in *Handbook of Inaesthetics* (2005b). According to Badiou, the relationship between art and philosophy has followed one of three schemata: "The first is what I will call the *didactic* schema. Its thesis is that art is incapable of truth, or that all truth is external to art" (2). Plato's opposition to poetry and art in his *Republic* is the perfect example of this understanding of art; the essence of art, in this way of thinking, "is conveyed in its public effect, and not in the artwork itself" (3). The contrary schema Badiou calls the *romantic* schema: "Its thesis is that art *alone* is capable of truth" (3), so that, according to this schema, "it is art itself that educates, because it teaches of the power of infinity held within the tormented cohesion of a form" (3). Badiou posits a third schema that he terms "the *classical* schema, of which one will say from the start that it *dehystericizes art*" (3). The exemplary figure here is Aristotle, who accepts Plato's judgment that art is incapable of truth but states that is not a problem because the purpose of art is not truth but pleasure and catharsis; that is, "Art has a therapeutic function, and not at all a cognitive or revelatory one" (4). What truth exists in art, according to this schema, amounts to an "'imaginarization' of truth, which is relieved of any instance of the **Real**"; this is "what the classical thinkers called 'verisimilitude' or 'likelihood'" (4). According to Badiou, the major recent trends of critical theory can be aligned along these three schemata, with **Marxist** thought tending to the didactic, German **hermeneutics** to the romantic, and **psychoanalysis** to the classical. Badiou responds to these three schemata, which he argues have dominated thought about art from Plato to the present, with a fourth schema, which he terms the inaesthetic, a new way of thinking about the relationship of art and philosophy: "Art is a thought in which artworks are the **Real** (and not the effect). And this thought, or rather the truths that it activates, are irreducible to other truths—be they scientific, political, or amorous. This also means that art, as a singular regime of thought, is irreducible to philosophy" (9). According to this way of thinking, truth is immanent to art—one need not look elsewhere for those truths—and art is perfectly singular—"These truths are given nowhere else than in art" (9). Badiou turns, in particular, to modernist literature (for example, the poetry of Stéphane Mallarmé and Samuel Beckett's *Worstward Ho*) to illustrate the notion of an artwork that transcends all referents in the objective world: "The modern poem is the opposite of a mimesis. In its operation, it exhibits an Idea of which both the **object** and objectivity represent nothing but pale copies" (21). In this way, art becomes for Badiou one of the privileged ways by which human **subjects** can transcend what Fredric Jameson (1972) terms "the prison-house of language": it gives us access to the undecidable, the indiscernible by which a **subject** comes into being in what Badiou terms an "**event**" (see **being and event**).

See also: **aesthetics**.

INCOMMENSURABILITY (INCOMMENSURABLE)

One thing that characterizes much **poststructuralist** and **postmodern** theory is the tendency to question grand or totalitarian narratives that would link together heterogeneous things. Instead, many such theorists argue that individuals, communities, cultures, or even **genres of discourse** are incommensurable, which is to say that they do not share the same standard of measurement. This situation can lead to a vision of society where conflict and politics are inescapable facts of the human condition. Judith Butler and others for example turn to the notion of "**radical democracy**," leading to a situation of "permanent political contest" (Butler 1993: 222). Jean-François Lyotard argues that conflict is an inescapable fact of our use of language and its incommensurable **phrase regimens** and **genres of discourse**: "genres are incommensurable, each has its own 'interests'" (1988a: 159). For this reason, "[t]here is conflict"; however, the conflict "is not between humans or between any other entities; rather these result from phrases" (1988a: 137). This stance is one reason why **poststructuralists** are sometimes critiqued, however unfairly, for their nihilism or their lack of ethical or moral standards. Lyotard, in response, sees the effort to impose one moral standard on all things as totalitarian and inherently unjust: "any attempt to state the law, for example, to place oneself in the position of enunciator of the universal prescription is obviously infatuation itself and absolute injustice" (Lyotard and Thébaud 1985: 99).

See also: **dissensus, wrong**.

Further reading: Butler 1993, 1997, 2000; Lyotard 1988a, 1988b; Lyotard and Thébaud 1985; J. H. Miller 1999.

INSTINCT (INSTINCTUAL)

According to **psychoanalysis**, an instinct is a pre-lingual bodily impulse that drives our actions. Sigmund Freud makes a distinction between instinct and the antithesis, conscious/unconscious; an instinct is pre-lingual and, so, can only be tangentially accessed by language, by an idea that represents the instinct. What is **repressed** is not properly the instinct itself but "the ideational presentation" of the instinct, which is just another way of saying that our deepest, primitive **drives** are beyond our ability to represent them. **Psychoanalysis** seeks to make sense of the **unconscious**, which is to some extent intelligible and, so, one step removed from instinct. According to Freud, there are two classes of instincts: (1) Eros or the sexual instincts, which he later saw as compatible with the self-preservation instinct; and (2) Thanatos or the death-instinct (see **death drive**), a natural desire to "re-establish a state of things that was disturbed by the emergence of life" (1923: 709). The death instinct, which he theorized in part as a response to the First World War, allowed Freud to explain man's capacity for murder and destruction.

See also: **repetition compulsion**.

INTERMEDIARIES

See **mediators and intermediaries**

INTERPELLATION

See **ideology**

INTERSECTIONALITY

This term is first theorized for **Critical Race Theory** and Black **Feminism** by Kimberlé Crenshaw, who argues that "The problem with **identity politics** is not that it fails to transcend difference, as some critics charge, but rather the opposite—that it frequently conflates or ignores intragroup differences." As she goes on to explain, "In the context of violence against women, this elision of difference in identity politics is problematic, fundamentally because the violence that many women experience is often shaped by other dimensions of their identities, such as **race** and **class**" (1991: 1242). The problem is that "**Feminist** efforts to politicize experiences of women and antiracist efforts to politicize experiences of people of color have frequently proceeded as though the issues and experiences they each detail occur in mutually exclusive terrains" (1242). The result is a double disempowerment when one considers an intersectional identity like a woman of color: "The failure of **feminism** to interrogate **race** means that the resistance strategies of **feminism** will often replicate and reinforce the subordination of people of color, and the failure of antiracism to interrogate **patriarchy** means that antiracism will frequently reproduce the subordination of women" (1252). As Patricia Hill Collins puts it, "The sexual politics of Black womanhood reveals the fallacy of assuming that gender affects all women in the same way—**race** and **class** matter greatly" (2000: 229). Even within a single person's life, intersecting markers of identity will affect that person differently at different times, as Collins explains:

> because oppression is constantly changing, different aspects of an individual U.S. Black woman's self-definitions intermingle and become more salient: Her **gender** may be more prominent when she becomes a mother, her **race** when she searches for housing, her social **class** when she applies for credit, her sexual orientation when she is walking with her lover, and her citizenship status when she applies for a job. In all of these contexts, her position in relation to and within intersecting oppressions shifts. (275)

Rather than follow an either/or approach to questions of identity, intersectionality considers the multiple markers of identity (**race**, **class**, **gender**, **sexuality**) that can together exacerbate exclusion and oppression in our culture. Crenshaw's and Collins's particular concern tends to be issues that affect black women but intersectionality can be and has been applied to other intersections of identity markers that could, otherwise, be theorized separately (e.g., queer black men), as Crenshaw suggests: "**race** can also be a coalition of straight and gay people of color, and thus serve as a basis for critique of churches and other cultural institutions that reproduce heterosexism" (1991: 1299). Collins makes this point as well: "Puerto Ricans, U.S White men, Asian American gays and lesbians, U.S. White women, and other historically identifiable groups all have distinctive histories that reflect their unique placement in intersecting oppressions" (2000: 227).

See also: **Matrix of Domination**.

Further reading: Collins 2000; Crenshaw 1991; Delgado and Stefancic 2001.

INTERTEXTUALITY

"Intertextuality" was coined by Julia Kristeva in her effort to understand Mikhail Bakhtin's concept of **dialogism** and to reconcile it with **semiotics**. As she explains in *Desire in Language* (1980), "By introducing the *status of the word* as a minimal structural unit, Bakhtin situates the **text** within history and society, which are then seen as **texts** read by the writer, and into which he inserts himself by rewriting them" (65). By this formulation, Kristeva explains, any **text**—including **subjectivity** itself— "is constructed as a mosaic of quotations; any **text** is the absorption and transformation of another." Kristeva therefore posits the "notion of *intertextuality*," which "replaces that of intersubjectivity" (66). The term was subsequently used widely by critical theorists to understand the "**textuality**" that wove together **discourses** from across periods and media. Michael Riffaterre in *Semiotics of Poetry* (1978) and *Fictional Truth* (1990) influentially reworks the concept in making sense of a given work's "subtext," which, he argues, functions like a work's **unconscious**: "This **unconscious** of the **text** is represented by the symbolism of the subtext and by the intertext this symbolism mobilizes" (1990: xvii). A few early theorists of the World Wide Web adopted the concept of intertextuality to make sense of hypertextual links (e.g., Landow 1997); see **Digital Humanities**.

Further reading: G. Allen 2000; Clayton and Rothstein 1991; Landow 1997; Orr 2003; Riffaterre 1978, 1990.

INTROJECTION

According to **psychoanalysis**, introjection is the internalization of authority. According to Sigmund Freud, when you introject the demands of your parents and, thus by extension, society, these demands become a part of your own psyche, which then becomes divided between social demands and your own **repressed**, socially unacceptable **desires** and needs. An endless process of self-policing occurs as the **super-ego** reinforces parental proscriptions long after the parental authority has ceased to make its demands.

INTROVERSION

According to psychoanalysis, introversion is a turn from reality to fantasy. Sigmund Freud borrowed this term from Carl Jung and defined it this way: "introversion denotes the turning away of the **libido** from the possibilities of real satisfaction and the hyper**cathexis** of phantasies which have hitherto been tolerated as innocent" (1953–74: 16.374). For Freud, an example of such introversion is art, since the artist turns away from real satisfaction to the life of fantasy.

JOUISSANCE

Jacques Lacan terms *"jouissance"* the lost plenitude of one's material bodily **drives** given up by the subject in order to enter the **symbolic order** and access the symbolic power of the **phallus**, something that occurs upon the adoption of language and acceptance of the rules of the **Name-of-the-Father**. When Lacan writes that the injunction of the **Super-ego** is "enjoy!" (for example, 1998: 3), he is underscoring the gap or **lack** in our sexual being that follows our entrance into the **symbolic order** of language and law. For this reason, *jouissance* is always in excess of and understood in contradistinction to **desire**, which is created by our entrance into language. **Desire**, according to Lacan, does not wish to be fulfilled, for to get too close to our **object** of desire (what Lacan terms the *objet petit a*) is potentially to see the real bodily *jouissance* that we find traumatic after our entrance into the symbolic order precisely because, by definition, *jouissance* cannot be named and therefore always exceeds language. In this sense, *jouissance* is quite properly "beyond the **pleasure principle**," which is why Julia Kristeva also aligns it with the **abject**.

See also: **Real**.

Further reading: Lacan 1998; Žižek 1994.

KITSCH

Kitsch is the reduction of aesthetic objects or ideas into easily marketable forms. Some theorists of **postmodernism** see the "kitschification" of culture as one symptom of the **postmodern** condition. The term can be as difficult to define as its companion term, **"camp,"** since there are so many disparate examples that can be cited as kitsch. Jean Baudrillard provides us with a useful definition: "The kitsch object is commonly understood as one of that great army of 'trashy' objects, made of plaster of Paris [*stuc*] or some such imitation material: that gallery of cheap junk—accessories, folksy knickknacks, 'souvenirs,' lampshades or fake African masks—which proliferate everywhere, with a preference for holiday resorts and places of leisure" (1998: 109–10). As Baudrillard goes on, "To the **aesthetics** of beauty and originality, kitsch opposes its *aesthetics of simulation*: it everywhere reproduces objects smaller or larger than life; it imitates materials (in plaster, plastic, etc.); it apes forms or combines them discordantly; *it repeats fashion* without having been part of the experience of fashion" (111). The kitsch object has certain common characteristics: (1) it tends to simplify and trivialize complex ideas by reducing them to black-and-white stereotypes; (2) it is oriented to the masses and thus towards a lowest-common denominator so that anyone can relate to it; (3) it is usually tied to mass consumption. As Baudrillard puts it, "This proliferation of kitsch, which is produced by industrial reproduction and the vulgarization at the level of objects of distinctive signs taken from all registers (the bygone, the 'neo,' the exotic, the folksy, the futuristic) and from a disordered excess of 'ready-made' signs, has its basis, like 'mass culture,' in the sociological reality of the consumer society" (1998: 110); (4) kitsch remains, on the whole, completely unselfconscious and without any political or critical edge. When kitsch becomes especially self-conscious it begins to tip over into **camp**.

Further reading: Baudrillard 1998; Călinescu 1987; Eco 2007; Friedlander 1984.

LABOR AND LABOR-POWER

Labor-power is the abstraction of human labor into something that can be exchanged for **money**, according to **Marxism**. The relation of labor-power to the actual labor of a private individual is analogous to the relation of **exchange value** to **use value**. The system of labor-power relies on the belief that the laborer chooses freely to enter into a contractual relationship with an employer, who purchases that worker's labor power as a **commodity** and then owns the goods produced by that worker. However, the worker is exploited insofar as he or she has no other option: the capitalist owns all the **means of production**. Also, the capitalist seeks to achieve the highest possible rate of **surplus value**, which "depends, in the first place, on the degree of exploitation of labour-power" (1867: 747). According to Karl Marx, the capitalist seeks to provide the laborer only enough money to subsist and to produce more laborers (through child-bearing).

See also: **capitalism**.

Further reading: Bottomore *et al.* 1983; Kolakowski 1978; Mandel 1972; Marx 1867; Marx and Engels 1848, 1932.

LACK

See **suture**

LANGUAGE GAME

Ludwig Wittgenstein developed this philosophical concept, arguing that language delimits what can be known and, so, what we know is determined by the rules of language. Our use of language in turn amounts to a series of "language games." Jean-François Lyotard developed the concept in several of his works. As he explains, what Wittgenstein "means by this term is that each of the various categories of utterance can be defined in terms of rules specifying their properties and the uses to which they can be put—in exactly the same way as the game of chess is defined by a set of rules determining the properties of each of the pieces, in other words, the proper way to move them" (1991: 10). All utterance subscribes to such rules, which are always "the object of a contract, explicit or not between players" (10); as a result, "every utterance should be thought of as a 'move' in a game" (10): "to speak is to fight, in the sense of playing, and **speech acts** fall within the domain of a general agonistics" (10). Part of that game is the creative play that seeks to recast rules or rework conventions, however much institutions (be it the army, the university, or the family) might seek to constrain what can be said and how to say it. Lyotard associates **postmodernism** with an explosion of language games that counters any claim to a single, legitimizing **grand narrative** for all possible language games: "That is what the **postmodern** world is all about. Most people have lost the nostalgia for the lost narrative" (41). What saves **postmodern** subjects from barbarity "is their knowledge that legitimation can only spring from their own linguistic practice and communicational interaction" (41). That is, they accept that all strategies are moves in a set of different language games and therefore are unwilling to impose the rules of any one language game (e.g., capitalist contract law or scientific **positivism**) onto all other possible language games.

See also: **dissensus, distribution of the sensible, incommensurability, metapolitics, phrase regimen**.

Further reading: Lyotard 1988a, 1991; Lyotard and Thébaud 1985; Wittgenstein 1958.

LANGUE AND *PAROLE*

Ferdinand de Saussure postulates this influential distinction in his 1916 *Course in General Linguistics*. It is a central element in the science of **semiotics**. *"Langue"* is the system governing the use of language, its rules, grammar, and structure. *"Parole"* refers to the actual use of specific words and phrases in context, with the words tied to specific, contingent referents and situations. Roland Barthes articulates the distinction well in his *Elements of Semiology* (1967), illustrating also the significance of the distinction for the study of culture and society:

> In working out this famous dichotomy, Saussure started from the "multiform and heterogeneous" nature of language, which appears at first sight as an unclassifiable reality the unity of which cannot be brought to light, since it partakes at the same time of the physical, the physiological, the mental, the individual and the social. Now this disorder disappears if, from this heterogeneous whole, is extracted a purely social object, the systematized set of conventions necessary to communication, indifferent to the *material* of the signals which compose it, and which is a *language (langue)*; as opposed to which *speech (parole)* covers the purely individual part of language (phonation, application of the rules and contingent combinations of signs). (13)

The distinction between *langue* and *parole* has contributed to a general linguistic turn in critical theory that Saussure's **semiotics** inspired.

See also: **signifier and signified, state of exception, structuralism, poststructuralism**.

Further reading: Barthes 1967; Saussure 1916; K. Silverman 1983.

LATE CAPITALISM

The term "late capitalism" originated with Werner Sombart (1863–1941), who, with Max Weber (1864–1920), was a member of the *Verein für Socialpolitik* (Social Policy Association) founded in 1873. It was later adopted and popularized by the **Frankfurt School** and refers to the form of capitalism that came to the fore in the modernist period and now dominates our own postmodern culture (see **postmodernism**).

This term tends to be preferred by critical theorists over "post-industrial society," a term used by Alain Touraine in *Post-Industrial Society* (1971) and Daniel Bell in *The Coming of Post-Industrial Society* (1974) to describe this same period. Bell's influential use of that term resembles critical theory's use of late capitalism. According to Bell, post-industrial society indicates the ways that our society has changed from a predominantly industrial society (factories, manufacturing, skilled labor for precision production and craft) to one oriented towards services (sales), as well as professional, managerial, and technical employment, supported by the increasing importance of both higher education and the communication network (cable, broadband, ISDN, the Internet) as well as **globalization**.

Although Bell does engage Karl Marx's work and has influenced thinkers on the Left, the term "late capitalism" is yet more closely aligned with post-**Marxist** thought. According to Jameson, the term first gains traction among theorists of the **Frankfurt School**, who "stressed two essential features: (1) a tendential web of bureaucratic control ... , and (2) the interpenetration of government and big business ('state capitalism') such that Nazism and the New Deal are related systems" (1991: xviii). Jameson argues that the term "late capitalism" now has "very different overtones from these" (xviii); indeed, Jameson dates the emergence of "late capitalism" in the 1950s, so that late capitalism for Jameson is ultimately coincident with and even synonymous with **postmodernism**: "the economic pre-paration of **postmodernism** or late capitalism began in the 1950s, after the wartime shortages of consumer goods and spare parts had been made up, and new products and new technologies (not least those of the media) could be pioneered" (xx). In turn, the psychic break that made possible the cultural (rather than merely economic) emergence of late-capitalist sensibilities occurred, according to Jameson, in the 1960s. Finally, the 1970s allowed the economic and the cultural side of **postmodern** late capitalism to come together: the economic system and the cultural "structure of feeling" "somehow crystallized in the great shock of the crises of 1971 (the oil crisis, the end of the international gold standard, for all intents and purposes the end of the great wave of 'wars of national liberation' and the beginning of the end of traditional communism)" (xx–xxi). In general, Jameson understands "late capitalism" as the pervasive condition of our own age, a condition that speaks both to economic and cultural structures: "What 'late' generally conveys is ... the sense that something has changed, that things are different, that we have gone through a transformation of the life world which is somehow decisive but incomparable with the older convulsions of modernization and industrialization, less perceptible and dramatic, somehow, but more permanent precisely because more thoroughgoing and all-pervasive" (1991: xxi).

According to Jameson, the new elements that **postmodernism** adds to the **Frankfurt School**'s version of late capitalism include:

(1) "[N]ew forms of business organization (multinationals, transnationals) beyond the monopoly stage" (1991: xviii–xix). Lenin's concept of the "monopoly stage" of capitalism now expands out beyond any national border and we see instead an internationalization of business beyond the older imperial model. In the new order of **capital**, multinational corporations are not tied to any one country but represent a form of power and influence greater than any one nation. That internationalization also applies to the **division of labor**, making possible the continued exploitation of workers from poor countries in support of multinational capital. Jameson refers to "the flight of production to advanced Third World areas, along with all the more familiar social consequences, including the crisis of traditional labor, the emergence of yuppies, and gentrification on a now-global scale" (1991: xix).

(2) "[A] vertiginous new dynamic in international banking and the stock exchanges (including the enormous Second and Third World debt)" (1991: xix). Through such a banking structure, the First World's multinational corporations maintain their control over the world market.

(3) "[N]ew forms of media interrelationship" (1991: xix). The media constitutes one of the more influential new products of late capitalism (print, Internet, television, film) and a new means for the capitalist take-over of our lives. Through the mediatization of culture, we become increasingly reliant on the media's version of our reality, a version of reality that is filled predominantly with capitalist values.

(4) "[C]omputers and automation" (1991: xix). Advances in computer automation have allowed for an unprecedented level of mass production, leading to ever greater profit-margins for multinational corporations.

(5) Planned obsolescence. As Jameson puts it, "the frantic economic urgency of producing fresh waves of ever more novel-seeming goods (from clothing to airplanes), at ever greater rates of turnover, now assigns an increasingly essential structural function and position to aesthetic innovation and experimentation" (1991: 5).

(6) American military domination. As Jameson writes in *Postmodernism*, "this whole global, yet American, **postmodern** culture is the internal and superstructural expression of a whole new wave of American military and economic domination throughout the world: in this sense, as throughout class history, the underside of culture is blood, torture, death, and terror" (1991: 5).

Some synonyms for "late capitalism" include "'multinational capitalism,' 'spectacle or image society,' 'media capitalism,' 'the world system,' even 'postmodernism' itself" (1991: xviii). Jameson, however, rejects the synonym "postindustrial society" because that term suggests that what we are seeing is a radical break from the forms of **capital** that existed in the nineteenth century (and thus, by implication, a break from Marx's understanding of **capital**). Jameson is more interested in perceiving a continuity from earlier forms of industrial society (even as he acknowledges the differences) and in affirming the continuing relevance of Marx's theories.

The concept of late capitalism or multinational capitalism is particularly important for **Global Studies**, which tries to make sense of this new **postmodern**, information society. As Michael Hardt and Antonio Negri argue in *Empire* (2000), what we are seeing today is "the decline of **nation-states** as boundaries that mark and organize the divisions in global rule. The establishment of a global society of control that smooths over the striae of national boundaries goes hand in hand with the realization of the world market and the real subsumption of global society under **capital**" (332). See **empire**.

*See also: **comprador***.

Further reading: Bell 1974; Hardt and Negri 2000; Jameson 1991; Kumar 1978; Mandel 1978; Touraine 1971.

LATENCY PERIOD

The latency period is the period of reduced sexuality that Sigmund Freud believed occurs between approximately age seven and adolescence. Freud claimed that children went through a "latency period" during which "we can observe a halt and retrogression in sexual development" (1953–74: 16.326). During this time, the child also begins the process of what Freud terms "infantile amnesia": the **repression** and estrangement of those earliest childhood memories that we find traumatic, evil and/or overly sexual. Freud warns, however, that "The latency period may ... be absent: it need not bring with it any interruption of sexual activity and sexual interests." (1953–74: 16.326)

See also: **psychosexual development**.

LATENT DREAM THOUGHTS

See **repression**

LGBTQ: LESBIAN, GAY, BISEXUAL, TRANSGENDER, AND QUEER OR QUESTIONING STUDIES

LGBTQ stands for lesbian, gay, bisexual, transgender, and queer or questioning, though the acronym is often found in a different order or with additional or fewer letters depending on the constitution of the group advocating for the rights of people with sexual orientations other than heterosexual (e.g., GLBT, LGBTQQ, etc.). LGBTQ is used by advocacy and support groups outside the academic community; "LGBTQ Studies" refers more specifically to the academic study of non-hetero sexuality and is sometimes referred to as "queer studies" or "sexual diversity studies."

Queer Studies or LGBTQ Studies has grown out of **queer theory**, and is sometimes difficult to distinguish from that earlier group of largely **poststructuralist** critics. Certainly the precepts of LGBTQ Studies are still influenced by and continue to develop the earlier theories of Adrienne Rich (see **compulsory heterosexuality**), Judith Butler (see **gender and sex**, **performativity**), Eve Sedgwick (see **epistemology of the closet**, **homosocial desire**), and Michel Foucault (see **bio-power**, **gender and sexuality**, **repressive hypothesis**). LGBTQ Studies could be said perhaps to coincide yet more directly with non-academic groups fighting for the recognition and equality of people of various sexualities; indeed, many university programs in LGBT or LGBTQ Studies include a service or advocacy component. LGBTQ Studies has also developed across a wide variety of disciplines (biology, sociology, sexology, the history of science, etc.), whereas **queer theory** has been most closely tied to literary theory and philosophy.

Further reading: Hall and Jagose 2013.

LIBIDO (LIBIDINAL)

The libido is our sexual **drive**, according to the **psychoanalysis** of Sigmund Freud. Freud believed that the sexual **drive** is as natural and insistent as hunger and that the libido manifests its influence as early as birth; however, our entrance into society and into what Jacques Lacan terms the **symbolic order** has led to the manifold **repression** of this bodily **drive**.

LIFEWORLD

This term is closely connected to Jürgen Habermas's theory of **communicative action**, although it has its roots in the **phenomenology** of Edmund Husserl (1859–1938). Husserl defines it in this way:

> In whatever way we may be conscious of the world as universal horizon, as coherent universe of existing objects, we, each "I-the-man" and all of us together, belong to the world as living with one another in the world; and the world is our world, valid for our consciousness as existing precisely through this "living together." We, as living in wakeful world-consciousness, are constantly active on the basis of our passive having of the world. (1936: 108)

For Habermas, "The structures of the lifeworld lay down the forms of the intersubjectivity of possible understanding. ... The lifeworld is, so to speak, the transcendental site where speaker and hearer meet, where they can reciprocally raise claims that their utterances fit the world (objective, social, or subjective), and where they can criticize and confirm those validity claims, settle their disagreements, and arrive at agreements" (1987: 2.126). Habermas thus sets his theory against the tendency of most critical theory to question any claim to universality or transcendentalism and to insist upon **incommensurability** between **subject** positions (see, for example, **differend** and **dissensus**). Habermas's lifeworld, by contrast, is a "transcendental site" insofar as it allows us to transcend all factional self-interest in the space of reasoned debate. Habermas is still committed to a neo-**Marxist** critique of modernity, in the tradition of Max Horkheimer's definition of critical theory (see **Introduction**), and, so, he still argues from within the precepts (and suspicions) of critical theory (indeed, he is associated with the **Frankfurt School** and studied under Horkheimer and Theodor Adorno); he just feels that such critique cannot be effective without a notion of a shared **lifeworld** and without the necessary presupposition that **communicative action** can occur successfully.

See also: **communicative reason, discourse ethics, public sphere**.

LIMINAL AND LIMINALITY

Liminal is derived from the Latin for threshold; critical theorists tend to be particularly interested in such threshold spaces, in-between spaces where one culture or language system intersects a completely different system. Unlike the notion of **incommensurability**, the liminal tends to mark instances where two sign systems intermingle, as in the similar concept of **hybridity**. Both liminality and **hybridity** are important concepts in the **postcolonial theory** of Homi Bhabha, who explores the messy intersections of colonial and native cultures or the intersection of different racial identities. As he explains,

> The representation of difference must not be hastily read as the reflection of *pre-given* ethnic or cultural traits set in the fixed tablet of tradition. The social articulation of difference, from the minority perspective, is a complex, on-going negotiation that seeks to authorize cultural **hybridities** that emerge in moments of historical transformation. (Bhabha 1994: 2)

Bhabha gives as an example the use of the stairwell and other architectural in-between spaces in the work of African-American artist, Renée Green: "The stairwell as liminal space, in-between the designations of identity, becomes the process of symbolic interaction, the connective tissue that constructs the difference between upper and lower, black and white" (Bhabha 1994: 4). According to Bhabha, such an "interstitial passage between fixed identifications opens up the possibility of a cultural **hybridity** that entertains difference without an assumed or imposed hierarchy" (4). A similar concept is explored in the work of **Critical Race Theory**, as in the concepts of **contact zone and transculturation** and **mimicry**.

Further reading: Bhabha 1994.

LITERARITY

This is a term coined by Jacque Rancière to support his notion that politics and **aesthetics** should be aligned since they follow the same principles: they are both concerned with determining what will be accepted as part of a communal way of speaking, doing, and making. Following the logic of what he terms "the aesthetic regime of the arts" (see **aesthetics**), Rancière is interested in breaking down distinctions between "high" and "low" or between fiction and history. As he writes, regarding "the relationship between literarity and historicity,"

> Political statements and literary locutions produce effects in reality. They define models of speech or action but also regimes of sensible intensity. They draft maps of the visible, trajectories between the visible and the sayable, relationships between modes of being, modes of saying, and modes of doing and making. They define variations of sensible intensities, perceptions, and the abilities of bodies. They thereby take hold of unspecified groups of people, they widen gaps, open up space for deviations, modify the speeds, the trajectories, and the ways in which groups of people adhere to a condition, react to situations, recognize their images. They reconfigure the map of the sensible by interfering with the functionality of gestures and rhythms adapted to the natural cycles of production, reproduction, and submission. Man is a political animal because he is a literary animal who lets himself be diverted from his "natural" purpose by the power of words. (2004: 39)

Rather than politicize art, Rancière argues that it is rather **aesthetics** that provides us with the most viable model for political change. Indeed, he sees in the "literarity that overflows the institution of literature" (2004: 39) a mechanism for constructing new political subjectivities that challenge the status quo.

LOCUTIONARY ACT

See **speech act and Speech–Act Theory**

LOGOCENTRISM

Jacques Derrida popularized the term "logocentrism," which refers to the desire for a transcendental **signifier** that can ground a metaphysics of presence. Derrida throughout his work questions the tendency of philosophy to "withdraw meaning, truth, presence, being, etc., from the movement of signification" (1976: 14). He argues that this maneuver is grounded in a theological metaphor whereby one imagines "a natural, eternal, and universal writing, the system of signified truth, which is recognized in its dignity," against which one contrasts "a certain fallen writing," a "finite and artificial inscription" (15). The maneuver, even when merely metaphorical, is ultimately part of a long theological tradition that privileges the word of God (*logos*) over actual writing: "The sign and divinity have the same place and time of birth," Derrida, for example, writes: "The age of the sign is essentially theological" (14). Such logocentrism is closely linked to **phonocentrism** since this metaphor of "natural writing," as opposed to the dead letter, tends to be "immediately united to the voice and to breath" (17). It also tends to ground a sense of stable, essential subjectivity: "the good and natural is the divine inscription in the heart and the soul; the perverse and artful is technique, exiled in the exteriority of the body" (17).

Derrida instead tends to see the relation between **signifier and signified** as problematic. He questions the desire to imagine a "**transcendental signified**" that absolutely links a signifier to a specific, unwavering meaning. Derrida concerns himself instead with the play of signification, which necessarily entails both the differences between words in the general structure of language and the need to defer meaning in the act of reading or hearing: "One could call *play* the absence of the transcendental signified as limitlessness of play, that is to say as the destruction of ontotheology and the metaphysics of presence" (50).

MANIFEST DREAM

See **repression**

MARGIN, MARGINAL, AND MARGINALIZATION

Critical theorists are often concerned with the ways **dominant**, **hegemonic** society excludes or marginalizes (sends to the margins) groups that do not conform to defined norms. That marginalization can be literally spatial, as it is in the colonial occupation of foreign lands explored by **Postcolonial Studies**, but more often we are talking about a metaphorical exclusion from what is characterized as a center of power. So, **feminists** examine how women are excluded from cultural, political, social, and economic equality with men, relegated instead to the marginal space of the private home; **LGBTQ** theorists examine how individuals who do not conform to heterosexual identity are discriminated against and defined as outside the norm, abnormal; **Critical Race Theory**, disability studies, and **Marxists** examine the various ways that racial minorities, the disabled, and the **proletariat**, respectively, are excluded from power. The goal in each case is to change society by addressing these forms of marginalization and fighting for the rights of the oppressed.

The critique of such marginalization is often aided by the **deconstruction** of **binary oppositions**, especially when one side of a binary is privileged over an excluded **Other**, e.g., male/female, heterosexual/homosexual, white/black. As in **deconstruction**, following Jacques Derrida's methodology of *différance*, one goal of such critique is to question society's very desire for norms and society's concomitant need to exclude those identities which in their difference serve, in fact, to define and stabilize the norm. Such work is influenced also by Michel Foucault's theorization of **power** and his **archaeological** methodology more generally. As **postcolonial** theorist Homi Bhabha explains,

> a range of contemporary critical theories suggest that it is from those who have suffered the sentence of history—subjugation, domination, diaspora, displacement—that we learn our most enduring lessons for living and thinking. There is even a growing conviction that the affective experience of social marginality—as it emerges in non-canonical cultural forms—transforms our critical strategies. It forces us to confront the concept of culture outside of *objets d'art* or beyond the canonization of the "idea" of **aesthetics**, to engage with culture as an uneven, incomplete production of meaning and value, often composed of **incommensurable** demands and practices, produced in the act of social survival. (Bhabha 1994: 172)

Indeed, a number of critical theorists have sought to propose alternative models for politics, signification, and identity that escape the center/margin opposition, including Alain Badiou's and Jacques Rancière's notions of **metapolitics**, Ernesto Laclau and Chantal Mouffe's understanding of **antagonism** and **radical democracy**, Jean-François Lyotard's notion of the **sublime,** and Homi Bhabha's own understanding of **liminality** and **hybridity**.

See also: **contact zone and transculturation, distribution of the sensible, mimicry**.

MARXISM

Marxism, a school of thought that concerns itself with **class** relations and the development of **capitalism**, responds to and develops the ideas in the nineteenth-century writings of Karl Marx (1818–83) and Friedrich Engels (1820–95). Marxism is complicated by the fact that Marx is by no means the only influence on this critical school; indeed, given the various sorts of political movements that have been inspired by this thinker (socialism, Trotskyism, communism, Leninism, Stalinism, Maoism, **radical democracy**, etc.), one despairs at trying to provide a fair and lucid overview. Add to that the fact that Marx himself changed his mind on various issues or sometimes expressed opinions that appear mutually exclusive, and one is faced with a rather high hurdle. Nonetheless, there are a number of Marxist thoughts and thinkers that have been especially influential on recent scholarly developments (particularly in literary, cultural, and political studies). The major distinction in Marxist thought that influences literary and cultural theory is that between traditional Marxists (sometimes, unfairly, called vulgar Marxists) and what are sometimes referred to as post-Marxists or neo-Marxists. What impels the shift from one to the other is the fact that Marx's predictions regarding the unification of the **proletariat** and worldwide revolution did not occur. As Ernesto Laclau and Chantal Mouffe explain, through this "crisis of Marxism, which served as the background to all Marxist debates from the turn of the century until the war," Marxism "finally lost its innocence" (1985: 18). The result was a growing theoretical complexity in thinking about the social. Laclau and Mouffe argue that the crisis "seems to have been dominated by two basic moments: the new awareness of the opacity of the social, of the complexities and resistances of an increasingly organized **capitalism**; and the fragmentation of the different positions of social **agents** which, according to the classical paradigm, should have been united" (18). Central Marxist concepts such as **hegemony**, **ideology**, and **dialectics** were completely rethought during this time period as a result. An important transitional school for Marxism is the **Frankfurt School**, so called because of the Institute for Social Research at the University of Frankfurt am Main. The school is associated with such influential thinkers as Max Horkheimer, Theodor Adorno, Herbert Marcuse, Walter Benjamin, and Jürgen Habermas, which is not to say that all these critical theorists were formally members of the Institute for Social Research.

Perhaps the most significant distinction that can be identified between traditional Marxism and neo- or post-Marxism is the understanding of **ideology**. Traditional Marxists tend to believe that it is possible to get past **ideology** to some essential truth (e.g., the stages of economic development). Post-Marxists, especially after Louis Althusser, tend to think of **ideology** in a way more akin to Jacques Lacan's **psychoanalysis**, as something that is so much a part of our culture and mental make-up that it actively determines what we commonly refer to as "reality." According to these post-Marxist critics, there may well be some hard kernel behind our obfuscating perceptions of reality but that kernel is by definition resistant to articulation. As soon as one attempts to articulate it, one is at risk of falling back into **ideology**. This understanding of **ideology** is what Fredric Jameson famously terms in the book of the same name (1972), the "prison-house of language," though in fact Jameson himself does not claim that it is easy to get from **ideology** to the real conditions of a society. Like Althusser, Jameson understands **history**, rather, as something that "can be apprehended only through its effects, and never directly as some reified force" (1981: 102).

Post-Marxists have also been forced to rethink Marx's analysis of nineteenth-century **capitalism** in light of the developments of the modern and **postmodern** periods, particularly the shift of the world's largest economies from industry and manufacturing to service, communication (including entertainment), and information. See **late capitalism** and **postmodernism**.

See also: **alienation, base and superstructure, commodity, commodity fetishism, cultural capital, division of labor, equivalent form, feudal society, field, ISAs, labor, means of production, mode of production, money, praxis, proletariat, relations of production, surplus value, tribal society, use value and exchange value, usury**.

Further reading: Bottomore *et al.* 1983; Eagleton 1991; Jameson 1971, 1981, 1991; Kolakowski 1978; Marx 1867; Marx and Engels, 1848, 1932; Nelson and Grossberg 1988; Williams 1958, 1977.

MATRIX OF DOMINATION

This is a term used in **Critical Race Theory** and Black **Feminism** to address the multiple structures that work to **marginalize**, oppress, or exploit identity groups. The concept seeks to address the structural mechanisms that contribute to the **marginalization** also of **intersectional** identities that bring together two or more identities, e.g., black women or queer black men. According to Patricia Hill Collins,

Intersectional paradigms remind us that oppression cannot be reduced to one fundamental type, and that oppressions work together in producing injustice. In contrast, the Matrix of Domination refers to how these intersecting oppressions are actually organized. Regardless of the particular intersections involved, structural, disciplinary, **hegemonic**, and interpersonal domains of **power** reappear across quite different forms of oppression. (2000: 18)

Any Matrix of Domination will change over time, opening up the possibility of successful political action, and it will differ from nation to nation, even locality to locality. A Matrix of Domination also works differently at different levels of experience. As Collins explains,

any particular matrix of domination is organized via four interrelated domains of **power**, namely the structural, disciplinary, **hegemonic**, and interpersonal domains. Each domain serves a particular purpose. The structural domain organizes oppression, whereas the disciplinary domain manages it. The **hegemonic** domain justifies oppression, and the interpersonal domain influences everyday lived experience and the individual consciousness that ensues. (276)

To clarify, the structural domain of power "encompasses how social institutions are organized to reproduce Black women's subordination over time" (277), including "the U.S. legal system, labor markets, schools, the housing industry, banking, insurance, the news media, and other social institutions" (272). In using the term "disciplinary domain," Collins is invoking Michel Foucault's sense of the term, **discipline**, and also **power**: "As a way of ruling that relies on bureaucratic hierarchies and techniques of surveillance, the disciplinary domain manages **power** relations" (280). Whereas "The structural and disciplinary domains of **power** operate through systemwide social policies managed primarily by bureaucracies," the **hegemonic** domain of **power**, by contrast, "aims to justify practices in these domains of **power**" and, so, "deals with **ideology**, **culture**, and consciousness" (284). Finally, the interpersonal domain of **power** addresses the everyday actions of individual people: "Whereas the structural domain of **power** organizes the macro-level of social organization with the disciplinary domain managing its operations, the interpersonal domain functions through routinized, day-to-day practices of how people treat one another. ... Such practices are systematic, recurrent, and so familiar that they often go unnoticed" (287).

See also: **whiteness as property**.

MEANS OF PRODUCTION

In Marxist theory, the means of production are the tools and raw material used to create a product. According to Karl Marx, what happens in **capitalism** is that the bourgeoisie gains control of all the means of production, making it necessary for the **proletariat** to sell their **labor** rather than the products of their hands, as was the case in **feudal** society.

See also: **base and superstructure, mode of production, relations of production, surplus value**.

Further reading: Marx 1867; Marx and Engels 1932.

MEDIATORS AND INTERMEDIARIES

The distinction between these terms is an important one for **Actor-Network Theory** (ANT). Bruno Latour defines an "intermediary" as "what transports meaning or force without transformation: defining its inputs is enough to define its outputs" (2005: 39). He argues that traditional sociology understands cause and effect in this way, which is to say unproblematically. With mediators, by contrast, "[t]heir input is never a good predictor of their output; the specificity has to be taken into account every time. Mediators transform, translate, distort, and modify the meaning or the elements they are supposed to carry" (39). A mediation is "an occurrence that is neither altogether a cause nor altogether a consequence, neither completely a means nor completely an end" (Latour 1999: 153). The example Latour gives in *Pandora's Hope* (1999) is that of a human holding and firing a gun. If we read the human holding the gun as an "intermediary," we see the gun as a "Neutral Tool under complete human control" (178); if, however, we read the human and the gun as mediators, we can begin to explore the full complexity of their interrelation: "If I define you by what you have (the gun), and by the series of associations that you enter into when you use what you have (when you fire the gun), then you are modified by the gun" (179). As Latour continues, the complexity of this interrelation affects both the **subject** and the **object**:

> This translation is wholly symmetrical. You are different with a gun in your hand; the gun is different with you holding it. You are another **subject** because you hold the gun; the gun is another **object** because it has entered into a relationship with you. (179)

Rather than "start with essences, those of **subjects** and those of **objects**," ANT theorists explore the ways "that neither **subject** nor **object** (nor their goals) are fixed" (Latour 1999: 180). ANT therefore tries always to multiply mediators, never taking for granted the forces causing an action to be performed by a social actor.

See also: **blackboxing, quasi-objects and quasi-subjects, things and Thing Theory**.

METADIEGETIC

See **diegesis**

METAPHORIC AND METONYMIC POLES

This is a distinction made by the Russian Formalist Roman Jakobson in his 1956 work, *Fundamentals of Language*, which was written with Morris Halle. Jakobson examines various kinds of aphasia (the loss of ability to understand or express speech, caused by brain damage) and concludes that all kinds of aphasia oscillate between two polar types. The impairment affects either "the faculty for selection and substitution or for combination and contexture" (76). The former affects the ability to see relations of similarity, as in the ability to create metaphors (substituting one thing for another similar thing as one does in figurative language, e.g., "he is the black sheep of the family"); the latter affects the ability to see relations of contiguity, as in metonymy (where one replaces a thing with something that is connected to it in space or time, e.g., "the pen is mightier than the sword" instead of "written words are mightier than military action"). Jakobson extrapolates from this observation to argue that individuals tend towards one or the other pole: "In normal verbal behavior both processes are continually operative, but careful observation will reveal that under the influence of a cultural pattern, personality, and verbal style, preference is given to one of the two processes over the other" (76). He then makes the same argument about literature (Romanticism and symbolism tend to the metaphoric pole, realism to the metonymic pole), about art (the "metonymical orientation of cubism" as opposed to the "patently metaphorical attitude" of the surrealist painters [78]); and, indeed, about "human behavior in general" (79). At the same time, he makes clear that, except in the example of people suffering from aphasia, the metaphoric and the metonymic poles normally work simultaneously, even if one is more dominant. As he explains about poetry, for example: "In poetry, where similarity is superinduced upon contiguity, any metonymy is slightly metaphoric and any metaphor has a metonymic tint" (1960: 370). The distinction between the metaphoric and metonymic poles has had an important influence on **semiotics** (with the metaphoric pole functioning in **paradigmatic** fashion, the metonymic pole in **syntagmatic** fashion) and also on **narratology**. See, for example, the work of Peter Brooks and Michael Riffaterre.

Further reading: P. Brooks 1985; Jakobson 1960; Jakobson and Halle 1956; Riffaterre 1978, 1990.

METAPOLITICS (METAPOLITICAL)

This is a term that has been popularized by both Jacques Rancière and Alain Badiou. Both philosophers seek in their concept of metapolitics to oppose parliamentary democracy, which they see as working against the demands of "truth." As Rancière for example writes,

> As far as justice goes, democracy only offers the theatrics of dispute. Offering a justice bogged down in the various forms of dispute and an equality flattened by the arithmetical counts of inequality, democracy is incapable of giving politics its true measure. (1999: 62)

Badiou is equally dismissive of democracy. As he writes, "It's certainly true that voting has little to do with truth. If our knowledge of planetary motion relied solely on suffrage as its protocol of legitimation, we would still inhabit a geocentric universe" (2005c: 15).

Rancière argues that metapolitics is opposed to two other ways of thinking politics: archipolitics and parapolitics. Archipolitics, exemplified by Plato's Republic, seeks to eliminate all discord ("mere factions, governments of discord" [Rancière 1999: 64]) by claiming that each person in a community is fulfilling his or her necessary function: "The activities of individual citizens are regulated in relation to their role in the organization of the communal body in such a way that everyone has a designated place and an assigned role. The democratic configuration of politics is thereby replaced by the police order of a living *nomos* that saturates the entire community and precludes any breaks in the social edifice" (Rancière 2004: 83). Parapolitics, exemplified by Aristotle's writings, instead locates politics in the "conflict over the occupation of 'offices,' the *arkhaï* of the city." Aristotle posits a center that "is the institutional apparatus of the *arkhaï* and the relationship of mastery played out in it, what the moderns will call power and for which Aristotle has no noun, only an adjective—*kurion*, the dominant element, the one who, by exercising dominion over others, gives the community its dominant characteristic, its own style" (Rancière 1999: 72). Artistotle thus comes closer to the system of parliamentary representation but the effect is, in fact, to integrate "the egalitarian anarchy of the dēmos into the constitutional order of the police" (Rancière 2004: 88); any apparent freedom in the system is really undercut by ensuring that power in fact always resides with the small percentage of people in control of the *arkhaï* of the city and, by extension, the police system of control. As Rancière writes, "This mimetic transformation of the dēmos into one of the parties of political litigation, as natural as it may seem to modern theories of sovereignty and the para-political tradition of social contract theory, masks the fact that the equality of the dēmos can never be adequately accounted for within the police order" (88). Metapolitics, as opposed to both archipolitics and parapolitics, seeks always to declare "a radical surplus of injustice or inequality in relation to what politics puts forward as justice or equality" (1999: 81). For Rancière, "The truth of politics is the manifestation of its falseness. It is the gap between any political process of naming or inscribing in relation to the realities subtending them" (82). Metapolitics, then, amounts to never-ending **ideological** critique on behalf of those who have no part in a given political system, and an effort to make these unrepresented individuals again visible within the **distribution of the sensible**: "Wherever the part of those who have no part is inscribed, however fragile and fleeting these inscriptions may be, a sphere of appearance of the demos is created, an element of the *kratos*, the power of the people, exists. The problem is to extend the sphere of this materialization, to maximize this power" (88).

Badiou's notion of metapolitics is similar, though he takes pains also to distinguish his notion from Rancière's. Indeed, he states, rather disingenuously, "I recognize myself in important parts of Rancière's work. And all the more so since I have the literally justifiable feeling of having largely anticipated, along with a few others, these parts" (2005c: 116). For Badiou, the essence of politics "is the prescription of a possibility in rupture with what exists" (24). Justice serves as one of his goals but always a notion of justice that resists objectification into "what exists": "The trouble with most doctrines of justice is their will to define what it is, followed by attempts to realise it. But justice, which is the philosophical name for the egalitarian political maxim, cannot be defined" (99). The problem, according to Badiou, is that

"Every definitional and programmatic approach to justice makes it into a dimension of State action" (100). Justice, when defined by the State, quickly turns "into its opposite: justice becomes a matter of harmonizing the interplay of conflicting interests. But justice, which is the theoretical name for an axiom of equality, necessarily refers to a wholly disinterested subjectivity" (100). Justice therefore can never be a "category of statist and social order" but rather "the name for those principles at work in rupture and disorder" (100). To seek for true equality "is to undo bonds, to desocialise thought, to affirm the rights of the infinite and the immortal against the calculation of interests" (104). For a true political **event** to occur (see **being and event** for Badiou's understanding of this term), one must first contest the notion that a State's power is "measureless, errant, unassignable. The political **event** puts an end to all this by assigning a visible measure to the excessive power of the State" (145). In the moment of action that constitutes the true political **event**, one must also act on behalf of all, without self-interest (thus affirming "the rights of the infinite and the immortal against the calculation of interests"): "Only politics is intrinsically required to declare that the thought that it is is the thought of all. This declaration is its constitutive prerequisite" (142). A properly political thought, in Badiou's sense of the term, "is topologically collective, meaning that it cannot exist otherwise than as the thought of all" (142).

Badiou argues that his position is different than Rancière's because of his emphasis that true politics exists in the moment of acting upon universal truths in the present. He therefore mentions his own involvement in an actual political group, Organisation Politique, at the time of writing *Abrégé de métapolitique* in 1998. As he writes, "the point from which a politics can be thought—which permits, even after the event, the seizure of its truth—is that of its actors, and not its spectators. It is through Saint-Just and Robespierre that you enter into this singular truth unleashed by the French Revolution, and on the basis of which you form a knowledge, and not through Kant or François Furet" (2005c: 23). According to Badiou, Rancière's work stops at **ideological** critique; Rancière does not "draw conclusions as to the possibility of politics, here and now" (111). In reading Rancière's work, according to Badiou, "You will come to know what politics must not be, you will even know what it will have been and no longer is, but never what it is within the **Real**, and still less what one must do in order for it to exist" (111). Badiou counters by arguing that "The central subjective figure of politics is the political militant, a figure totally absent from Rancière's system" (122).

See also: **antagonism**, **dissensus**, **radical democracy**.

METONYMIC POLE

See **metaphoric and metonymic poles**

MICROAGGRESSION

See **Critical Race Theory**

MIMICRY

This term is used in postcolonial studies to make sense of those instances where the colonized **Other** mimics elements of dominant, colonial identity. According to Homi Bhabha, such mimicry at once mirrors elements of colonial authority and also threatens that authority because it is always adopted with a difference: "colonial mimicry is the desire for a reformed, recognizable **Other**, *as a subject of a difference that is almost the same, but not quite*. Which is to say, that the **discourse** of mimicry is constructed around an *ambivalence*" (1994: 86). Mimicry, then, is "the sign of a double articulation" (86). It can be a way for colonial authority to appropriate the **Other** as an agent of its control and surveillance, as in the **comprador**; however, because it still betrays "a difference that is almost the same," mimicry is also "the sign of the inappropriate … , a difference or recalcitrance which … poses an immanent threat to both 'normalized' knowledges and disciplinary powers" (86). Bhabha's examples therefore occupy an "area between mimicry and mockery, where the reforming, civilizing mission is threatened by the displacing **gaze** of its disciplinary double" (86).

See also: **hybridity, contact zone and transculturation, liminality, parody**.

MIRROR STAGE

According to Jacques Lacan, the "mirror stage" refers to the moment in a child's **psychosexual development** (around 6 to 18 months of age) when he or she identifies with his or her own image (what Lacan terms the "Ideal-I" or "**ideal ego**"). For Lacan, this act marks the primordial recognition of one's self as "I," although at a point "before it is objectified in the dialectic of identification with the **other**, and before language restores to it, in the universal, its function as **subject**" (1977: 2). In other words, this recognition of the self's image precedes the entrance into language, after which the **subject** can understand the place of that image of the self within a larger social order. The mirror stage is necessary for the next stage, since to recognize yourself as "I" is like recognizing yourself as **other** ("yes, that person over there is me"); this act is thus fundamentally self-alienating. Indeed, for this reason your feelings towards the image were mixed, caught between hatred ("I hate that version of myself *because* it is so much better than me") and love ("I want to be like that image"). In this way, Lacan's mirror stage corresponds very loosely to Freud's **anal-sadistic phase** (which Freud associated with the ages 2–4). In the **anal-sadistic phase**, the child is similarly caught between passive and active impulses, between sadism and masochism, between exhibitionism and voyeurism. Lacan's "Ideal-I" is important precisely because it represents to the subject a simplified, bounded form of the self, as opposed to the turbulent chaotic perceptions, feelings, and needs felt by the infant. This "primordial Discord" (Lacan 1977: 4) is particularly formative for the **subject**, that is, the discord between, on the one hand, the idealizing image in the mirror and, on the other hand, the reality of one's body between 6 and 18 months ("the signs of uneasiness and motor unco-ordination of the neo-natal months" [Lacan 1977: 4]): "The *mirror stage* is a drama whose internal thrust is precipitated from insufficiency to anticipation—and which manufactures for the **subject**, caught up in the lure of spatial identification, the succession of phantasies that extends from a fragmented body-image to a form of its totality that I shall call orthopaedic—and, lastly, to the assumption of the armour of an alienating identity, which will mark with its rigid structure the **subject**'s entire mental development" (4). According to Lacan, this misrecognition or *méconnaissance* (seeing an **ideal-ego** where there is a fragmented, chaotic body) subsequently "characterizes the **ego** in all its structures" (6). In particular, this creation of an ideal version of the self gives pre-verbal impetus to the creation of **narcissistic** phantasies in the fully developed **subject**. It establishes what Lacan terms the "**imaginary order**" and, through the **imaginary**, continues to assert its influence on the subject even after the subject enters the next stage of **psychosexual development**, the **symbolic order**.

MODE OF PRODUCTION

"Mode of production" refers to everything that goes into the production of the necessities of life, including the "productive forces" (**labor**, instruments, and raw material) and the "**relations of production**" (the social structures that regulate the relation between humans in the production of goods). According to Karl Marx and Friedrich Engels, for individuals, the mode of production is "a definite form of expressing their life, a definite *mode of life* on their part. As individuals express their life, so they are. What they are, therefore, coincides with their production, both with *what* they produce and *how* they produce" (1932: 42). The mode of production therefore affects all aspects of mental and social life: "The mode of production of material life conditions the social, political and intellectual life process in general" (Marx and Engels 1962: 1.363).

See also: **base and superstructure**.

MONEY OR THE MONEY-FORM

The money-form is the **commodity** chosen to function as the **universal equivalent** for all other **commodities**. The actual form of money is a "matter of accident," Karl Marx explains; in the development of society, "The money-form comes to be attached either to the most important articles of exchange from outside, which are in fact the primitive and spontaneous forms of manifestation of the **exchange value** of local products, or to the object of utility which forms the chief element of indigenous alienable wealth, for example cattle" (1867: 183). **Capitalist** society turned to gold and silver because precious metals fulfill the necessary functions of the **universal equivalent**: "Only a material whose every sample possesses the same uniform quality can be an adequate form of appearance of value, that is a material embodiment of abstract and therefore equal human **labour**." Also, "the money **commodity** must be capable of purely quantitative differentiation"; it "must therefore be divisible at will, and it must also be possible to assemble it again from its component parts. Gold and silver possess these properties by nature" (184). Once gold and silver take on the role of money-form they are separated from their real **use value** (e.g., as filling in teeth or as raw material in luxury goods) and function almost exclusively as **exchange value**; it becomes an ideal value, which is why it is so easy for this function to be taken over by paper money (though the paper used for making money is, in and of itself, useless). Money performs a similar function on all things exchanged for it: "Money is the absolutely alienable **commodity**, because it is all other **commodities** divested of their shape, the product of their universal **alienation**" (205). In other words, money is the means by which material use values are "transubstantiated," as Marx sometimes put it, into **exchange value**, thus alienating all **commodities** from the **labor** that really gives value to **commodities**. Slavoj Žižek is particularly helpful in making sense of why, even when we know that paper money is nothing but an **alienation** of real **labor**, it still holds power over us as if power inhered in the worthless sheet of paper itself: "When individuals use money, they know very well that there is nothing magical about it—that money, in its materiality, is simply an expression of social relations" (1989: 31). The problem, as Žižek explains, is that "in their social activity itself, in what they are *doing*, they are *acting* as if money, in its material reality, is the immediate embodiment of wealth as such. They are **fetishists** in practice, not in theory" (31).

See also: **commodity fetishism**, **ideology**.

NAME-OF-THE-FATHER

The "name of the father" refers to the laws and restrictions that control both your **desire** and the rules of communication, according to Jacques Lacan. The Name-of-the-Father is closely bound up with the **super-ego**, the Phallus, the **symbolic order**, and the **Oedipus complex**. As Lacan writes, "It is in the *name of the father* that we must recognize the support of the symbolic function which, from the dawn of history, has identified his person with the figure of the law" (1977: 67). According to Lacan, the Name-of-the-Father has a perverse shadow double in the **Father of Enjoyment**.

NARCISSISM (NARCISSISTIC)

Narcissism is self-love, a concept that is particularly important in **psychoanalysis**. Ideally, according to Sigmund Freud, the **libido** directs its energies to objects ("**object**-libido"), including eventually one's love-**object**. However, the libido can also attach itself to the **ego** ("ego-libido") to the exclusion of external object-**cathexes**. This situation leads, according to Freud, to narcissistic behavior and to narcissistic **neuroses** such as megalomania. Jacques Lacan makes narcissism an even more central aspect of the human psyche, aligning it with what he terms the "**imaginary order**," one of the three major structures of the psyche for Lacan (along with the **Real** and the **symbolic order**). Lacan suggests that, whereas the zero form of sexuality for animals is copulation, the zero form of sexuality for humans is masturbation. The act of sex for humans is so much caught up in our fantasies (our idealized images of both ourselves and our sexual partners) that it is ultimately **narcissistic**. As Lacan puts it, "That's what love is. It's one's own **ego** that one loves in love, one's own **ego** made real on the **imaginary** level" (1991: 142).

NARRATIVE AND NARRATOLOGY

The study of narrative is particularly important because narrative constitutes one of the primary ways we construct meaning in general. As Hayden White puts it, "far from being one code among many that a culture may utilize for endowing experience with meaning, narrative is a meta-code, a human universal on the basis of which transcultural messages about the nature of a shared reality can be transmitted" (1987: 1). Having said that, White also makes clear that the understanding of space and time that we tend to associate with narrative is, in fact, of rather recent invention. To illustrate his point, White examines how medieval annals and Renaissance chronicles understand time and space differently than do nineteenth-century histories. Looking at the *Annals of Saint Gall*, which are about the eighth, ninth, and tenth centuries of our era, White points out:

> Although this text is "referential" and contains a representation of temporality ... it possesses none of the characteristics that we normally attribute to a story: no central subject, no well-marked beginning, middle, and end, no peripeteia, and no identifiable narrative voice. In what are, for us, the theoretically most interesting segments of the text, there is no suggestion of any necessary connection between one event and another. (1987: 6)

Rather than dismiss the annalist's version of history as primitive, White argues "not that the chronicle is a 'higher' or more sophisticated representation of reality than the annals, but that it is merely a different kind of representation, marked by a desire for a kind of order and fullness in an account of reality that remains theoretically unjustified, a desire that is, until shown otherwise, purely gratuitous" (1987: 17). White goes on to reject history's claims to **empirical** objectivity altogether; indeed, he illustrates in *Metahistory* (1973) and elsewhere (1978, 1992) the ways that different histories in fact follow generic conventions borrowed from literature and that they thus restructure the historical world according to **ideological** parameters. White's work reflects a general distrust among critical theorists of both **positivist**, **empirical** history and what Jean-François Lyotard terms "**grand narratives**," those overarching and totalizing **narratives** by which we make sense of how we came to our present moment. Walter Benjamin goes so far as to state that "There is no document of civilization which is not at the same time a document of barbarism" (1968: 256) since traditional histories normally only tell the history of the victors. According to Benjamin, the **historical materialist** therefore "regards it as his task to brush **history** against the grain" (257).

In a rather different vein, Mikhail Bakhtin is another critic who explores how the very structure of narrative changes as we move from earlier forms like the epic and the romance to the nineteenth-century novel. As Bakhtin explains,

> all of the action in a Greek romance, all the events and adventures that fill it, constitute time-sequences that are neither historical, quotidian, biographical, nor even biological and maturational. Actions lie outside these sequences, beyond the reach of that force, inherent in these sequences, that generates rules and defines the measure of a man. In this kind of time, nothing changes: the world remains as it was, the biographical life of the heroes does not change, their feelings do not change, people do not even age. This empty time leaves no traces anywhere, no indications of its passing. (1981: 91)

Nineteenth-century narratives, by contrast, concretize both space and time in such a way that cause and effect are inextricably bound together, a development that Bakhtin explores through his concept of the **chronotope**.

In contrast to such diachronic analyses of changes in narrative form, narratology (the science of narrative) tends to analyze the synchronic narrative structures that order our perception of both cultural artifacts and the world around us in any given **text** or in any given social situation, including our very understanding of time and space. Influenced heavily by **structuralism** and **semiotics**, narratologists explore the underlying structures of any given narrative, beginning with the structural distinction between **story and discourse**. They build on this distinction to explore the larger structural dynamics of narrative form, as in Algirdas Julien Greimas's analysis of the "*fundamental semantics and grammar*" (1976b: 65) of narrative (see **Greimassian square**) and Roland Barthes's examination in *S/Z* (1974) of the underlying codes that secretly structure our reading of any **text** (see **hermeneutic and proairetic codes**). Narratologists often provide a taxonomy (a scheme of classification) for all narrative elements, as in the work of Gérard Genette (1980, 1988), Paul Ricoeur (1984, 1985, 1988, 1991) and

Tzvetan Todorov (1969). Others follow in the **semiotic** tradition of Ferdinand de Saussure (see **signifier and signified**) to provide the basic, irreducible narrative elements of cultural systems, as in the work of Vladimir Propp (1968), Claude Lévi-Strauss (1963; see **binary opposition**) and Roland Barthes (1972).

Given the prevalence and importance of narrative media in our lives (television, film, fiction), narratology is a useful foundation to have before one begins analyzing popular **culture** and, indeed, Roland Barthes's examinations of popular culture (1972, 1977) helped to establish **Cultural Studies** as a viable field of study.

See also: **archaeology, cognitive map, diegesis,** *pétits récits,* **phrase regimen, suture, utopia**.

Further reading: Abbott 2008; Bakhtin 1981; Bal 1997; Barthes 1972, 1974, 1977; P. Brooks 1985; Chatman 1978; Cohen and Shires 1988; Genette 1980, 1988; Lévi-Strauss 1963; D. A. Miller 1981; Prince 1982, 2003; Propp 1968; Ricoeur 1984, 1985, 1988, 1991; Todorov 1969; White 1973, 1978, 1987.

NATION, NATION-STATE, NATIONHOOD, AND NATIONALISM

The definition of these terms would seem to be obvious but critical theorists have, over the last 50 years, problematized and elucidated the coming into being and current functioning of nations and nationhood. In general, "nation-state" generally refers to modern nations and all the State Apparatuses and **Ideological State Apparatuses**— as Louis Althusser terms them—that constitute nations after 1800 and even more so after 1900, including the police system, military, judiciary, educational systems, bureaucracy, and government. "Nation" by contrast is a more nebulous term. As Timothy Brennan puts it,

> As for "nation," it is both historically determined and general. As a term it refers both to the modern nation-state and to something more ancient and nebulous—the *"natio"*—a local community, domicile, family, condition of belonging. The distinction is often obscured by nationalists who seek to place their own country in an "immemorial past" where it's [sic] arbitrariness cannot be questioned. (1990: 45)

That is to say that "nation" is inextricably bound up not with the material facts of a demonstrable object in the real world but with **ideology**. And, indeed, as an **ideology**, "nation" and especially "nationalism" do tend to be used to shore up **hegemonic** power structures in any nation-state and to quell antagonism. As Étienne Balibar puts it, "national states, whose integrity suffers from internal conflicts that threaten its survival (regional conflicts, and especially class conflicts), project beneath their political existence to a pre-existing 'ethnic' or 'popular' unity (into the past, into the depths of 'civil' society)." This pre-existing unity usually takes the form of "a more or less mythical origin (linguistic, religious, cultural, racial)" (1990: 331) and tends to be articulated in terms of language and race (350–54).

The imaginary nature of nationhood is influentially argued by Benedict Anderson in *Imagined Communities: Reflections on the Origin and Spread of Nationalism* (1991). He defines "nation" as "an imagined political community—and imagined as both inherently limited and sovereign" (6). It is "*imagined* because the members of even the smallest nation will never know most of their fellow-members, meet them, or even hear of them, yet in the minds of each lives the image of their communion" (6). It is "imagined as *limited* because even the largest of them, encompassing perhaps a billion living human beings, has finite, if elastic, boundaries, beyond which lie other nations" (7). It is imagined as *sovereign* because, "Coming to maturity at a stage of human history when even the most devout adherents of any universal religion were inescapably confronted with the living *pluralism* of such religions," nations could "dream of being free, and, if under God, directly so. The gage and emblem of this freedom is the sovereign state" (7). Nation thus takes many of its cues from religion and from religion's imagining of an eternity beyond any one individual's death: "If nation-states are widely conceded to be 'new' and 'historical,' the nations to which they give political expression always loom out of an immemorial past, and, still more important, glide into a limitless future" (12). Finally, "it is imagined as *community*, because, regardless of the actual inequality and exploitation that may prevail in each, the nation is always conceived as a deep, horizontal comradeship" that "makes it possible, over the past two centuries, for so many millions of people, not so much to kill, as willingly to die for such limited imaginings" (7).

By thinking of "nation" as an ideological fiction, **Cultural Studies** has examined the important role of literature and other cultural products in the formation of any given national identity. It has often taken its cue from Benedict Anderson's analysis of "the basic structure of two forms of imagining which first flowered in Europe in the eighteenth century: the novel and the newspaper" (1991: 24–25), both of which, according to Anderson, contributed to the new sense of temporality that ushered in the new concept of "nation." Lacanian psychoanalysis has similarly explored the psychodynamics behind nationalist and totalitarian movements, following the lead of Slavoj Žižek in such works as *For They Know Not What They Do: Enjoyment as a Political Factor* (1991a) and *Did Somebody Say Totalitarianism?* (2001). As Žižek writes, nationalist ideology tends to construct "a myth of Origins—of an epoch preceding oppression and exploitation when the Nation was *already there* (the Khmer kingdom in Cambodia, India before English colonialism, Ireland before the Protestant invasion, and so on)—the past is trans-coded as Nation that already existed and to which we are supposed to return through a liberation struggle" (1991a: 214).

Nation has also been an important concept for **Postcolonial Studies**, if a fraught one. While accepting the implicit critique of nationalism characteristic of Cultural Studies, postcolonial theorists also must acknowledge the importance of national consciousness in the struggles for independence of nations formerly under colonial rule. One of the founding texts of **Postcolonial Studies**, Frantz Fanon's *The Wretched of the Earth*, first published in 1961 (in French), spends a large portion of the book discussing "The Pitfalls of National Consciousness," the title of Chapter Three. The problem arises, he argues, when nationalization is understood to mean simply "the transfer into native hands of those unfair advantages which are a legacy of the colonial period" (1963: 124). He also explores how quickly nationalism passes to "ultra-nationalism, to chauvinism, and finally to racism" (127): "The racial prejudice of the young national bourgeoisie is a racism of defence, based on fear. Essentially it is no different from vulgar tribalism, or the rivalries between septs or confraternities" (132). And yet, Fanon does not abandon the notion of nationalism but rather seeks to redefine it as the will of all: "Individual experience, because it is national and because it is a link in the chain of national existence, ceases to be individual, limited and shrunken and is enabled to open out into the truth of the nation and of the world" (160); however, it is important that such national consciousness also be tied to real, everyday people and experience: "In the same way that during the period of armed struggle each fighter held the fortune of the nation in his hand, so during the period of national construction each citizen ought to continue in his real, everyday activity to associate himself with the whole of the nation, to incarnate the continuous dialectical truth of the nation and to will the triumph of man in his completeness here and now" (160). Fanon concludes by arguing that "If man is known by his acts, then we will say that the most urgent thing today for the intellectual is to build up his nation" (199). As Brennan puts it, "If European nationalism was a project of *unity* on the basis of conquest and economic expediency, insurgent or popular nationalism ... is for the most part a project of consolidation following an act of *separation* from Europe. It is a task of reclaiming community from within boundaries defined by the very power whose presence denied community" (1990: 58).

This tension is explored, influentially, in the essay collection, *Nation and Narration*, edited by Homi K. Bhabha (1990b). Bhabha himself, in his essay for the collection, "DissemiNation," proposes a "cultural construction of nationness as a form of social and **textual** affiliation" (292), one that is always double, both pointing to an authoritarian, totalizing vision of origin and to the quotidian, day-to-day reality of the people (what Bhabha terms the "locality of culture," a concept he explores more fully in *The Location of Culture* [1994]): "We then have a contested cultural territory where the people must be thought in a double-time; the people are the historical 'objects' of a nationalist pedagogy, giving the discourse an authority that is based on a pre-given or constituted historical origin or event; the people are also the '**subjects**' of a process of signification that must erase any prior or originary presence of the nation-people to demonstrate the prodigious, living principle of the people as that continual process by which the national life is redeemed and signified as a repeating and reproductive process" (1990b: 297). "Nation" is thus conceived as at once authoritarian and **performative**: "In place of the polarity of a prefigurative self-generating nation itself and extrinsic **Other** nations, the **performative** introduces a temporality of the 'in-between' through the 'gap' or 'emptiness' of the **signifier** that punctuates linguistic difference" (299). Such "counter-narratives" of the nation "that continually evoke and erase its totalizing boundaries—both actual and conceptual— disturb those ideological manoeuvres through which '**imagined communities**' are given essentialist identities" (300). Bhabha, in his Foreword to a 2005 edition of Frantz Fanon's *The Wretched of the Earth*, also acknowledges how **postmodern** globalization affects the way postcolonial studies understands nation: "while it was the primary purpose of decolonization to repossess land and territoriality in order to ensure the security of national polity and global equity, **globalization** propagates a world made up of virtual transnational domains and wired communities that live vividly through webs and connectivities 'on line.' In what way, then, can the once colonized woman or man become figures of instruction for our global century?" (2005: xi). Bhabha goes on to argue that one can find in Fanon's work "a postcolonial consciousness based on a 'dual emergence' of national sovereignty and international solidarity" (xxvi) and that one needs to ensure postcolonial theorists can engage with the realities of our **postmodern** global world system.

Marxism problematizes the idea of nation given that the goal of Karl Marx's communism was the transcendence of national boundaries in the transnational struggle on behalf of a global exploited **proletariat**, hence the name given to the first congress and alliance of socialist parties formed by Marx and Friedrich Engels in 1864, the "First International," not to mention the left-wing anthem adopted by the "Second International," "The Internationale," with its refrain: "Let us group together, and tomorrow/ The Internationale/ Will be the human race." The concept of "nation" is also problematized in **Global Studies**, given that the emergent **postmodern** reality of an inter-connected world driven by the logic of **late capitalism** has created a situation where national identity is arguably less important than transnational (e.g., cosmopolitan) myths of identity, where nations are less powerful than transnational corporations or transnational entities like the World Bank, the International Monetary Fund, or the United Nations. As Michael Hardt and Antonio Negri influentially argue in *Empire* (2000),

> It is certainly true that, in step with the processes of globalization, the sovereignty of nation-states, while still effective, has progressively declined. The primary factors of production and exchange— money, technology, people, and goods—move with increasing ease across national boundaries; hence the nation-state has less and less power to regulate these flows and impose its authority over the economy. Even the most dominant nation-states should no longer be thought of as supreme and sovereign authorities, either outside or even within their own borders. (xi)

The result, according to Hardt and Negri, is "a global order, a new logic and structure of rule—in short, a new form of sovereignty" (xi), which they name "**Empire**" (see **empire**).

Further reading: B. Anderson 1991; Balibar 1990; Bhabha 1990b, 2005; Brennan 1990; Fanon 1963, 1967; Hardt and Negri 2000; Žižek 1991a, 2001.

NATURE (NATURALIZE, NATURALIZATION)

In his *Keywords* (1983), **Cultural Materialist** Raymond Williams claims that "Nature is perhaps the most complex word in the language." He goes on to explain:

It is relatively easy to distinguish three areas of meaning: (i) the essential quality and character *of* something; (ii) the inherent force which directs either the world or human beings or both; (iii) the material world itself, taken as including or not including human beings. Yet it is evident that within (ii) and (iii), though the area of reference is broadly clear, precise meanings are variable and at times even opposed. The historical development of the word through these three senses is important, but it is also significant that all three senses, and the main variations and alternatives within the two most difficult of them, are still active and widespread in contemporary usage. (219)

Williams later states that "Any full history of the uses of nature would be a history of a large part of human thought" (221). That history would include a few important transitions in thought regarding Williams's sense "(iii)," which is sometimes difficult to distinguish from (i) and (ii). In particular, we see a development in the history of ideas from: (1) an earlier sense of the "state of nature" as barbarous, from which civilization must work hard to establish and protect itself (e.g., in Thomas Hobbes [1588–1679] but continuing through to Immanuel Kant [1724–1804], who argues in *Toward Perpetual Peace* [1795] that "The state of nature ... is not a state of peace among human beings who live next to one another but a state of war" [72]); (2) to a "state of nature" that is either benign in relation to or actively superior to civilization, the place where one can find the secret order of the universe (as in the scientific theories of Isaac Newton [1642–1727] or the philosophy of John Locke [1632–1704]). The Romantic period (1789–1832) slightly modified this second sense: nature was now seen as a state of perfection from which civilization perversely departs and to which one must go for renewal and truth (e.g., the work of Jean-Jacques Rousseau [1712–78] and William Wordsworth [1770–1850], followed by the writing of the so-called Transcendentalists in the American tradition, especially Ralph Waldo Emerson [1803–82], Henry David Thoreau [1817–62] and Margaret Fuller [1810–50]). Of course, Charles Darwin (1809–82) impacted our understanding of nature yet again if in different, sometimes opposing ways. Because of evolution, nature is "red in tooth and claw," as Alfred Lord Tennyson (1809–92) puts it in his poem, "In Memoriam"; one can read that in a negative sense (civilization must protect us from nature) or in a positive sense (we must follow the logic of natural selection, as the eugenics movement argued). Our understanding of nature is transformed yet again in the twentieth century, particularly after human population and technology accelerate global warming and the extinction of countless species, impelling the rise of **Ecocriticism**.

I rehearse this complicated history because we can read these diverse senses of nature in critical theory: the dangerous and threatening version that civilization must continually work to **repress**, as in the **psychoanalysis** of Sigmund Freud and, to a lesser extent, Jacques Lacan; or a liberating version of the state of nature that offers us the **utopic** possibility of an escape from the **ideological** obfuscations of **capitalist** or **patriarchal** society, as in some of the writings of Karl Marx or in Julia Kristeva's notions of **chora** and the **genotext**.

Most commonly, critical theory is concerned with the increasing tendency in the eighteenth century and then especially in the nineteenth century for scientists, doctors, politicians, and reformers to argue that certain aspects of human behavior are "natural," so that departures from that natural norm require administration and correction. According to Michel Foucault, the increasing concern especially with **sexuality** in the nineteenth century (which brings together the individual body and the species body through a regulated ideal of **heteronormative** reproduction) leads to a new order of social control that he terms **bio-politics and bio-power**. Giorgio Agamben builds on this argument in his theorization of **bare life and *homo sacer***.

In the new way of thinking that followed the Enlightenment, one sees not only **gender and sex** but also **race** and even **class** as "natural," at once inevitable and part of a set of **binary oppositions** that one must seek to regulate (male vs. female, Occidental vs. Oriental, eugenically pure vs. racialized **Other**, bourgeois morality vs. working-class degeneracy). Critical theorists reject such naturalized distinctions, arguing that even those categories that have—in fact only recently, since the eighteenth century—come to be seen as natural or inherent (especially, **race**, **sex**, and **class**) are in fact arbitrary, **discursive**, **performative**, and **ideological**. In this, critical theorists sometimes borrow **poststructuralist** techniques for dismantling **binary oppositions** and for questioning the effort to posit a presence or center to ground the play of signification (see **signifier and signified**). As **deconstructionist** Jacques Derrida for example argues in *Of Grammatology* (1976), "there has never been anything but writing"; "the absolute present, Nature" has "never existed" so "that what opens meaning and language is writing as the disappearance of natural presence" (159). Other **poststructuralist** key concepts follow suit (see **discourse**, **differend**, **incommensurability**, **language game**, **logocentrism**, **phrase regimen**, **sublime**, **supplement**, **trace**). One can see the same rejection of naturalized identity positions in

feminism (see also **patriarchy, performativity**), **queer theory** (see also **compulsory heterosexuality, queer temporality**), the critique of **ideology** (see also **distribution of the sensible, doxa, field, habitus**), theories of **subjectivity, Actor-Network Theory** and its influences (see also **assemblage and assemblage theory, Body without Organs, quasi-objects and quasi-subjects, rhizome**), **psychoanalysis** (see also **imaginary order, Real, suture, symbolic order**), **Postcolonial Studies** and **Critical Race Theory** (see also **subaltern**), even **Speculative Realism** (see also **factiality**).

See also: **parody, repressive hypothesis**.

NEGATIVE DIALECTICS

See **dialectic**

NEO-COLONIAL (NEO-COLONIALISM)

See **Postcolonial Studies**

NEO-IMPERIAL (NEO-IMPERIALISM)

See **Postcolonial Studies**

NEO-MARXISM (NEO-MARXIST)

See **Marxism**

NEUROSIS (NEUROSES, NEUROTIC)

According to **psychoanalysis**, neurosis refers to the formation of behavioral or psychosomatic **symptoms** as a result of the return of the **repressed**. A neurosis represents an instance where the **ego**'s efforts to deal with its desires through **repression, displacement**, etc. fail: "A person only falls ill of a neurosis if his **ego** has lost the capacity to allocate his **libido** in some way" (Freud 1953–74: 16.387). The failure of the **ego** and the increased insistence of the **libido** lead to **symptoms** that can be as bad or worse than the conflict they are designed to replace. We should keep in mind, however, that **repression** is a normal aspect of **psychosexual development**, according to Sigmund Freud; neurosis too need not in every instance be seen as negative. Freud writes that there are cases in which the physician himself must admit that the solution of a conflict by a neurosis is one of the most harmless and most tolerable socially (16.382); indeed, Freud goes so far as to argue that even "ostensibly healthy life is interspersed with a great number of trivial and in practice unimportant **symptoms**" (16.457). The neurotic that needs treatment simply has more debilitating **symptom**-formations that prevent enjoyment and active achievement in life. A **psychosis**, by contrast, refers to when a patient has completely lost touch with reality. Freud originally distinguished between neurosis and **psychosis** in the following way: "In neurosis the **ego** suppresses part of the **id** out of allegiance to reality, whereas in **psychosis** it lets itself be carried away by the **id** and detached from a part of reality" (1953–74: 5.202).

In neurosis, the **ego** generally perceives "an advantage through illness," as Freud terms it; the symptom, that is, allows the psyche to side-step the conflict between its **ego** and its **id** through a **symptom** that allows it to experience pleasure in an alternate (if often debilitating) fashion. The **symptom** is a substitute for the **instinctual** impulse but one that is so reduced, displaced, and distorted that it is often not recognizable as a gratification but looks more like a compulsion or even an illness, for example, the obsessional neurotic's compulsion to clean. Once such a **symptom** is put in place, the **ego** will often reinforce it by rationalizing and taking advantage from the behavior (it is good to be clean; look how much more conscientious I am than others). The more ingrained and rationalized a **symptom** becomes, the more resistant it will be to the psychoanalytical cure.

Neuroses can be caused (1) by internal impulses that are improperly **repressed** by the **ego** and that, therefore, find alternative expression; or (2) by external traumatic events (a sexual encounter, sexual abuse, war trauma). Usually, a combination of (1) and (2) is required for the neurosis to manifest itself; however, Freud soon came to realize that the line between fantasy (1) and reality (2) can be difficult to determine and, so, "we should equate phantasy and reality"; indeed, we should "not bother to begin with whether the childhood experiences under examination are the one or the other," for *"in the world of neurosis it is psychical reality which is the decisive kind"* (1953–74: 16.368). In other words, memories of childhood trauma (incest with the father, viewing one's parents copulating [what Freud terms the "primal phantasy"]) can sometimes be completely constructed (pure fantasy) and yet nonetheless function as traumatically as if they had actually happened.

According to Freud, there are a number of classes of neuroses: (1) **Narcissistic** neuroses: megalomania, melancholia. Freud saw these neuroses as particularly difficult to cure because the patient has developed in such a way as to refuse interaction with other people, thus making a talking cure with an analyst difficult. (2) **Transference** neuroses or "psycho-neuroses": when one's desire for an external object is transferred to fantasies that then take the place of real sexual gratification. Included under this general category are **hysteria** and obsessional neuroses, where a sexual impulse is substituted by obsessive thoughts and compulsive behaviors (e.g., obsessive cleaning or minutely repeated ceremonial acts). (3) Traumatic neuroses: given that he experienced the results of the First World War, Freud was especially familiar with the neuroses caused by the trauma of war; however, any number of traumas can lead to neuroses (e.g., sexual assault, a mother's departure). See **death drive**, **repetition compulsion**, and **transference**. What distinguishes traumatic neuroses from other neuroses is the fact that the cause of the symptoms does not stem, for the most part, from the unconscious or psychological conflicts but from an actual (and, often, immediate) traumatic event.

The treatment of neurosis consists of making conscious some of the unconscious until "we transform the pathogenic conflict into a normal one for which it must be possible somehow to find a solution" (1953–74: 16.435). However, simply stating the "truth" of a patient's neurosis is often not enough, since the work of **repression** is such that the patient may hear the analyst's words but not believe them or perhaps allow the "truth" to stand alongside a continuing illness. A good example of this tendency for the truth to stand alongside the **symptom** is in **fetishism**. To counter this tendency, the psychoanalytic cure seeks to overcome the **transference** by returning to the actual memory that is being repressed: "It has been the physician's endeavour to keep this **transference** neurosis within the narrowest limits: to force as much as possible into the channel of memory and to allow as little as possible to emerge as repetition" (Freud 1953–74: 18.19).

Further reading: Laplanche and Pontalis 1973.

NEW CRITICISM AND NEW FORMALISM

New Criticism, a term derived from John Crowe Ransom's *The New Criticism* (1941), was a **structuralist** theory that was particularly influential in the 1940s and 1950s. The approach provided critics of literature with interpretative techniques of "close reading" that never ceased to be used in the study of literature, although the movement was eclipsed by the rise of **poststructuralism**, **Reader-Response Criticism**, **Marxist** and **Feminist** criticism, and **Cultural Materialism** in the 1960s and 1970s, followed by **New Historicism**, **Cultural Studies**, **queer theory**, **Critical Race Theory**, and so on, all of which concerned themselves with issues such as **race**, **class**, **gender, and sexuality** that were outside the purview of the New Critics. The New Critics sought to stay true to the formal elements of any given work of literature, which they regarded as independent of the intentions of the author (what the New Critics W. K. Wimsatt and Monroe Beardsley termed the "Intentional Fallacy" [1954]), the response of the reader (the "Affective Fallacy") or the historical context of the work (the "Historical Fallacy"). Instead, New Critics concerned themselves with such **formalist** concerns as paradox, ambiguity, irony, and tension. Influential critics of the school include, in addition to those already mentioned, Allen Tate, Cleanth Brooks, and Robert Penn Warren.

Beginning with works like Garrett Stewart's *Reading Voices* (1990), Susan Wolfson's *Formal Charges* (1997), Isobel Armstrong's *The Radical Aesthetic* (2000) and Jonathan Loesberg's *A Return to Aesthetics* (2005), a movement termed "New Formalism" has developed recently, often aiming to bring together **structuralist** technique and the historical concerns of critical theory from the last 50 years—"an historically informed **formalist** criticism" (1), as Susan Wolfson puts it, borrowing a phrase from James Breslin. According to Stewart, "what would be **formalist** about a return to textual theory is exactly what would equip it for registering the *forms* of cultural dissemination in both the literary instance and its alternative **discursive** modes" (16). This return to formal concerns generally does not reject the "Affective Fallacy" nor does it reject the insights of **poststructuralism**. As Stewart continues, "Among the foreseeable gains to be made by reconceiving the purposes of so-called stylistic study in light of **poststructuralist** linguistics would not be to recover the shibboleth of 'style' and the methodologies of its specification from writer to writer but rather to retrieve the fact of writing itself—and precisely in its inseparability from **reading**—from amid the welter of cultural 'inscriptions' now under scrutiny" (18). A good starting point is Susan Wolfson's 2000 special issue of *Modern Language Quarterly*, later published as *Reading for Form* (2006), which includes an article by Stewart. Many articles and collections have followed, with alternative terms proposed: Caroline Levine's "Strategic Formalism" (2006), Herbert F. Tucker's "Tactical Formalism" (2006) or the still-to-be-published special issue of *Modern Language Quarterly* (2015) on "Historical Poetics" (edited by V. Joshua Adams, Joel Calahan, and Michael Hansen), which will include articles by C. Levine, Simon Jarvis, Yopie Prins, and others who have begun to explore **formalist** issues along these new lines.

See also: **agency, author**.

Further reading: Adams *et al.* 2015; Armstrong 2000; Bogel 2013; C. Brooks 1947; Brooks and Warren 1938, 1943; Hošek and Parker 1985; Lentricchia 1980; Lentricchia and DuBois 2003; C. Levine 2006; Levinson 2007; Loesberg 2005; Ransom 1941; Stewart 1990, 2009; Tate 1940; Thiele and Tredennick 2013; Tucker 2006; Wellek and Warren 1949; Wimsatt 1954; Wolfson 1997.

NEW FORMALISM

See **New Criticism and New Formalism**

NEW HISTORICISM AND CULTURAL MATERIALISM

There are a number of similarities between New Historicism and Cultural Materialism, so it is helpful to think of them together. Both New Historicists and Cultural Materialists are interested in recovering lost histories and in exploring mechanisms of repression and subjugation. The major difference is that New Historicists, largely based at American universities, tend to concentrate on those at the top of the social hierarchy (i.e., the church, the monarchy, the upper-classes). Cultural Materialists, largely based at British universities, tend to concentrate on those at the bottom of the social hierarchy (the lower-classes, women, and other marginalized peoples). New Historicists tend to draw on Foucauldian **archaeology** (see **apparatus, bio-politics, panoptic**, and **power**) and Geertzean anthropology (see **thick description**) given their interest in governments, institutions, and culture, while Cultural Materialists tend to rely on economics and sociology given their interest in **class**, economics, and **commodification**, and are particularly inspired by the work of Raymond Williams (see **class, culture** and **dominant, residual and emergent**), Louis Althusser (see **Ideological State Apparatuses, ideology, psychoanalysis, subject**), and Antonio Gramsci (see **class, hegemony, praxis, subaltern**). New Historicists are, like the Cultural Materialists, interested in questions of circulation, negotiation, profit and exchange, i.e., how activities that purport to be above the market (including literature) are in fact informed by the values of that market; however, New Historicists take this position further by then claiming that all cultural activities may be considered as equally important texts for historical analysis: contemporary trials of hermaphrodites or the intricacies of map-making may inform a Shakespeare play as much as, say, Shakespeare's literary precursors. New Historicism is also more specifically concerned with questions of **power** and **culture** (especially the messy commingling of the social and the cultural or of the supposedly autonomous **subject** and the cultural/political institutions that in fact produce that **subject**).

Part of the difficulty of summarizing New Historicism is that a number of different approaches to **history** and **culture** often get lumped together under the category of the yet larger umbrella term, **Cultural Studies**. The effort to define "New Historicism" is certainly not helped by the fact that some of the most prominent New Historicists, like Stephen Greenblatt and Alan Liu, either reject or critique the methodologies of and even the very term "New Historicism"; see Greenblatt 1989 and Liu 1989a. Nonetheless, this critical school and the journal associated with it, *Representations*, have been hugely influential on scholarship of the last three decades.

While acknowledging that "'the New Historicism' remains a phrase without an adequate referent" (1989: xi) given the heterogeneity of approaches attributed to the school, H. Aram Veeser contends that "for all its heterogeneity, key assumptions continually reappear and bind together the avowed practitioners" (1989: xi). He helpfully lists these as follows:

(1) That every expressive act is embedded in a network of material practices;
(2) that every act of unmasking, critique, and opposition uses the tools it condemns and risks falling prey to the practice it exposes;
(3) that literary and non-literary "**texts**" circulate inseparably;
(4) that no discourse, imaginative or archival, gives access to unchanging truths nor expresses inalterable human nature;
(5) finally, … that a critical method and a language adequate to describe culture under capitalism participate in the economy they describe. (1989: xi)

Although he begins by stating that New Historicism is "no doctrine at all" (1989: 1), Stephen Greenblatt provides a similar list of "practices" that characterize New Historicist investigation: (1) one should begin with specific details, anecdotes, and examples in order to avoid a totalizing version of history; (2) one should proceed from such details to illustrate how they are tied up with larger contradictory forces in a given time period, no matter how apparently innocuous the detail may seem at first; (3) one should remain self-conscious about one's methodologies, thus resisting "a historicism based upon faith in the transparency of signs and interpretative procedures" (1989: 12); (4) one should be suspicious of liberatory narratives: everything is, on some level, caught up in the circulations of power in a given time period; and (5) all cultural products, whether they are high art, political documents, personal letters, or trash, are a part of larger **discursive** structures and, so, can offer clues to the **ideological** contradictions of a given time period.

Both Veeser's and Greenblatt's essays appear in *The New Historicism*, edited by Veeser, a collection that helped to define the movement. A similar collection helped to define Cultural Materialism in Britain: *Political Shakespeare*, edited by Jonathan Dollimore and Alan Sinfield, with an Afterword by Raymond Williams. Like Veeser and Greenblatt for New Historicism, Dollimore and Sinfield provide in their Foreword to the collection a list of critical practices that they characterize as Cultural Materialist, specifically "historical context, theoretical method, political commitment and **textual** analysis." They elaborate as follows:

> Historical context undermines the transcendent significance traditionally accorded to the literary **text** and allows us to recover its histories; theoretical method detaches the **text** from immanent criticism which seeks only to reproduce its own terms; socialist and feminist commitment confronts the conservative categories in which most criticism has hitherto been conducted; **textual** analysis locates the critique of traditional approaches where it cannot be ignored. (1985: vii)

They state also that the goal is to reject the sense of "**culture**" as "cultured" in favor of the analytical sense used in the social sciences, especially anthropology: this approach to culture "seeks to describe the whole system of significations by which a society or a section of it understands itself and its relations with the world" (vii). The "materialism" in "cultural materialism" should be understood as "opposed to 'idealism,'" they explain; "it insists that culture does not (cannot) transcend the material forces and **relations of production**. Culture is not simply a reflection of the economic and political system, but nor can it be independent of it" (viii). Following in the tradition of critical theory as defined by the Frankfurt School (see **Introduction**),

Dollimore and Sinfield also underscore that the goal of this criticism is political, oriented towards the improvement of the world: Cultural Materialism "registers its commitment to the transformation of a social order which exploits people on grounds of race, gender and class" (viii).

Further reading: Dollimore 1985; Dollimore and Sinfield 1985; Greenblatt 1989; Liu 1989a, 1989b; K. Ryan 1996; Veeser 1989; Williams 1958, 1995.

OBJECT, OBJECTIFICATION, AND *OBJET PETIT A*

Feminist critics are particularly concerned with the objectification of women, which is to say the reduction of another person—with all her own needs, opinions, and independent actions—into an object for the male, desiring gaze, as in, for example, **scopophilia**. Women are thus deprived of **agency** and self-constitution, becoming instead the objects of male fantasy or mirrors for a man's articulation of his own identity (see also **Other** and **suture**).

In **psychoanalysis**, "object" often refers to the object of one's sexual **desire**: Sigmund Freud, for example, refers to one's "object-choice," the earliest one being the mother (and before her the mother's breast). Freud also refers to "object-**cathexes**," objects that have been imbued with a sexual charge. "Object-choice" should be carefully distinguished from **identification**. Jacques Lacan develops this understanding of the object into his concept of the *objet petit a*, the "object-cause" of our **desire**. The *objet petit a* is a way for us to establish coordinates for our own **desire**, by which we establish the screen that separates us from the **Real**. At the heart of **desire** is a misrecognition of fullness where there is really nothing but a screen for our own **narcissistic** projections. It is that **lack** at the heart of **desire** that ensures we continue to desire, according to Lacanian psychoanalysis. To come too close to our object of desire threatens to uncover the **lack** that is, in fact, necessary for our **desire** to persist, so that, ultimately, **desire** is most interested not in fully attaining the object of desire but in keeping our distance, thus allowing desire to persist. Because **desire** is articulated through fantasy, it is driven by its own impossibility.

See also: **Gaze, quasi-objects and quasi-subjects, things and Thing Theory**.

OEDIPUS COMPLEX (OEDIPAL)

For Sigmund Freud, the "Oedipus complex" refers to the childhood desire to have the mother and to kill the father. Freud describes the source of this complex in his *Introductory Lectures* of 1916–17 (Twenty-First Lecture): "You all know the Greek legend of King Oedipus, who was destined by fate to kill his father and take his mother to wife, who did everything possible to escape the oracle's decree and punished himself by blinding when he learned that he had none the less unwittingly committed both these crimes" (1953–74: 16.330). According to Freud, Sophocles' play, *Oedipus Rex*, illustrates a formative stage in each individual's **psychosexual development**, when the young child transfers his love **object** from the breast (the **oral phase**) to the mother. At this time, the child desires the mother and resents (even secretly desires to murder) the father. (The Oedipus complex is closely connected to the **castration complex**.) Such primal desires are, of course, quickly **repressed** but, even among the mentally sane, they will arise again in dreams or in literature. Among those individuals who do not progress properly into the **genital phase**, the Oedipus complex, according to Freud, can still be playing out its psychodrama in various displaced, abnormal, and/or exaggerated ways. Gilles Deleuze and Félix Guattari influentially critique Freud's Oedipal model in their *Anti-Oedipus* (1983); see **schizoanalysis**.

ORAL PHASE

According to Sigmund Freud, the oral phase is the earliest phase in a child's **psychosexual development**, during which time the mouth and lips take on an erotic charge (roughly 0–2 years of age). The first sexual **object**, according to Freudian **psychoanalysis**, is the mother's breast, followed by the mother herself. In dealing with the loss of the breast, the young child of the oral phase naturally turns, for example, to thumb-sucking in order to compensate for the loss of gratification (see **psychosexual development**).

ORIENTALISM

Edward W. Said, in his influential book, *Orientalism*, argues that Orientalism is "a way of coming to terms with the Orient that is based on the Orient's special place in European Western experience" (1978: 1). The Orient, according to Said, represents one of Europe's "deepest and most recurring images of the **Other**" (1) and "has helped to define Europe (or the West) as its contrasting image, idea, personality, experience" (1–2). As **Other**, the Orient is consistently represented by Orientalism in negative terms that are then given **discursive** coherence: "one of the important developments in nineteenth-century Orientalism was the distillation of essential ideas about the Orient—its sensuality, its tendency to despotism, its aberrant mentality, its habits of inaccuracy, its backwardness—into a separate and unchallenged coherence" (205). Said defines three main ways that Orientalism manifests itself: (1) Orientalism as a field of study, whereby "Anyone who teaches, writes about, or researches the Orient ... is an Orientalist" (2); (2) Orientalism as "a style of thought" affecting writers in many disciplines that is "based upon an ontological and epistemological distinction made between 'the Orient' and (most of the time) 'the Occident'" (2); and (3) Orientalism "as a Western style for dominating, restructuring, and having authority over the Orient" (3). Because of these various ways that the Orient has been delimited by **discourse**, "the Orient was not (and is not) a free subject of thought or action" (3). Rather, the "relationship between Occident and Orient is a relationship of power, of domination, of varying degrees of a complex **hegemony**" (5). For that reason, Said argues, "It is therefore correct that every European, in what he could say about the Orient, was consequently a racist, an imperialist, and almost totally ethnocentric" (204).

Said's book helped to establish the methodology of **Cultural Studies**, for Said argues throughout that one cannot easily separate cultural or academic work from political questions and issues. He also concerns himself with Orientalism as a representation (rather than any "real" Orient), illustrating how "these representations rely upon institutions, traditions, conventions, agreed-upon codes of understanding for their effects, not upon a distant and amorphous Orient" (1978: 22). Following Said, **postcolonial** critics are particularly sensitive to the ways that the foreign **"other"** is represented, be it in terms of culture, race, sexuality or even economics. As Gayatri Chakravorty Spivak puts it, the "benevolent first-world appropriation and reinscription of the Third World as an **Other** is the founding characteristic of much third-worldism in the U.S. human sciences today" (1988a: 289).

See also: **contact zone and transculturation**, **hybridity**, **liminality**, **mimicry**, **Postcolonial Studies**, **subaltern**.

Further reading: Ballantyne 2002; Breckenridge and van der Veer 1993; Codell and Macleod 1998; Dallmayr 1996; Hoeveler and Cass 2006; Lockman 2009; Said 1978; B. S. Turner 1994.

THE OTHER, THE BIG OTHER, AND OTHERING

Critical theorists are particularly committed to opposing **binary oppositions** where one side is seen as privileged over or defining itself against an Other (often capitalized), for example, male/female, Occident/Orient, center/margin. See **binary opposition**, **Orientalism**, and **phallocentrism**. Through such **binary oppositions**, Homi Bhabha explains, "The Other loses its power to signify, to negate, to initiate its historic desire, to establish its own institutional and oppositional discourse" (1994: 31). Often borrowing maneuvers from deconstruction (see *différance*), critical theorists seek instead to unveil and critique the effort to establish a "sovereign **Subject**" over and against a constitutive Other.

Gayatri Chakravorty Spivak develops the term into her own concepts of "othering" and "worlding." In her essay, "The Rani of Sirmur," she argues that the turning of foreign lands and people into an Other for the European, colonial master occurs not just in official documents or high culture but also in everyday interactions between colonialists and the indigenous population in India during the nineteenth century. Her point is that "the 'Colonizing Power' is far from monolithic—that its class-composition and social positionality are necessarily heterogeneous" (1985: 254). She examines, for example, the letters of a minor functionary, Captain Geoffrey Birch, who through the simple act of traveling across India with a native escort engages "in consolidating the self of Europe by obliging the native to **cathect** the space of the Other on his home ground. He is worlding *their own world*, which is far from mere uninscribed earth, anew, by obliging *them* to domesticate the alien as Master" (253). She borrows the term "worlding" from Martin Heidegger's essay, "The Origin of the Work of Art," where Heidegger suggests that a work of art establishes a world over and against the earth (understood as yet "uninscribed"). Spivak's point is that, when one is talking about colonial occupation, the European **Subject** "worlds" or violently recreates the already inscribed or meaningful world of the native subject, thus making him "Other," and that this act occurs at all levels of society: "What I am trying to insist on here is that the agents of this cartographic transformation in the narrow sense are not only great names like Vincent Van Gogh, but small unimportant folk like Geoffrey Birch, as well as the policymakers. I am also suggesting that the necessary yet contradictory assumption of an uninscribed earth which is the condition of possibility of the worlding of a world generates the force to make the 'native' see himself as 'other'" (253–54). Through the mere act of traveling across the Indian landscape, "the figure of the European on the hills is being reinscribed from stranger to Master, to the sovereign as Subject with a capital S, even as the native shrinks into the consolidating subjected subject in the lower case" (254).

Jacques Lacan gives "other" a different valence in his **psychoanalysis**. He argues that at what he terms the **mirror stage** of psychosexual development (6–18 months) the **subject** first understands that it is "other" than the mother, from whom the **subject** did not properly distinguish itself before this stage. For Lacan, the act of recognizing oneself in the mirror marks the primordial recognition of one's self as "I," although at a point "before it is objectified in the dialectic of identification with the other, and before language restores to it, in the universal, its function as **subject**" (1977: 2). The next stage—when the subject does fully enter into language and what Lacan terms the **symbolic order**—then establishes a relation between the subject and what Lacan terms the "big Other" (the entire system of language and convention into which we are born): at that point, the **subject** is reduced into an empty signifier ("I") within the field of the "Other," which Lacan capitalizes to distinguish this function from any single other person. See **symbolic order**.

A few critical theorists have also explored the ethical and moral nature of our relation to the Other, including Mikhail Bakhtin in his early philosophical work translated into English as *Art and Answerability* (1990), a philosophical disquisition that clearly informs his later concept of **dialogism**; **poststructuralist** Jacques Derrida in *Politics of Friendship* (1997), *Of Hospitality* (2000), and other late writings; Jürgen Habermas in his theorization of the **public sphere** of rational debate and his concepts of **communicative action** and **discourse ethics**; theorists positing a new principle of **cosmopolitanism** in the current age of **globalization**; Alain Badiou's theorization of love in *Being and Event* (2005a) and *In Praise of Love* (2012); Paul Ricoeur's **phenomenological** understanding of oneself *as* another in his book of the same name: "*Oneself as Another* suggests from the outset that the selfhood of oneself implies otherness to such an intimate degree that one cannot be thought of without the other, that instead one passes into the other" (1992: 3); and Emmanuel Levinas's understanding of our ineluctable debt to what he terms the "face" of the Other: "It is precisely in this call to my responsibility by the face that summons me, that demands me, that claims me—it is in this questioning that the other is my neighbor" (1998: 146).

Further reading: Badiou 2005a, 2012; Bakhtin 1990; Bhabha 1994; Derrida 1997, 2000; Gilbert and Gubar 1984; Habermas 1987, 1991, 1993, 1999; Lacan 1968, 1977, 1981, 1991; Levinas 1991, 1998, 2003; Ricoeur 1991, 1992; Spivak 1985, 1987, 1988a; Žižek 1989, 1991b.

PANOPTIC, PANOPTICON, AND CARCERAL

Michel Foucault sought throughout his work to make sense of the structural differences between contemporary society and the society that preceded us. He has been particularly influential precisely because he tends to overturn accepted wisdom, illustrating the dangers inherent in those Enlightenment reforms that were designed to correct the barbarity of previous periods (the elimination of dungeons, the modernization of medicine, the creation of the public university, etc.). As Foucault illustrates, each process of modernization entails disturbing effects with regard to the **power** of the individual and the control of government. Indeed, his most influential work, *Discipline and Punish: The Birth of the Prison* (1977a), paints a picture of contemporary society that sometimes resembles George Orwell's *1984*. He explores the ways that government has claimed ever greater control over and enforcement of ever more private aspects of our lives.

In particular, Foucault explores the transition from what he terms a "culture of spectacle" to a "carceral culture." Whereas in the former, punishment was effected on the body in public displays of torture, dismemberment, and obliteration, in the latter punishment and discipline become internalized and directed to the constitution and, when necessary, rehabilitation of social subjects. Jeremy Bentham's nineteenth-century prison reforms provide Foucault with a representative model for what happens to society in the nineteenth century. (Bentham's *"Panopticon"* was published in 1791; however, he continued to write about discipline and punishment into the nineteenth century, with *Panopticon versus New South Wales* coming out in 1812.) Bentham argued that the perfect prison would be structured in such a way that cells would be open to a central tower. In the model, individuals in the cells do not interact with each other and are constantly confronted by the panoptic tower (pan = all; optic = seeing). They cannot, however, see when a person is in the tower; they must believe that they could be watched at any moment: "the inmate must never know whether he is being looked at at any one moment; but he must be sure that he may always be so" (Foucault 1977a: 201).

Bentham saw this prison reform as a model for how society should function. To maintain order in a democratic and capitalist society, the populace needs to believe that any person could be surveilled at any time. In time, such a structure would ensure that the people would soon internalize the panoptic tower and police themselves: "He who is subjected to a field of visibility, and who knows it, assumes responsibility for the constraints of **power**; he makes them play spontaneously upon himself; he inscribes in himself the **power** relation in which he simultaneously plays both roles; he becomes the principle of his own subjection" (202–3). This system of control has, arguably, been aided in our own culture by new technological advancements that allow federal agencies to track a person's movement and behavior (the Internet, telephones, cell phones, social security numbers, the census, ATMs, credit cards, and the ever increasing number of surveillance cameras in urban spaces). By carceral culture, Foucault refers to a culture in which the panoptic model of surveillance has been diffused as a principle of social organization, affecting such disparate things as the university classroom; urban planning (organized on a grid structure to facilitate movement but also to discourage concealment); hospital and factory architecture; and so on. As Foucault puts it, the Panopticon

> is polyvalent in its applications; it serves to reform prisoners, but also to treat patients, to instruct schoolchildren, to confine the insane, to supervise workers, to put beggars and idlers to work. It is a type of location of bodies in space, of distribution of individuals in relation to one another, of hierarchical organization, of disposition of centres and channels of **power**, of definition of the instruments and modes of intervention of **power**, which can be implemented in hospitals, workshops, schools, prisons. Whenever one is dealing with a multiplicity of individuals on whom a task or a particular form of behaviour must be imposed, the panoptic schema may be used. (1977a: 205)

"The panoptic schema, without disappearing as such or losing any of its properties, was destined to spread throughout the social body," Foucault explains; "its vocation was to become a generalized function" (1977a: 207). The ultimate result is that we now live in the panoptic machine: "We are neither in the amphitheatre, nor on the stage, but in the panoptic machine, invested by its effects of **power**, which we bring to ourselves since we are part of its mechanism" (217).

Some of the effects of this new model of organization include:

(1) The internalization of rules and regulations. As we **naturalize** rules, society could be said to become less willing to contest unjust laws. Of course, Foucault has Nazi Germany in mind when he thinks about conformity; however, studies of American society (Zimbardo 2007; Milgram 1974) have suggested that Americans are, in fact, just as willing to follow authorities even when it means doing violence to innocent subjects.

(2) Rehabilitation rather than cruel and unusual punishment. This reform was implemented because of nineteenth-century outcries over the inhumane treatment of prisoners and the insane. Foucault, however, questions the subsequent emphasis on the "normal," which entails the enforcement of the status quo on ever more private aspects of our lives (for example, **sexuality**).

(3) Surveillance into ever more private aspects of our lives, which, once again, is aided by new surveillance technology.

(4) Information society. All of this surveillance and information-gathering leads, of course, to huge challenges for the organization and retrieval of data. Perhaps the very move of society into this new mode of social organization made the invention of the computer inevitable because it allows us to organize ever more vast amounts of data.

(5) Bureaucracy. A new white-collar labor force is necessary to set up the procedures for information retrieval and storage. This form of organization encourages a separation from real people since it turns individuals into statistics and paperwork. A classic example is Nazi Germany's Adolf Eichmann and what Hannah Arendt in *Eichmann in Jerusalem* (1963) terms the "banality of evil."

(6) Efficiency. Value is placed on the most efficient means of organizing data and individuals to effect the mass production and dissemination of more goods and information, even if at the expense of exploitation or injustice.

(7) Specialization. Members of the workforce are organized into increasingly specialized fields, so much so that we increasingly rely on other "experts" to complete tasks that had previously been shared or had simply been common knowledge (the preparation of meats and other food products, building construction, transportation, etc.).

Further reading: T. J. Armstrong 1992; Bender 1987; Dean 1999; Foucault 1977a, 1980, 1982; Milgram 1974; D. A. Miller 1988; Zimbardo 2007.

PARADIGMATIC

See **syntagmatic and paradigmatic**

PARADIGM SHIFT

Thomas Kuhn proposed this concept in his influential work, *The Structure of Scientific Revolutions* (1962). In it, he argues that scientists are able only to see those elements in the universe that fit into a given set of rules about how the universe is supposed to operate (the "paradigm"). At moments of scientific crisis (when a particular problem forces scientists to question their current paradigm), those rules change, allowing scientists to see completely new things when looking at the same set of data that they had examined before the paradigm shift (e.g., the shift from a Ptolemaic to a Copernican universe). Kuhn thus challenges a **positivist** understanding of scientific investigation, illustrating how the supposedly objective, neutral form of **empirical** observation that undergirds scientific experimentation is, in fact, to some extent **ideological**. We do not have complete, direct access to a real world of objects; rather, "when paradigms change, the world itself changes with them" (111). That is, insofar as "paradigm changes do cause scientists to see the world of their research-engagement differently" and "In so far as their only recourse to that world is through what they see and do, we may want to say that after a revolution scientists are responding to a different world" (111).

See also: **archaeology, being and event**.

PARAPRAXIS (PARAPRAXES)

See **unconscious**

PARODY (PARODIC)

According to Linda Hutcheon, one of the main features distinguishing postmodernism from modernism is the fact that it "takes the form of self-conscious, self-contradictory, self-undermining statement" (1989: 1). One way of creating this double or contradictory stance on any statement is the use of parody, for example, citing a convention only to make fun of it. As Hutcheon explains, "Parody—often called ironic quotation, **pastiche**, appropriation, or **intertextuality**—is usually considered central to **postmodernism**, both by its detractors and its defenders" (93). Unlike Fredric Jameson, who considers such **postmodern** parody as a symptom of the age, one way in which we have lost our connection to the past and to effective political critique, Hutcheon argues that "through a double process of installing and ironizing, parody signals how present representations come from past ones and what **ideological** consequences derive from both continuity and difference" (93). Hutcheon thus sets herself against the prevailing view among many **postmodern** theorists: "The prevailing interpretation is that **postmodernism** offers a value-free, decorative, de-historicized quotation of past forms and that this is a most apt mode for a culture like our own that is oversaturated with images" (94). Hutcheon insists, instead, that such an ironic stance on representation, genre, and **ideology** serves to *politicize* representation, illustrating the ways that interpretation is ultimately ideological. Parody de-doxifies, to use a favorite term of Hutcheon's; it unsettles all **doxa**, all accepted beliefs and ideologies. Rather than see this ironic stance as "some infinite regress into **textuality**" (95), Hutcheon values the resistance in such **postmodern** works to totalizing solutions for society's con-tradictions; she values **postmodernism**'s willingness to question all **ideological** positions, all claims to ultimate truth.

Such a willingness to play with society's contradictions means that "parody is doubly coded in political terms: it both legitimizes and subverts that which it parodies" (1989: 101); however, this position does not mean that the critique is not effective: postmodern parody "may indeed be complicitous with the values it inscribes as well as subverts, but the subversion is still there" (106). Hutcheon at one point likens such an ironic position to the convention of the inverted comma:

> It is rather like saying something whilst at the same time putting inverted commas around what is being said. The effect is to highlight, or "highlight," and to subvert, or "subvert," and the mode is therefore a "knowing" and an ironic—or even "ironic"—one. **Postmodernism**'s distinctive character lies in this kind of wholesale "nudging" commitment to doubleness, or duplicity. In many ways it is an even-handed process because **postmodernism** ultimately manages to install and reinforce as much as undermine and subvert the conventions and presuppositions it appears to challenge. Nevertheless, it seems reasonable to say that the post-modern's initial concern is to de-naturalize some of the dominant features of our way of life; to point out that those entities that we unthinkingly experience as "**natural**" (they might even include **capitalism**, **patriarchy**, liberal humanism) are in fact "cultural"; made by us, not given to us. (1989: 1–2)

Through such an ironic play with society's contradictions, post-modern parody forces us to question a number of other traditional assumptions about the aesthetic product: (1) the notion of artistic originality and the cult of personality that surrounds the artist; (2) the assumption that **subjectivity** is stable, coherent, or self-determining;

(3) the capitalist principles of ownership and property; (4) all contentions that meaning or identity is **natural** rather than artificial; (5) the belief that one can know **history** the way it really was (to echo a famous **empiricist** formulation of the German historian, Leopold von Ranke); (6) the belief that there is such a thing as a neutral or non-**ideological** position; and (7) the claim that one can secure an autonomous yet still effective realm for the **aesthetic** product, separate from either a mass audience or the mass market.

In such critiques, postmodern parody resembles modernist parody, which, Hutcheon acknowledges, can be found "in the writing of T. S. Eliot, Thomas Mann, and James Joyce and the painting of Picasso, Manet, and Magritte" (1989: 99). What **postmodernist** parody questions, however, is the "Unacknowledged modernist assumptions about closure, distance, artistic autonomy, and the apolitical nature of representation" (99). It is more willing to break down distinctions between "reality" and "fiction," as in such disparate works as Christa Wolf's *No Place on Earth*, E. L. Doctorow's *Ragtime*, Timothy Findlay's *Famous Last Words*, and Woody Allen's *Zelig* (a postmodern generic trait that Hutcheon terms "**historiographic metafiction**"). It is also more willing to incorporate mass-market forms in its critique, with photography and film serving as two especially noteworthy examples. As Hutcheon puts it, "**Postmodernism** is both academic and popular, élitist and accessible" (44). It is thanks to such contradictions that **postmodernism** can mount a successful critique. Whereas Jameson condemns all Hollywood film as contributing to the problems of **late capitalism**, Hutcheon offers another way of valuing such work: "**Postmodern** film does not deny that it is implicated in capitalist **modes of production**, because it knows it cannot. Instead it exploits its 'insider' position in order to begin a **subversion** from within, to talk to consumers in a **capitalist** society in a way that will get us where we live, so to speak" (1989: 114).

Parody is also an important concept in Mikhail Bakhtin's work on the **carnivalesque** tradition and on the **dialogic** and **polyphonic** novel: "Parody ... is an integral element in Menippean satire and in all carnivalized genres in general. To the pure genres (epic, tragedy) parody is organically alien; to the carnivalized genres it is, on the contrary, organically inherent" (Bakhtin, 1984a: 127). Bakhtin provides a particularly helpful chart of the various levels of dialogization in *Problems of Dostoevsky's Poetics* (1984a), ranging from the most monologic discourse ("Direct, unmediated discourse") through "discourse of a represented person" to various forms of what Bakhtin terms "double-voiced discourse": stylization, narration, parody, and "discourse with a sideward glance" (199).

Parody has also been an important genre and concept in the examination of African-American and **postcolonial** literature, appearing for example in Mary Louise Pratt's notions of the **contact zone and transculturation** and in Homi Bhabha's theorization of **hybridity**, **liminality**, and **mimicry**, for which Bakhtin's work serves as touchstone. Also building on Bakhtin's work, Henry Louis Gates sees parody and pastiche as central elements of the African-American tradition of literature. As he explains in *The Signifying Monkey* (1988),

Black **texts** Signify upon other black **texts** in the tradition by engaging in what Ellison has defined as implicit formal critiques of language use, of rhetorical strategy. Literary Signification, then, is similar to parody and pastiche, wherein parody corresponds to what I am calling motivated Signification while pastiche would correspond roughly to unmotivated Signification. By motivation I do not mean to suggest the lack of intention, for parody and pastiche imply intention, ranging from severe critique to acknowledgment and placement within a literary tradition. Pastiche can imply either homage to an antecedent **text** or futility in the face of a seemingly indomitable mode of representation. Black writers Signify on each other's **texts** for all of these reasons, and the relations of Signification that obtain between and among black **texts** serve as a basis for a theory of formal revision in the Afro-American tradition. (xxvii)

In his concept of "Signifyin(g)," Gates seeks to establish an alternative relation to signification in the African-American tradition, one that always troubles the simple relation of **signifier** to **signified** by offering always a double-voiced, often parodic relation to monologic signification: "Signifyin(g)," he writes, "is black double-voicedness" (51). Gates also illustrates that this tradition of parody and double-voicedness has existed in the non-European African and Caribbean tradition for centuries, thus completely separate from Bakhtin's exclusively Eurocentric understanding of the **carnivalesque**.

Further reading: Bakhtin 1981, 1984a, 1984b; Gates 1988; Hutcheon 1988, 1989.

PAROLE

See *langue* **and** *parole*

PASTICHE

Fredric Jameson's concept of "pastiche" is usefully contrasted with Linda Hutcheon's understanding of postmodern **parody**. Whereas Hutcheon sees much to value in **postmodern** literature's stance of parodic self-reflexivity, seeing an implicit political critique and historical awareness in such parodic works, Jameson characterizes **postmodern parody** as "blank parody" without any political bite. According to Jameson, parody has, in the **postmodern** age, been replaced by pastiche: "Pastiche is, like parody, the imitation of a peculiar or unique, idiosyncratic style, the wearing of a linguistic mask, speech in a dead language. But it is a neutral practice of such mimicry, without any of parody's ulterior motives, amputated of the satiric impulse, devoid of laughter" (1991: 17). Jameson sees this turn to "blank parody" as a falling off from modernism, where individual authors were particularly characterized by their individual, "inimitable" styles: "the Faulknerian long sentence, for example, with its breathless gerundives; Lawrentian nature imagery punctuated by testy colloquialism; Wallace Stevens's inveterate hypostasis of nonsubstantive parts of speech ('the intricate evasions of as')"; etc. (16). In postmodern pastiche, by contrast, "Modernist styles ... become postmodernist codes" (17), leaving us with nothing but "a field of stylistic and discursive heterogeneity without a norm" (17). Postmodern cultural productions therefore amount to "the cannibalization of all the styles of the past, the play of random stylistic allusion, and in general what Henri Lefebvre has called the increasing primacy of the 'neo'" (18).

In such a world of pastiche, we lose our connection to history, which gets turned into a series of styles and superseded genres, or **simulacra**: "The new spatial logic of the **simulacrum** can now be expected to have a momentous effect on what used to be historical time" (1991: 18). In such a situation, "the past as 'referent' finds itself gradually bracketed, and then effaced altogether, leaving us with nothing but **texts**" (18). We can no longer understand the past except as a repository of genres, styles, and codes ready for **commodification**.

Jameson points to a number of examples:

(1) The way that postmodern architecture "randomly and without principle but with gusto cannibalizes all the architectural styles of the past and combines them in overstimulating ensembles" (1991: 19).

(2) The way nostalgia film or *la mode rétro* represents the past for us in hyperstylized ways (the 1950s in George Lucas's *American*

Graffiti; the Italian 1930s in Roman Polanski's *Chinatown*); in such works we approach "the 'past' through stylistic connotation, conveying 'pastness' by the glossy qualities of the image, and '1930s-ness' or '1950s-ness' by the attributes of fashion" (1991: 19). The "history of **aesthetic** styles" thus "displaces '**real**' history" (20). Jameson sees this situation as a "symptom of the waning of our historicity, of our lived possibility of experiencing history in some active way" (21).

(3) The way that **postmodern** historical novels (those works Hutcheon characterizes as "**historiographic metafiction**") represent the past through pop images of the past. Jameson gives E. L. Doctorow's *Ragtime* as a perfect example: "This historical novel can no longer set out to represent the historical past; it can only 'represent' our ideas and stereotypes about that past (which thereby at once becomes 'pop history')" (1991: 25). In such works, according to Jameson, "we are condemned to seek **History** by way of our own pop images and **simulacra** of that history, which itself remains forever out of reach" (25).

PATRIARCHY (PATRIARCHAL)

Etymologically meaning "rule of the father," patriarchy is a term used by critical theorists to designate the ways society is structured so as to give power to men. That power is manifested not only in the political and economic spheres (the so-called "glass ceiling") but also in the various ways that culture at large is constructed to privilege men over women: stereotypes that set up uneven **binary oppositions**, for example, the alignment of women with nature, domesticity, emotion, or passivity and men with science, the public sphere, reason, or aggressivity; a **scopophillic** sexualization of women that reduces them to passive **objects** of the male **gaze**; and even language itself, with its privileging of the male pronoun to represent groups of mixed gender (e.g., the original *Star Trek* opening, "where no man has gone before"). **Feminists** have addressed all of these manifestations of patriarchy. In addition to seeking equality for women in politics, leadership, and economic wages, **feminists** have examined the ways cultural representations and social structures have oppressed (and are still oppressing) women. Influenced by **poststructuralism**, some **feminists** in the 1970s and 1980s suggested that all language is structured in such a way as to privilege patriarchy. Julia Kristeva (see **chora**), Hélène Cixous (see *écriture féminine*), and Luce Irigaray (see **phallocentrism**) all reworked Jacques Derrida's **deconstruction** of **logocentrism** in order to question the "**phallogocentrism**" of patriarchal discourse at large, calling for a use of language that privileges instead the fluid, sensual, and agrammatical.

More recent critical theory (so-called "third wave" **feminism**) has increasingly questioned first- and second-wave **feminism**'s almost exclusive concentration on male/female **binary oppositions**. The concern is that **feminism**'s concentration on patriarchy alone keeps theorists from acknowledging the many other identity markers (e.g., race, class, and sexuality) that, when coupled with **gender** stereotypes, yet more egregiously oppress particular groups of people (see especially **Critical Race Theory**, **intersectionality**, and **Matrix of Domination**). **LGBTQ** theorists argue that by concentrating exclusively on the male/female **binary opposition** suggested by the term "patriarchy," earlier **feminists** have ignored and thus excluded all the other identities represented by the acronym **LGBTQ**, that is, lesbian, gay, bisexual, transgender, and queer or "questioning."

Further reading: Butler 1990a, 1990b, 1993; Collins 2000; Crenshaw 1991; Gilbert and Gubar 1984; Gilligan and Richards 2008; Mies 1986; Moghadam 1996; Spivak 1985, 1987, 1988a, 1988b; Swarr and Nagar 2010; Walby 1986, 1990.

PERFORMATIVITY (PERFORMATIVE)

This term is particularly associated with the theorist Judith Butler, who is influenced by Lacanian psychoanalysis, **phenomenology** (Edmund Husserl, Maurice Merleau-Ponty, George Herbert Mead, etc.), structural anthropology (Claude Lévi-Strauss, Victor Turner, Clifford Geertz, etc.) and **Speech–Act Theory** (particularly the work of J. L. Austin and John Searle) in her understanding of the "performativity" of our identities. All of these theories explore the ways that social reality is not a given but is continually created as an illusion "through language, gesture, and all manner of symbolic social sign" (1990b: 270). A good example in **Speech–Act Theory** is what Austin terms perlocutionary speech acts, those speech acts that actually *do* something rather than merely *represent* something. The classic example is the "I pronounce you man and wife" of the marriage ceremony. In making that statement, a person of authority changes the status of a couple within an intersubjective community; those words actively change the existence of that couple by establishing a new marital reality: the words *do* what they say. As Butler explains, "Within **speech act theory**, a performative is that discursive practice that enacts or produces that which it names" (1993: 13). A speech act can produce that which it names, however, only by reference to the law (or the accepted norm, code, or contract), which is cited or repeated (and thus performed) in the pronouncement.

Butler takes this formulation further by exploring the ways that linguistic constructions create our reality *in general* through the speech acts we participate in every day. By endlessly citing the conventions and ideologies of the social world around us, we enact that reality; in the performative act of speaking, we "incorporate" that reality by enacting it with our bodies, but that "reality" nonetheless remains a social construction (at one step removed from what Jacques Lacan distinguishes from reality by the term, "the **Real**"). In the act of performing the conventions of reality, by embodying those fictions in our actions, we make those artificial conventions appear to be **natural** and necessary. By enacting conventions, we do make them "real" to some extent (after all, our **ideologies** have "real" consequences for people) but that does not make them any less artificial. In particular, Butler concerns herself with those "gender acts" that similarly lead to material changes in one's existence and even in one's bodily self: "One is not simply a body, but, in some very key sense, one does one's body and, indeed, one does one's body differently from one's contemporaries and from one's embodied predecessors and successors as well" (1990b: 272). Like the performative citation of the conventions governing our perception of reality, the enactment of gender norms has "real" consequences, including the creation of our sense of **subjectivity,** but that does not make our **subjectivity** any less constructed. We may believe that our **subjectivity** is the source of our actions, our **agency**, but Butler contends that our sense of independent, self-willed **subjectivity** is really a retroactive construction that comes about only through the enactment of social conventions.

Butler therefore understands gender to be "*a corporeal style,* an 'act,' as it were" (1990b: 272). That style has no relation to essential "truths" about the body but is strictly **ideological**. It has a history that exists beyond the **subject** who enacts those conventions:

> The act that one does, the act that one performs, is, in a sense, an act that has been going on before one arrived on the scene. Hence, gender is an act which has been rehearsed, much as a script survives the particular actors who make use of it, but which requires individual actors in order to be actualized and reproduced as reality once again. (1990b: 272)

What is required for the **hegemony** of **heteronormative** standards to maintain power is our continual repetition of such **gender** acts in the most mundane of daily activities (the way we walk, talk, gesticulate, etc.). For Butler, the distinction between the personal and the political or between private and public is itself a fiction designed to support an oppressive status quo: our most personal acts are, in fact, continually being scripted by **hegemonic** social conventions and **ideologies**.

Butler underscores **gender**'s constructed nature in order to fight for the rights of oppressed identities, those identities that do not conform to the artificial—though strictly enforced—rules that govern normative heterosexuality. If those rules are not **natural** or essential, Butler argues, then they do not have any claim to justice or necessity. Since those rules are historical and rely on their continual citation or enactment by **subjects**, then they can also be challenged and changed through alternative performative acts. As Butler puts it, "If the 'reality' of gender is constituted by the performance itself, then there is no recourse to an essential and unrealized '**sex**' or '**gender**' which gender performances ostensibly express" (1990b: 278). For this reason, "the transvestite's gender is as fully real as anyone whose performance complies with social expectations" (278).

See also: **LGBTQ Studies**.

Further reading: Butler 1990a, 1990b, 1993, 1997, 2000; Ehlers 2012; Jagger 2008; Sedgwick 2003.

PERLOCUTIONARY ACT

See **speech act and Speech–Act Theory**

PERVERSION, PERVERSITY, AND POLYMORPHOUS PERVERSITY

Perversion refers to the pursuit of "abnormal" sexual **objects**. Sigmund Freud at one point lists five forms of perversion, which is to say five ways that an individual "differs from the normal": "first, by disregarding the barrier of species (the gulf between men and animals); secondly, by overstepping the barrier against disgust; thirdly, that against incest (the prohibition against seeking sexual satisfaction from near blood-relations); fourthly, that against members of one's own sex; and fifthly, the transferring of the part played by the genitals to other organs and areas of the body" (1953–74: 15.208). He makes clear that a young child will not recognize any of these five points as abnormal—and only does so through the process of education. For this reason, he calls children "polymorphously perverse" (15.209). **Queer theory** and then **LGBTQ Studies** have been quite critical of Freud's understanding of perversion, proposing alternative models for the understanding of human **sexuality**.

Further reading: de Lauretis 1994; Penny 2006.

PETITS RÉCITS

According to Jean-François Lyotard, **postmodernism** is character-ized by a questioning of all **grand narratives** (progress, liberation, salvation, truth) in favor of the *petit récit* or "little narrative." As he writes, "In contemporary society and culture—**postindustrial society**, **postmodern** culture—the question of the legitimation of knowledge is formulated in different terms. The **grand narrative** has lost its credibility, regardless of what mode of unification it uses, regardless of whether it is a speculative narrative or a narrative of emancipation" (1991: 37). Lyotard argues that all claims to truth are really moves in a **language game** and that the goal of a **postmodern** approach to science would be "to point out these metaprescrip-tives (science's 'presuppositions') and to petition the players to accept different ones" (65). No metaprescriptive can be said to be common to all **language games**; the very notion of universal consensus is suspect. All that remains is an "inexhaustible" (67) profusion of new small narratives in an unending play that seeks always to counter the terrorism whereby one set of rules is imposed on other **language games**.

See also: **dissensus, incommensurability, phrase regimen**.

PHALLIC PHASE

According to Sigmund Freud, the phallic phase is the third phase in a child's **psychosexual development**, when pleasure is oriented towards the phallus and urination (roughly 4–7 years of age). For young girls, the clitoris serves the same function as the penis, acccording to Freud. The trauma connected with this phase is that of **castration**, which makes this phase especially important for the resolution of the **Oedipus complex** (see **psychosexual development**).

PHALLOCENTRISM AND PHALLOGOCENTRISM

"Phallocentrism" or "phallogocentrism" is the privileging of the masculine (the phallus) in understanding meaning or social relations. This term
evolved from **deconstructionists** who questioned the "**logocentrism**"
of Western literature and thought, i.e., the belief in the centrality of logos,
understood as cosmic reason (affirmed in ancient Greek philosophy as the
source of world order and intelligibility) or, in the Christian version, the
self-revealing thought and will of God. The term is also associated with
Lacanian **psychoanalysis**, which understands the entrance of **subjects**
into language as a negotiation of the phallus and the **Name-of-the-
Father** (see **symbolic order**). The problem, according to **feminist**
theorists, is that Freudian and Lacanian psychoanalysis read all **desire** in
terms of the male phallus, including female **desire**, which is reduced in
Sigmund Freud to penis envy. As Luce Irigaray explains,

> The fact remains that "penis-envy" must above all be interpreted
> as a symptomatic index—laid down as a law of the economy of
> woman's sexuality—of the pregnancy of the desire for the same,
> whose guarantee, and transcendental signifier or signified, will be
> the phallus. The Phallus. If it were not so, why not *also* analyze
> the "envy" for the vagina? For the uterus? Or the vulva? Etc. ...
> But finally, in Freud, sexual pleasure boils down to being plus or
> minus one sex organ: the penis. And sexual "otherness" comes
> down to "not having it." Thus, woman's lack of penis and her
> envy of the penis *ensure the function of the negative*, serve as repre-
> sentatives of the negative, in what could be called a *phallocentric*—or
> phallotropic—dialectic. (1985a: 51–52)

Following the tenets of **deconstruction**, feminists recast the notion of
logocentrism to illustrate how all Western languages, in all their features,
are utterly and irredeemably male-engendered, male-constituted, and
male-dominated. **Discourse** is "phallogocentric" because it is centered
and organized throughout by implicit recourse to the phallus both as its
supposed ground (or logos) and as its prime signifier and power source.
Some **feminists** extend phallocentrism to what they characterize as a
male form of writing, with regard not only to vocabulary and syntax, but
also to rigorous rules of logic, the proclivity for fixed classifications and
oppositions, and the criteria for what we take to be valid evidence and
objective knowledge (see *écriture feminine*). Feminine writing, by contrast, is aligned with multiplicity, flux, uncertainty, play, laughter, creativity, and the breaking of grammatical rules.

See also: **chora**.

Further reading: Cixous 1976, 1986; Irigaray 1985a, 1985b; Kristeva 1984; Showalter 1985; Slipp 1993.

PHENOMENOLOGY

Phenomenology refers to a branch of critical theory first developed by Edmund Husserl (1859–1938) that examines the structures of consciousness, particularly as a subject's first-person point of view grasps an experience or object of perception. It was later developed by such thinkers as Martin Heidegger (1889–1976), Jean-Paul Sartre (1905–80), and Maurice Merleau-Ponty (1908–61). Phenomenology is generally concerned with an "intentional" consciousness that, as Husserl argues, is always oriented towards the world of objects. It contends that those objects can be grasped by consciousness in their real immediacy; it also argues that an essential aspect of our subjectivity is our ability empathetically to anticipate and understand other subjects' apperception of our own subjectivity, thus allowing us to understand our own subjectivity objectively. After the linguistic turn in philosophy (see **signifier and signified**) and the rise of **poststructuralism**, critical theory increasingly argued that the **subject** is, by definition, separated from the real world of **objects** because of our reliance on language and **ideology** (see the **Real**) and that the relation between **subjects** tends towards **incommensurability** (see **differend, dissensus**). Not surprisingly, phenemonology therefore fell increasingly out of favor. Nonetheless, a few influential thinkers have continued to explore a phenomenological understanding of our relation to **objects** and to **others**, particularly Paul Ricoeur (see **utopia, Other**) and Emmanuel Levinas (see **Other**). Phenomenology has also influenced **Reader-Response Criticism**, particularly through the work of George Poulet (1902–91).

See also: **hermeneutics**.

Further reading: Husserl 1936, 1999; Levinas 1991, 1998, 2003; Luft and Overgaard 2012; Merleau-Ponty 2004; Ricoeur 1991, 1992; Sokolowski 2000.

PHENOTEXT

See **genotext and phenotext**

PHONOCENTRISM (PHONOCENTRIC)

This term, which is closely tied to the comparable term "**logo-centrism**," was popularized by Jacques Derrida, who questioned philosophy's tendency to privilege the spoken voice over writing, to argue for the "absolute proximity of voice and being, of voice and the meaning of being, of voice and the ideality of meaning" (1976: 12). Derrida argues, by contrast, that such maneuvers are grounded on theological mystification and that it is, rather, the logic of writing that precedes such obfuscating maneuvers. Derrida makes the apparently impossible statement that "language is first ... writing" (37). Although writing is clearly a technology that was introduced around 4,000 BCE, Derrida claims that "oral language already belongs to this writing" (55). To make such a claim, Derrida must modify the very concept of writing, arguing for an "arche-writing" that functions to **deconstruct** "presence" in the same way that writing did upon its introduction to human culture: arche-writing "is that very thing which cannot let itself be reduced to the form of *presence*" (57). All meaning-making in fact begins with the arbitrariness of the sign (see **signifier and signified**), according to Derrida, which is to say that there is no necessary or essential thing connecting any word and that which it signifies, just as the marks on a page of writing have no necessary connection to the phonetic sounds or things to which they refer. The written marks that make up the word "tree" are arbitrary, a product of mere convention but so too are the spoken sounds we speak in saying the English word "tree." There is no transcendental or essential operation by which the word "tree," regardless of whether it be written or spoken, is connected to that which it signifies, however much the history of philosophy is replete with efforts to establish such a connection. For Derrida, then, "[t]his arche-writing would be at work not only in the form and substance of graphic expression but also in those of nongraphic expression. It would constitute not only the pattern uniting form to all substance, graphic or otherwise, but the movement of the sign-function linking a content to an expression, whether it be graphic or not" (60). The arbitrary sounds that make up the spoken word "tree" are no different than the **trace** of writing, which is throughout the history of philosophy commonly denigrated in favor of spoken speech.

See also: **binary opposition**, *différance*, **poststructuralism**, **supplement**, **text and textuality**.

PHRASE REGIMEN, PHRASE UNIVERSE, AND GENRE OF DISCOURSE

Jean-François Lyotard establishes his argument about the **differend** by claiming that language is made up of various sets of rules that allow us to make sense of the world or to judge right and wrong. In this, he is particularly inspired by Ludwig Wittgenstein, who argued that language delimits what can be known and, so, that what we know is determined by the rules of language, amounting to a series of what Wittgenstein terms **language games**. Both Wittgenstein and Lyotard are thus part of what Lyotard refers to as "[t]he 'linguistic turn' of Western philosophy" (1988a: xiii). For Lyotard, "[a] phrase, even the most ordinary one, is constituted according to a set of rules (its regimen)" (xii), hence "phrase regimen." Lyotard provides a number of examples of these: "reasoning, knowing, describing, recounting, questioning, showing, ordering, etc." (xii). In each of these phrases, the regimen determines (1) the referent of the phrase; (2) its sense; (3) its addressee; and (4) its addressor: "The disposition of a phrase universe consists in the situating of these four elements in relation to each other" (14).

Lyotard's main point is that "[p]hrases from heterogeneous regimens cannot be translated from one into the other"; they can only be "linked one onto the other in accordance with an end fixed by a genre of discourse" (1988a: xii). A "genre of discourse," then, refers to the generic rules by which we link phrase regimens in order to achieve some goal. For example, a "dialogue links an ostension (showing) or a definition (describing) onto a question; at stake in it is the two parties coming to an agreement about the sense of a referent." As he goes on to explain, "Genres of discourse supply rules for linking together heterogeneous phrases, rules that are proper for attaining certain goals: to know, to teach, to be just, to seduce, to justify, to evaluate, to rouse emotion, to oversee" (xii). The problem is that there is no "universal genre of discourse" (xii) that can regulate conflicts between what Lyotard ultimately sees as **incommensurable** genres of discourse.

The stakes are high for Lyotard since his ultimate goal is "[t]o refute the prejudice anchored in the reader by centuries of humanism and of 'human sciences' that there is 'man,' that there is 'language,' that the former makes use of the latter for his own ends, and that if he does not succeed in attaining these ends, it is for want of good control over language 'by means' of a 'better' language" (1988a: xiii). (On the importance of humanism, see **Introduction**.) Reality itself is uncertain, in Lyotard's formulation, since it can only ever exist as a result of linguistic rules about referentiality. As Lyotard explains, "Reality is not what is 'given' to this or that '**subject**,' it is a state of the referent (that about which one speaks) which results from the effectuation of establishment procedures defined by a unanimously agreed-upon protocol, and from the possibility offered to anyone to recommence this effectuation as often as he or she wants" (1988a: 4). A "phrase universe," then, is the version of reality delineated by the rules of a given phrase regimen. Lyotard also questions whether the **subject** of an utterance is independent of the phrases he or she uses. He wonders, in fact: is it perhaps "that phrases or silences take place (happen, come to pass), presenting universes in which individuals x, y, you, me are situated as the addressors of these phrases or silences?" (11). He thus wonders whether we are in control of language or whether it is, in fact, language that constitutes us as **subjects**. In these ways, Lyotard can be read as opposed to Jürgen Habermas's belief in the possibility of **communicative reason** and **communicative action**, questioning instead any effort to establish what he terms a "**grand narrative**" that seeks to make sense of or rule what are in fact **incommensurable** genres of discourse; at best, all we have are *petits récits*, or little stories tied to particular situations and ways of understanding the world. To impose one narrative or one set of rules to all genres of discourse is, for Lyotard, "totalitarian" (5) and, indeed, it's no coincidence that Lyotard offers as his first example of a **differend** the Holocaust witness who cannot "prove" the existence of the gas chamber because anyone who saw one was, by consequence of the gas chamber's use, killed.

See also: **dissensus, distribution of the sensible, metapolitics.**

Further reading: Lyotard 1988a, 1988b.

PLEASURE PRINCIPLE AND REALITY PRINCIPLE

According to the **psychoanalysis** of Sigmund Freud, "pleasure principle" is the desire for immediate gratification, "reality principle" the deferral of that gratification. Quite simply, the pleasure principle drives one to seek pleasure and to avoid pain; however, as one grows up, one begins to learn that sometimes one must endure pain and defer gratification because of the exigencies and obstacles of reality: "An **ego** thus educated has become 'reasonable'; it no longer lets itself be governed by the pleasure principle, but obeys the *reality principle*, which also at bottom seeks to obtain pleasure, but pleasure which is assured through taking account of reality, even though it is pleasure postponed and diminished" (1953–74: 16.357).

POLYMORPHOUS PERVERSITY

See **perversion**

POLYPHONY (POLYPHONIC)

Mikhail Bakhtin argues that in what he terms Fyodor Dostoevsky's polyphonic novels we see the culmination of a **carnivalesque**, **dialogic** tradition that can be traced backwards to Menippean satire and Socratic dialogues. In a work like Dostoevsky's *Notes from Underground*, we have, according to Bakhtin, *"authentic polyphony"* (1984a: 178), whereby the author gives up all pretense of monologic, centralizing authority: "In Dostoevsky almost no word is without its intense sideward glance at someone else's word" (1984a: 203).

POSITIVISM (POSITIVIST) AND EMPIRICISM (EMPIRICIST)

Critical theorists will sometimes refer to the positivist approach to reality. In so doing, they refer to a position promulgated by August Comte (1798–1857) that only recognizes "observable phenomena and empirically verifiable scientific facts and laws," thus "rejecting inquiry into ultimate causes or origins as belonging to outmoded metaphysical or theological stages of thought" (*OED*). The position is used to support the ultimate value of scientific investigation, accompanied by the belief "that every cognitively meaningful proposition can be scientifically verified or falsified" (*OED*). Theorists apply the term to any philosophical position that claims we can only know the world through scientific investigation and that we should therefore dismiss everything else. "Positivism" is occasionally used as a simple synonym for empiricism, which it certainly supports; that is, the belief that truth can only be derived from direct observation of the real world. This empirical position is adopted in the discipline of history by Leopold von Ranke (1795–1886), Comte's contemporary. According to Ranke, who defined his methodology against the **dialectical** thinking of Georg Wilhelm Friedrich Hegel (1770–1831), a true historian must rely only on primary sources and should eschew all theorizing. Ranke famously synopsized the empirical approach to history in his claim to represent history *"wie es eigentlich gewesen"* (as it actually happened).

The positivist and empiricist position is countered by critical theorists on a number of fronts: Thomas Kuhn examines what he terms "**paradigm shifts**" in science (e.g., Ptolemy to Copernicus or the theory of relativity to quantum mechanics) in order to illustrate that science itself can only "see" those things that fit a given paradigm of thought so that the central premise of positivism is false. Max Weber assumes an anti-positivist position, arguing that the very philosophy of positivism is itself an **ideology** that supports the rise of **capitalism** and modernism through its emphasis on rationalization and secularization. Jean-François Lyotard considers positivism a **language game** among many other language games that are **incommensurable** with each other. Bruno Latour and **Actor-Network Theory** refuse the distinction between the natural world of objects and the human world of representation, exploring instead those hybrid **mediators** that Latour terms **quasi-objects** and **quasi-subjects**. Dominick LaCapra examines the limit-case of the Holocaust to argue that it is impossible to represent the past the way it actually happened—we should instead approach the past in a **transferential** way that considers our psychic health in the present. Walter Benjamin argues that a **historical materialist** must reject Ranke's empiricist position and instead "seize hold of a memory as it flashes up at a moment of danger" (1968: 255); Benjamin's **historical materialist** therefore considers the past not as a "sequence of events like the beads of a rosary" but, rather, examines the relation of the past to the present, "the constellation which his own era has formed with a definite earlier one" (1968: 263). **Speculative Realism** and **Thing Theory** seek to return to the real objects of the world but in a "speculative" way that eschews the more simplistic formulas of positivism and empiricism.

See also: **factiality**, **quasi-objects and quasi-subjects**.

Further reading: Benjamin 1968; Comte 1848; Kuhn 1962; LaCapra 1987, 1994, 1998; Latour 1993, 1999, 2005; Lyotard 1988a; Ranke 1981; Weber 1930.

POSTCOLONIAL STUDIES (POSTCOLONIALISM)

Postcolonial Studies is a critical theory that examines both colonial subjugation and the impact of that subjugation on **ethnic** identities even after previously colonized states have achieved national independence. In other words, although the "post" in "postcolonial" may suggest a concern only with states after independence, Postcolonial Studies examines all the mechanisms whereby imperial colonialism functioned in the past as well as its after-effects in the present. Although the theory has its roots in earlier writers, especially Frantz

Fanon (1925–61), the critical school gained cohesion and prominence during the rise of **poststructuralism**; indeed, the most influential theorists of the last 50 years, Edward Said, Gayatri Chakravorty Spivak, Homi Bhabha, and Mary Louise Pratt, all adopted precepts of **poststructuralism**, especially the **deconstructionist** critique of **binary oppositions**, in the theorization of their key concepts (see **contact zone**, **hybridity**, **liminal and liminality**, **mimicry**, **orientalism**, **othering**, **subaltern**, **transculturation**, and **worlding**). Postcolonial critics are also strongly influenced by **Marxism**, **feminism**, **Cultural Studies**, **psychoanalysis**, and the theoretical concepts of Michel Foucault (especially **discipline**, **discourse**, and **power**), all the while being wary and quite critical of the Eurocentric tendencies of these theories. As Gayatri Chakravorty Spivak, for example, states of Foucault's work, "Foucault is a brilliant thinker of **power**-in-spacing, but the awareness of the topographical reinscription of imperialism does not inform his presuppositions. ... The clinic, the asylum, the prison, the university—all seem to be screen-allegories that foreclose a reading of the broader narratives of imperialism" (1988a: 290–91). In other words, Foucault's concentration on Western institutional developments (the clinic, the asylum, the prison, the university) keeps him from seeing how **power** and **discipline** affect the world outside of Europe.

In general, postcolonial theorists examine and critique the various ways that dominant, Eurocentric culture maintains its **hegemony** by defining itself against—and thus circumscribing the **discursive** possibilities of—the **Other**. It also examines the ways that colonized peoples assert their **subjectivities**, define their **ethnicities**, and trouble the colonizer's **hegemonic discourses**. In addition to examining colonialism and its effects, Postcolonial Studies examines the continuing influence of colonizing, imperial powers through other means than direct military and political control even after the independence of the colonized state. The term "neocolonialism," coined by Kwame Nkrumah (1965), or "neo-imperialism," is often used to describe this continuing influence by other means. As Nkrumah defines his concept, "The essence of neo-colonialism is that the State which is subject to it is, in theory, independent and has all the outward trappings of international sovereignty" but "In reality its economic system and thus its political policy is directed from outside" (ix). For example, as Nkrumah goes on, "The neo-colonial State may be obliged to take the manufactured products of the imperialist power to the exclusion of competing products from elsewhere" or "Control over government policy in the neo-colonial State may be secured by payments towards the cost of running the State, by the provision of civil servants in positions where they can dictate policy, and by monetary control over foreign exchange through the imposition of a banking system controlled by the imperial power" (ix–x). The result of such neo-colonialism "is that foreign capital is used for the exploitation rather than for the development of the less developed parts of the world" (x).

By examining such neo-colonial or neo-imperial mechanisms, **Postcolonial Studies** abuts **Global Studies**, which is also concerned with the economic, cultural, and **ideological** mechanisms by which the "First World" dominates the rest of the world. The area of investigation in **Global Studies** tends, however, to move beyond the interests of single **nation-states** to explore the ways that multinational corporations and global entities like the World Bank or the International Monetary Fund—along with the cultural support for the new world system in the entertainment and communication industries or the military support for it in transnational coalitions, embargoes, and drone strikes—are creating new power structures and forms of dominance in **late capitalism**. Indeed, many theorists have identified a shift in Postcolonial Studies following Michael Hardt and Antonio Negri's work *Empire* (2000), in which the authors go so far as to claim that "Imperialism is over" and that "No nation will be world leader in the way modern European nations were" (xiv) because of the realities of today's multinational, global system. As Ania Loomba, Suvir Kaul, Matti Bunzl, Antoinette Burton, and Jed Esty put it in the introduction to their *Postcolonial Studies and Beyond* (2005),

> Some scholars view postcolonial methods and vocabularies as out of step with an intellectual scene increasingly carved up by such rubrics as the information age (the so-called digital divide), transnational capital, globalization, and alternative modernities. What, then, is the value of postcolonial studies in our globalizing world, and does it have a viable future beyond its existing life span, identified by Vilashini Cooppan in this volume as the period from Edward Said's *Orientalism* (1978) to Michael Hardt and Antonio Negri's *Empire* (2000)? (2)

In response to work in Global Studies, recent postcolonial theorists have developed a complex understanding of both **nation** and **empire**, one that takes into account the new realites of the information age and of multinational and **late capitalism**. They have also moved beyond an exclusive focus on **nation** and **nationalism** or on the **binary opposition**, Occident/Orient, to explore the complex **ethnic** identities that characterize not only the current, postcolonial world order but also aspects of the colonial past, including: diasporic populations; hybrid, multi-ethnic cultures; cultural influences across national borders; and non-military forms of cultural, social, or economic control and resistance.

See also: **culture, fetishism**.

Further reading: Ashcroft *et al.* (2007); Bhabha 1990b, 1994; Breckenridge and v. d. Veer 1993; During 1998, 2000; Fanon 1963, 1967; Gikandi 2001; Krishnaswamy and Hawley 2008; Lazarus 2004; Loomba 2005; Loomba *et al.* 2005; Nkrumah 1965; Olson and Worsham 1999; Pratt 1991, 1992; Said 1978; Spivak 1985, 1987, 1988a, 1988b; Tiffin and Lawson 1994; Wilson, Sandru and Welsh 2010.

POST-INDUSTRIAL SOCIETY

See **late capitalism**

POST-MARXISM

See **Marxism**

POSTMODERNISM AND POSTMODERN THEORY

It is useful to distinguish between "postmodernism," those cultural and theoretical works that share certain postmodern traits or that examine the postmodern age, and "postmodernity," the historical age in which we live. See **postmodernity** for those elements that critical theorists see as characterizing our current postmodern age. Here, I will concentrate first on postmodern cultural works and then postmodern theory.

One of the problems in dealing with postmodernism is in distin- guishing it from modernism. In many ways, postmodern artists and theorists continue the sorts of experimentation that we can also find in modernist works, including the use of self-consciousness, **parody**, irony, fragmentation, generic mixing, ambiguity, and the breakdown between high and low forms of expression. In this way, postmodern artistic forms can be seen as an extension of modernist experimentation; and, indeed, some theorists do not read a break between the two. Jean-François Lyotard goes so far as to argue that "A work can become modern only if it is first postmodern. Postmodernism thus understood is not modernism at its end but in the nascent state, and this state is constant" (1991: 79). However, others prefer to represent the move into postmodernism as a more radical break, one that is a result of new ways of representing the world, including television, film, and the computer. Many date **postmodernity** from the 1960s when we witnessed the rise of postmodern architecture; some point to the 1950s, as does Lyotard in his *Postmodern Condition* (1991: 3); still others prefer to see the Second World War as the radical break from modernity that ushers in the postmodern, since the horrors of the Holocaust revealed at this time how "progressive" advancements like democracy, science, higher education, high culture, a modern judicial system, and religion failed to protect Weimar Germany from the events of the 1930s and 40s. The very term "postmodern" was, in fact, first used to describe our current age in the 1940s by the historian, Arnold Toynbee, though he looked backwards to the cusp of what we now term the modern period as the point when we first moved from modernism (which he instead dates 1475–1875) into post-modernism. See my **Introduction** to this book for the logic of Toynbee's proposed historical trajectory.

Some of the things that distinguish postmodern aesthetic work from modernist work are as follows:

(1) Extreme self-reflexivity. We find this in modernist cultural works, but postmodernists tend to be more playful, even irreverent, which has allowed the technique to enter into mainstream cultural works, for example the way the *Scream* series of movies has characters debating the generic rules behind the horror film. In modernism, self-reflexivity tended to be used by "high" artists in difficult works; in postmodernism, self-reflexive strategies can be found in both high art and everything from *Seinfeld* to music videos. In postmodern architecture, this effect is achieved by keeping visible internal structures and engineering elements (pipes, support beams, building materials, etc.).

(2) Irony and parody. Connected to the former point, is the tendency of postmodern artists, theorists, and culture to be playful or **parodic**. The art works of Andy Warhol and Roy Lichtenstein are good examples. Pop culture and media advertising also abound with examples; indeed, shows or films will often step outside of mimetic representation altogether in order to parody themselves in mid-stride. See **pastiche** and **parody**.

(3) A breakdown between high and low cultural forms. Whereas some modernists experimented with this same breakdown, even the modernists that played with pop forms (e.g., James Joyce and T. S. Eliot) tended to be extremely difficult to follow in their experimentations. Postmodernists, by contrast, often employ pop and mass-produced objects in more immediately understandable ways, even if their goals are still often complex (e.g., Andy Warhol's commentary on mass production and on the commercial aspects of "high" art through his famous, exact reproduction of a set of Cambell's Soup cans). We should, however, keep in mind that Warhol is here clearly following in the *modernist* tradition of "ready-mades," initiated by Marcel Duchamp, who used everyday objects in his art exhibits (including, for example, a urinal for his work, *Fountain*).

(4) Retro **pastiche**. Postmodernists and postmodern culture tend to be especially fascinated with styles and fashions from the past, which they will often use completely out of their original context. Postmodern architects for example will juxtapose baroque, medieval, and modern elements in the same room or building. In pop culture, think of the endlessly recycled television shows of the past that are then given new life on the big screen. Fredric Jameson and Jean Baudrillard tend to read this tendency as a symptom of our loss of connection with historical temporality (see **pastiche, schizophrenia, simulacra**).

(5) A questioning of **grand narratives**. Lyotard sees the breakdown of the narratives that formerly legitimized the status quo as an important aspect of the postmodern condition; in fact, he defines "postmodern" in the very first pages of his *Postmodern Condition* "as incredulity toward metanarratives" (1991: xxiv). Of course, modernists also questioned metanarratives, including such traditional concepts as law, religion, subjectivity, and nationhood; what appears to distinguish postmodernism is that such questioning is no longer particularly associated with an avant-garde intelligentsia. Postmodern artists will employ pop and mass culture in their critiques and pop culture itself tends to play with traditional concepts of temporality, religion, and subjectivity. Think of the popularity of **queer** issues in various media forms or the tendency of, say, Madonna videos to question traditional Christianity ("Like a Prayer"), **gender** divisions ("What It Feels like for a Girl"), **capitalism** ("Material Girl"), and so on. Whether such pop **deconstructions** have any teeth is one of the debates still raging among postmodern theorists.

(6) Visuality and the **simulacrum** working against temporality. Given the predominance of visual media (TV, film, media advertising, the computer), both postmodern art and postmodern culture gravitate towards visual (often even two-dimensional) forms, as in the "cartoons" of Roy Lichtenstein. A good example of this, and of the breakdown between "high" and "low" forms, is Art Spiegelman's *Maus*, a Pulitzer-prize-winning rendition of Vladek Spiegelman's experiences in the Holocaust, which Art (his son) chooses to present through the medium of comics or what is now commonly referred to as the "graphic novel." Another symptom of this tendency is a general breakdown in **narrative** linearity and temporality. Many point to the style of MTV videos as a good example. As a result, Baudrillard and others have argued (for example, through the notion of the **simulacrum**) that we have lost all connection to reality or history. This diagnosis may help to explain why we are so fascinated with reality television. Pop culture also keeps coming back to the idea that the line separating reality and representation or the real world and the dream world has broken down (*Wag the Dog*, *Dark City*, the *Matrix*, the *Truman Show*, *Inception*, etc.).

(7) **Late capitalism**. There is also a general sense that the world has been so taken over by the values of **capitalist** acquisition that alternatives no longer exist. One symptom of this fear is the predominance of paranoia narratives in pop culture (*Blade Runner*, *X-Files*, *The Matrix*, *Minority Report*). This fear is, of course, aided by advancements in technology, especially surveillance technology, which creates the sense that we are always being watched. The global nature of multinational capitalism (see **Global Studies**) also contributes to the sense that there is no clear adversary that one can combat (hence Jameson's insistence on the importance of **cognitive maps** and **utopic** thinking).

(8) Disorientation. MTV culture is sometimes cited as an example as is postmodern architecture, which attempts to disorient the subject entering its space. Another example may be the popularity of films that seek to disorient the viewer completely through the revelation of a truth that changes everything that came before (*The Sixth Sense*, *The Others*, *Unbreakable*, *Memento*, *The Matrix*, even *The Lego Movie*).

Theorists of postmodernism tend to respond to postmodern **aesthetic** work and to the postmodern age more generally in two opposing ways: one camp tends to paint the current situation as **dystopic**;

another camp is celebratory of postmodern **aesthetic** work and theory, arguing that they succeed in safeguarding us from the darker elements of the postmodern condition.

On the **dystopic** side, Jameson, in his magisterial work, *Postmodernism, or, the Cultural Logic of Late Capitalism* (1991), has offered us a particularly influential analysis of our current postmodern condition. Like Baudrillard, whose concept of the **simulacrum** he adopts, Jameson is highly critical of our current historical situation; indeed, he paints a rather **dystopic** picture of the present, which he associates, in particular, with a loss of our connection to **history**. What we are left with is a fascination with the present that approximates **schizophrenia**. According to Jameson, **postmodernity** has transformed the historical past into a series of emptied-out stylizations (what Jameson terms **pastiche**) that can then be **commodified** and consumed. The result is the threatened victory of **capitalist** thinking over all other forms of thought.

Jameson contrasts this postmodern situation with the modernist situation that has been superseded. Whereas modernism still believed in "some residual zones of 'nature' or 'being,' of the old, the older, the archaic" and still believed that one could "do something to that nature and work at transforming that 'referent'" (1991: ix), **postmodernity** has lost a sense of any distinction between the **Real** and **Culture**. For Jameson, **postmodernity** amounts to "an immense dilation of [culture's] sphere (the sphere of **commodities**), an immense and historically original acculturation of the **Real**" (x). Whereas "modernism was still minimally and tendentially the critique of the **commodity** and the effort to make it transcend itself," **postmodernity** "is the consumption of sheer **commodification** as a process" (x). That apparent victory of **commodification** over all spheres of life marks **postmodernity**'s reliance on the "cultural logic of **late capitalism**."

Baudrillard has proven to be an important influence on postmodern theorists and artists, making his presence felt from Jameson's *Postmodernism* to the Wachowskis' *The Matrix*. Like Jameson, Baudrillard paints a rather bleak picture of our current postmodern condition, arguing that we have lost contact with the "**real**" in various ways, that we have nothing left but a continuing fascination with its disappearance. His vision is highly **dystopic**. In Baudrillard's version of **postmodernity**, there is hardly any space for opposition or resistance because of the supreme **hegemony** of the controlling system: "Everywhere, always, the system is too strong: **hegemonic**" (1994: 163). Baudrillard's vision, then, is one of supreme nihilism and melancholia: "Melancholia is the inherent quality of the mode of the disappearance of meaning. ... And we are all melancholic" (162). The problem is that "The system is itself also nihilistic, in the sense that it has the power to pour everything, including what denies it, into indifference" (163). When reading Baudrillard on **postmodernity**, one sometimes gets the sense that we have already lost, that Baudrillard is merely pointing out the various ways that consumer society and the **simulacrum** have won in their colonization of all "reality." The only way out is radical violence and revolution.

In contrast to this dystopic strain, other postmodern theorists see postmodern strategies as valuable, even liberatory. Lyotard argues that what distinguishes the postmodern world is that people have "lost the nostalgia" for **grand narratives** and, so, are willing to test the boundaries of all existing **language games**. "Postmodern science," for example, "by concerning itself with such things as undecidables, the limits of precise control, conflicts characterized by incomplete information, '*fracta*,' catastrophes, and pragmatic paradoxes—is theorizing its own evolution as discontinuous, catastrophic, nonrectifiable, and paradoxical," thus "changing the meaning of the word *knowledge*" (1991: 60).

Linda Hutcheon does not deny that **postmodernity** and postmodernism are "inextricably related" (1989: 26); however, she wants to maintain the possibility that postmodernism's cultural works could be successful in achieving a critical distance from the problems of our contemporary age. Where Hutcheon departs from critics of **postmodernity** is by underscoring the ways that postmodern cultural works engage in effective political critiques of the postmodern world around us: "critique is as important as complicity in the response of cultural postmodernism to the philosophical and socio-economic realities of **postmodernity**: postmodernism here is not so much what Jameson sees as a systemic form of **capitalism** as the name given to cultural practices which acknowledge their inevitable implication in **capitalism**, without relinquishing the power or will to intervene critically in it" (26). Hutcheon therefore explores a wide variety of works from various genres and media to illustrate how the cultural works of postmodernism effect their critique of the present.

Although Hutcheon acknowledges that postmodernism borrows some strategies from modernism (e.g., self-consciousness and self-reflexivity), she argues that postmodernism does differ from modernism in important ways and that it is this difference from the modernist project that exemplifies the critical potential of postmodern cultural work. For one, Hutcheon points out that postmodern works tend to be critical of "modernism's elitist and sometimes almost totalitarian modes of effecting ... 'radical change'—from those of Mies van der

Rohe to those of Pound and Eliot, not to mention Céline" (1989: 26–27). Hutcheon points out how modernists pursued radical change without acknowledging the price that must be paid for the more extremist positions assumed by modernist authors (e.g., fascism, futurism, primitivism, anarchism, etc.). She also questions how effective elitist modernist projects could ever be as political critique.

If there is one thing that especially distinguishes postmodernism from modernism, according to Hutcheon, it is postmodernism's relation to mass culture. Whereas modernism "defined itself through the exclusion of mass culture and was driven, by its fear of contamination by the consumer culture burgeoning around it, into an elitist and exclusive view of **aesthetic formalism** and the autonomy of art" (1989: 28), postmodern works are not afraid to renegotiate "the different possible relations (of complicity and critique) between high and popular forms of culture" (28). In *The Politics of Postmodernism* (1989), she gives postmodern photography as a perfect example, since it "moves out of the hermeticism and **narcissism** that is always possible in self-referentiality and into the cultural and social world, a world bombarded daily with photographic images" (29). Those contemporary works that are particularly autonomous and auto-referential Hutcheon tends to call "late modernist" (27) rather than postmodernist because, as she argues, "These formalist extremes are precisely what are called into question by the historical and social grounding of postmodern fiction and photography" (27). The other techniques that Hutcheon associates with postmodern cultural works include: the de-**naturalization** of the **natural** (i.e., a refusal to present "what is really *constructed* meaning as something *inherent* in that which is being represented" [1989: 49]); the questioning of the distinction between fiction and **history** (thus subscribing to the **poststructuralist** contention that so-called "objective," **empiricist, positivist** history is, in fact, just as affected by generic and **ideological** constructs or the artificial structures of **narrative** form as is fiction—Hutcheon coins the term **historio-graphic metafiction** for postmodern works that mix **history** and fiction); a rejection of **grand narratives** (in favor of what Lyotard terms *petits récits* or little stories—multiple and even contradictory histories rather than "**History**"); an acknowledgement of the present's influence on our knowledge of the past; a recognition of our reliance on **textuality** (documents, written histories, etc.) and on the limited perspectives of individuals in understanding the past or even any event in the present; and the de-**naturalization** of **gender and sex**. Along with the breakdown between high and low cultural forms, the most important strategy that for Hutcheon distinguishes postmodern

aesthetic works from modernist works is **parody**. According to Hutcheon, such strategies allow postmodern works to maintain a continual and effective critique of **postmodernity** without, at the same time, ever falling prey to the belief that one can ever *completely* escape complicity with the **ideologies** that determine our sense of reality in the postmodern condition.

Some theorists go even further in celebrating aspects of post-modernism. Donna Harraway for example adopts irony as a "rhetorical strategy and a political method" (1991: 149) in her turn to the **cyborg** as a postmodern strategy and a model for the program of "socialist-**feminism**." Whereas "[f]rom one perspective, a cyborg world is about the final imposition of a grid of control on the planet," Harraway posits another perspective from which "a cyborg world might be about lived social and bodily realities in which people are not afraid of their joint kinship with animals and machines, not afraid of per-manently partial identities and contradictory standpoints" (1991: 154). For her, the **cyborg** exemplifies a laudatory postmodern self that breaks boundaries and no longer believes in traditional **binary oppositions**.

Further reading: Baudrillard 1988, 1994, 1998; Călinescu 1987; Harraway 1991; Harvey 1989; Hassan 1987; Hutcheon 1988, 1989; Jameson 1991; Jenks 1991; Lyotard 1991, 1993; Mandel 1978; Rosenau 1992; H. J. Silverman, 1990; B. S. Turner 1994; Vattimo 1988.

POSTMODERNITY

Linda Hutcheon is very careful to distinguish between "postmodernity" and "**postmodernism**." The former she understands to mean "the designation of a social and philosophical period or 'condition'" (1989: 23), specifically the period or "condition" in which we now live. The latter she associates with *cultural* expressions of various sorts, including "architecture, literature, photography, film, painting, video, dance, music" (1) and so on (see **postmodernism**). Indeed, Hutcheon argues that the reason why critics have been led to such disparate opinions about the "postmodern" is because of the conflation of these two disparate if associated domains (socio-historical on the one hand, **aesthetic** on the other hand). By distinguishing between the two domains, Hutcheon offers a critique of Fredric Jameson's influential attack against the postmodern: "The slippage from postmoder*nity* to postmoder*nism* is constant and deliberate in Jameson's work: for him **postmodernism** *is* the 'cultural logic of late capitalism'" (25). Jameson tends to see postmodern art and theory as merely reinforcing the many things he finds distressing in postmodern culture, particularly the conditions of multinational **late capitalism**. I should add that Hutcheon does in fact agree with other critics about many of the elements that characterize our current moment in time or postmodern*ity*.

See **postmodernism** for an articulation of the differences between some theorists of postmodern culture. In this section, I will lay out some of the elements that, according to postmodern critical theorists, characterize postmodernity:

(1) A world dominated by the logic of **capitalism** and consumerism, which has no regard for the rights of oppressed laborers or the ravagement of the natural world. A culture of consumption has so much taken over our ways of thinking that all reality is filtered through the logic of **exchange value** and advertising. As Jean Baudrillard writes, "Our society thinks itself and speaks itself as a consumer society. As much as it consumes anything, it consumes itself as consumer society, as idea. Advertising is the triumphal paean to that idea" (1998: 193).

(2) The proliferation of trashy, **kitsch**, mass-market products, which, according to Baudrillard, contribute to our society of **simulation** and consumerism.

(3) A society increasingly under the scrutiny of government agencies that insist on casting their disciplining gaze ever deeper into our private lives.

(4) An increasing reliance on technologies that separate us from other people and the natural world, thus feeding into our sense of atomism and unease.

(5) An emphasis on flat, spatial representations (screens, statistics, ads) that serve to sever us from our former sense of temporality and **history**. The **media** are an important part of this characteristic of postmodernity. The fact that movies and television (the media) keep turning to history and to various "retro" recreations of the past is merely a symptom (a **reaction formation**, Sigmund Freud would say) for the loss of **history**. Indeed, such media works continue the process of forgetting history; as Baudrillard writes of the NBC miniseries *Holocaust*, "One no longer makes the Jews pass through the crematorium or the gas chamber, but through the sound track and image track, through the universal screen and the microprocessor. Forgetting, annihilation, finally achieves its **aesthetic** dimension in this way—it is achieved in retro, finally elevated here to a mass level" (1994: 49). Television, film,

and the Internet separate us from the **real** even as they seek to reproduce it more fully or faithfully: "The hyperreality of communication and of meaning. More real than real, that is how the **real** is abolished" (Baudrillard 1994: 81).

(6) A culture increasingly dominated by **simulacra** (computer images, commercial advertising, Hollywood idealizations, commercial mass reproduction, televisuality, and technological replications of all stripes), thus contributing to our sense of separation from the **real**.

(7) The loss of history. As Baudrillard puts it, "**History** is our lost referential, that is to say our myth." He goes on to say that "The great event of this period, the great trauma, is this decline of strong referentials, these death pangs of the **real** and of the rational that open onto an age of **simulation**" (1994: 43).

(8) Ironic distance from the real world. Although Hutcheon believes this distance can be positive when turned into **parody**, Jameson and Baudrillard see it as a symptom of the postmodern condition. Like Jameson, Baudrillard argues that the **parodic**, self-conscious, self-reflexive elements of pop-cultural forms only aid in their **capitalist** complicity:

> This false distance is present everywhere: in spy films, in Godard, in modern advertising, which uses it continually as a cultural allusion. It is not really clear in the end whether this "cool" smile is the smile of humour or that of commercial complicity. This is also the case with pop, and its smile ultimately encapsulates all its ambiguity: it is not the smile of critical distance, but the smile of *collusion*. (1998: 121)

(9) Secondary orality. Whereas literacy rates had been rising steadily from the introduction of print through the modern period, postmodern society has seen a reversal in this trend as more and more people are now functionally illiterate, relying instead on an influx of oral media sources: television, film, radio, etc. The culture still very much relies on print to create these media outlets (hence the term *secondary* orality); however, it is increasingly only a professional, well-educated class that has access to full print and computer literacy. An ever-larger percentage of the population merely ingests orally the media that is being produced.

Further reading: Baudrillard 1988, 1994, 1998; Călinescu 1987; Harvey 1989; Hassan 1987; Hutcheon 1988, 1989; Jameson 1991; Lyotard 1991, 1993; Mandel 1978; Rosenau 1992; Turner 1994; Vattimo 1988.

POSTSTRUCTURALISM

Closely associated with **postmodernism**, poststructuralism is a term that encompasses a group of largely French and American theorists who grew to prominence in the second half of the twentieth century. As the term suggests, poststructuralists are closely tied to the **structuralist** theorists they question. **Deconstruction** is perhaps the most well-known poststructuralist school of thought. According to Jacques Derrida, the history of Western science and philosophy is a history of efforts to limit the "play" of structure by referring structure "to a point of presence, a fixed origin" (1978: 278). As he goes on, "It could be shown that all the names related to fundamentals, to principles, or to the center have always designated an invariable presence—*eidos*, *archē*, *telos*, *energeia*, *ousia* (essence, existence, substance, subject) *alētheia*, transcendentality, consciousness, God, man, and so forth" (279–80). According to Derrida, a "rupture" occurred over the course of the twentieth century after which "it was necessary to begin thinking that there was no center, that the center could not be thought in the form of a present-being, that the center had no natural site, that it was not a fixed locus but a function, a sort of nonlocus in which an infinite number of sign-substitutions came into play" (1978: 280). This was the point, particularly after the publication of Ferdinand de Saussure's *Course in General Linguistics* in 1916, when "language invaded the universal problematic, the moment when, in the absence of a center or origin, everything became **discourse**—provided we can agree on this word—that is to say, a system in which the central signified, the original or transcendental signified, is never absolutely present outside a system of differences" (1978: 280). Derrida also mentions as significant influences Friedrich Nietzsche's "critique of metaphysics"; the "Freudian critique of self-presence, that is, the critique of consciousness, of the **subject**, of self-identity and of self-proximity or self-possession" (see **psychoanalysis**); and Martin Heidegger's "destruction of metaphysics, of onto-theology, of the determination of Being as presence" (280). For Derrida's ideas, see, in particular, *bricolage*, *différance*, **logocentrism**, **phonocentrism**, **supplement**, **teleology**, and **trace**.

All poststructuralists who followed Derrida shared with him a desire to question any claim to absolute metaphysical truth or the **naturalization** of presence and **teleology**. The approach was therefore particularly influential on critical theorists seeking to contest dominant and hegemonic claims about the **naturalization** of concepts such as **gender and sex**, **race** and **class**, in particular **feminism** and theorists of **gender and sex** (Judith Butler, Hélène Cixous, Barbara Johnson,

Luce Irigaray, Eve Sedgwick; see *écriture féminine*, **epistemology of the closet, homosocial desire, performativity**, and **phallocentrism**); **postcolonial** theorists and theorists of **race** (Homi Bhabha, Kimberlé Crenshaw, Gayatri Chakravorty Spivak; see **Critical Race Theory, hybridity, liminal and liminality, mimicry**, and **subaltern**); and **Marxist** theorists of **class** (Ernesto Laclau and Chantal Mouffe; see **antagonism, articulation, hegemony**, and **radical democracy**). Poststructuralism has also greatly influenced many **postmodern** theorists (Jean Baudrillard, Gilles Deleuze, Félix Guattari, Linda Hutcheon, Jean-François Lyotard, Avital Ronell; see **assemblage, body without organs, differend, grand narrative, historiographic metafiction, incommensurability, language game, parody,** *petits récits*, **phrase regimen, rhizome, schizoanalysis, schizophrenia, simulacra, sublime**, and **wrong**). Other significant theorists associated with poststructuralism and deconstruction include Paul de Man and J. Hillis Miller. Michel Foucault is sometimes associated with poststructuralism, though his concerns with **power** and **government** lead him to different conclusions and areas of investigation (see **apparatus, archaeology, author, bio-politics and bio-power, discipline, discourse, heterotopia, panoptic, repressive hypothesis**). The **psychoanalysis** of Jacques Lacan and Julia Kristeva has also been characterized as poststructuralist (see **psychosexual development**).

See also: **agency, binary opposition,** *langue* and *parole*, **semiotics, signifier and signified**.

Further reading: Attridge *et al.* 1987; de Man 1979, 1983; Derrida 1976, 1978, 1982; Harari 1980; Johnson 1987; Lyotard 1988a, 1994; Lyotard and Thébaud 1985; J. H. Miller 1977, 1985, 1991, 1995; Ronell 1989, 1994; Sturrock 1979; Young 1981.

POWER

The issues of power and disempowerment concern many of the theorists discussed in this *Key Concepts* book; however, the most significant theorist looking at the issue of power is Michel Foucault, who addressed the relation of power to knowledge and subjectivity throughout his career. Although this concept seems as if it should be self-explanatory, it has in fact been inflected by its re-definition in the work of this influential theorist. In his work, Foucault argues that power is not merely physical force but a pervasive human dynamic determining our relationships to others; one need only think of how one acts differently the moment someone enters a room in which one had previously been alone. Power is also not necessarily "bad," because it can also be productive; we may be willing, for example, to assign to certain people the power to organize an activity because we know they are capable of helping us actually accomplish the task at hand. We could also say that power is essential to a just society; all people exert a certain power over us insofar as we defer to their needs and desires. The moment we cease to acknowledge this power that an other has over us, then we deny that other's humanity (and human rights.) As Foucault puts it, "slavery is not a power relationship when man is in chains" (1982: 221). However, power also refers to the (often surreptitious) ways in which a dominant group exerts its influence over others. Though this **hegemonic** power may (at some end point) rely on the threat of punishment, it does not necessarily rely on actual physical enforcement on a day-to-day basis. Imagine this scenario, for example: you are driving over a flat country landscape at night and you reach a stoplight; there is no one else that you can see for miles, and yet do you not feel obliged to stop for the light?

Foucault's understanding of power changes between his early work on institutions (*Madness and Civilization, The Birth of the Clinic, Discipline and Punish*) and his later work on **sexuality** and **governmentality**. In the early work, Foucault sometimes gives a sense that power somehow inheres in institutions themselves rather than in the individuals that make those institutions function. What Foucault explores in those books is how the creation of modern **disciplines**, with their principles of order and control, tends to "disindividualize" power, making it seem as if power inheres in the prison, the school, the factory, and so on. The **Panopticon** becomes Foucault's model for the way other institutions function: the **Panopticon** "is an important mechanism, for it automatizes and disindividualizes power. Power has its principle not so much in a person as in a certain concerted distribution of bodies, surfaces, lights, gazes; in an arrangement whose internal mechanisms produce the relation in which individuals are caught up" (1977a: 202). Indeed, Bentham's goal was to create an architectural idea that, ultimately, could function on its own; it did not matter who exactly operated the machine: "Any individual, taken almost at random, can operate the machine: in the absence of the director, his family, his friends, his visitors, even his servants" (1977a: 202). The idea of **discipline** itself similarly functions as an abstraction of the idea of power from any individual: "'**Discipline**' may be identified neither with an institution nor with an apparatus; it is a type of power, a modality for its exercise, comprising a whole set of instruments, techniques, procedures, levels of application, targets; it is a 'physics' or an 'anatomy' of power, a technology" (1977a: 215). Bureaucracies, like disciplines, contribute to the process of disindividuation since they promote the facelessness of the bureaucrat ("I'm just doing my job"; "I'm just a cog in the machine") and tend to continue functioning even after major revolutions; after the fall of Nazi Germany, for example, the general bureaucratic structure, and most of its workers, remained in place.

The effect of this tendency to disindividualize power is the perception that power resides in the machine itself (the "panoptic machine"; the "technology" of power) rather than in its operator. For this reason, one can finish reading Foucault's *Discipline and Punish* with the paranoid feeling that we are powerless before such an effective and diffuse form of social control. Foucault makes clear in his later work, however, that power ultimately does inhere in individuals, including those that are surveilled or punished. It is true that contemporary forms of disciplinary organization allow ever larger numbers of people to be controlled by ever smaller numbers of "specialists"; however, as Foucault explains in "The Subject and Power" (1982), "something called Power, with or without a capital letter, which is assumed to exist universally in a concentrated or diffused form, does not exist. Power exists only when it is put into action" (219). Foucault therefore makes clear that, in itself, power "is not a renunciation of freedom, a transference of rights, the power of each and all delegated to a few" (220). Indeed, power is *not* the same as violence because the opposite pole of violence "can only be passivity" (220). By contrast, "a power relationship can only be articulated on the basis of two elements which are each indispensable if it is really to be a power relationship: that 'the other' (the one over whom power is exercised) be thoroughly recognized and maintained to the very end as a person who acts; and that, faced with a relationship of power, a whole field of responses, reactions, results, and possible inventions may open up" (220). Power always entails a set of actions performed upon another person's actions and reactions. Although violence may be a part of some power relationships, "In itself the exercise of power is not violence" (220); it is "always a way of acting upon an acting **subject** or acting **subjects** by virtue of their acting or being capable of action" (220).

Foucault therefore turns in his later work to the concept of "**government**" in order to explain how power functions. The turn to this concept of "**government**" allowed Foucault to include a new element to his understanding of power: freedom. "Power is exercised only over free subjects, and only insofar as they are free" (1982: 221), Foucault explains. Indeed, recalcitrance thus becomes an integral part of the power relationship: "At the very heart of the power relationship, and constantly provoking it, are the recalcitrance of the will and the intransigence of freedom" (1982: 221–22). Foucault thus provides us with a powerful model for thinking about how to fight oppression when one sees it: "the analysis, elaboration, and bringing into question of power relations and the 'agonism' between power relations and the intransitivity of freedom is a permanent political task inherent in all social existence" (1982: 223).

Foucault's understanding of power in his later work comes closer to Max Weber's understanding of power, which is developed especially in Pierre Bourdieu's theories about **culture** (see **cultural capital, doxa, habitus, field**).

See also: **antagonism, apparatus, bare life** and *homo sacer*, **Matrix of Domination, radical democracy**.

Further reading: T. J. Armstrong 1992; Collins 2000; Dreyfus and Rabinow 1983; Foucault 1975, 1977a, 1980, 1982, 1990, 1991c; Rose 1999; Weber 1921.

PRAXIS

This term is used particularly by **Marxist** theorists to distinguish their political goals from "mere theorizing." That is, such critical theorists seek not only to *theorize* aspects of a given society but also to effect *practical*, political change. The term can also be distinguished from **ideology**. As Antonio Gramsci writes, for example,

> There is ... a fundamental difference between the philosophy of praxis and other philosophies: other ideologies are non-organic creations because they are contradictory, because they aim at reconciling opposing and contradictory interests. ... The philosophy of praxis, on the other hand, does not aim at the peaceful resolution of existing contradictions in history and society but is rather the very theory of these contradictions. It is not the instrument of government of the dominant groups in order to gain the consent of and exercise **hegemony** over the **subaltern** classes; it is the expression of these **subaltern** classes who want to educate themselves in the art of government and who have an interest in knowing all truths, even the unpleasant ones, and in avoiding the (impossible) deceptions of the upper class and—even more—their own. (1995: 395–96)

Praxis is therefore closely tied to the roots of critical theory in the **Frankfurt School**, which understood its goal as the transformation of society for the better and the vigilant application of ideological critique to everything, including their own theories (see **Introduction**).

PRECONSCIOUS

The preconscious refers, in Sigmund Freud, to the parts of the brain that are readily available to the conscious mind, although not currently in use. Freud used this term to make clear that the **repressed** is a part of the **unconscious**, not all of it, which is to say that the **repressed** does not comprise the whole **unconscious**. Many facts, memories, etc. are not actively engaged by the conscious mind but remain available for possible use at a future time. The preconscious refers to those facts of which we are not currently conscious but which exist in latency and can be easily called up when needed. Other facts, memories, etc. are *actively* **repressed** by the conscious mind and thus are not accessible to the mind except by way of the psychoanalytical "talking cure."

PROAIRETIC

See **hermeneutic and proairetic codes**

PROJECTION

Scapegoating is a good example of projection. The term refers to the act of cutting off from oneself what the **super-ego** perceives as "bad" (e.g., weakness or homosexual desire) and *projecting* that quality or **desire** onto someone else "over there" where it can be condemned, punished, etc.

PROLETARIAT

"Proletariat" refers to the "lower" or "working" classes after the rise of **capitalism**, the members of which must sell their **labor** in order to earn a living. According to Karl Marx, since the members of the proletariat do not own the products of their **labor** and do not have free access to the **means of production** or to the means of communication, they are alienated both from the products they produce and from each other (see **alienation**). Note that some post-Marxists (for example, Ernesto Laclau and Chantal Mouffe) have argued that the working classes are, in fact, much more stratified than acknowledged by traditional

Marxists, with the differences between skilled labor and unskilled labor being as significant as the difference between the lower and middle classes.

PROPOSITION

See **articulation**

PSYCHOANALYSIS

Psychoanalytical Criticism aims to show that a literary or cultural work is always structured by complex and often contradictory human desires. Whereas **New Historicism** and Marx-inspired **Cultural Materialism** analyze public power structures in terms of the **culture** as a whole, psychoanalysis analyzes microstructures of power within the individual and within small-scale domestic environments. That is, it analyzes the interiority of the self as well as the self's kinship systems. By analyzing the formation of the individual, psychoanalysis also helps us to understand the formation of **ideology** at large—and can therefore be extended to the analysis of various cultural and societal phenomena. Indeed, for this reason, psychoanalysis has been especially influential over the last three decades in **cultural studies**, film studies, and **Marxist** criticism.

Psychoanalysis is complicated by the fact that it has undergone numerous transformations at the hands of influential individual psychoanalysts and psychoanalytical critics. It is therefore necessary to differentiate between individual thinkers. Regarding the study of literature and culture, the most influential theorists are Sigmund Freud (1856–1939), Jacques Lacan (1901–81), Julia Kristeva (1941–), and, building on Louis Althusser's use of Lacan for **Marxist** critique, Slavoj Žižek (1949–).

Most people are familiar with at least some of Freud's ideas given the important influence he has had on the literature and culture of the twentieth century. Indeed, many of Freud's key terms have now entered common parlance, terms such as **repression**, **libido**, **super-ego**, **fetishism**, the **unconscious,** and so on; for this very reason, however, it is important to take the popular definitions of such terms with a grain of salt, which is to say that the terms were often much more complex in Freud's thinking than popular culture tends to acknowledge.

Lacan has proven to be an important influence on contemporary scholarship as well, particularly for **feminists**, film theorists, and cultural critics. Although Lacan used some of the general premises of Freudian psychoanalysis, he rethought elements of Freudian theory and also came up with his own terms and ideas to explain various psychiatric phenomena. Whereas Freud tended to hew closely to issues of **sexuality** in a biological sense, Lacan argued that "the unconscious is structured like a language." For this reason, he eschewed terms that suggested a "natural" or "essential" reason for psychic processes (instincts, appetites, etc.) and opted instead for terms that underlined how psychic processes are always artificially constructed, like language or **ideology**. Following this general premise, Lacan broke from the Freudian school and established his own complex set of structures to explain the functioning of **ideology** and thought in general. See, especially, **Real**, **Imaginary Order**, and **Symbolic Order**.

Kristeva began her own studies under Roland Barthes and was heavily influenced by the **structuralists** associated with the Tel Quel group (including Michel Foucault, Philippe Sollers, and Roland Barthes himself). Her interest in psychoanalysis was also inspired by Lacan's **structuralist** re-interpretation of Freud, although Kristeva has also carefully distinguished her own ideas from those of Lacan. Kristeva was particularly critical of what she saw as an inherent misogyny in Lacan's and Freud's theories; her own system of thinking therefore attempts to rethink sexual development in such a way as to value the importance of the feminine. For this reason, she has been especially influential on theories of **gender and sex**. Each individual book by Kristeva has tended to concentrate on and rethink a specific concept (e.g., the abject or mourning and melancholia) and has thus often influenced critical understandings of the terms under discussion (see especially **abject** and **chora**).

Psychoanalysis has also proven important for **Marxist** critics. Louis Althusser influentially reworked Lacan's understanding of the **Real** for a **Marxist** critique of **ideology**, arguing that the **Real** corresponds to the class **antagonisms** that are repressed in order to maintain the current way of structuring reality. **Ideology** for Althusser is aligned with Lacan's understanding of "reality," the fantasy world we construct for ourselves after we become speaking beings; as such, it is impossible to get outside of **ideology**: "**ideology** has always-already interpellated individuals as **subjects**, which amounts to making it clear that individuals are always-already interpellated by **ideology** as **subjects**" (2001: 119). Building on Lacan, Althusser's thesis is that "*Ideology represents the imaginary relationship of individuals to their real conditions of existence*" (109). That is, "it is not their real conditions of existence, their real world, that 'men' 'represent to themselves' in **ideology**"; rather, it is the "*imaginary nature*" of their relation to those conditions of existence that is represented to them there (111). "What is represented in ideology," Althusser explains further, "is therefore not the system of the real relations which govern the existence of individuals, but the imaginary relation of those individuals to the real relations in which they live" (111). In this way of thinking, confronting the **Real** is as traumatic as it is in Lacan and just as impossible to articulate (since it is outside of what can be said in language).

Other **Marxist** theorists have adopted this way of understanding the **Real** of history, for example Fredric Jameson, Ernesto Laclau, and Chantal Mouffe (see **history**). Slavoj Žižek is perhaps the most influential recent **Marxist** critic adopting Lacanian concepts for his critique of **ideology**. For Žižek, "All 'culture' is in a way a **reaction-formation**, an attempt to limit, canalize—to *cultivate* this imbalance, this traumatic kernel, this radical **antagonism** through which man cuts his umbilical cord with nature, with animal homeostasis" (1989: 5). To understand the social field and **history** itself, we must acknowledge "an original 'trauma,' an impossible kernel which resists symbolization, totalization, symbolic integration. Every attempt at symbolization-totalization comes afterwards: it is an attempt to **suture** an original cleft—an attempt which is, in the last resort, by definition doomed to failure" (6). By this logic, all the terms that in Freud and Lacan tend to be applied to a single individual (in the psychoanalytical talking cure) can just as effectively be applied to society at large, and, indeed, Freud does that himself in his works *Civilization and Its Discontents* (1929) and *Totem and Taboo* (1912–13).

An influential critique of the Freudian and Lacanian understanding of **desire** and the **unconscious** can be found in the work of Gilles Deleuze and Félix Guattari, particularly *Anti-Oedipus* (1983) and *A Thousand Plateaus* (1987). Deleuze and Guattari propose an alternative form of psychoanalysis that they term **schizoanalysis**, arguing against the patriarchal and "arborescent" structures—"the phallus-tree" (1987: 17)—of traditional approaches. By contrast, schizoanalysis "treats the **unconscious** as an acentered system, in other words, as a machinic network of finite automata (a **rhizome**), and thus arrives at an entirely different state of the **unconscious**" (1987: 18).

PSYCHOSEXUAL DEVELOPMENT

Each of the major psychoanalytical theories (Freudian, Lacanian, Kristevan) offers a narrative of how we developed our consciousness over the course of our childhood. Jacques Lacan and Julia Kristeva largely build on and modify Sigmund Freud's earlier and highly influential model. Freud established a rigid model for the "normal" sexual development of the human subject, which he terms the "**libido** development." Despite the rigidity of Freud's model, one should note that anyone can be arrested at or insufficiently grow out of any of the primal stages, leading to various **neurotic symptoms** in adult life (see **fixation** and **regression**). Here is your story, as told by Freudian, Lacanian, and Kristevan psychoanalysis, with the ages provided as very rough approximations since Freud, Lacan, and Kristeva changed their minds about the actual dates of the various stages and also acknowledged that development varied between individuals. Stages can even overlap or be experienced simultaneously:

0–2 years of age

Early in your development, according to Freud, all of your desires were oriented towards your lips and your mouth, which accepted food, milk, and anything else you could get your hands on (the **oral phase**). The first object of this stage was, of course, the mother's breast; the **libidinal** drive could then be transferred to auto-erotic objects (thumb-sucking). The mother thus logically became your first "love-**object**," already a **displacement** from the earlier **object** of desire (the breast). When you first recognized the fact of your father, you dealt with him by identifying yourself with him; however, as the sexual wishes directed to your mother grew in intensity, you became possessive of your mother and secretly wished your father out of the picture (the **Oedipus complex**). This **Oedipus complex** plays out throughout the next two phases of development.

According to Lacan, the first six months of this first stage of psycho-sexual development is when you were closest to the pure materiality of existence, or what Lacan terms "the **Real**." Kristeva refers to these first months as the **chora**; at this stage, according to Kristeva, you were purely dominated by your **drives** (both life drives and the **death drive**). Even at this early stage, according to Lacan, your body began to be fragmented into specific erogenous zones (mouth, anus, penis, vagina), aided by the fact that your mother tended to pay special attention to these body parts. This "territorialization" of the body could already be seen as a falling off, an imposition of boundaries and, thus, the neo-natal beginning of socialization (a first step away from the **Real**). Indeed, this fragmentation was accompanied by **identification** with those things perceived as fulfilling your **lack** at this early stage: the mother's breast, her voice, her gaze. Since these privileged external objects could not be perfectly assimilated and could not, therefore, ultimately fulfill your **lack**, you already began to establish the psychic dynamic (fantasy vs. **lack**) that would control the rest of your life.

From about 6 to 18 months, Lacan argues that you underwent a "mirror stage," which was a crucial moment in your development. The "mirror stage" entails a "libidinal dynamism" (1977: 2) caused by the young child's identification with his own image (what Lacan terms the "Ideal-I" or "**ideal ego**"). For Lacan, this act marks the primordial recognition of one's self as "I," although at a point before entrance into language and the **symbolic order**. This stage's misrecognition or *méconnaissance* (seeing an **ideal ego** where there is a fragmented, chaotic body) subsequently "characterizes the ego in all its structures" (1977: 6). In particular, this creation of an ideal version of the self gives pre-verbal impetus to the creation of **narcissistic** fantasies in the fully developed **subject**. That fantasy image of ourselves can be filled in by others who we may want to emulate in our adult lives (role models, etc.), anyone that we set up as a mirror for ourselves. The mirror stage thus establishes what Lacan terms the "**imaginary order**" and, through the imaginary, continues to assert its influence on the subject even after the subject enters the **symbolic order**.

Kristeva posits that between the **chora** and the **mirror stage** occurs a crucial pre-linguistic stage that she associates with the **abject**. During this time in your development, you began to establish a separation between yourself and the maternal, thus creating those boundaries between self and other that must be in place before the entrance into language: "The abject confronts us ... with our earliest attempts to release the hold of *maternal* entity even before ex-isting outside of her, thanks to the autonomy of language. It is a violent, clumsy breaking away, with the constant risk of falling back under the sway of a power as securing as it is stifling" (1982: 13). Like the subject's confrontation with death, the threat of falling back into the pre-linguistic stage of the **chora** strikes him or her with fear and horror because it means giving up all the linguistic structures by which we order our social world of meaning. Kristeva sees the stage of abjection as "*a precondition of narcissism*" (1982: 13), which is to say, a precondition for the narcissism of the **mirror stage**, which directly follows.

2–4 years of age

Following the **oral phase**, according to Freud, you entered the **anal-sadistic phase**, which is split between active and passive impulses: the impulse to mastery, on the one hand, which can easily become cruelty; the impulse to **scopophilia** (love of gazing), on the other hand. This phase was roughly coterminous with a new auto-erotic **object**: the rectal orifice (hence, the term "**sadistic-anal phase**"). According to Freud, your pleasure in defecation at this stage was connected to your pleasure in creating something of your own, a pleasure that for women is later transferred to child-bearing.

According to Lacan, the acquisition of language during this stage of development further separated you from a connection to the **Real** (from the actual materiality of things). Once you entered into the differential system of language, it forever afterwards determined your perception of the world around you, so that the intrusion of the **Real**'s materiality becomes a traumatic event, albeit one that is quite common because our version of "reality" is built over the chaos of the **Real** (both the materiality outside you and the chaotic impulses inside you). By acquiring language, you entered into what Lacan terms the "**symbolic order**"; you were reduced into an empty signifier ("I") within the field of the **Other**, which is to say, within a field of language and culture (which is always determined by those others that came before you). That linguistic position, according to Lacan, is particularly marked by **gender** differences, so that all your actions were subsequently determined by your sexual position (which, for Lacan, does not have much to do with your "real" sexual urges or even your sexual markers but by a linguistic system in which "male" and "female" can only be understood in relation to each other in a system of language).

Kristeva adopts Lacan's model but makes the mother a much more central part of our psychosexual development: "As the addressee of every demand, the mother occupies the place of alterity. Her replete body, the receptacle and guarantor of demands, takes the place of all **narcissistic**, hence **imaginary**, effects and gratifications; she is, in other words, the **phallus**" (1984: 47). Kristeva also adds to Lacan her sense that language is ultimately a **fetish**, which for Freud is your reaction to the mother's lack of a penis. Language, for Kristeva, is an effort to cover over the **lack** inherent in your relation to not only death, materiality, and the **abject** but also the maternal **chora**: "It is perhaps unavoidable that, when a **subject** confronts the factitiousness of **object** relation, when he stands at the place of the want that founds it, the **fetish** becomes a life preserver, temporary and slippery, but nonetheless indispensable. But is not exactly language our ultimate and inseparable **fetish**?" (1982: 37).

4–7 years of age

Finally, according to Freud, you entered the **phallic phase**, when the penis (or the clitoris, which, according to Freud, stands for the penis in the young girl) became your primary **object-cathexis**. In this stage, the child becomes fascinated with urination, which is experienced as pleasurable, both in its expulsion and retention. The trauma connected with this phase is that of **castration**, which makes this phase especially important for the resolution of the **Oedipus complex**. Over this time, you began to deal with your separation anxieties (and your all-encompassing egoism) by finding symbolic ways of representing and thus controlling the separation from (not to mention your desire for) your mother. You also learned to defer bodily gratification when necessary. In other words, your **ego** became trained to follow the **reality principle** and to control the **pleasure principle**, although this ability would not be fully attained until you passed through the **latency period**. In resolving the **Oedipus complex**, you also began to identify either with your mother or your father, thus determining the future path of your sexual orientation. That identification took the form of an **"ego-ideal**," which then aided the formation of your **"super-ego"**: an internalization of the parental function (which Freud usually associated with the father) that eventually manifested itself in your conscience (and sense of guilt).

The **Oedipus complex** is just as important for Lacan as it is for Freud, if not more so. The difference is that Lacan maps that complex onto the acquisition of language, which he sees as analogous. The process of moving through the **Oedipus complex** (of being made to recognize that you cannot sleep with or even fully "have" your mother) is your way of recognizing the need to obey social strictures and to follow a closed differential system of language in which we understand "self" in relation to "others." In this linguistic rather than biological system, the "phallus" (which, in Lacan, must always be understood not to mean "penis") comes to stand in the place of everything the **subject** loses through its entrance into language (a sense of perfect and ultimate meaning or plenitude, which is, of course, impossible) and all the power associated with what Lacan terms the "symbolic father" and the **"Name-of-the-Father"** (laws, control, knowledge). Like the phallus's relation to the penis, the **"Name-of-the-Father"** is much more than any actual father; in fact, it is ultimately more analogous to those social structures that control our lives and that interdict many of our actions (law, religion, medicine, education). After you pass through the **Oedipus complex**, the position of the phallus (a position within that differential system) can be assumed by most anyone (teachers, leaders, even the mother) and, so, to repeat, is not synonymous with either the biological father or the biological penis.

Kristeva reads the castration complex as the final separation of the **subject** from the mother: "The discovery of **castration** ... detaches the **subject** from his dependence on the mother, and the perception of this **lack** [*manque*] makes the phallic function a symbolic function—*the* symbolic function." As she goes on, "This is a decisive moment fraught with consequences: the **subject**, finding his identity in the symbolic, *separates* from his fusion with the mother, *confines* his **jouissance** to the genital, and transfers semiotic motility onto the **symbolic order**" (1984: 47)

7–12 years of age

Next, according to Freud, followed a long "**latency period**" during which your sexual development was more or less suspended and you concentrated on **repressing** and **sublimating** your earlier desires and thus learned to follow the **reality principle**. During this phase, you gradually freed yourself from your parents (moving away from the mother and reconciling yourself with your father) or by asserting your independence (if you responded to your incestuous desires by becoming overly subservient to your father). You also moved beyond your childhood egoism and sacrificed something of your own **ego** to others, thus learning how to love others.

13 years of age onward (or from puberty on)

Your development over the **latency period** allowed you to enter the final **genital phase**, according the Freud. At this point, you learned to desire members of the opposite sex and to fulfill your **instinct** to procreate and thus ensure the survival of the human species.

Women and psychosexual development

One thing "you" have surely noticed is the decidedly masculine bent of Freud's and Lacan's story of sexual development. Indeed, Freud often had difficulty incorporating female desire into his theories, leading to his famous, unanswered question: "what does a woman want?" As Freud states late in life, "psychology too is unable to solve the riddle of femininity" (1953–74: 22.116). It is for this reason that many feminists have criticized Freud's ideas and one reason why some feminists interested in psychoanalysis have turned instead to Kristeva. To explain women, Freud argued that young girls followed more or less the same psychosexual development as boys. Indeed, he argues paradoxically that "the little girl is a little man" (22.118) and that the entrance into the **phallic phase** occurs for the young girl through her "penis-equivalent," the clitoris. In fact, according to Freud, the young girl, also experiences the **castration-complex**, with the difference that her tendency is to be a victim of what Freud terms "penis-envy," a desire for a penis as large as a man's. After this stage, according to Freud, the woman has an extra stage of development when "the clitoris should wholly or in part hand over its sensitivity, and at the same time its importance, to the vagina" (22.118). According to Freud, the young girl must also at some point give up her first **object**-choice (the mother and her breast) in order to take the father as her new proper **object**-choice. Her eventual move into heterosexual femininity, which culminates in giving birth, grows out of her earlier infantile desires, with her own child now taking "the place of the penis in accordance with an ancient symbolic equivalence" (22.128).

For Lacan too, the anatomical differences between boys and girls lead to a different trajectory for men and women. Men achieve access to the privileges of the phallus, according to Lacan, by denying their last link to the **Real** of their own **sexuality** (their actual penis); for this reason, the **castration complex** continues to function as a central aspect of the boy's psychosexual development for Lacan. In accepting the dictates of the **Name-of-the-Father**, which is associated with the symbolic phallus, the male subject denies his sexual needs and, forever after, understands his relation to others in terms of his position within a larger system of rules, gender differences, and **desire**. Since women do not experience the **castration complex** in the same way (they do not have an actual penis that must be denied in their access to the **symbolic order**), Lacan argues that women are not socialized in the same way, that they remain more closely tied to what Lacan terms "*jouissance*," the lost plenitude of one's bodily **drives** given up by the male subject in order to access the symbolic power of the **phallus**. Women are thus at once more lacking (never accessing the **phallus** as fully) and more full (having not experienced the loss of the penis as fully). Regardless, what defines the position of both the man and the woman in this schema is above all **lack**, even if that **lack** is articulated differently for men and women.

Kristeva gives greater centrality to women throughout her theories about psychosexual development. She also argues that the semiotic **chora** continually returns even after our entrance into the **symbolic order**; indeed, we should understand communicative language as founded upon an underlying semiotic substratum, which she terms the **genotext**; see **genotext and phenotext**. She reads art, in particular, as a "semiotization of the **symbolic**" and argues that it "represents the flow of **jouissance** into language" (1984: 79). Like Kristeva, **screen theory** has reworked Lacan for the purpose of **feminist** critique, as in the work of Teresa de Lauretis, Laura Mulvey, and Kaja Silverman (see **scopophilia**, **suture**).

Further reading: Bowie 1991; de Lauretis 1984; Fink 2007; Freud 1916–17, 1923, 1932, 1953–74; E. A. Kaplan 2000; Kristeva 1980, 1982, 1984; Lacan 1968, 1977, 1981, 1991, 1992, 1998; Laplanche and Pontalis 1973; Mulvey 1989; K. Silverman 1988; Žižek 1989, 1991b.

PSYCHOSIS

Psychosis is a mental condition whereby the patient completely loses touch with reality. Sigmund Freud originally distinguished between **neurosis** and psychosis in the following way: "In **neurosis** the **ego** suppresses part of the **id** out of allegiance to reality, whereas in psychosis it lets itself be carried away by the **id** and detached from a part of reality" (1953–74: 5.202).

PUBLIC SPHERE

Jürgen Habermas traces the development of our modern notion of the public sphere to the rise of mercantile **capitalism** and bourgeois society in the eighteenth century. The concept is tied to his notion of **communicative action**. Habermas is interested in this new bourgeois public sphere "as the sphere of private people come together as a public," eventually creating a space where private individuals (i.e., those not officially involved in public office) could "debate over the general rules governing relations in the basically privatized but publicly relevant sphere of commodity exchange and social labor" (1999: 27). He examines, for example, the role of salons, learned societies, and, especially, coffee houses in the seventeenth and eighteenth centuries. In such forums for discussion, a new principle was proposed, even if it was applied unevenly at first: "they preserved a kind of social intercourse that, far from presupposing the equality of status, disregarded status altogether. The tendency replaced the celebration of rank with a tact befitting equals" (36). This process continued into the nineteenth century, aided by the rise of a mass market in books; the proliferation of journals and periodicals; a general rise in literacy rates, newspapers; and, eventually, the establishment of libraries and a system of public education. As a result, a new understanding of the "public" emerged, one that included "all private people, persons who—insofar as they were propertied and educated—as readers, listeners, and spectators could avail themselves via the market of the objects that were subject to discussion" (37). In his theory of **communicative action**, Habermas wishes to reconstitute this model for rational, critical debate, thus salvaging the public sphere from those forces that threaten its destruction in the contemporary age, particularly the commercialization of private activities:

> When leisure was nothing but a complement to time spent on the job, it could be no more than a different arena for the pursuit of private business affairs that were not transformed into a public communication between private people. ... When the laws of the market governing the sphere of **commodity** exchange and of social **labor** also pervaded the sphere reserved for private people as a public, rational-critical debate had a tendency to be replaced by consumption, and the web of public communication unraveled into acts of individuated reception, however uniform in mode. (1999: 161)

Habermas refers to this change as the "structural transformation of the public sphere," the title of his first major work. Unlike coffee-house culture of the eighteenth century, the new culture of consumption, aided and abetted by the mass media, creates a situation where individuals are deprived of opportunities to enter into critical debate with other private individuals. What has occurred today, then, is that "The sounding board of an educated stratum tutored in the public use of reason has been shattered" (1999: 175).

See also: **discourse ethics**.

Further reading: Calhoun 1992; Habermas 1999.

PUNCTUALISATION

See **blackboxing**

QUASI-OBJECTS AND QUASI-SUBJECTS

According to Bruno Latour, our society is now having an ever more difficult time maintaining the **positivist** distinction between the **natural** world of **objects** and the human world of representations:

So long as Nature was remote and under control, it still vaguely resembled the constitutional pole of tradition, and science could still be seen as a mere intermediary to uncover it. Nature seemed to be held in reserve, transcendent, inexhaustible, distant enough. But where are we to classify the ozone hole story, or global warming or deforestation? Where are we to put these hybrids? Are they human? Human because they are our work. Are they natural? Natural because they are not our doing. Are they local or global? Both. (Latour 1993: 50)

To designate such "hybrids," where it is hard to distinguish between the human and a natural order understood as separate from us as **subjects**, Latour borrows a term from Michel Serres (1987): quasi-objects. Through this maneuver, he rejects the tendency of scientists and sociologists to keep separate the world of **objects** and the world of **subjects**. According to Latour, critics tend to claim that our very understanding of objects is determined by **ideology** (the **subject** is all, and we are, therefore, separated from the **Real**) while, at the same time, they "denounce, and debunk and ridicule" any "naïve belief in the freedom of the human **subject** and society": "This time they use the **nature** of things—that is the indisputable results of the sciences—to show how it determines, informs and moulds the soft and pliable wills of the poor humans" (Latour 1993: 53). Latour rejects both sides, both the pure objective world of things and the perfectly subjective world of ideology, in favor of hybrid phenomena that test the distinction:

Of quasi-objects, quasi-subjects, we shall simply say that they trace networks. They are real, quite real, and we humans have not made them. But they are collective because they attach us to one another, because they circulate in our hands and define our social bond by their very circulation. (Latour 1993: 89)

Such quasi-objects and quasi-subjects are not completely subjective nor completely objective but, rather, underscore the indelible networks that interlink the world of real objects and the human world of language, **ideology** and **subjectivity**. In this maneuver, Latour rejects the **positivist** distinction between observers and the observed as well as the **postmodern** argument whereby we are "locked into language alone, or imprisoned in social representation alone" (Latour 1993: 90).

See also: **mediators and intermediaries**, **blackboxing**, **Thing Theory**.

Further reading: Latour 1993; Serres 1987.

QUEER STUDIES

See **LGBTQ Studies**

QUEER TEMPORALITY

A number of **queer theorists** have suggested that queer identity entails a completely different sense of temporality than that understood by **subjects** subscribing to normative heterosexuality, a "queer temporality," a phrase first coined by Stephen Barber and David Clark in "Queer Moments" (2002), the opening essay of the edited collection, *Regarding Sedgwick*. Before and after that book, there were a number of theoretical works that sought to develop the notion of an alternative queer time or even queer space. As Judith Halberstam puts it in her book, *In a Queer Time and Place* (2005), "what has made queerness compelling as a form of self-description in the past decade or so has to do with the way it has the potential to open up new life narratives and alternative relations to time and space" (1–2). Other works that explore the notion of a queer temporality or queer historiography or queer **historical materialism** include Carolyn Dinshaw's *Getting Medieval: Sexualities and Communities, Pre- and Postmodern* (1999), Christopher Nealon's *Foundlings: Lesbian and Gay Historical Emotion before Stonewall* (2001), Annemarie Jagose's *Inconsequence: Lesbian Representation and the Logic of Sexual Sequence* (2002), Lee Edelman's *No Future: Queer Theory and the Death Drive* (2004), Carla Freccero's *Queer/Early/Modern* (2006), Elizabeth Freeman's *Time Binds: Queer Temporalities, Queer Histories* (2010), Jane Gallop's *The Deaths of the Author: Reading and Writing in Time* (2011), and E. L. McCallum and Mikko Tuhkanen's edited collection, *Queer Times, Queer Becomings* (2011). According to Edelman, society tends to assume that there is one way to think about the **subject**'s relation to the future, that is, one tied to the family and heterosexual reproduction. The commonly expressed phrase, "we must fight for the sake of our children," assumes a **heteronormative** understanding of time and temporality. Freeman makes the same point about the family photograph, which often revolves around pictures of children: such photographs "inserted the family into, and made the family into an image of, the nationalist march of 'progress'" by merging "the secularized, quasi-sacred time of **nature** and family with the homogeneous, empty time across which national destiny moved" (2010: 22). For both Edelman and Freeman, queerness entails a different approach to time precisely because, as Freeman puts it, "blacks, homosexuals, and other deviants" have been aligned "with threats to the forward movement of individual or civilizational development" (24). For Edelman, *"queerness,"* partly as a result of that imposed deviancy, "names the side of those *not* 'fighting for the children,' the side outside the consensus by which all politics confirms the absolute value of reproductive futurism" (3). Edelman instead aligns "queerness" with the logic of the **death drive**, as Jacques Lacan rethinks it for ethics, thus proposing a relationship to **history** (and our future) that is non-**teleological**. Rather than "reinforce some positive social value" (6), what Edelman terms "queer negativity" finds its value "in its challenge to value as defined by the social, and thus in its radical challenge to the very value of the social itself" (6).

See also: **LGBTQ Studies**.

Further reading: Barber and Clark 2002; Dinshaw 1999; Edelman 2004; Freccero 2006; Freeman 2010; Gallop 2011; Halberstam 2005; Hall and Jagose 2013; Jagose 2002; McCallum and Tuhkanen 2011; Nealon 2001.

QUEER THEORY (QUEER THEORIST)

Queer theory is tied to a group of theorists who established the early critical techniques for the analysis of non-**heteronormative** sexual identity, especially Adrienne Rich (see **compulsory heterosexuality**), Judith Butler (see **gender and sex**, **performativity**), Eve Kosofsky Sedgwick (see **epistemology of the closet**, **homosocial desire**), and Michel Foucault (see **bio-power**, **gender and sexuality**, **repressive hypothesis**). Coincident with the ascendency of **poststructuralism** in the 1990s, in fact inaugurated to some extent by a 1990 conference at the University of California, Santa Cruz, for which Theresa de Lauretis coined the term, queer theory is closely tied to such **poststructuralist** theoretical approaches as **deconstruction**, **Speech–Act Theory**, **discourse analysis**, and Lacanian **psychoanalysis**. Indeed, for many queer theorists, "queer" is less a particular identity formation (the **identity politics** of being a gay man, for example) than it is a commitment to rejecting what are seen as the heterocentric myths of **agency** and **naturalized subjectivity** in favor of an understanding of identity (and even bodily **sex**) as constructed, **performative**, **discursive**—in short, **ideological**. (Some queer theorists go so far as to suggest that "queer" entails a completely different sense of temporality than that assumed by **heteronormativity**: see **queer temporality**.) Lee Edelman in *Homographesis* (1994) for example aligns "queer" with

Jacques Derrida's project to **deconstruct** all myths of presence or center (see *différance*): "gay male **sexuality** will be seen to occupy a position much like that of 'writing' in the Western philosophical tradition—a tradition that enshrines, as Derrida has argued, a metaphysics of presence bespeaking its **phonocentric** orientation" (xv). As Edelman goes on, "Like writing, gay male **sexuality** comes to occupy the place of the material prop, the excessive element, of representation: the superfluous and arbitrary thing that must be ignored, repressed, or violently disavowed in order to represent representation itself as **natural** and unmediated" (xvi).

In this, Edelman follows Butler's rejection of any "**identity politics**" that seeks "a full confession of the contents of any given identity category" (1993: 221). "When some set of descriptions is offered to fill out the content of an identity, the result is inevitably fractious" (221), she argues. For Butler, then, "women" must be understood as "a permanent site of contest, or as a **feminist** site of agonistic struggle," which is to say that "there can be no closure on the category"; indeed, "for politically significant reasons, there ought never to be" (221). After all, a delimitation of "women" to some **natural**, biological category, e.g., heterosexuality, would impose what Rich calls a **compulsory heterosexuality** and Foucault the disciplining function of **bio-power**; Butler's point is that the delimitation of the category to, say, lesbianism or to *any* "foreclosed" self-description of identity is no less delimiting and fractious. Instead, one must "learn a double movement: to invoke the category and, hence, provisionally to institute an identity and at the same time to open the category as a site of permanent political contest" (222).

Queer theory is very closely tied to (often characterized as a part of and, indeed, hard to distinguish from) **LGBTQ Studies**, which is sometimes referred to as **queer studies**. It certainly influences and inspires many of the critics associated with **LGBTQ Studies**; however, because of **LGBTQ**'s connection to non-academic advocacy groups and to disciplines beyond the English and Philosophy departments where queer theory is dominant, **LGBTQ Studies** does not always share the same **poststructuralist** concerns regarding the value of **identity politics**.

Further reading: Butler 1990a, 1990b, 1993, 1997; de Lauretis 1984, 1994; Dinshaw 1999; Edelman 1994, 2004; Elfenbein 1999; Foucault 1990; Freccero 2006; Freeman 2010; Gallop 2011; Halberstam 2005, 2011; Hall and Jagose 2013; Jagose 2002; McCallum and Tuhkanen 2011; Nealon 2001; Rich 1980; Sedgwick 1990, 2003.

RACE AND ETHNICITY

As with **class** or **gender and sex**, it is important to keep in mind that racial distinctions, as we now understand them, are in fact of recent invention. Today, race tends to be understood as "the major groupings of mankind, having in common distinct physical features" (*OED*); however, this sense of the term "race" does not appear until the eighteenth century and does not become fully instantiated until the nineteenth. That instantiation was aided by Charles Darwin's evolutionist theories, which eventually inspired the eugenics movement at the end of the nineteenth century and into the twentieth century, not to mention the violence perpetrated in the name of racial purity throughout the twentieth century. As Lerone Bennett for example explains in *The Shaping of Black America*, "race did not have the same meaning in 1619," the year the first African slaves were sold into captivity on American soil, "that it has today." As he clarifies, "The first white settlers were organized around concepts of class, religion, and nationality, and they apparently had little or no understanding of the concepts of race and slavery" (1975: 10). By looking to a time before contemporary notions of race are postulated, critical theorists are able to illustrate that race is by no means a biological fact but rather a **discursive** creation, an **ideology**, albeit one that has, of course, had real, material effects.

Some theorists have argued that the contemporary concepts of race and racism are a direct result of developments in the nineteenth century, including Enlightenment philosophy, imperial expansion, and the rise of capitalism. Just at the moment when Enlightenment principles of inalienable rights would seem to make slavery unthinkable (remember that it was acceptable in, say, ancient Greece where it was not tied to race), we see the growth of the African slave trade and its use in the plantation system of America and the West Indies. We also witness at this time a rush of colonial expansion, including the brutal oppression and exploitation of colonized peoples. As Helen Scott explains in "Was There a Time before Race?" (2002), the way around the new ideology of "personal liberty and freedom" was to define "slaves as property, rather than as people," thus placing "the property rights of the planter above the individual rights of the slave" (173), a development that is explored especially by **Critical Race Theory** (see **whiteness as property**). Similarly, by defining the colonial **Other** as racially inferior, even subhuman, one could legitimize the brutality of colonial occupation or, later in the twentieth century, the mistreatment of immigrant labor.

257

Postcolonial theorists often turn to the **discursive** instantiation of racial **ideology**, underscoring at once the **hegemonic** power of such representations of the **Other** and their artificiality or arbitrariness, as in Edward Said's influential analysis of *Orientalism* (1978). Indeed, influenced by **poststructuralist** theory, they are careful of any claim to fix the identity of an oppressed group, as in Gayatri Chakravorty Spivak's demands for **subaltern** subjectivity in her provocatively titled essay, "Can the **Subaltern** Speak?" (1988a). Instead, what tends to be underscored are the spaces where identities are blurred or mixed, as in the key concepts of **contact zone and transculturation**, **hybridity**, **intersectionality**, **liminality**, and **mimicry**. So, in seeking to theorize an Afro-American tradition of literature, Henry Louis Gates underscores the "double-voicedness" and "double play" that black forms of literature "bore to white forms," often through the mechanisms of **parody** and **pastiche**. He terms this general form of signification "Signifyin(g)" (1988: xxiv), a practice that contests the monolithic and homogeneous.

Cornel West could be said to explore a similar notion of heterogeneity in his writings on race. As he states, "Distinctive features of the new cultural politics of difference are to trash the monolithic and homogeneous in the name of diversity, multiplicity, and heterogeneity; to reject the abstract, general, and universal in light of the concrete, specific, and particular; and to historicize, contextualize, and pluralize by highlighting the contingent, provisional, variable, tentative, shifting, and changing" (1993: 203–4). In the different arena of Birmingham School **Cultural Studies**, Stuart Hall similarly seeks to contest any monolithic or homogeneous sense of race or even racism by adopting Antonio Gramsci's key concepts (**hegemony**, **war of position**, **war of maneuver**) in his exploration of race in contemporary **culture**: "In the analysis of particular historical forms of racism, we would do well to operate at a more concrete, historicized level of abstraction (i.e., not racism in general but racisms)" (1986: 23).

Instead of making claims about biological race or any essentialist notion of racial identity, theorists are more likely to turn to the concept of ethnicity in order to understand group identity, particularly in the sense articulated well by Richard Schermerhorn: "a collectivity within a larger society having real or putative common ancestry, memories of a shared historical past, and a cultural focus on one or more symbolic elements defined as the epitome of their peoplehood" (1970: 12). This approach underscores the **discursive** make-up of group identity and can function as an empowering form of self-constitution for **subaltern** groups. Rather than isolate **subaltern** groups, the idea behind this understanding of ethnicity is that we all construct our identities through such "symbolic elements," including "kinship patterns, physical contiguity ... , religious affiliation, language or dialect forms, tribal affiliation, nationality, phenotypical features, or any combination of these" (Schermerhorn 1970: 12), as well as cultural values and cultural practices such as art, literature, and music. As Stuart Hall puts it, rejecting any essentialist notion of ethnicity, "In my terminology, everybody has an ethnicity because everybody comes from a cultural tradition, a cultural context, an historical context; it is the source of their self-production, so everybody has an ethnicity" (Drew 1999: 228). One must always be careful, however, to underscore that certain ethnic communities are disadvantaged with regard to other, dominant communities. The goal is to understand and contest how **hegemonic** groups define themselves against those ethnic identities that are then discursively **marginalized** as **Other**.

See also: **identity politics**.

Further reading: D. A. Bell 1973; Bennett 1975; Drew 1999; Fanon 1967; Gates 1988; S. Hall 1986; Malik 1996; Said 1978; Schermerhorn 1970; H. Scott 2002; Spivak 1988a, 1988b; West 1993, 2001.

RADICAL DEMOCRACY

Ernesto Laclau and Chantal Mouffe propose this concept in their work, *Hegemony and Socialist Strategy* (1985). In order effectively to counter what they identify as the "new **hegemonic** project ... of liberal-conservative discourse" (175), they offer "radical democracy" as an "Alternative for a New Left," the subtitle of the last section of their book. Their argument is that past **Marxist** thinkers have fallen prey to "essentialist apriorism, the conviction that the social is **sutured** at some point, from which it is possible to fix the meaning of any event independently of any **articulatory** practice" (177). In particular, they question "*classism*: that is to say, the idea that the working **class** represents the privileged agent in which the fundamental impulse of social change resides"; "*statism*—the idea that the expansion of the role of the state is the panacea for all problems"; and "*economism* ... —the idea that from a successful economic strategy there necessarily follows a continuity of political effects which can be clearly specified" (177). Rejecting these myths, Laclau and Mouffe seek to posit "a plurality of political spaces" (137): "In a given social formation, there can be a variety of **hegemonic** nodal points" (139), which, they make clear, is not the same as proposing "either pluralism or the total diffusion of power within the social" (142). Rather, they wish to bring together disparate democratic struggles through the logic of "family resemblance" or "equivalence," with the ultimate goal of creating a new **hegemony**:

> The strengthening of specific democratic struggles requires ... the expansion of chains of equivalence which extend to other struggles. The equivalential **articulation** between anti-racism, anti-sexism, and anti-capitalism, for example, requires a **hegemonic** construction which, in certain circumstances, may be the condition for the consolidation of each one of these struggles. The logic of equivalence, then, taken to its ultimate consequences, would imply the dissolution of the autonomy of the spaces in which each one of these struggles is constituted; not necessarily because any of them become subordinated to others, but because they have all become, strictly speaking, equivalent symbols of a unique and indivisible struggle. (182)

That struggle must be seen as endless for this diversity of democratic struggles can never "be led back to a point from which they could all be embraced and explained by a single **discourse**" (1985: 191).

See also: **antagonism, articulation, dominant, hegemony**.

REACTION FORMATION

Reaction formation refers to the blocking of **desire** by its opposite. "Reaction formation" is the term Sigmund Freud uses to describe the mechanism whereby the **ego** *reacts* to the impulses of the **id** by creating an antithetical formation that blocks repressed **cathexes**. For example, someone who feels homosexual desire might **repress** that desire by turning it into hatred for all homosexuals

See also: **substitute-formation**.

READER, READING AND READER-RESPONSE CRITICISM

In contrast to **structuralists** or **New Critics**, who are more concerned with the decontextualized formal structures of a given work, Reader-Response Criticism argues that one cannot understand a text without taking into account how the reader at a given period or in a given situation constructs the work in the act of reading. Early exploration of the relation between a work and the reader's interpretation or reconstruction of the work can be found in **phenomenology** and **hermeneutics** and some early Reader-Response Criticism borrows directly from these traditions, as in the work of George Poulet (1902–91), especially *Studies in Human Time* (1956) and *The Interior Distance* (1959). However, current critical theory is most influenced by the Reader-Response Criticism of the 1960s and 1970s, especially the work of Stanley Fish, Wolfgang Iser, Hans-Robert Jauss and Roland Barthes.

As Fish characterizes his early challenges to **New Criticism**'s refusal to consider either the author's intention or the reader's response, what were termed the Intentional and Affective Fallacies, respectively, "I challenged the self-sufficiency of the text by pointing out that its (apparently) spatial form belied the temporal dimension in which its meanings were actualized, and I argued that it was the developing shape of that actualization, rather than the static shape of the printed page, that should be the object of critical description" (1980: 2). As he goes on, "In practice, this resulted in the replacing of one question— what does it mean?—by another—what does this do?—with 'do' equivocating between a reference to the action of the text *on* a reader and the actions performed *by* a reader as he negotiates (and, in some sense, actualizes) the text" (3). Iser similarly argues that what matters is "what literature *does* and not what it *means*" (1979: 360), or, as Barthes puts it, "writing is not the communication of a message which starts from the author and proceeds to the reader; it is specifically the voice of reading itself: *in the text, only the reader speaks*" (1974: 151). In order to avoid the argument that interpretation is, then, the result of "an independent and arbitrary will" (1980: 11) and thus relativisitic or even anarchic, Fish argues that the reader's interpretative strategies "proceed not from him but from the interpretative community of which he is a member." Fish goes on to define this notion of "interpretative community": "Interpretative communities are made up of those who share interpretative strategies not for reading but for writing texts, for constituting their properties. In other words these strategies exist prior to the act of reading and therefore determine the shape of what is read rather than, as is usually assumed, the other way around" (1980: 14).

Iser builds on **Speech-Act Theory** to argue that the act of reading entails a **performative** instantiation of any given work. Following the linguistic turn of **semiotics** (see **signifier and signified**), Iser argues that, when we are talking about the "representational function of fictional language," "there *is* no given object except for the sign itself." As a result, "The iconic signs of literature constitute an organization of **signifiers** which do not serve to designate a **signified** object, but instead designate *instructions* for the *production* of the **signified**" (1979: 367). The reader, in this formulation, "is essential to the fulfillment of the **text**, for materially speaking this exists only as a potential reality—it requires a '**subject**' (i.e., a reader) for the potential to be actualized" (368). Like Fish, Iser avoids intepretative relativity by arguing that both authors and readers—both speakers and recipients—rely on "conventions" or a "repertoire" common to both, "procedures accepted by both, and the willingness of both to participate in the speech action" (370).

Jauss—building on the **hermeneutical** work of Hans-Georg Gadamer, particularly Gadamer's notion of the "fusion of horizons"— argues that literary interpretation always entails a negotiation between what he terms the synchronic "horizon of expectations" of the work's own time and the horizon of expectations of the present, which opens up the diachronic evolution of interpretative practices over the course of literary history: "the interpreter must bring his own experience into play, since the past horizon of old and new forms, problems and solutions, is only recognizable in its further mediation, within the present horizon of the received work" (1982: 175). As he continues, "The historicity of literature comes to light at the intersections of diachrony and synchrony" (177).

Barthes argues in *S/Z* (1974) that we are all constrained by the shared codes we use to "write" any given text in the act of reading. In addition to the "**hermeneutic and proairetic codes**" that impel the temporality of reading in **narrative**, any text is shot through with what Barthes terms "semes," "symbols" and "cultural codes" or "cultural citations." Barthes also makes a distinction between what he terms the "classic" text, which tends to limit the play of interpretation, and the "modern text," which Barthes terms "writerly" because it invites the reader actively to create the work: "This is the problem facing modern writing: how breach the wall of utterance, the wall of origin, the wall of ownership?" (45).

Other critics that have influenced or are influenced by Reader-Response Criticism include Mikhail Bakhtin, particularly his theorization of the **dialogic** relation between text and reader; reception study, especially as explored by critics of the history of the book (e.g., Robert Darnton); and **Cultural Studies** (e.g., the work of Janice Radway). **Feminism**, **queer theory**, **psychoanalysis**, **Marxism**, **Discourse Studies**, **Critical Race Theory**, Pierre Bourdieu's socio-anthropology (see **cultural capital**, **field**)—indeed, most contemporary theory—could be said to explore the codes and ideologies by which readers are constructed and, in turn, construct the world (and texts) around them.

Most recently, the rise of the **Digital Humanities** has impacted the notion of reading, leading to Franco Moretti's notion of "distant reading," explored in a book of the same name (2013), whereby computational modeling and the quantitative analysis of huge amounts of data (so-called data mining) replaces **New Criticism**'s "close reading" precisely because of the computer's ability to be much more comprehensive in its analysis of either a given moment's synchronic breadth of published material or changes in literary works over time (diachronic development). Rather than privilege the individual reader's **performative** instantiation of a given text in a given context, do we not learn more about literary history or history itself, he asks, if we ingest vast amounts of data that are then presented to us in the form of "graphs, maps and trees," the title of Moretti's 2005 book on "abstract models for literary history"? Steven Ramsay in *Reading Machines* (2011), N. Katharine Hayles in *How We Think* (2012) and Matt Jockers in *Macroanalysis* (2013) all explore a similar notion of reading and interpretation. Citing the rise of the **Digital Humanities** as one major impetus, Stephen Best and Sharon Marcus (2009) identify a general shift in critical theory from a **Marxist** or Freudian "**symptomatic** reading" model "that took meaning to be hidden, **repressed**, deep, and in need of detection and disclosure by an interpreter" (1) to a version of interpretation that they term "surface reading." As they write, "In the last decade or so, we have been drawn to modes of reading that attend to the surfaces of texts rather than plumb their depths" (1–2) and they give a number of examples of this trend, including the methodology of distant reading itself.

Some Digital Humanists take the "writerly" dimension of criticism in the age of computers yet further. Jauss's horizon of expectation for example gets recast by Jerome McGann as the TEI or XML "mark up" that all interpretation entails. As he puts it in *Radiant Textuality* (2001), "Every text descending to us is not only marked text, it is multiply and ambiguously marked" (206), which is why, according to McGann, texts are never "self-identical," for "it is the operation of marking that divides the text from itself" (206). Reading is "*performative*" (206) and that **performativity** can extend to what McGann terms the "deformance" made possible by computer analysis, a concept also explored by Ramsay in *Reading Machines* (2011). In the "dialogue between the computer and the human beings who are teaching it how to read," we will "inevitably constitute a set of (de)formations full of surprises for the rule-givers," McGann writes. As he goes on, "What those surprising readings will be cannot be predicted, but that they will come is ... as certain as the fact that no text is commensurate with itself" (207). McGann applies the same principle to any interpretative reading; as he puts it, "we may usefully regard all criticism and interpretation as deformative" (127).

Further reading: Best and Marcus 2009; Darnton 2001, 2008; Fish 1980; Hayles 2012; Iser 1979; Jauss 1982; Jockers 2013; Machor and Goldstein 2001; McGann 2001; Moretti 2005, 2013; Poulet 1956, 1959; Radway 1997; Ramsay 2011; Suleiman and Crosman 1980; Tompkins 1980.

THE REAL

The "Real" refers to the state of nature from which we have been forever severed by our entrance into language, according to Lacanian **psychoanalysis**. Only as neo-natal children were we close to this state of nature, a state in which there is nothing but need. A baby needs and seeks to satisfy those needs with no sense of separation between itself and the external world or the world of others. For this reason, Jacques Lacan sometimes represented this state of nature as a time of fullness or completeness that is subsequently lost through the entrance into language. The primordial animal need for copulation (for example, when animals are in heat) similarly corresponds to this state of nature. There is a need followed by a search for satisfaction. As far as humans are concerned, however, "the **real** is impossible," as Lacan was fond of saying. It is impossible insofar as we cannot express it in language because the very entrance into language marks our irrevocable separation from the Real. Still, the Real continues to exert its influence throughout our adult lives as it is the rock against which all our fantasies and linguistic structures ultimately fail. The Real for example continues to erupt whenever we are made to acknowledge the materiality of our existence, an acknowledgement that is usually perceived as traumatic (since it threatens our very "reality"), although it also drives Lacan's sense of *jouissance*. The Real works in tension with the **imaginary order** and the **symbolic order**. In *The Ethics of Pyschoanalysis* (1992), Jacques Lacan builds on Freud's concept of **death drive** to articulate his understanding of our ethical relationship to each other through our negotiation of the Real.

See also: **abject**, **repetition compulsion**.

Further reading: Lacan 1968, 1977, 1992; Žižek 1989, 1991b, 1997; Zupančič 2000.

REALITY PRINCIPLE

See **pleasure principle and reality principle**

REAL TIME

In film, "real time" refers to a sequence that takes exactly as long to view as it does to occur in the **diegetic** "reality" of the film. The television series, *24*, attempted to present the viewer with real time for each of its 24 episodes, with the action in each episode lasting exactly one hour. The exact time of the story action is therefore equal to the time it takes to view that action. The show made up for tediousness by jumping between actions occurring at the same time. In general, film or video rarely attempts to present you with real time since the most interesting aspects of a narrative tend to reside in the **discursive** reorganization of the chronological **story**.

REGRESSION

Regression refers to the psychic reversion to childhood **desires**, according to **psychoanalysis**. When normally functioning **desire** meets with powerful external obstacles, which prevent satisfaction of those desires, the **subject** sometimes regresses to an earlier phase in normal **psychosexual development**. "Regression," as a term, is closely connected to the term, **fixation**; the stronger one's fixations on earlier sexual **objects** (e.g., the mouth, the anus), the more likely that a subject will regress to an earlier phase when confronted with obstacles to heterosexual satisfaction. Example: a normally functioning woman is dumped by her boyfriend and starts over-eating (thus regressing to the **oral phase**). Regression can result either in **neurosis** (if accompanied by **repression**) or in **perversion**: "A regression of the **libido** without **repression** would never produce a **neurosis** but would lead to a **perversion**" (Freud 1953–74: 16.344).

RELATIONS OF PRODUCTION

This term is used in **Marxist** criticism and derives from Karl Marx's own work. It is related to the notions of **base and superstructure**. As Marx writes, "In the social production of their life, men enter into definite relations that are indispensable and independent of their will, relations of production which correspond to a definite stage of development of their material productive forces" (Marx and Engels

1962: 1.362–63). These relations of production correspond, then, to the economic **base** of a society, which, according to Marx, drives other aspects of our existence, including not only law and politics but also, Marx suggests, consciousness and ideology (the **superstructure**). As he writes, "The sum total of these relations of production constitutes the economic structure of society, the real foundation, on which rises a legal and political **superstructure** and to which correspond definite forms of social consciousness" (1.363).

See also: **class, ideology, labor, means of production, surplus value**.

REPETITION COMPULSION

According to **psychoanalysis**, repetition compulsion refers to the mind's tendency to repeat traumatic events in order to deal with them; Sigmund Freud began to formulate this idea when he dealt with the experiences of shell-shocked veterans of the First World War. The repetition can take the form of dreams, storytelling. or even hallucination. Freud would eventually understand this compulsion as closely tied up with the **death drive**. The famous example of repetition compulsion that Freud gives in *Beyond the Pleasure Principle* (1920) is of a boy aged one and a half who enjoyed playing a game in which he would throw objects out of view while exclaiming "o-o-o-o," which Freud and the boy's mom took to mean "fort" (gone). When playing with a wooden reel tied to a string, the boy would (1) throw the reel over the edge of his curtained cot while exclaiming "o-o-o-o"; then (2) pull the reel back into view, hailing "its reappearance with a joyful 'da' ['there']" (1953–74: 18.15). Freud interpreted this game as the child's effort to master unpleasurable experience (specifically, the departure of his mother, to whom he was especially attached). What struck Freud is the fact "that the unpleasurable nature of an experience does not always unsuit it for play" (18.17). The process of **transference** in the psychoanalytical talking cure follows a similar structure, Freud realized.

REPRESSION (TO REPRESS, THE REPRESSED)

Repression refers to the **ego**'s mechanism for suppressing its **instinctual** impulses. According to Sigmund Freud, the very act of entering into civilized society entails the repression of various archaic, primitive desires. Each person's **psychosexual development** includes the surpassing of previous "love-**objects**" or "object-**cathexes**" that are tied to earlier sexual phases (the **oral phase**, the **anal–sadistic phase**, etc.); however, even well-adjusted individuals still betray the insistent force of those earlier desires through dreams, literature, or "Freudian slips"; hence the term, "return of the **repressed**." In less well-adjusted individuals, who remain **fixated** on earlier **libido** objects or who are driven to abnormal **reaction formations** or **substitute formations**, two possibilities exist: (1) **perversion**; or (2) **neurosis**. Rejected libidinal longings can thus manifest themselves as any number of **symptoms**.

In other words, for Freud, repression is a normal part of human development; indeed, the analysis of dreams, literature, jokes, and "Freudian slips" illustrates the ways that our secret desires continue to find outlet in perfectly well-adjusted individuals. However, when we are faced with obstacles to the satisfaction of our **libido**'s **cathexis**, when we experience traumatic events, or when we remain **fixated** on earlier phases of our development, the conflict between the **libido** and the **ego** (or between the **ego** and the **super-ego**) can lead to alternative sexual discharges.

The source of our sexual discharges is the **libido**, which seeks to **cathect** (or place a charge on) first one's bodily parts (e.g., the lips and mouth in the **oral phase**) and then external objects (e.g., the breast and then the mother in the **oral phase**). Freud terms this "**object**-libido." The **libido** can also get caught up in the **ego**, which leads to **narcissism**. A normal part of **psychosexual development** is the overcoming of early childhood **narcissism** (the belief, for example, that everything revolves around one's own desires).

Both healthy dreams and unhealthy symptoms follow a similar logic when confronted with repression. Let's take dreams as our first example. Freud calls the dream we remember upon waking the "manifest dream"; according to Freud, the manifest dream is already a **reaction-formation** or **substitute-formation** that hides what he calls the "latent dream-thoughts." Repression, which Freud sometimes calls the "dream-censor" in his discussion of dreams, is continually reworking the latent dream-thoughts, which are then forced to assume toned-down, distorted, or even unrecognizable forms. Freud calls this translation of latent dream-thoughts into the manifest dream the "dream work." The two main ways that repression reworks the primitive impulses of the latent dream-thoughts is by way of **condensation** (1) or **displacement** (2), the two main forms of "dream distortion":

(1) In **condensation**, multiple dream-thoughts are combined and amalgamated into a single element of the manifest dream; according to Freud, every situation in a dream seems to be put

together out of two or more impressions or experiences. One need only think about how people and places tend to meld into composite figures in our dreams.

(2) In **displacement**, the affect (emotions) associated with threatening impulses are transferred elsewhere (displaced), so that, for example, apparently trivial elements in the manifest dream seem to cause extraordinary distress while "what was the essence of the dream-thoughts finds only passing and indistinct representation in the dream" (1953–74: 22.21). For Freud, "**Displacement** is the principle means used in the *dream-distortion* to which the dream-thoughts must submit under the influence of the censorship" (22.21).

Some of these condensations and displacements become so ingrained in the **id** (the reservoir of inherited human knowledge) that they take on the quality of rigid symbols, which have similar meanings for all humans, according to Freud. These are multiple and various—and can be found elaborated in Freud's *Interpretation of Dreams* (1900). As one example among many, Freud writes that "in a woman's dreams [a cloak] stood for a man" (1953–74: 22.24). Such symbols also find expression in literature, religion, and mythology, so, for example, Freud writes how in the ancient marriage ceremony of the Bedouins, the bridegroom covers the bride in a special cloak called an "aba" and at the same time states the following ritual words: "Henceforth none save I shall cover thee!" (22.24). The job of dream interpretation is to translate the manifest dream back into its constituent, if buried, dream-thoughts.

The interpretation of **symptoms** follows a similar path; the goal is to determine the repressed sexual desires or traumatic events that are causing the abnormal behavior to occur. As with the dream-work, psychological **symptoms** are often **condensations** or **displacements** (caused by repression) of deeper, unconscious impulses or buried memories.

Further reading: Freud 1900, 1912–13, 1915, 1916–17, 1923, 1929, 1932; Laplanche and Pontalis 1973.

REPRESSIVE HYPOTHESIS

According to common wisdom, we witness an increasing discourse of **repression** that develops hand in hand with the rise of **capitalism**, culminating finally in the pervasive stereotype of the Victorian as "imperial prude" (Foucault 1990: 1.3). Michel Foucault in his *History of Sexuality* (1990) raises three doubts about this repressive hypothesis: (1) "Is sexual repression truly an established historical fact?" (1.10); (2) "Are prohibition, censorship, and denial truly the forms through which **power** is exercised in a general way, if not in every society, most certainly in our own?" (1.10); (3) "Was there really a historical rupture between the age of repression and the critical analysis of **repression**?" (1.10).

Foucault points out that the rise of **repression** that is generally believed to begin in the seventeenth century leads not to silence but to "a veritable discursive explosion" (1.17). Yes, the discussion of **sexuality** was restricted in certain areas (the family, the school, etc.) but that restriction was accompanied by "a steady proliferation of **discourses** concerned with **sex**—specific **discourses**, different from one another both by their form and by their object: a **discursive** ferment that gathered momentum from the eighteenth century onward" (1.18). Far from silence, we witness "an institutional incitement to speak about [**sex**], and to do so more and more; a determination on the part of the agencies of **power** to hear it spoken about, and to cause it to speak through explicit articulation and endlessly accumulated detail" (1.18). The effect of all this rational **discourse** about **sex** was the increasing encroachment of state law into the realm of private **desire**: "one had to speak of [**sex**] as of a thing to be not simply condemned or tolerated but managed, inserted into systems of utility, regulated for the greater good of all, made to function according to an optimum. **Sex** was not something one simply judged; it was a thing one administered" (1.24).

Our continual call to speak of **sexuality** in the present age (on television, in popular music, etc.) is, therefore, not significantly different from the ways state power imposed its regulations in the eighteenth and nineteenth centuries: through the continual demand for **discourse**. Foucault also argues that censorship is not the primary form through which **power** is exercised; rather, it is the incitement to speak about one's **sexuality** (to experts of various sorts) in order better to regulate it. Indeed, silence itself can be read as caught up in a larger **discourse** about sexuality:

> Silence itself—the things one declines to say, or is forbidden to name, the discretion that is required between different speakers— is less the absolute limit of **discourse**, the other side from which it is separated by a strict boundary, than an element that functions alongside the things said, with them and in relation to them

within over-all strategies. ... There is not one but many silences, and they are an integral part of the strategies that underlie and permeate discourses. (Foucault 1990: 1.27)

Foucault gives the example of eighteenth-century secondary schools. Sex was not supposed to be spoken of in such institutions; however, for this very reason, one can read the preoccupation with **sexuality** in all aspects of such schools: "The space for classes, the shape of the tables, the planning of the recreation lessons, the distribution of the dormitories ... , the rules for monitoring bedtime and sleep periods— all this referred, in the most prolix manner, to the **sexuality** of children" (1.28). And a whole industry of experts (doctors, educators, school-masters, etc.) were, indeed, consulted regularly on the matter of **sex** in order to regulate all the times, spaces, and activities of the school.

Foucault does not question the fact of **repression**; he questions, rather, why **sexuality** "has been so widely discussed, and what has been said about it" (1.11). His goal is to "define the regime of **power-**knowledge-pleasure that sustains the **discourse** on human **sexuality** in our part of the world" (1.11), what he terms the "polymorphous techniques of **power**" (1.11).

RESIDUAL

See **dominant, residual and emergent**

RHIZOME (RHIZOMATIC)

Gilles Deleuze and Félix Guattari in *A Thousand Plateaus* (1987) turn to "rhizomes" in their effort to contest the usual binary, centered structures of taxonomic and scientific thinking, which they align with what they term the "root-book" (5), while countering the multiplicity of the modernist critique of the root-book, which they align with what they term the "radicle-system, or fascicular root" (5) and which they see as not "radical" enough. The term, "rhizome," for them applies not just to the subterranean stems of plants but to any **assemblage** that does not conform to the metaphor of the root-book and that is instead "an acentered, nonhierarchical, nonsignifying system without a General and without an organizing memory or central automaton, defined solely by a circulation of states" (21); their examples include the book, music, ant colonies, human thought, the city of Amsterdam, and the relationship between a wasp and an orchid. As they explain in *A*

Thousand Plateaus, the principles of a rhizomatic structure are as follows: (1) principles of connection and heterogeneity; "any point of a rhizome can be connected to anything other, and must be" (7) as opposed to the fixed structure of a tree or root; (2) a principle of multiplicity: "There is no unity to serve as a pivot in the object, or to divide in the subject. ... A multiplicity has neither **subject** nor **object**, only determinations, magnitudes, and dimensions that cannot increase in number without the multiplicity changing in nature" (8); (3) a principle of asignifying rupture: "A rhizome may be broken, shattered at a given spot, but it will start up again on one of its old lines, or on new lines" (9); and (4) Principles of cartography and decalcomania: "a rhizome is not amenable to any structural or generative model. It is a stranger to any idea of genetic axis or deep structure" (12). In contrast to such "tracing," Deleuze and Guattari propose the idea of "maps": "The map is open and connectable in all of its dimensions; it is detachable, reversible, susceptible to constant modification. It can be torn, reversed, adapted to any kind of mounting, reworked by an individual, group, or social formation" (12). The rhizome is by definition never stable: "It is a question of a model that is perpetually in construction or collapsing, and of a process that is perpetually prolonging itself, breaking off and starting up again" (20). As a result, "A rhizome has no beginning or end; it is always in the middle, between things, interbeing, *intermezzo*" (25) or, to add the term that becomes the title of their book, plateau: "A plateau is always in the middle, not at the beginning or the end" (21).

See also: **assemblage**, **Body without Organs**.

SCHIZOANALYSIS

"Schizoanalysis" is a neologism coined by Gilles Deleuze and Félix Guattari in *Anti-Oedipus* (1983) to characterize their rejection of Freudian models for identity. Unlike psychoanalysis, "which confines every **desire** and statement to a genetic axis or overcoding structure," schizoanalysis "rejects any idea of pretraced destiny, whatever name is given to it—divine, anagogic, historical, economic, structural, hereditary, or syntagmatic" (1987: 13). The problem with traditional psychoanalysis, according to Deleuze and Guattari, is that "it subjects the **unconscious** to arborescent structures, hierarchical graphs, recapitulatory memories, central organs, the phallus, the phallus-tree—not only in its theory but also in its practice of calculation and treatment" (17). By contrast, schizoanalysis "treats the **unconscious** as an acentered system, in other words, as a machinic network of finite automata (a **rhizome**), and thus arrives at an entirely different state of the **unconscious**" (18).

"**Desire**," then, is understood differently by Deleuze and Guattari than it is by Sigmund Freud or Jacques Lacan. Rather than see **desire** as that which separates us from the **Real** after our entrance into language, Deleuze and Guattari wish to argue that **desire** is in fact aligned with the **Real**: "We maintain that the social field is immediately invested by **desire**, that it is the historically determined project of **desire**, and that libido has no need of any mediation or sublimation, any psychic operation, any transformation, in order to invade and invest the productive forces and the **relations of production**. *There is only **desire** and the social, and nothing else*" (1983: 29). See also **schizophrenia**.

In particular, Deleuze and Guattari wish to reject the Freudian reduction of all human activity to the Oedipal scenario: "By boxing the life of the child up within the **Oedipus complex**, by making familial relations the universal mediation of childhood, we cannot help but fail to understand the production of the **unconscious** itself, and the collective mechanisms that have an immediate bearing on the **unconscious**" (1983: 48–49). Beyond the Oedipal scenario, according to Deleuze and Guattari, there exists "desiring-production—the machines of **desire** that no longer allow themselves to be reduced to the structure [of the Oedipal scenario] any more than to persons, and that constitute the **Real** in itself, beyond or beneath the **Symbolic** as well as the **Imaginary**" (52–53). The schizophrenic best exemplifies this new understanding of **desire** released from the Oedipal scenario, according to Deleuze and Guattari: "Wouldn't it be better to schizophrenize—to schizophrenize the domain of the unconscious as well as the sociohistorical domain, so as to shatter the iron collar of Oedipus and rediscover everywhere the force of desiring-production; to renew, on the level of the **Real**, the tie between the analytic machine, desire, and production?" (53). Schizophrenia, then, is not a "'breakdown'" for Deleuze and Guattari but, rather, "a 'break-through,' however distressing and adventurous: breaking through the wall or the limit separating us from desiring-production, causing the flows of desire to circulate" (362).

See also: **assemblage, Body without Organs**.

Further reading: Buchanan and MacCormack 2008; Deleuze and Guattari 1983, 1987; Holland 1999.

SCHIZOPHRENIA

A few critics have made the argument that the **postmodern** condition is analogous to schizophrenia. Fredric Jameson in his *Postmodernism* (1991) argues that the **postmodern** condition results in a loss of connection to history and is "increasingly dominated by space and spatial logic." As he goes on, "If, indeed, the subject has lost its capacity actively to extend its pro-tensions and re-tensions across the temporal manifold and to organize its past and future into coherent experience, it becomes difficult enough to see how the cultural productions of such a **subject** could result in anything but 'heaps of fragments' and in a practice of the randomly heterogeneous and fragmentary and aleatory" (25). Jameson turns to Jacques Lacan's understanding of schizophrenia to characterize this situation: "I have found Lacan's account of schizophrenia useful here not because I have any way of knowing whether it has clinical accuracy but chiefly because—as description rather than diagnosis—it seems to me to offer a suggestive aesthetic model" (26). Jameson does not claim we are schizophrenics, only that our new ways of making sense of time and space resemble schizophrenia. In particular, he is interested in Lacan's description of schizophrenia "as a breakdown in the signifying chain, that is, the interlocking syntagmatic series of signifiers which constitutes an utterance or a meaning" (26). Normally, meaning is constructed "by the movement from **signifier** to signifier" (26) but in schizophrenia the relationship between signifiers breaks down: "when the links of the signifying chain snap, then we have schizophrenia in the form of a rubble of distinct and unrelated signifiers" (26). This situation in turn has an effect on the schizophrenic's understanding of the self: "If we are unable to unify the past, present, and future of the sentence, then we are similarly unable to unify the past, present, and future of our own biographical experience or psychic life" (27). The schizophrenic is thus reduced to nothing but a "series of pure and unrelated presents in time" (27). Jameson reads a similar understanding of signification, subjectivity, and spatiality in the **postmodern** work of John Cage, Samuel Beckett, Language Poetry, and the artwork of Nam June Paik (28–31) or in postmodern society's loss of connection to history and subsequent enthrallment with the euphoric present.

Gilles Deleuze and Félix Guattari similarly align our current stage of **late capitalism** with schizophrenia: "Capitalism tends toward a threshold of decoding that will destroy the socius in order to make it a **body without organs** and unleash the flows of desire on this body as a deterritorialized field. Is it correct to say that in this sense schizophrenia is the product of the capitalist machine … ?" (1983: 33). Unlike Jameson, however, Deleuze and Guattari wish to make the case for a positive and even heroic schizophrenic, one who is aligned with their privileged term, "**body without organs**," and who offers them a model for their own "**schizoanalysis**." **Capitalism** in fact continually seeks to counter the schizophrenic tendencies of its own nature, according to Deleuze and Guattari: "The more the **capitalist** machine deterritorializes, decoding and axiomatizing flows in order to extract surplus value from them, the more its ancillary apparatuses, such as government bureaucracies and the forces of law and order, do their utmost to reterritorialize" (34–35) through their reintroduction of such centripetal, "territorializing" notions as "States, nations, families" (34). Deleuze and Guattari instead offer the schizophrenic as the ideal limit of **capitalism**: "The schizophrenic deliberately seeks out the very limit of **capitalism**: he is its inherent tendency brought to fulfillment, its surplus product, its **proletariat**, and its exterminating angel. He scrambles all the codes and is the transmitter of the decoded flows of **desire**" (35).

See also: **assemblage, rhizome**.

SCOPOPHILIA (SCOPOPHILIC)

Etymologically, "scopophilia" means the love of looking. The term, as used in feminist film criticism, is heavily influenced by both Freudian and Lacanian **psychoanalysis**. In **Screen Theory**, "scopophilia" refers to the predominantly male gaze of Hollywood cinema, which enjoys **objectifying** women, turning them into passive objects to be looked at (rather than subjects with their own voice and subjectivity). As Laura Mulvey explains,

> In a world ordered by sexual imbalance, pleasure in looking has been split between active/male and passive/female. The determining male gaze projects its fantasy onto the female figure, which is styled accordingly. In their traditional exhibitionist role women are simultaneously looked at and displayed, with their appearance coded for strong visual and erotic impact so that they can be said to connote *to-be-looked-at-ness*. (1989: 19)

The other side of this dynamic is the identification that occurs between the male spectator and the active male figure on the screen: "As the spectator identifies with the main male protagonist, he projects his look onto that of his like, his screen surrogate, so that the power of the male protagonist as he controls events coincides with the active power of the erotic look, both giving a satisfying sense of omnipotence" (Mulvey 1989: 20). This two-fold dynamic is ultimately subtended by a threat of **castration** that, according to Lacanian film theorists, drives the fantasy of traditional cinema since the occluded secret of film is that it is actually the camera that is doing the looking for us; we are not in control.

See also: **suture**.

Further reading: E. A. Kaplan 2000; Mulvey 1989; Padva and Buchweitz 2014; K. Silverman 1983, 1988.

SCREEN THEORY

See **suture**

SEMIOLOGY

See **semiotics**

SEMIOTIC SQUARE

See **Greimassian square**

SEMIOTICS (SEMIOLOGY, SEMIOTICIAN)

Semiotics is the science of signs, particularly as signs are understood after the so-called "linguistic turn" in critical theory that occurred after the publication of Ferdinand de Saussure's *Course in General Linguistics* in 1916. "Semiology" was coined by Saussure (1857–1913); however, "semiotics" is the more common term used in referring to this critical school, despite the fact that that term was actually coined by John Locke (1632–1704). Semiotics is interested in the production of meaning; although it is closely associated with linguistics, it opens its sights to all sign systems, including non-verbal signs. As Saussure explains,

A science that studies the life of signs within society is conceivable; it would be a part of social psychology and consequently of general psychology; I shall call it *semiology* (from Greek *sēmeîon* 'sign'). Semiology would show what constitutes signs, what laws govern them. Since the science does not yet exist, no one can say what it would be; but it has a right to existence, a place staked out in advance. Linguistics is only a part of the general science of semiology; the laws discovered by semiology will be applicable to linguistics, and the latter will circumscribe a well-defined area within the mass of anthropological facts. (1916: 16)

Saussure's invitation to examine sign systems beyond linguistics has proven influential, allowing for the application of semiological principles to the study of culture at large, as in the semiological **Cultural Studies** of Roland Barthes. Indeed, according to Barthes, his approach to culture in *Mythologies* was a direct result of reading Saussure:

> This book has a double theoretical framework: on the one hand, an **ideological** critique bearing on the language of so-called mass-culture; on the other, a first attempt to analyse **semiologically** the mechanics of this language. I had just read Saussure and as a result acquired the conviction that by treating "collective representations" as sign-systems, one might hope to go further than the pious show of unmasking them and account *in detail* for the mystification which transforms petit-bourgeois culture into a universal **nature**. (1972: 9)

Cultural Studies, Cultural Materialism, and **postmodernism** have all been influenced by such a semiological understanding of the system of signs in their approach to **culture** at large, as has anthropology through the influential work of Claude Lévi-Strauss, who applied Saussurian semiological principles to that discipline (see **binary opposition**), and then, later, Clifford Geertz (see **thick description**). The approach has influenced **poststructuralists** as much as **structuralists**.

Many critical theorists see in the advent of semiotics a general "linguistic turn" in the study of culture and society. As Jonathan Culler explains in outlining the general implications of semiotics, "we come to think of our social and cultural world as a series of sign systems, comparable with languages. What we live among and relate to are not physical objects and events; they are objects and events with meaning" (1981: 25). In the extreme, this approach to society sees human **agents** as necessarily separated from the **Real** because of our reliance on language and various other sign systems for our very understanding of reality, as in Jacques Lacan's **psychoanalysis** of the **subject**, Jean-François Lyotard's theorization of **language games** and **phrase regimens,** or Louis Althusser's understanding of **ideology**. **Marxist** critic Fredric Jameson in the book of the same name critiques this position as the "prison house of language" (1972).

In this way, Saussure is more closely tied to critical theory's understanding of semiotics than is the still influential semiotic thinker, Charles Sanders Peirce (1839–1914), Saussure's contemporary. Peirce sought to establish more determinately than does Saussure the relation between sign and object, thus rejecting what Saussure posits as the arbitrariness of the linguistic sign (see **signifier and signified**). For Peirce, "A sign is an object which stands for another to some mind" (1991: 141) and that connection is fixed by three preconditions: (1) the "material quality" of the sign (e.g., a "printed word is black"); (2) "a physical connection between every sign and its object"; Peirce argues that the connection is as concrete as the physical connection that links a weathervane and the wind (141); that is, "there is a real causal connection between the sign and the thing signified" (142); and (3) a perceiving mind who considers the sign as sign: "if it is not a sign to any mind it is not a sign at all" (142); again, Peirce sees this connection as fixed and causal: "Our ideas have also a causal connection with the things that they represent without which there would be no real knowledge" (143). Saussure, by contrast, is more concerned with the system of differences by which any term comes to achieve meaning. What matters, then, is the structure behind the system of languages (what Saussure terms *langue*) rather than any individual use of language (*parole*), any physical connection between the sign and its referent, or the causal **agency** of either a **subject** or even an objective world of things. For Saussure, "in language there are only differences"; that is, "Whether we take the **signified** or the **signifier**, language has neither ideas nor sounds that existed before the linguistic system, but only conceptual and phonic differences that have issued from the system" (1916: 120). Rather than say, with Peirce, that our ideas have "a causal connection with the things that they represent," Saussure argues that meaning only ever derives from the structural system of language:

> Instead of pre-existing ideas then, we find in all the foregoing examples *values* emanating from the system. When they are said to correspond to concepts, it is understood that the concepts are purely differential and defined not by their positive content but negatively by their relations with the other terms of the system. Their most precise characteristic is in being what the others are not. (117)

As Saussure states baldly, "There are no pre-existing ideas, and nothing is distinct before the appearance of language" (112). It is worth pointing out, however, that Jacques Derrida reads in Peirce a methodology that is more akin to his own theory of **deconstruction**: "Peirce goes very far in the direction that I have called the **de-construction** of the **transcendental signified**, which, at one time or another, would place a reassuring end to the reference from sign to sign" (1976: 49). The reason is that, unlike Saussure, Peirce does not privilege speech over writing and instead sees everything as a set of symbols or signs: "We think only in signs," Peirce argues, "So it is only out of symbols that a new symbol can grow" (1960: 2.169).

Such a linguistic turn has influenced a number of critical theorists who have, consequently, questioned to what extent we can understand ourselves as **agents** of our actions, given how reliant we are on semiosis for the construction of meaning. If the relation between **signifier** and **signified** is completely arbitrary, as Saussure claims, and meaningful action only derives from a system of differences and deferrals that is determined by our use of semiotic systems, especially language, then we can even question whether we can experience the **real** world outside of our semiotic systems. Even that which we experience as tied to the somatic fact of our bodies may in fact follow the logic of a system of differences, as semiotician Algirdas Julien Greimas for example argues regarding our passions in *The Semiotics of Passions* (1993). As he concludes, "for semiotic vision there remains a horizon beyond which it cannot reach, the horizon that separates the 'world of meaning' from the 'world of being'" (218). See **Greimassian square**.

The semiotic approach to culture and society has influenced a number of critical theories, including **psychoanalysis** (see **abject**, **chora**, **desire**, **Gaze**, **imaginary order**, **mirror stage**, **Other**, **psychosexual development**, **Real**, **schopophilia**, **subject**, **suture**, **symbolic order**, and **super-ego**); ideological critique (see **archaeology**, **articulation**, **class**, **discourse**, **hegemony**, **history**, **ideology**, and **radical democracy**); Cultural Studies (see **cultural capital**, **culture**, **discourse**, **doxa**, **field**, and **habitus**), and the study of **race** and **sex** (see **Critical Race Theory**, *écriture féminine*, **feminism**, **hybridity**, **intersectionality**, **Matrix of Domination**, **liminality**, **mimicry**, **Orientalism**, **Other**, **performativity**, **Postcolonial Studies**, **subaltern**, and **whiteness as property**).

See also: **poststructuralism**, **structuralism**, **text and textuality**.

Further reading: Barthes 1967, 1972, 1977; Culler 1981; Derrida 1976; Eco 1976, 1986; Greimas 1976a, 1993; Hernadi 1978; Jameson 1972; Lévi-Strauss 1963; Saussure 1916; K. Silverman 1983.

SEX AND SEXUALITY

See **gender and sex**

SIGN

See **semiotics** and **signifier and signified**

SIGNIFIER AND SIGNIFIED

A "signifier" refers to any sign's physical form (for example, any written or spoken word); a "signified" refers to the meaning conveyed by that sign. The distinction has been particularly significant for critical theory in the wake of Ferdinand de Saussure's work, *Course in General Linguistics* (1916), where Saussure theorizes the "arbitrary nature of the sign" and the differential nature of language and meaning-production. Saussure here argues that "sign" should be understood as a relation between what he terms "signified" and "signifier." He then posits two "primordial characteristics" of the linguistic sign. The first principle is that "The bond between the signifier and the signified is arbitrary" (67). As he explains, "The idea of 'sister' is not linked by any inner relation-ship to the succession of sounds *s-ö-r* which serves as its signifier in French; that it could be represented equally by just any other sequence is proved by differences among languages and by the very existence of different languages: the signified 'ox' has as its signifier *b-ö-f* on one side of the border and *o-k-s* (*Ochs*) on the other" (67–68). Saussure extends this observation about the arbitrariness of the sign to all communication, not just language: "every means of expression used in society is based, in principle, on collective behavior or—what amounts to the same thing—convention" (68). Meaning derives, then, not from any intrinsic connection between a signifier and the thing it signifies, including any worldly referent, but rather from the differences between terms in any given language system. As Saussure explains,

> Instead of pre-existing ideas then, we find in all the foregoing examples *values* emanating from the system. When they are said to correspond to concepts, it is understood that the concepts are

purely differential and defined not by their positive content but negatively by their relations with the other terms of the system. Their most precise characteristic is in being what the others are not. (117)

As signs are arbitrary, so also are they necessarily differential, their meanings established not by referents or any one signified but by differences from other opposing meanings in a structural system. Saussure therefore argues that "*Arbitrary* and *differential* are two correlative qualities" (118).

This thesis logically leads to Saussure's second principle of the linguistic sign: "the linear nature of the signifier," that is, that signification occurs only over a span of time. If meaning only occurs as we understand a term's difference from other opposing terms, then meaning can only occur over time, over what Saussure terms a "syntagm": "In the syntagm a term acquires its value only because it stands in opposition to everything that precedes or follows it, or to both" (123).

Saussure's emphasis on the differential structures of language over referentiality influenced a number of **structuralist** theorists in various disciplines. Claude Lévi-Strauss, a structural anthropologist, for example states that, "in accordance with the Saussurean principle," "nothing compels, a priori, certain sound-clusters to denote certain objects" (1963: 92). He then goes on to establish the unconscious **binary oppositions** by which cultures are, in fact, structured. **Poststructuralists** adopt Saussure's linguistic turn, arguing that we are necessarily separated from reality because of our reliance on language to structure everything we know; however, they push Saussure's theories further, questioning any desire to fix the play of signification by positing stable centers for the production of meaning, including Saussure's own privileging of the spoken word over writing, which Jacques Derrida **"deconstructs"** in Part I of his book, *Of Grammatology* (1976). According to Derrida, "It could be shown that all the names related to fundamentals, to principles, or to the center have always designated an invariable presence—*eidos*, *archē*, *telos*, *energeia*, *ousia* (essence, existence, substance, subject) *alētheia*, transcendentality, consciousness, God, man, and so forth" (1978: 279–80). Derrida terms the signified that fixes the play of signification a "transcendental signified" and argues, building on Saussure, that one must concentrate instead on *différance*, the deferrals and differences that constitute the play of signification in the actual act of reading or interpreting. According to Derrida, "The absence of the transcendental signified extends the domain and the play of signification infinitely" (280).

Like Derrida, Henry Louis Gates questions what he sees as Saussure's resistance to play in the relationship between signifier and signified, and argues that one can best understand and theorize an African-American literary tradition by examining not only Saussure's standard understanding of signification (the relation of signifier to signified) but an alternative sense of "Signifyin(g)" in literature of the black vernacular:

> Signifyin(g) concerns itself with … the chaos of what Saussure calls "associative relations," which we can represent as the playful puns on a word that occupy the **paradigmatic** axis of language and which a speaker draws on for figurative substitutions. These substitutions in Signifyin(g) tend to be humorous, or function to name a person or a situation in a telling manner. Whereas signification depends for order and coherence on the exclusion of unconscious associations which any given word yields at any given time, Signification luxuriates in the inclusion of the free play of these associative rhetorical and semantic relations. (1988: 49)

A similar sense of play on the level of the signifier can be found in Homi K. Bhabha's theorization of **hybridity** and in Mikhail Bakhtin's theorization of **dialogism**, **heteroglossia**, and **polyphony**.

See also: **parody**.

Further reading: Bakhtin 1981, 1984a, 1986; Barthes 1967; Culler 1975; Derrida 1976, 1978, 1982; Gates 1988; Saussure 1916; K. Silverman 1983.

SIMPLE ABSTRACTION

Karl Marx uses this term in the *Grundrisse* (written 1857–58, published in 1941) to designate a concept that appears simple in common usage—his specific example here is "labor"—but that, in fact, hides a complex **dialectical–materialist** reality. As Marx puts it, "the most general abstractions arise only in the midst of the richest possible concrete development" (1973: 104). We should be wary, then, in using any term that "appears as common to many, to all" (104); society "by no means begins only at the point where one can speak of it *as such*" (106). Simple abstractions thus contribute to what Marx terms the "false consciousness" of **ideology**.

See also: **base and superstructure, ideology**.

SIMULACRA (SIMULACRUM) AND SIMULATION

A simulacrum refers to something that replaces reality with its representation. Jean Baudrillard in *Simulacra and Simulation* (1994) defines this term as follows: "Simulation is no longer that of a territory, a referential being, or a substance. It is the generation by models of a **real** without origin or reality: a hyperreal" (1–2). Fredric Jameson provides a similar definition: the simulacrum's "peculiar function lies in what Sartre would have called the *derealization* of the whole surrounding world of everyday reality" (1991: 34). According to Baudrillard, with whom the term is most closely associated, what has happened in **postmodern** culture is that our society has become so reliant on models and maps that we have lost all contact with the real world that preceded the map. Reality itself has begun merely to imitate the model, which now precedes and determines the real world: "The territory no longer precedes the map, nor does it survive it. It is nevertheless the map that precedes the territory—precession of simulacra—that engenders the territory" (1994: 1). According to Baudrillard, when it comes to postmodern simulation and simulacra, "It is no longer a question of imitation, nor duplication, nor even **parody**. It is a question of substituting the signs of the real for the **real**" (2). Baudrillard is not merely suggesting that **postmodern** culture is artificial, because the concept of artificiality still requires some sense of reality against which to recognize the artifice. His point, rather, is that we have lost all ability to make sense of the distinction between **nature** and artifice. To clarify his point, he argues that there are three "orders of simulacra": (1) in the first order of simulacra, which he associates with the pre-modern period, the image is a clear counterfeit of the **real**; the image is recognized as just an illusion, a place marker for the real; (2) in the second order of simulacra, which Baudrillard associates with the industrial revolution of the nineteenth century, the distinctions between the image and the representation begin to break down because of mass production and the proliferation of copies. Such production misrepresents and masks an underlying reality by imitating it so well, thus threatening to replace it (e.g., in photography or **ideology**); however, there is still a belief that, through critique or effective political action, one can still access the hidden fact of the real; (3) in the third order of simulacra, which is associated with the **postmodern** age, we are confronted with a *precession* of simulacra; that is, the representation *precedes* and *determines* the **real**. There is no longer any distinction between reality and its representation; there is only the simulacrum.

Baudrillard points to a number of phenomena to explain this loss of distinctions between "reality" and the simulacrum:

(1) Media culture. Contemporary media (television, film, magazines, billboards, the Internet) are concerned not just with relaying information or stories but with interpreting our most private selves for us, making us approach each other and the world through the lens of these media images. We therefore no longer acquire goods because of real needs but because of **desires** that are increasingly defined by commercials and commercialized images, which keep us at one step removed from the reality of our bodies or of the world around us.

(2) **Exchange Value**. According to Karl Marx, the entrance into **capitalist** culture meant that we ceased to think of purchased goods in terms of **use value**, in terms of the real uses to which an item will be put. Instead, everything began to be translated into how much it is worth, into what it can be exchanged for (its **exchange value**). Once money became a "**universal equiva- lent**," against which everything in our lives is measured, things lost their material reality (real-world uses, the sweat and tears of the laborer). We began even to think of our own lives in terms of money rather than in terms of the real things we hold in our hands: how much is my time worth? How does my conspicuous consumption define me as a person? According to Baudrillard, in the **postmodern** age, we have lost all sense of **use value**: "It is all **capital**" (1981: 82).

(3) Multinational capitalism. As the things we use are increasingly the product of complex industrial processes, we lose touch with the underlying reality of the goods we consume. Not even national identity functions in a world of multinational corporations. According to Baudrillard, it is **capital** that now defines our identities. We thus continue to lose touch with the material fact of the laborer, who is increasingly invisible to a consumer oriented towards retail outlets or the even more impersonal Internet. A common example of this is the fact that most consumers do not know how the products they consume are related to real-life things. How many people could identify the actual plant from which is derived the coffee bean? Starbucks, by contrast, increasingly defines our urban realities (see **late capitalism**).

(4) Urbanization. As we continue to develop available geographical locations, we lose touch with any sense of the natural world. Even natural spaces are now understood as "protected," which is

to say that they are defined in contradistinction to an urban "reality," often with signs to point out just how "real" they are. Increasingly, we expect the sign (behold nature!) to precede access to nature.

(5) Language and **Ideology**. Baudrillard illustrates how in such subtle ways language keeps us from accessing "reality." The earlier understanding of ideology was that it hid the truth, that it represented a **"false consciousness,"** as **Marxists** phrase it, keeping us from seeing the real workings of the state, of economic forces, or of the dominant groups in power. (This understanding of **ideology** corresponds to Baudrillard's second order of simulacra.) **Postmodernism**, on the other hand, understands **ideology** as the support for our very perception of reality. There is no outside of **ideology**, according to this view, at least no outside that can be articulated in language. Because we are so reliant on language to structure our perceptions, any representation of reality is always already **ideological**, always already constructed by simulacra.

Further reading: Baudrillard 1981, 1988, 1994, 1998; Jameson 1991.

SKAD (SOCIOLOGY OF KNOWLEDGE APPROACH TO DISCOURSE)

See **discourse**

SOCIAL CAPITAL

See **cultural capital, social capital, and symbolic capital**

SPECULATIVE REALISM

"Speculative Realism" is a term that has been applied to a group of philosophers (Quentin Meillassoux, Ray Brassier, Iain Hamilton Grant, and Graham Harman) who, although they differ on some fundamental points, all seek to contest what they see as the anthropomorphism of philosophy after Immanuel Kant (1724–1804). They are influenced by the work of Bruno Latour, the leading proponent of **Actor-Network Theory**, and the work of Gilles Deleuze. As Harman explains, "Rather than a unified school, Speculative Realism has always been a loose umbrella term for four markedly different

positions: my own object-oriented philosophy, Ray Brassier's elim-
inative nihilism, Iain Hamilton Grant's cyber-vitalism, and Quentin
Meillassoux's speculative materialism" (2010: 1). They are "realist"
insofar as they reject Kant's position that philosophy cannot discuss
reality in itself (only reality as it exists "for us," that is, potentially
distorted by our delimited powers of perception and understanding)
and they are "speculative" insofar as "none of them merely defend a
dull commonsense realism of genuine trees and billiard balls existing
outside the mind, but a darker form of 'weird realism' bearing little
resemblance to the presuppositions of everday life" (Harman 2010: 2).

Quentin Meillassoux's book, *After Finitude* (2008), has proven to
be an important touchstone for the movement, even as aspects of
Meillassoux's argument are occasionally critiqued by the other philosophers of this school of thinking. Meillassoux's two-fold thesis is as
follows: "on the one hand, we acknowledge that the sensible only
exists as a **subject**'s relation to the world; but on the other hand, we
maintain that the mathematizable properties of the **object** are exempt
from the constraint of such a relation, and that they are effectively in the
object in the way in which I conceive them, whether I am in relation
with this **object** or not" (3). In other words, although it is true that
sensible properties ("sonorous, visual, olfactory, etc." [1]) result from a
"relation between the world and the living creature I am" (2)—what
Meillassoux terms "secondary qualities"—it is also true that we can
posit "primary qualities" which "are supposed to be inseparable from
the **object**, properties which one supposes to belong to the thing even
when I no longer apprehend it" (3).

According to Meillassoux, such a thesis is impossible, indefensible if
one follows the logic of post-Kantian philosophy:

> It is an indefensible thesis because thought cannot get outside itself
> in order to compare the world as it is "in itself" to the world as it is
> "for us," and thereby distinguish what is a function of our relation
> to the world from what belongs to the world alone. Such an
> enterprise is effectively self-contradictory, for at the very moment
> when we think of a property as belonging to the world in itself,
> it is precisely the latter that we are thinking, and consequently
> this property is revealed to be essentially tied to our thinking about
> the world. We cannot represent the "in itself" without it becoming
> "for us," or as Hegel amusingly put it, we cannot "creep up on"
> the object "from behind" so as to find out what it is in itself—
> which means that we cannot know anything that would be
> beyond our relation to the world. (3–4)

As there is no direct access to the "thing in itself," according to post-Kantian philosophy, there can be no "naïve realism" (4). Even the "mathematical properties of the object" (e.g., length, width, movement, depth, figure, size) must be "conceived as dependent upon the **subject**'s relation to the given—as a form of representation for the orthodox Kantian, or as an act of **subjectivity** for the **phenomenologist**, or as a specific formal language for the analytical philosopher, and so on" (4). Lacanian **psychoanalysis**, **poststructuralist** thought, and even Jürgen Habermas's theories of **communicative action** could be said to follow suit as they all posit our inaccessibility to the **Real** and/or our reliance on language to determine our relation to the real world. Harman refers to all such theories as part of the "linguistic turn" in philosophy (2010: 93), which he seeks to counter with his "**object**-oriented philosophy." According to Meillassoux, in such theories "inter-subjectivity, the consensus of a community, supplants the adequation between the representations of a solitary **subject** and the **thing** itself as the veritable criterion of objectivity, and of scientific objectivity more particularly. Scientific truth is no longer what conforms to an in-itself supposedly indifferent to the way in which it is given to the **subject**, but rather what is susceptible of being given as shared by a scientific community" (2008: 4–5).

The problem with this linguistic turn, according to Harman, is that it does not get us beyond the human-centered metaphysics of pre-Kantian philosophy: "The ostensibly revolutionary transition from consciousness to language still leaves humans in absolute command at the center of philosophy" but in a way that has led philosophy to renounce "its claim to have anything to do with the world itself" (2010: 94). In other words, "the relation between humans and apples is assumed to be philosophically more significant than the relations between apples and trees, apples and sunlight, or apples and wind" (147). Harman therefore argues that "The root duality of the universe is not made up of **subject** and **object**, or even Dasein and world, but of *objects and relations*" (156).

For Brassier, this leads to a principle of nihilism that he sees as the logical result of the "disenchantment of the world" begun by the Enlightenment and that he presents as "an invigorating vector of intellectual discovery, rather than a calamitous diminishment." As he goes on, "nihilism is not … a pathological exacerbation of sub-jectivism, which annuls the world and reduces reality to a correlate of the absolute ego, but on the contrary, the unavoidable corollary of the realist conviction that there is a mind-independent reality, which, despite the presumptions of human **narcissism**, is indifferent to our existence and oblivious to the 'values' and 'meanings' which we would drape over it in order to make it more hospitable" (2007: xi).

Speculative Realism insists, then, on the primary qualities of **objects** outside of any relation to the human **subject** who perceives those objects. At the same time, it does not ask us to return to the "naïve realism" of pre-Kantian metaphysics: "we have no desire to call into question the contemporary desuetude of metaphysics," Meillassoux writes, "For the kind of dogmatism which claims that this God, this world, this history, and ultimately this actually existing political regime necessarily exists, and must be the way it is—this kind of *absolutism* does indeed seem to pertain to an era of thinking to which it is neither possible nor desirable to return" (2008: 34). The "speculative" part of speculative realism addresses the rejection of such naïve realism in favor of the following seeming paradox in Meillassoux: "*we must uncover an absolute necessity that does not reinstate any form of absolutely necessary entity.* In other words, we must think an absolute necessity without thinking anything that *is* absolutely necessary," which is to say that "it is possible to envisage an *absolutizing* thought that would not be *absolutist*" (34). See **factiality**.

Meillassoux wishes to counter the belief that we are unable "to gain access to the absolute ground of what is" (2008: 42) while refusing to fall prey to any absolutist claim about what that "is" actually *is*. Meillassoux thus runs counter to **postmodern** thought, which will "dismiss every variety of universal as a mystificatory relic of the old metaphysics" (43). **Postmodernists**, according to Meillassoux, will always insist that "the correlations which determine 'our' world ... be identified with a situation anchored in a determinate era of the history of being, or in a form of life harbouring its own **language-games**, or in a determinate cultural and interpretative community, etc." (43). That is, the **postmodernist** argues that any claim to know the world cannot help but be **ideological** in some way. The problem with this situation, according to Meillassoux is that, by stating it can no longer say anything about the absolute, philosophy "has inadvertently justified belief's claim to be the *only* means of access to the absolute" (46). The result is what Meillassoux terms the "fideism" or religiosity of contemporary "anti-metaphysical scepticism": "it is our conviction that the contemporary end of metaphysics is nothing other than the victory of such a fideism ... over metaphysics" (46). By questioning every claim that one can know the absolute truth about anything, **postmodern** theory, according to Meillassoux, has in its skepticism made all faiths equally valid: "The modern man is he who, even as he stripped Christianity of the **ideological** (metaphysical) pretension that its belief system was superior to all others, has delivered himself body and soul to the idea that all belief systems are equally legitimate in matters of veracity" (48). By not believing in any absolute, such thinking leaves us with nothing but beliefs, in other words: "In leaving the realm of metaphysics, the absolute seems to have been fragmented into a multiplicity of beliefs that have become indifferent, all of them equally legitimate from the viewpoint of knowledge, and this simply by virtue of the fact that they themselves claim to be nothing *but* beliefs" (47). Speculative realism asserts that there *are* absolute primary qualities for the objective **real** that exist outside of our ability to perceive or describe them while refusing any dogmatic claim that any one absolute is the ultimate ground for meaning (see **factiality**): "Against dogmatism, it is important that we uphold the refusal of every metaphysical absolute, but against the reasoned violence of various fanaticisms, it is important that we re-discover in thought a modicum of absoluteness" (49).

See also: **correlationism, factiality, positivism and empiricism, things**.

Further reading: Brassier 2007; Garcia 2014; Grant 2008; Harman 2010, 2011; Meillassoux 2008; Žižek 2012.

SPEECH ACT AND SPEECH-ACT THEORY

For critical theory, the term "speech act" normally refers to J. L. Austin's theorization of what he termed "speech acts" in *How to Do Things with Words* (1962), a concept later developed in the work of John Searle. Moving away from the tendency of linguistics to concentrate on the structure behind language (see *langue* **and** *parole*), Austin influentially concerns himself with the context of any utterance. As he explains, "Once we realize that what we have to study is *not* the sentence but the issuing of an utterance in a speech situation, there can hardly be any longer a possibility of not seeing that stating is performing an act" (139). The relation between **signifier and signified** is not perfectly stable because "Reference depends on knowledge at the time of utterance" (144). You can make a given constative statement (a declaration that something is the case, e.g., "the road is clear"); however, the force of that statement and its effect on an actual addressee (the two aspects of a **performative** utterance) will change depending on the context: "It is essential to realize that 'true' and 'false,' like 'free' and 'unfree,' do not stand for anything simple at all; but only for a general dimension of being a right or proper thing to say as opposed to a wrong thing, in these circumstances, to this audience, for these purposes and with these intentions" (145).

To clarify his point, Austin divides speech acts into three levels of the utterance: (1) A *locutionary act* refers to constative statements whereby "meaning is equivalent to sense and reference" (100); "in saying something," to put this another way, "we perform a *locutionary act*, which is roughly equivalent to uttering a certain sentence with a certain sense and reference, which again is roughly equivalent to 'meaning' in the traditional sense" (109). Linguistics tends to stop at this function of language; however, Austin argues that we must distinguish the meaning of an utterance from its "force" and its "effect," the two aspects of a performative utterance. (2) An *illocutionary act* refers to the force of the utterance, the *intended* effect of the utterance, "the act of attempting or purporting (or affecting or professing or claiming or setting up or setting out) to perform a certain illocutionary act" (105). Austin argues that this act must be distinguished from the *achieved* effect of the act, "the act of successfully achieving or consummating or bringing off such an act" (106). (3) The achieved effect is the *perlocutionary act*; that is, the performative *effect* on a specific individual in a specific context, "what we bring about or achieve *by* saying something, such as convincing, persuading, deterring, and even, say, surprising or misleading" (109). The classic example of a perlocutionary act is the "I pronounce you man and wife" of the marriage ceremony. In making that statement, a person of authority changes the status of a couple within an intersubjective community; those words actively change the existence of that couple by establishing a new marital reality: the words *do* what they say.

One of the radical conclusions that Austin makes is that it is ultimately difficult to distinguish among these three acts, for, as he asks, "When we issue any utterance whatsoever, are we not 'doing something'?" (92). Austin therefore concludes that "in general the locutionary act as much as the illocutionary is an abstraction only: every genuine speech act is both" (147) such that a constative statement like "He did not do it" is exactly on a level with the more clearly illocutionary statements "I argue that he did not do it" or "I suggest that he did not do it" or "I bet that he did not do it" and so on (134). One can also say that any sentence also does something, has some effect on specific individuals and, so, can be characterized also as a perlocutionary act.

Poststructuralist Jacques Derrida builds on Searle's Speech-Act Theory in *Margins of Philosophy* (1982). He questions Austin's distinction between "felicitous" and "infelicitous" utterances because such a distinction assumes "a free consciousness present for the totality of the operation, of an absolutely full meaning that is master of itself: the teleological jurisdiction of a total field whose *intention* remains the organizing center" (323). Derrida instead underscores in any utterance "a general citationality—or rather, a general iterability—without which there would not even be a 'successful' performative" (325). As Derrida asks, "Could a **performative** statement succeed if its formulation did not repeat a 'coded' or iterable statement, in other words if the expressions I use to open a meeting, launch a ship or a marriage were not identifiable as *conforming* to an iterable model, and therefore if they were not identifiable in a way as 'citation'?" (326). That citationality or iterability is an inescable aspect of language because of the arbitrariness of the sign (see **signifier and signified** and *différance*). "Given this structure of iteration," Derrida explains, "the intention which animates utterance will never be completely present in itself and its content" (326). In the "Law of Genre" (1980), Derrida develops his understanding of the speech act into a general theory of genre.

Building on both Austin's and Derrida's understanding of the speech act, Judith Butler in *Gender Trouble* (1990a), *Bodies That Matter* (1993) and *Excitable Speech* (1997) develops a theory of **performativity** that greatly influenced both **feminism** and **queer theory**.

Further reading: Austin 1962; Butler 1990a, 1993, 1997; Derrida 1980, 1982; Felman 1983; J. H. Miller 2001; Pratt 1977; Searle 1969, 1979.

STATE

See **nation, nation-state, nationhood, and nationalism**

STATE APPARATUSES

See **Ideological State Apparatuses (ISAs)**

STATE OF EXCEPTION

This term is theorized by Giorgio Agamben as a way of making sense of what is traditionally referred to in English as "martial law," that is, those moments of crisis when juridical law is suspended. The term is originally theorized by Carl Schmitt who defines "sovereign" as "he who decides on the state of exception" (Agamben 1998: 11), which is to say that "the sovereign, having legal power to suspend the validity of the law, legally places himself outside the law" (Agamben 1998: 15). Agamben purposively chooses the term, "state of exception," instead of "martial *law*" in order to make clear that "[t]he state of exception is not a special kind of law (like the law of war); rather, insofar as it is a suspension of the juridical order itself, it defines law's threshold or limit concept" (2005: 4). One example is the USA Patriot Act issued on 26 October 2001, because that act created "a legally unnamable and unclassifiable being"; captured Taliban in Afghanistan do not "enjoy the status of POWs as defined by the Geneva Convention" nor even "the status of persons charged with a crime according to American laws" (3): "Neither prisoners nor persons accused, but simply 'detainees,' they are the object of a pure de facto rule, of a detention that is indefinite not only in the temporal sense but in its very nature as well, since it is entirely removed from the law and from judicial oversight" (3–4). The problem, according to Agamben, is that since the First World War, this state of exception has increasingly become common practice, even "a paradigm of government," which therefore threatens to destroy democracy and the distinction among legislative, executive, and judicial powers" (7). Agamben argues that when law and its state of exception "tend to coincide in a single person," as in dictatorship, "when the state of exception, in which they are bound and blurred together, becomes the rule, then the juridico-political system transforms itself into a killing machine" (86), as it did in Nazi Germany and as, Agamben fears, may be happening today because of "the working of the machine that is leading the West toward global civil war" (87).

According to Agamben, the state of exception is in fact a constitutive aspect of the very possibility of law (and, as such, is tied to his related concept, **bare life**), so Agamben is ultimately questioning a tradition of thinking about law (and its exception) that goes back to ancient Greece; in other words, there is something inherently problematic, he argues, in the way law has always established its legitimacy, which is precisely what opens up the sort of abuse of law and government that characterizes the modern period, with its unprecedented genocides. He goes even further: the relation of the rule and its exception is at the heart of how we make sense of the world. In this, Agamben aligns himself with a **deconstructionist** understanding of signification. Language, he argues, functions in a similar way given the way our use of it relies on an understanding of *langue*'s opposition to *parole*. "*Langue*" refers to language as pure potentiality, as a set of structural rules, or, as Agamben puts it, "the pure potentiality to signify, withdrawing itself from every concrete instance of speech" (1998: 21). By contrast, *parole* refers to the concrete instance of speech, which necessarily includes the messy "noise" of context, each actual use of words necessarily different from every other use. As Agamben explains, "Here the sphere of law shows its essential proximity to that of language. Just as in an occurrence of actual speech, a word acquires its ability to denote a segment of reality only insofar as it is also meaningful in its own not-denoting (that is, as *langue* as opposed to *parole*, as a term in its mere lexical consistency, independent of its concrete use in discourse), so the rule can refer to the individual case only because it is in force, in the sovereign exception, as pure potentiality in the suspension of every actual reference" (1998: 20).

See also: **apparatus**.

Further reading: Agamben 1998, 2005, 2011; de la Durantaye 2009; Lechte and Newman 2013.

STORY AND DISCOURSE

The distinction between "story" and "discourse" is an important one for **narratology**. (Russian Formalists use instead the Russian terms "*fabula*" and "*sjužet*.") "Story" refers to the actual chronology of events in a narrative, which usually needs to be reconstructed after watching or reading a narrative; discourse refers to the manipulation of that story in the presentation of the narrative. These terms refer, then, to the basic structure of all narrative form. Story usually needs to be reconstructed from a **narrative** because most stories are not told chronologically, the way they *actually* occurred in the time-space (or **diegetic**) universe of the narrative being read. The closest a film narrative ever comes to pure story is in what is termed "**real time**." In literature, it's even harder to present material in real time. One example occurs at the end of the *Odyssey* (Book XXIII); Odysseus here presents the story of his adventures to Penelope in almost pure "story" form, that is, in the chronological order of occurrence. Stories are rarely recounted in this fashion, however. So, for example, in the *Odyssey*, we do not begin at the chronological start of the story but *in medias res* (in the middle of things), when Odysseus is about to be freed from the isle of Calypso (which actually occurs nearly at the end of the chronological story that Odysseus relates to Penelope in Book XXIII). In narratology, "discourse" has been extended to encompass all the material an author adds to a story: similes, metaphors, the form of narration, the choice between verse or prose, and so on; after all, these stylistic choices do not change the chronological sequence of events as they occur in narrative, only our access to those story elements in the time of reading. In film, such manipulations are extended to include framing, cutting, camera movement, camera angles, extra-**diegetic** music, and so on.

One might be tempted to understand "story" as coming first and the "discourse" as the subsequent reworking of that story for the benefit of a story's narration; however, many **poststructuralist** narratologists have questioned that understanding, going so far as to argue that "story" is nothing but an enabling fiction in our reading—that, really, all we ever actually have is "discourse." Jonathan Culler gives the example of Sophocles' *Oedipus Rex*, where early in the play there is some question about whether Laius was killed by a single person or a gang of robbers. Culler is interested in the fact that this alternative possibility for the death of Laius is never explored and that Oedipus instead assumes he is the guilty party, without being given additional evidence about what happened that night:

> Once we are well into the play, we know that Oedipus must be found guilty, otherwise the play will not work at all; and the logic to which we are responding is not simply an esthetic logic that affects readers of literary works. Oedipus, too, feels the force of this logic. It had been prophesied that Oedipus would kill his father; it had been prophesied that Laius would be killed by his son; Oedipus admits to having killed an old man at what may have been the relevant time and place; so when the shepherd reveals that Oedipus is in fact the son of Laius, Oedipus leaps to the conclusion, and every reader leaps with him, that he is in fact the murderer of Laius. His conclusion is based not on new evidence concerning a past deed but on the force of meaning, the inter-weaving of prophesies and the demands of narrative coherence. The convergence of discursive forces makes it essential that he become the murderer of Laius, and he yields to this force of meaning. Instead of saying, therefore, that there is a sequence of past events that are given and which the play reveals with certain detours, we can say that the crucial event is the product of demands of signification. Here meaning is not the effect of a prior event but its cause. (1981: 174)

Peter Brooks makes similar arguments in his psychoanalytically inspired work of narratology, *Reading for the Plot* (1985). As he writes, "We must ... recognize that the apparent priority of *fabula* to *sjužet* is in the nature of a mimetic illusion, in that the *fabula*—'what really happened'—is in fact a mental construction that the reader derives from the *sjužet*, which is all that he ever directly knows" (13). He goes on to illustrate the structuring force of a given narrative's ending, illustrating how "the end writes the beginning and shapes the middle" (22).

Further reading: Brooks 1985; Chatman 1978; Cohen and Shires 1988; Culler 1981.

STRUCTURALISM (STRUCTURALIST)

Structuralism, sometimes called Formalism, refers to a variety of critical theories that have in common a desire to understand the interrelation of elements as part of a larger system or "structure" rather than examination of those elements in isolation from their structural function. In structural linguistics, for example, what matters is not the meaning of words in isolation or in their original context (e.g., their referentiality) but rather the system of differences by which meaning-production is achieved or the decontextual system of rules that organizes the apparent complexity of everyday usage. The tendency, then, is to approach language, history, narrative, or cultural systems at large in an atemporal, synchronic fashion. For critical theory, the most influential critics in structural linguistics and **semiotics** are Ferdinand de Saussure, Roman Jakobson, Algirdas Julien Greimas, Roland Barthes, and Émile Benveniste (see **Greimassian square, hermeneutic and proairetic codes,** *langue* **and** *parole*, **signifier and signified, syntagmatic and paradigmatic**); in anthropology, Claude Lévi-Strauss (see **binary opposition**); in history and the history of ideas, Michel Foucault (see **apparatus, archaeology, author, discipline, discourse, government, heterotopia, panoptic,** and **repressive hypothesis**); in psychoanalysis, Jacques Lacan (see **desire, Gaze, imaginary order, mirror stage, Name-of-the-Father, narcissism, psychosexual development, the Real, super-ego, suture,** and **the unconscious**). **Poststructuralism,** including **deconstruction,** builds on the insights of structuralism but questions the desire for a totalizing system that structuralist theorists appear to exhibit in their work.

See also: **New Criticism and New Formalism, narrative and narratology.**

Further reading: Barthes 1967; Culler 1975; Dreyfus and Rabinow 1983; Foucault 1966, 1972; Hernadi 1981; Jameson 1972; Kurtzweil 1980; Lacan 1968, 1977, 1981; Lévi-Strauss 1963; Saussure 1916; Sturrock 1979.

SUBALTERN

The term "subaltern" originally meant simply: of inferior rank or status (as in the military); however, the term has been largely taken over by **Postcolonial Studies**. Antonio Gramsci first defines "subaltern" for critical theory by applying the term to any group that is excluded from the dominant **hegemony** of a society and is thus denied the same benefits of the dominant class. Gramsci was interested in writing a history of the subaltern classes, thus countering the tendency of traditional history to represent only the history of the dominant group.

The term was adopted by a "Subaltern Studies" group of critics, largely historians tied to the publication, *Subaltern Studies: Writings on South Asian History and Society*, which was edited by the historian Ranajit Guha. This group sought to provide an alternative history of South Asia that represented oppressed groups of people. As Edward Said explains in the Foreword to the collection, *Selected Subaltern Studies*, "Guha's claim for the group of scholars his editorship had gathered together was relatively simple—that hitherto Indian history had been written from a colonialist and elitist point of view, whereas a large part of Indian history had been made by the subaltern classes, and hence the need for a new historiography which these scholars were now going to write" (1988: v). Said explains that, according to Guha, what is missing in the story that is usually told about Indian independence from British rule "is the constitutive role of an enormous mass of subaltern Indians, the urban poor and the peasants, who throughout the nineteenth century and earlier, resisted British rule in terms and modes that were quite distinct from those employed by the elite" (vi). Or, in Guha's own words, "parallel to the domain of elite politics there existed throughout the colonial period another domain of Indian politics in which the principal actors were not the dominant groups of the indigenous society or the colonial authorities but the subaltern classes and groups constituting the mass of the labouring population and the intermediate strata in town and country—that is, the people" (1988: 40).

Gayatri Chakravorty Spivak in her essay, "Can the Subaltern Speak?" (1988a) influentially critiqued certain essentializing tendencies and phrasings in the writings of the Subaltern Studies group, particularly their tendency here and there to articulate a subaltern consciousness and common voice, to assume "that there *is* a pure form of consciousness" (286). As she asks, "With what voice-consciousness can the subaltern speak?" (285). Spivak argues that "a nostalgia for lost origins can be detrimental to the exploration of social realities within the critique of imperialism" (291) because that nostalgia threatens to reproduce the same strategies by which dominant discourse excludes anything that does not fit into a stable "ethnocentric **Subject**" (292), a **Subject** that is, in fact, only ever retroactively constructed as a myth and stable cause or author through our use of language. Formerly the English translator of Jacques Derrida's *Of Grammatology*, Spivak argues for the implementation of **deconstructionist** strategies in **post-colonial** critique in order to ensure that **postcolonial** critics do not reproduce the linguistic strategies that ultimately benefit Eurocentric, "First World" and elitist **hegemonies**. As she explains in "Subaltern Studies" (1988b), her Introduction to *Selected Subaltern Studies*, "If ... the restoration of the subaltern's subject-position in history is seen by the historian as the establishment of an inalienable and final truth of things, then any emphasis on sovereignty, consistency, and logic will ... inevitably objectify the subaltern and be caught in the game of knowledge as **power**" (16). She argues instead that "the arena of the subaltern's persistent emergence into **hegemony** must always and by definition remain heterogenous to the efforts of the disciplinary historian. The historian must persist in *his* efforts in this awareness, that the subaltern is necessarily the absolute limit of the place where **history** is narrativized into logic" (16).

In both "Subaltern Studies" and "Can the Subaltern Speak?" Spivak also questions the exclusion of women from the work of the Subaltern Studies group: "Male subaltern and historian are ... united in the common assumption that the procreative sex is a species apart, scarcely if at all to be considered a part of civil society" (1988b: 28). As she puts it in "Can the Subaltern Speak?" "If, in the context of colonial production, the subaltern has no history and cannot speak, the subaltern as female is even more deeply in shadow" (1988a: 287).

Homi Bhabha has influentially sought to rethink the notion of **nation** to open up a space for subaltern identity. Resisting any authoritarian myth of **nation**, there always exists, according to Bhabha, the singular site of any one person's performance of nation-ness, a liminal space that necessarily resists all totalization: "The aim of cultural difference is to re-articulate the sum of knowledge from the perspective of the signifying *singularity* of the 'other' that resists totalization—the repetition that will not return as the same, the minus-in-origin that results in political and discursive strategies where adding-*to* does not add-up but serves to disturb the calculation of **power** and knowledge, producing other spaces of subaltern signification" (1990a: 312).

See also: **Orientalism, race and ethnicity**.

Further reading: Bhabha 1990a; Chakrabarty 2002; Gramsci 1992, 1995, 2000; Guha 1988; Mignolo 2000; Spivak 1985, 1987, 1988a, 1988b.

SUBJECT AND SUBJECTIVITY

The examination of "subjectivity" begins in philosophy's effort to understand the preconditions for subjecthood, from René Descartes's *cogito ergo sum* (I think, therefore I am) to Immanuel Kant's positing of a "transcendental subject" of "pure apperception" as the *a priori* precondition for human thought, "independent of all experience" (Kant 1781: 45). As Kant explains, "I term ... an examination of the manner in which conceptions can apply *a priori* to objects, the *transcendental deduction* of conceptions, and I distinguish it from the **empirical** deduction, which indicates the mode in which a conception is obtained through experience and reflection thereon" (45). Kant thus establishes a separation between the "transcendental subject" and the "*ding an sich*" or the "thing in itself," the world of objects, a position not dissimilar to statements in critical theory about our separation from the **Real** (a contention that **Speculative Realism**, however, rejects). Kant also thus establishes a unitary and originary Subject that appears to be fully in control of itself and of its apperceptions, a precept that critical theory rejects: "It is in all acts of consciousness one and the same, and unaccompanied by it, no representation can exist *for me*. The unity of this apperception I call the transcendental unity of self-consciousness, in order to indicate the possibility of *a priori* cognition arising from it" (49).

Critical theorists question Kant's notion of a "transcendental subject" while still using the term "subject" rather than person or individual in describing human culture, politics, history, and society. The use of the term, though, has a different valence after the "linguistic turn" in critical theory that occurred especially after the publication of Ferdinand de Saussure's *Course in General Linguistics* in 1916. After Saussure, many critical theorists began to see language not as the tool of transcendental subjects who are completely in control of their thoughts but rather as the inherited system of arbitrary rules and conventions by which we construct reality, including the very concept of a conscious human subject. See **signifier and signified**. Such critical theorists tend, in fact, to be suspicious of what they characterize as the myth of the "sovereign subject," a consciousness that is completely in control of its thoughts and actions, as a king would be of his subjects. Instead, they turn to the system of rules that, especially through language, constructs what we take for granted as **natural**. "Subject" is thus turned into a linguistic function, as in the subject of a sentence. As the **semiotician** Roland Barthes puts it, "language knows a 'subject,' not a 'person,' and this subject, empty outside of the very enunciation which defines it, suffices to make language 'hold together'" (1977: 145).

Michel Foucault influentially builds on this way of thinking in order to explore the ways that the very notion of a "subject," with all of its attendant characteristics (reason, sexuality, self-discipline), develops over the course of history through linguistic structures that Foucault terms **discourse**. As he writes, "the subject should not be entirely abandoned. It should be reconsidered, not to restore the theme of an originating subject, but to seize its functions, its intervention in **discourse**, and its system of dependencies" (1977b: 148). This shift in focus allows Foucault to ask different questions of the subject and to articulate a different understanding of its development in **history**:

> We should suspend the typical questions: how does a free subject penetrate the density of things and endow them with meaning; how does it accomplish its design by animating the rules of **discourse** from within? Rather, we should ask: under what conditions and through what forms can an entity like the subject appear in the order of **discourse**; what position does it occupy; what functions does it exhibit; and what rules does it follow in each type of discourse? In short, the subject (and its substitutes) must be stripped of its creative role and analysed as a complex and variable function of **discourse**. (148)

Poststructuralists like Jacques Derrida go even further, critiquing the very notion of The Subject (with capital letters) as a totalizing concept that seeks always to shut down the play of interpretation opened up by the **différance** of writing. As Derrida states in his contribution to the collection, *Who Comes after the Subject?*: "There has never been The Subject for anyone" and "The subject is a fable" (Cadava *et al.* 1991: 102). Similarly, Jean-François Lyotard rejects the notion of an independent, originating subject, arguing that we are in fact only ever "subject to" **phrase regimens**, **genres of discourse**, and **language games**.

The notion of the Subject has also been influenced by the **psychoanalytical** work of Jacques Lacan, who applied the linguistic turn in **semiotics** to Sigmund Freud's theories of the **unconscious**.

According to Lacan, the human subject's entrance into language and the **symbolic order** entails a separation from the *ding an sich*, which Lacan designates as the **Real** (see **psychosexual development**). Since the very notion of the subject is reliant on a system of language that is outside and precedes the self (what Lacan terms the "big **Other**"), the notion of subjective, causal agency is only ever a fantasy that is constructed over a lack (see **suture**). For this reason, Lacan uses the "matheme," $, to designate the Subject. The subject is, by necessity, "barred," never fully in control of itself. The **Marxist** theorist Louis Althusser adopts this Lacanian understanding of the subject to make sense of how **ideology** functions, arguing that "*the category of the subject is only constitutive of all ideology insofar as all ideology has the function (which defines it) of 'constituting' concrete individuals as subjects*" (2001: 116). Althusser proceeds to argue that "you and I are *always already* subjects, and as such constantly practice the rituals of ideological recognition, which guarantee for us that we are indeed concrete, individual, distinguishable and (naturally) irreplaceable subjects" (117). That process functions by what Althusser terms "interpellation": "The existence of ideology and the hailing or interpellation of individuals as subjects are one and the same thing" (118), he explains. In interpellation, we are hailed (say, when we are simply walking down a street) and we respond to that hail by turning around. According to Althusser, "By this mere one-hundred-and-eighty-degree physical conversion, [the individual] becomes a *subject*" (118). Althusser goes on to make clear that such interpellation is merely the function of being a subject in language, so that "an individual is always-already subject, even before he is born" (119). See **ideology**.

See also: **agency**, **author**.

Further reading: Althusser 2001; T. J. Armstrong 1992; Barthes 1977; Cadava *et al.* 1991; Foucault 1977b; Gagnier 1991; Gelpi 1992; D. E. Hall 2004; Lacan 1981; K. Silverman 1983; Žižek 1999.

SUBLATION

See **dialectic**

SUBLIMATION

In psychoanalysis, sublimation refers to the redirection of sexual desire to "higher" aims. Freud saw sublimation as a protection against illness, because it allowed the subject to respond to sexual frustration (lack of gratification of the sexual impulse) by taking a new aim that, though still "genetically" (1953–74: 16.345) related to the sexual impulse, is no longer properly sexual but social. In this way, civilization has been able to place "social aims higher than the sexual ones, which are at bottom self-interested" (16.345). This is not to say that the "free mobility of the **libido**" (16.346) is ever fully contained: "sublimation is never able to deal with more than a certain fraction of **libido**" (16.346).

SUBLIME

Although there were earlier theorizations of the sublime (e.g., Longinus's), the understanding of the sublime that critical theory engages was first theorized by Immanuel Kant (1724–1804) and Edmund Burke (1729–97), who both distinguished the sublime from the beautiful. The beautiful is that in nature which can be admired calmly and appreciated for its surface appearance (color, depth, material, balance). The sublime, by contrast, is that in nature which is so much greater than man that it breaks down man's ability to make sense of things. In part because of this breakdown in meaning, the attraction of the sublime actually includes a certain degree of fear on the part of the beholder, although a fear not so immediate that it traumatizes. Thomas Weiskel usefully suggests that the sublime, as it is explained in Kant, actually has three phases. We begin, in the first phase, with "the state of normal perception or comprehension" where "[n]o discrepancy or dissonance interrupts representation, the smooth correspondence of inner and outer" (1976: 23). In the second phase, upon confrontation with the sublime object or experience, "the habitual relation of mind and object suddenly breaks down" (23) and we find ourselves facing a feeling of radical indeterminacy where all meaning breaks down. There is also a "third, or reactive, phase of the sublime moment," according to Weiskel, when "the mind recovers the balance of outer and inner by constituting a fresh relation between itself and the [sublime] object such that the very indeterminacy which erupted in phase two is taken as symbolizing the mind's relation to a transcendent order" (24). The sublime experience thus becomes proof of some greater reality that eliminates the threat of indeterminacy, be it imagination or nature or god.

Some critical theorists have sought to characterize the work of **poststructuralist** and **postmodern** theory as an effort to stay locked continuously in phase two of the sublime experience. One essay collection edited by Hugh J. Silverman and Gary E. Aylesworth even takes as its title *The Textual Sublime: Deconstruction and Its Differences* (1990). As Silverman writes in the introduction, "The **textual** sublime puts all claims to rigid limits under a shadow of doubt" (xii) and, so, serves as a possible model for **deconstruction** itself.

The notion of the sublime is particularly important in the work of Jean-François Lyotard, who turns to the concept as the mechanism by which a **postmodernist** seeks to counter any effort to impose the rules of one **language game** on all others. As he writes, "Modern **aesthetics** is an aesthetic of the sublime, though a nostalgic one. ... The **postmodern** would be that which, in the modern ... searches for new presentations ... in order to impart a stronger sense of the unpresentable" (1991: 81). The sublime for Lyotard, then, is the mechanism by which postmodernists seek always to counter every effort to impose one **grand narrative** on all others: "Let us wage a war on totality," he writes in the final lines of *The Postmodern Condition* (1991), "let us be witnesses to the unpresentable" (82).

See also: **abject**.

Further Reading: Burke 1756; Kant 1764, 1790; Librett 1993; Lyotard 1988b, 1991, 1994; Weiskel 1976.

SUBSTITUTE-FORMATION

In **psychoanalysis**, a substitute-formation is a result of **repression** and the subsequent return of the **repressed** in an alternate form. For example, in childhood anxiety-**hysteria**, the child is often working through a **libidinal** attitude to—and fear of—his or her father: "After **repression**, this impulse vanishes out of consciousness: the father does not appear in consciousness as an **object** for the **libido**. As a substitute for him we find in a corresponding situation some animal which is more or less suited to be an object of dread" (Freud 1915: 426). The substitute-formation thus follows the path of **displacement**.

See also: **reaction formation**.

SUPER-EGO

In **psychoanalysis**, the super-ego is the faculty that seeks to police what it deems unacceptable desires; it represents all moral restrictions and is the "advocate of a striving towards perfection" (Freud 1953–74: 22.67). Originally, the super-ego had the task of **repressing** the

Oedipus complex and, so, it is closely caught up in the psycho-dramas of the **id**; it is, in fact, a **reaction-formation** against the primitive **object**-choices of the **id**, specifically those connected with the **Oedipus complex**. The young heterosexual male deals with the **Oedipus complex** by identifying with and internalizing the father and his prohibitions: "The super-ego retains the character of the father, while the more intense the **Oedipus complex** was and the more rapidly it succumbed to **repression** (under the influence of discipline, religious teaching, schooling and reading), the more exacting later on is the domination of the super-ego over the **ego**—in the form of conscience or perhaps of an unconscious sense of guilt" (Freud 1923: 706). Given its intimate connection with the **Oedipus complex**, the super-ego is associated with the dread of **castration**. As we grow into adulthood, various other individuals or organizations will take over the place of the father and his prohibitions (the church, the law, the police, the government). Because of its connection to the **id**, the super-ego has the ability to become *excessively* moral and thus lead to destructive effects, a function that in Lacanian psychoanalysis is represented by the father of enjoyment.

In Lacanian psychoanalysis, the super-ego is closely tied to the functioning of the **symbolic order** and serves not so much to prohibit desire as to enable it. For this reason, Jacques Lacan is careful to distinguish human desire from animal sexuality (see **desire**). In a sense, our **desire** is never properly our own, but is created through fantasies that are caught up in cultural **ideologies** rather than material **sexuality**. For this reason, according to Lacan, the command that the super-ego directs to the subject is, of all things, "Enjoy!" That which we may believe to be most private and rebellious (our **desire**) is, in fact, regulated, even commanded, by the **super-ego**.

Further reading: Freud 1923, 1932; Lacan 1991; Žižek 1989, 1991b.

SUPERSTRUCTURE

See **base and superstructure**

SUPPLEMENT

According to Jacques Derrida, language lacks "a center which arrests and grounds the play of substitutions" (1978: 289) that in fact makes up the act of meaning-making (see **différance**). We may attempt to ground meaning by positing a center or a **transcendental signified** like the **subject** or God but such meaning is always added after the play of language and, so, constitutes a supplement: "The movement of signification adds something, which results in the fact that there is always more, but this addition is a floating one because it comes to perform a vicarious function, to supplement a lack on the part of the **signified**" (289). Before all centers that might seek to stabilize meaning (the **subject**, consciousness, origin, **teleology**, God), there is this **lack** that language seeks to supplement. Derrida aligns this play of supplementarity with writing, arguing paradoxically that "*There is nothing outside of the text* [there is no outside-**text**; *il n'y a pas de hors-texte*]" (1976: 158). As he explains, "there has never been anything but writing; there have never been anything but supplements, substitutive significations which could only come forth in a chain of differential references, the '**real**' supervening, and being added only while taking on meaning from a **trace** and from an invocation of the supplement, etc." (158).

See also: **phonocentrism**, **trace**, **différance**.

SURFACE READING

See **reader, reading, and Reader-Response Criticism**

SURPLUS VALUE

Surplus value is the surplus produced over and above the actual cost of hiring a laborer, which is translated into profit in **capitalism**. According to Karl Marx, the actual value of a product is commensurate with the amount of **labor** that went into the production of that product. What happens in **capitalism** is that laborers are put in the position whereby they must sell not their labor but their **labor-power**, the abstraction of human labor into something that can be exchanged for **money**. They must do this because they do not own the **means of production** and, indeed, have no other way to earn a subsistence living. Laborers are then paid a fixed amount for their **labor**, just enough for them to subsist and produce more laborers (so many dollars per hour); however, the capitalist manages to derive greater value out of the products of these laborers than it costs to purchase their **labor-power**. The cost of **labor-power** remains more or less constant whereas the capitalist manages to get laborers to produce ever more products over the course of a day through the use of machines and the implementation of strategies of efficiency (e.g., the assembly line). Laborers are paid a minimum wage, but they are thus able to create products worth many times that amount, even after the cost of material and machines is calculated. The system is set up so that it appears that laborers enter into this situation out of their own free will; however, as they have no other option, the situation is one of exploitation that is not so different from slavery. The reason for this is that the capitalist owns: (1) the **means of production**, (2) the worker's **labor-power**, and also (3) the product that is thus produced. Capitalists are able to buy **labor-power**, which is then turned into **commodities** to be sold at a profit on the market. Rather than exchange a **commodity** for money in order to buy another **commodity** of use to the consumer (selling in order to buy), the capitalist buys **labor-power** in order to sell the products of that **labor-power** at a profit margin (surplus value). The capitalist is thus driven by profit-making in and of itself, without regard to **use value** or the suffering of the laborer.

Further reading: Bottomore *et al.* 1983; Foley 1986; Mandel 1972; Marx 1867; Marx and Engels 1932.

SUTURE

"Suture" is a concept that was first proposed by Jacques-Allain Miller, building on the **psychoanalytic** work of Jacques Lacan. According to Miller, "suture" is, most basically, "the relation of the **subject** to the chain of its **discourse**" (1977: 25). For Lacanian psychoanalysts, the **subject** constructs itself only retroactively by telling itself the fiction that it was from the start the **agent** of its own **discourse** when in fact the **subject** was created by that very **discourse**, as a linguistic function: "in so far as the signifying chain is concerned, it is on the level of its effects and not of its cause that consciousness is to be situated" (33). For that reason, the "matheme" (i.e., symbol) for the **subject**, S, is always written with a bar across it, the *sujet barré*: $. The subject is barred, which is to say constituted over a lack, both because it is not fully in control of itself (split as it is between the conscious and **unconscious**) and because it is a stand-in for a foundational **lack** initiated by our entrance into language. Language opens up a space that is much greater than us—the field of signification that exceeds us and was ongoing before we were ever born. Lacan refers to this aspect of language as the "discourse of the **Other**," which is the field of the

Symbolic Order. Suture occurs in the space between the **Symbolic Order** and the **Imaginary Order** where we create stand-ins for the self, the **ego-ideal**. The function of suture, then, goes a little beyond merely pointing out the **lack** inherent in our relation to language; it speaks to the "filling in" of the **subject**, the mechanism by which the **subject** appears to gain fullness and consistency, however imaginary. As Stephen Heath explains, "the 'I' is a division but joins all the same, the stand-in is the lack in the structure but nevertheless, simultaneously, the possibility of a coherence, of the *filling in*. At the end of the suturing function is the **ego**, the *me*" (1977: 56). The heart of the problem is that, in order to become meaningful, the **subject** must use language, by which act the **subject** departs from the **Real** to accept an **imaginary** stand-in for itself, e.g., a personal name or a pronoun ("I," "me"), that at once constitutes the **subject** within the larger field of language and speaking **subjects** (the **Symbolic Order**) and cannot help but underscore the **lack** inherent in all language: it is never *really* the thing to which it claims to refer. "Suture" in this sense has been used by theorists to describe any maneuver whereby what is in fact a linguistic effect is instead claimed to be caused by an originary **subject**.

First applied to cinema by Jean-Pierre Oudart, the term has been influential in film theory, particularly as articulated in the journal *Screen*, which is why this Lacanian way of approaching film is sometimes referred to as Screen Theory. Like Jacques-Allain Miller's notion of suture, suture in film "is the name given to the procedures by means of which cinematic **texts** confer **subjectivity** upon their viewers" (K. Silverman 1983: 195). The shot/reverse shot sequence in film (e.g., in a dialogue between two characters) is particularly significant in thinking about suture and the issue of the viewer's **subjectivity**. As Kaja Silverman explains, "The shot/reverse shot formation is a cinematic set in which the second shot shows the field from which the first shot is assumed to have been taken. The logic of this set is closely tied to certain 'rules' of cinematic expression, in particular the 180° rule, which dictates that the camera not cover more than 180° in a single shot" because of "the assumption that a complete camera revolution would be 'unrealistic,' defining a space larger than the 'naked eye' would normally cover" (201). The idea is to deny the fact that we rely on a piece of technology, the camera, to do the looking for us. The shot/reverse shot cinematic sequence allays our suspicion that someone else is controlling what we see and "in such a manner that the cinematic illusion remains intact: Shot 1 shows a space which may or may not contain a human figure (e.g. the wall of a building, a view of the

ocean, a room full of people), being careful not to violate the 180°
rule. Shot 2 locates a spectator in the other 180° of the same circular
field, thereby implying that the preceding shot was seen through the
eyes of a figure in the cinematic narrative" (K. Silverman 1983: 202).
Through such tricks of camera editing, "the gaze which directs our
look seems to belong to a fictional character rather than to the
camera" (202). In that fictional character, who takes over the power
of the occluded camera, we find an ideal surrogate for ourselves and
compensation for our feeling of **lack**. We thus mark out a space for
our own **subjectivity**. As Silverman explains, "The operation of
suture is successful at the moment that the viewing **subject** says, 'Yes,
that's me,' or 'That's what I see'" (205).

In most traditional cinema, any feeling of **lack** we cannot help but
feel is further mitigated by the fact that the dominant cinematic **gaze**
is usually aligned with male characters in positions of authority, often
looking at sexualized, passive, female **objects** of **desire** (themselves
representatives of the very **lack** threatening the male viewer—see
scopophilia). This act of **identification** helps us to forget the
mechanical look of the camera and our own invested look at the screen.
As Kaja Silverman explains, "This sleight-of-hand involves attributing to
a character within the fiction qualities which in fact belong to the
machinery of enunciation: the ability to generate narrative, the omnipotence and coercive **gaze**, the castrating authority of the law" (1983:
232). Laura Mulvey explains further: "As the spectator identifies with
the main male protagonist, he projects his look onto that of his like,
his screen surrogate, so that the power of the male protagonist as he
controls events coincides with the active power of the erotic look,
both giving a satisfying sense of omnipotence" (1989: 20). Through
such mechanisms, the viewer sutures the **lack** that, according to these
Lacanian **feminists**, threatens in the experience of any cinematic
presentation.

Mulvey argues that there are, in fact, three looks implied by film:
(1) the look of the camera itself; (2) the look of the audience watching
the film; and (3) the look of the characters on screen. "The conventions
of narrative film," Mulvey explains, "deny the first two and subordinate
them to the third, the conscious aim being always to eliminate intrusive
camera presence and prevent a distancing awareness in the audience"
(1989: 25). Being reminded of the first two looks, according to
Mulvey, functions as a form of **castration**, destroying the fantasy of
power and control given to us by traditional film. Traditional cinema
responds to this threat by "suturing over the wound of **castration**
with **narrative**. However, it is only by inflicting the wound to begin

with that the viewing **subject** can be made to want the restorative of meaning and **narrative**" (Silverman 1983: 204).

Further reading: Heath 1977; E. A. Kaplan 2000; J.-A. Miller 1977; Mulvey 1989; K. Silverman 1983.

SYMBOL

In **psychoanalysis**, symbols are elements in the world that have come to hold specific, if **repressed**, sexual meaning for the human species. According to Sigmund Freud, the **displacements** and **condensations** effected by **repression** can sometimes take on such rigid form that they take on the quality of symbols, which, according to Freud, have similar meanings for all humans. In other words, such **repressions** become phylogenetic: they speak to the whole development of the human race and constitute a racial heritage. For this reason, Freud sometimes referred to the **id** as the inheritance of the species. C. G. Jung broke from Freud in 1913 and pursued this aspect of psychoanalytical theory, in particular.

SYMBOLIC CAPITAL

See **cultural capital, social capital, and symbolic capital**

SYMBOLIC ORDER

In Lacanian psychoanalysis, the symbolic order is the social world of linguistic communication, intersubjective relations, knowledge of ideological conventions, and the acceptance of the law (also called the "big Other"; see **Other**). Once a child enters into language and accepts the rules and dictates of society, the child is able to deal with others. The acceptance of language's rules is aligned with the **Oedipus complex**, according to Jacques Lacan. The symbolic is made possible because of one's acceptance of the **Name-of-the-Father**, those laws and restrictions that control both your **desire** and the rules of communication. Through recognition of the **Name-of-the-Father**, a person is able to enter into a community of others. The symbolic, through language, is "the pact which links ... subjects together in one action. The human action *par excellence* is originally founded on the existence of the world of the symbol, namely on laws and contracts" (1991: 230). The symbolic order works in tension with the **imaginary**

order and the **Real**. It is closely bound up with the **super-ego** and the phallus.

Whereas the **Real** concerns need and the **imaginary order** concerns demand, the symbolic order is all about desire, according to Lacan (see **desire**). Once we enter into language, our **desire** is forever afterwards bound up with the play of language. We should keep in mind, however, that the **Real** and the **Imaginary** continue to play a part in the evolution of human desire within the symbolic order. The fact that our fantasies always fail before the **Real**, for example, ensures that we continue to desire; **desire** in the symbolic order could, in fact, be said to be our way to avoid coming into full contact with the **Real**, so that desire is ultimately most interested not in obtaining the **object** of **desire** but, rather, in reproducing itself. The **narcissism** of the **Imaginary** is also crucial for the establishment of **desire**, according to Lacan:

> The primary imaginary relation provides the fundamental framework for all possible erotism. It is a condition to which the **object** of Eros as such must be submitted. The **object** relation must always submit to the **narcissistic** framework and be inscribed in it. (1991: 174)

For Lacan, love begins here; however, to make that love "functionally realisable" (to make it move beyond scopophilic **narcissism**), the subject must reinscribe that **narcissistic** imaginary relation into the laws and contracts of the symbolic order: "A creature needs some reference to the beyond of language, to a pact, to a commitment which constitutes him, strictly speaking, as an other, a reference included in the general or, to be more exact, universal system of interhuman symbols." As he goes on, "No love can be functionally realisable in the human community, save by means of a specific pact, which, whatever the form it takes, always tends to become isolated off into a specific function, at one and the same time within language and outside of it" (1991: 174). The **Real**, the **Imaginary**, and the Symbolic thus work together to create the tensions of our psychodynamic selves. See also **psychosexual development**.

Further reading: Bowie 1991; Lacan 1968, 1977, 1981, 1991; Žižek 1989, 1991b.

SYMBOLIC VIOLENCE

See **field**

SYMPTOM

In **psychoanalysis**, a symptom is a behavior or bodily abnormality that is caused by the return of the **repressed**. According to **psychoanalysis**, insistent **desires** that the individual feels must be **repressed** will often find alternative paths toward satisfaction and therefore manifest themselves as symptoms. Sigmund Freud defines a symptom in this way: "A symptom is a sign of, and a substitute for, an instinctual satisfaction which has remained in abeyance; it is a consequence of the process of **repression**" (1953–74: 20.91). Symptoms tend to be activities that are detrimental or perhaps only useless to one's life. In extreme cases, such symptoms "can result in an extraordinary impoverishment of the **subject** in regard to the mental energy available to him and so in paralysing him for all the important tasks of life" (16.358).

SYNTAGMATIC AND PARADIGMATIC

According to Ferdinand de Saussure, relations between linguistic terms are either what he terms "syntagmatic" or "associative." Semioticians later used the binary set, "syntagmatic" and "paradigmatic," to refer to the same distinction and it is these terms that have since been adopted by critical theory to describe, on the one hand, the act of reading or viewing a given sequence ("syntagmatic") and, on the other hand, our ability at the same time to associate multiple items with any one thing we read or view ("paradigmatic"). Saussure elaborates in this way: On the one hand, Saussure explains, words "acquire relations based on the linear nature of language because they are chained together. This rules out the possibility of pronouncing two elements simultaneously" (1916: 123). In other words, we must, by necessity, speak words one at a time (we can't say or read two things simultaneously); as a result, we must defer understanding of the full sense of any given phrase or sentence until we have spoken or read all the words in that sequence: "In the syntagm a term acquires its value only because it stands in opposition to everything that precedes or follows it, or to both" (123). On the other hand, Saussure explains, any single word we use is "associated" with any number of other words: "For instance, the French word *enseignement* 'teaching' will unconsciously call to mind a host of other words (*enseigner* 'teach,' *renseigner* 'acquaint,' etc.; or *armament* 'armament,' *changement* 'amendment,' etc.; or *éducation* 'education,' *apprentissage* 'apprenticeship,' etc.)" (123). Any single word is thus "the point of convergence of an indefinite number of co-ordinated terms" (126) that can be suggested by similar sounds or by analogy.

Also, any one word automatically calls to mind its opposite, an insight that for example inspires Algirdas Julien Greimas's understanding of the **Greimassian square**. The syntagmatic is closely aligned with *parole*, the paradigmatic with *langue*.

See also: **metaphoric and metonymic poles**.

Further reading: Barthes 1967; Saussure 1916.

TELEOLOGY (*TELOS*, TELEOLOGICAL)

According to Jacques Derrida, one tends to impose meaning on a **text** by positing a closural endpoint (a *telos*; Greek for "end" or "goal") that arrests the movement of *différance* that in fact impels our acts of reading and interpretation. The notion of a totality (for example, complete knowledge of a given thing) is therefore tied to teleology: "if meaning is meaningful only within a totality, could it come forth if the totality were not animated by the anticipation of an end, or by an intentionality which, moreover, does not necessarily and primarily belong to a consciousness?" (Derrida 1978: 26). Structure, for Derrida, also entails a notion of *telos*: "If there are structures, they are possible only on the basis of the fundamental structure which permits totality to open and overflow itself such that it *takes on meaning* by anticipating a *telos* which here must be understood in its most indeterminate form" (26).

Grand narratives offer teleologies that help to explain and also **naturalize** the current world order. **Dialectical materialists**, **postmodernists**, and **poststructuralists** all critique this temptation; Jean-François Lyotard for example turns instead to *pétits récits* or little stories that never subordinate other **language games** and **phrase regimens** to one way of conceiving historical development (see **history**).

See also: **signifier and signified**, **poststructuralism**, **utopia**.

TEXT AND TEXTUALITY

When critical theorists use the term "text," they are purposively avoiding terms such as "book" or "work" since the former suggests a self-enclosed, self-sufficient, or autonomous object whereas the latter suggests a product of a determining **agency** or **author**. Critical theorists often adopt a **semiotic** approach to cultural products instead, following Ferdinand de Saussure's understanding of semiology or

semiotics as "*A science that studies the life of signs within society*" (1916: 16). In this understanding of the sign (see **signifier and signified**), "text" is not delimited to writing but to any sign system, an approach to signs that has greatly influenced **Cultural Studies** and all its related schools (**New Historicism, Cultural Materialism, Discourse Studies**, etc.), as well as anthropology through the work of Claude Lévi-Strauss (see **binary opposition**) and Clifford Geertz (see **thick description**). By using "textuality" rather than "writing," critical theorists extend their analysis of signs to all aspects of society. Indeed, **poststructuralists** go so far as to reject Saussure's distinction between oral speech and writing in his *Course in General Linguistics* (1916). **Deconstructionist** Jacques Derrida instead argues, influentially, that "*There is nothing outside of the text* [there is no outside-text; *il n'y a pas de hors-texte*]" (1976: 158). Everything, including speech follows the logic of sign systems; that is, the connection between **signifiers** and **signifieds** is arbitrary. We make sense of signs only by way of the structural differences between terms (see *différance*) and in the **performative** repetition of conventions over the time of interpretation, with **transcendental signifieds** like **nature, author, subject, telos**, or origin only ever imposed retroactively as a fiction.

By approaching signs in this way, critical theorists seek to examine the codes and rules by which we construct the "reality" of the world around us. Some go so far as to argue that, because of our reliance on language, we can only ever know signifying texts and that the **Real**, the **natural** world of real **things**, is beyond intelligibility; as psycho-analyst Jacques Lacan therefore puts it, "the **real** is impossible." All we can know is what Lacan terms the **symbolic order** of signs and conventions. In other words, everything we can know and express (which is pretty much everything) is caught up in **ideology**.

This approach to textuality underscores the arbitrariness and **performative** nature of conventions that may be perceived as necessary or **natural**. Critical theorists instead examine the **hegemonic** rules that govern our use of signs, seeking always to speak and fight for the exploited and **marginalized**. Michel Foucault's theorization of **discourse** and **discipline** has been particularly influential in this regard, as has Pierre Bourdieu's examination of the ways we establish **cultural capital** in an always **ideological** (and therefore arbitrary) "field of power" (see **field**).

The notion of textuality has also been challenged and transformed by the **Digital Humanities** given recent changes in the material nature of text after the digital revolution (e.g., hypertext, the data-base, the semantic web). Although some critics see in hypertext an instantiation of **deconstructive** principles (e.g., Ulmer 1994, Landow 1997), others have been inspired by this transformation in the medium of communication to reconsider the material substratum of not only current forms of media but also of the history of the book. Jerome McGann has been particularly influential in both regards through his work on textual editing (McGann 1983a, 1985a, 1985b) and on the digital revolution (McGann 2001, 2002, 2004, 2013).

See also: **Actor-Network Theory, articulation, assemblage and assemblage theory, Body without Organs, correlationism, culture, distribution of the sensible, doxa, factiality, habitus, history, intertextuality, *langue* and *parole*, logocentrism, Matrix of Domination, phonocentrism, phrase regimen, supplement, suture, trace**.

Further reading: Culler 1975, 1981; Derrida 1976, 1978, 1982; Harari 1980; Landow 1997; Loizeaux and Fraistat 2002; McGann 1983a, 1985a, 1985b, 2001, 2002, 2004, 2013; Melville and Readings 1995; M.-L. Ryan 1999; Silverman and Aylesworth 1990; Tiffin and Lawson 1994; Ulmer 1994; Young 1981.

THEORY OF MIND

See **Cognitive Studies**

THICK DESCRIPTION

This concept, originating in the work of Gilbert Ryle and then theorized by anthropologist Clifford Geertz in his influential work *The Interpretation of Cultures* (1973), has had a formative influence on **New Historicism** and **Cultural Studies** more generally. Geertz explains that his concept of culture "is essentially a **semiotic** one" (5), which is to say that he reads all human behavior as "symbolic action—action which, like phonation in speech, pigment in painting, line in writing, or sonance in music, signifies" (10). The anthropologist, through such a "**semiotic** approach to culture," seeks to gain "access to the conceptual world in which our subjects live so that we can, in some extended sense of the term, converse with them" (24). To do so, the anthropologist must adopt a "microscopic" approach to his material. That is, according to Geertz, "cultural theory ... is not its own master": "As it is unseverable from the immediacies thick description presents, its freedom to shape itself in terms of its internal logic is rather limited. What generality it contrives to achieve grows out of the delicacy of its distinctions, not the sweep of its abstractions" (25). Geertz attempts, then, as he does for example in the famous last essay of *The Interpretation of Cultures*, "Deep Play: Notes on the Balinese Cockfight," to provide microscopically detailed descriptions of the social interactions of a given **culture** before offering up an interpretation of how those actions reveal a generalizable sign system about that **culture**. "What the ethnographer is in fact faced with," Geertz explains, "is a multiplicity of complex conceptual structures, many of them superimposed upon or knotted into one another, which are at once strange, irregular, and inexplicit, and which he must contrive somehow first to grasp and then to render" (10).

THINGS AND THING THEORY

This approach to culture and society grows out of a special issue of *Critical Inquiry* edited by Bill Brown in 2001. There, Brown makes a distinction between **objects** and things: "We look through **objects** because there are codes by which our interpretative attention makes them meaningful, because there is a **discourse** that allows us to use them as facts" (Brown 2001: 4); that is, **objects** function within a dialectic of **subject** and **object** that undergirds our system of language; they are understood as meaningful and stable because of their relation to the **subjects** who perceive them. According to Brown, "things" fall to some extent outside that dialectic:

> A *thing*, in contrast, can hardly function as a window. We begin to confront the thingness of objects when they stop working for us: when the drill breaks, when the car stalls, when the windows get filthy, when their flow within the circuits of production and distribution, consumption and exhibition, has been arrested, however momentarily. The story of objects asserting themselves as things, then, is the story of a changed relation to the human **subject** and thus the story of how the thing really names less an object than a particular **subject–object** relation. (2001: 4)

Brown goes on to point out other peculiarities of our use of "things," for example our tendency to use them to designate that for which we have no name, the thingamabob, the thingamajig. It can also designate "an amorphous characteristic or a frankly irresolvable enigma: 'There's a thing about that poem that I'll never get'" (Brown 2001: 4). In such ways, "*things* is a word that tends, especially at its most banal, to index a certain limit or **liminality**, to hover over the threshold between the nameable and unnameable, the figurable and unfigurable, the identifiable and unidentifiable" (4–5). Thing is thus at once that which is "baldly encountered" but also "some thing not quite apprehended" (5), somehow outside the relation of **subject** and **object**. As Brown puts it, "Things lie beyond the grid of intelligibility the way mere things lie outside the grid of museal exhibition, outside the order of **objects**" (5). The Thing in this sense is close to Jacques Lacan's understanding of the **Real**, as Brown himself suggests (5). Thing Theory is also influenced by **Actor-Network Theory**, especially the work of Bruno Latour.

See also: **assemblage**, **quasi-objects and quasi-subjects**, **speculative realism**.

Further reading: Brown 2001, 2002; Freedgood 2006; Garcia 2014; Plotz 2005.

TRACE

This concept of Jacques Derrida's is closely tied to that of *différance*; indeed, Derrida writes, at one point, that "*[t]he (pure) trace is differance*" (1976: 62). In "trace," Derrida points to the play of language that always-already precedes meaning and any stable **binary oppositions**. That is, before we can make sense of anything, we must *defer* meaning as we work through the *differences* between signifiers (see **différance** and **signifier and signified**). This play always-already precedes all ontologies, epistemologies, and theologies, all efforts to stop the endless deferrals that, in fact, enable meaning production. In opposition to this trace, the history of philosophy tends to posit some stabilizing center for its orderly systems, a center that is at once "within the structure and outside it" (1978: 279)—as both its ground and transcendental guarantee. That center, according to Derrida, has received "different forms or names": "The history of metaphysics, like the history of the West, is the history of these metaphors and metonymies," which seek to fix "Being as *presence* in all senses of this word" (279). The trace—like the analogous terms in Derrida's work, **différance**, **arche-writing**, pharmakon, and specter—abandons "all reference to a *center*, to a *subject*, to a privileged *reference*, to an *origin*, or to an absolute *archia*" (286). The trace is "not a presence but the **simulacrum** of a presence that dislocates itself, displaces itself, refers itself"; it therefore "has no site—erasure belongs to its structure" (1972: 24).

TRANSCENDENTAL SIGNIFIED

See **signifier and signified**

TRANSCULTURATION

See **contact zone and transculturation**

TRANSFERENCE (TRANSFERENTIAL)

In **psychoanalysis**, transference is the **displacement** of one's unresolved conflicts, dependencies, and aggressions onto a substitute **object** (e.g., substituting a lover, spouse, etc. for one's parent). This operation can also occur in the psychoanalytical talking cure, when a patient transfers onto the analyst feelings that were previously directed to another **object**. By working through this transference of feelings onto the analyst, the patient can come to grips with the actual cause of their feelings. The fact of transference points to an important fact about the nature of trauma: the compulsion of the human psyche to repeat traumatic events over and over again (hence the term "**repetition compulsion**"). Previously, Sigmund Freud believed that the repetition of childhood impulses in the talking cure (transference) allowed the patient to discharge his or her **repressed** sexual feelings and, so, must bring a degree of pleasure even when disguised as hate or frustration; however, Freud had to acknowledge that "the compulsion to repeat also recalls from the past experiences which include no possibility of pleasure, and which can never, even long ago, have brought satisfaction even to **instinctual** impulses which have since been repressed" (1953–74: 18.20). Freud therefore concludes that one must theorize a "compulsion to repeat" that "seems more primitive, more elementary, more instinctual than the **pleasure principle** which it over-rides" (18.23), that is, the **death drive**. That compulsion often works through the mechanism of transference, which Freud sees as a "universal phenomenon of the human mind" and, so, not delimited to the talking cure.

Dominick LaCapra has adopted the concept of transference for the study of historical trauma, particularly the Holocaust. His goal is "a basic reconceptualization of historical self-understanding and practice" (1987: 224). He sees the transferential situation occurring in "the very relation of the historian to the 'object' of study": "'Transference' offers a better way of understanding a 'dialogic' relation to the past than do standard, round-robin debates about objectivity or subjectivity, truth or relativism" (228). Indeed, he argues that "one way to define **positivism** is as a denial of transference" (1994: 47); that is, **positivists** are concerned with representing—and believe they *can* represent—the past the way it actually happened. Events like the Holocaust—"so extreme that they seem unclassifiable and threaten or tempt one with silence" (47)—require a different approach to the past, one that includes the notion of "working through" the traumatic event by way of transferential repetition (as opposed to denying the event or acting out in some destructive way). According to LaCapra, "What is not confronted critically does not disappear; it tends to return as the repressed" (1992: 126). His solution, then, is "a modified mode of repetition offering a measure of critical purchase on problems and responsible control in action that would permit desirable change"; as he goes on, working-through "is thus intimately bound up with the possibility of ethically responsible action and critical judgment on the part of someone who strives for the position of an agent and may thereby counteract his or her experience of victimhood and the incapacitating effects of trauma" (1998: 186).

Further reading: Freud 1932; LaCapra 1987, 1992, 1994, 1998; Laplanche and Pontalis 1973.

TRIBAL SOCIETY

Tribal society is a primitive stage in the development of society during which there are no social classes, according to Karl Marx. Tribal society is instead structured around kinship relations, with hunting the province of men and domestic work the province of women. The tribal form, according to Marx and Friedrich Engels, is quite elementary, "a further extension of the natural division of labour existing in the family" (1932: 44). During this stage, it is, however, possible to see a slave culture established (the beginning of **class** relations), particularly as the population increases, leading to "the growth of wants" and the growth of relations with outside civilizations (through war or barter).

UNCANNY *(UNHEIMLICH)*

The "uncanny" is a term that is theorized by Sigmund Freud in an essay of the same name (1919). It is "related to what is frightening— to what arouses dread and horror" (135), Freud explains. It applies both to a subset of horror (in literature and, now, film) and to an experience that we can feel in our own lives. Freud explains that the *unheimlich* is connected to the *heimlich* (*heim* is home in German, *heimlich* is familiar, belonging to the home, but also secret), for, as Freud writes, "this uncanny is in reality nothing new or alien, but something which is familiar and old-established in the mind and which has become alienated from it only through the process of **repression**" (142). Indeed, the fear associated with the uncanny tends to arise when we are made to believe as real beliefs either from our childhood or earlier stages in the development of human civilization that have since been dismissed (magic, the evil eye, the reanimation of the dead, and so on): "As soon as something *actually happens* in our lives which seems to confirm the old, discarded beliefs we get a feeling of the uncanny" (148). The uncanny also applies to the uncanny return of "repressed infantile complexes, from the **castration complex**, womb-fantasies, etc.," though Freud states that "experiences which arouse this kind of uncanny feeling are not of very frequent occurrence in real life" (149).

The uncanny is closely tied to repetition, which can create the feeling of the uncanny in us. Freud for example writes of the experience of being brought to the same place again and again by chance or the repetition of a single number several times over the course of a day, which then creates the sensation of being subjected to some evil power or secret meaning: "it is only this factor of involuntary repetition which surrounds what would otherwise be innocent enough with an uncanny atmosphere, and forces upon us the idea of something fateful and inescapable when otherwise we should have spoken only of 'chance'" (138). The uncanny therefore applies to a particular class of frightening things "in which the frightening element can be shown to be something repressed which *recurs*. This class of frightening things would then constitute the uncanny; and it must be a matter of indifference whether what is uncanny was itself originally frightening or whether it carried some *other* affect" (142). Freud develops this idea in *Beyond the Pleasure Principle* and his later writings through his concepts of **death drive** and **repetition compulsion**.

The term, "uncanny," has been given a different valence in the postcolonial work of Homi Bhabha. In *The Location of Culture* (1994), Bhabha draws on Freud's suggestion that the uncanny is "something that ought to have remained hidden but has come to life" (142). He uses this aspect of the uncanny to discuss those troubling passages of postcolonial fiction that bring to light repressed histories in such a way as to break down the separation of the private and the public, the home and the world: "it captures something of the estranging sense of the relocation of the home and the world—the unhomeliness—that is the condition of extra-territorial and cross-cultural initiations" (9). Indeed, Bhabha states that "the 'unhomely' is a paradigmatic colonial and postcolonial condition" (9). The "generalizing subject of civil society, comprising the 'individual' that is the support for its universalist aspiration" (10), seeks to establish a vision of the civilized by forgetting or disavowing a superseded zone of messy uncertainty and commingling (what Bhabha terms the **hybrid** and the **liminal**). **Postcolonial** fiction responds by making the forgotten and disavowed recur through uncanny effects.

Further reading: Bhabha 1994; Castle 1995; Freud 1919; Masschelein 2011.

UNCONSCIOUS

According to Sigmund Freud, humanity's very movement into civilized society and the child's analogous introduction to that society require the **repression** of our primitive (but still very insistent) desires; these primitive desires are thus relegated to the unconscious. Indeed, for this reason, he argues in *Civilization and Its Discontents* (1929) that all of civilized society is a **substitute-formation**, of sorts, for our atavistic **instincts** and **drives**. As he puts it in *Introductory Lectures on Psycho-Analysis* (First Lecture, originally given in 1915), "we believe that civilization is to a large extent being constantly created anew, since each individual who makes a fresh entry into human society repeats this sacrifice of instinctual satisfaction for the benefit of the whole community" (1953–74: 15.23). What happens instead, as he goes on to explain, is that those "primitive impulses," of which the sexual impulse is the strongest, are sublimated or "diverted" towards other goals that are "socially higher and no longer sexual" (15.23). Our **instincts** and primitive impulses are thus **repressed**; however, Freud believed that the sexual impulse was so powerful that it continually threatened to "return" and thus disrupt our conscious functioning (hence the now-famous term, "the return of the repressed"). Freud also believed that there was a relation between the child's develop-ment and the development of the species. As he explains, "The prehistory into which the dream-work leads us back is of two kinds— on the one hand, into the individual's prehistory, his childhood, and on the other, in so far as each individual somehow recapitulates in an abbreviated form the entire development of the human race, into phylogenetic prehistory too" (15.199). Such statements are what inspired C. G. Jung, who was originally an important member of

Freud's Psycho-Analytic Association; Jung broke away in 1913 and formed his own brand of Jungian psychoanalysis. One can see what must have inspired Jung when one reads in Freud that "symbolic connections, which the individual has never acquired by learning, may justly claim to be regarded as a phylogenetic heritage" (15.199).

According to Freud, it is the insistent return of the **repressed** that can explain numerous phenomena that are normally overlooked: not only our dreams but also what has come to be called "Freudian slips" (what Freud himself called "parapraxes"). According to Freud, there is a "psychology of errors"; that slip of the tongue or that slip of the pen, "which have been put aside by the other sciences as being too unimportant" (15.27), become for Freud the clues to the secret functioning of the unconscious. Indeed, he likens his endeavor to "a detective engaged in tracing a murder" (15.27). The mentally unwell add to these clues numerous other obsessions and mental symptoms. See **repression**.

To make sense of this dynamic, Freud proposed a depth-model for the functioning of the mind, a model now so much a part of culture that it is difficult to appreciate just how transformative this new way of thinking about the **subject** really was for the development of civilization as a whole. Freud's model was also important because it argued that the difference between the sane and the ill is only a matter of degree: "if you look at the matter from a theoretical point of view and ignore this question of degree you can very well say that we are *all* ill, that is, **neurotic**—since the preconditions for the formation of **symptoms** can also be observed in normal people" (16.358).

Freud began with the division, conscious/unconscious, to which he also sometimes added the term, "**preconscious**"; he soon turned, however, to a tripartite version of that depth model (it is worth noting that for a time psychoanalysis was referred to as "depth-psychology"):

Super-ego
Ego
Id

The **id** is the great reservoir of the **libido**, from which the **ego** seeks to distinguish itself through various mechanisms of **repression**. Because of that **repression**, the **id** seeks alternative expression for those impulses that we consider evil or excessively sexual, impulses that we often felt as perfectly natural at an earlier or archaic stage and have since **repressed**. These **repressed** memories are often translated, according to Freud, into "screen-memories" that the ego is then able to remember: "the **ego** has the task of bringing the influence of the external world to bear upon the **id** and its tendencies, and endeavours to substitute the **reality-principle** for the **pleasure-principle** which reigns supreme in the **id**" (1923: 702). Whereas the **ego** is oriented towards perceptions in the real world, the **id** is oriented towards internal **instincts**; whereas the **ego** is associated with reason and sanity, the **id** belongs to the passions. The **ego**, however, is never able fully to distinguish itself from the **id**, of which the **ego** is, in fact, a part, which is why in his pictorial representation of the mind Freud does not provide a hard separation between the **ego** and the **id**. In fact, Freud argues at various places that there exists an unconscious of the **ego** and an unconscious of the **super-ego** even as there is an unconscious element to the **id**: "If ... we are faced with the case where the patient under analysis is not conscious of his resistance, then it must be either that the **super-ego** and **ego** can operate unconsciously in quite important situations, or, which would be far more significant, that parts of both **ego** and **super-ego** themselves are unconscious. In both cases we should have to take account of the disturbing view that the **ego** (including the **super-ego**) does not by any means completely coincide with the conscious, nor the **repressed** with the unconscious" (1932: 835).

Jacques Lacan's contribution to the notion of the unconscious is to approach it as completely determined by language, which structures our entrance into what Lacan terms the **symbolic order**. According to Lacan, one must always distinguish between reality (the fantasy world we convince ourselves is the world around us) and the **Real** (a materiality of existence beyond language and thus beyond expressibility). The development of the subject, in other words, is made possible by an endless misrecognition of the **Real** because of our need to construct our sense of "reality" in and through language. So much are we reliant on our linguistic and social version of "reality" that the eruption of pure materiality (of the **Real**) into our lives is radically disruptive. And yet, the **Real** is the rock against which all of our artificial linguistic and social structures necessarily fail. It is this tension between the **Real** and our social laws, meanings, conventions, desires, etc. that determines our psychosexual lives, according to Lacan. Not even our unconscious escapes the effects of language, which is why Lacan argues that "the unconscious is structured like a language" (1981: 203). Lacan thus follows the linguistic turn in critical theory, examining the **structuralist** oppositions that order our psychic lives.

In this, Lacan builds on such **semiotic** critics as Ferdinand de Saussure to show how language is a system that makes sense only within its own internal logic of differences: the word, "father," only makes sense in terms of those other terms it is defined with or against (mother, "me," law, the social, etc.). See **signifier and signified**. As Kaja Silverman puts it, "the **signifier** 'father' has no relation whatever to the physical fact of any individual father. Instead, that **signifier** finds its support in a network of other **signifiers**, including 'phallus,' 'law,' 'adequacy,' and 'mother,' all of which are equally indifferent to the category of the **real**" (1983: 164). In such a linguistic system, anyone, regardless of actual sexuality, can assume the function of the phallus or what Lacan terms the **Name-of-the-Father**.

Further reading: Bowie 1991; Freud 1923, 1929, 1932; Lacan 1968, 1977, 1981, 1991; Laplanche and Pontalis 1973; Žižek 1989, 1991b.

UNHEIMLICH

See **uncanny**

UNIVERSAL EQUIVALENT

As explored by Karl Marx and **Marxist** theory, a universal equivalent is an object that is the measure by which all **commodities** are compared and exchanged on the market (see **commodity**). In **capitalism**, this function is eventually taken over by **money**, first precious metals, then paper money, eventually credit (i.e., without the exchange of any material thing that in itself is valuable).

USE VALUE AND EXCHANGE VALUE

Karl Marx distinguishes between the use value and the exchange value of the **commodity**. Use value is inextricably tied to "the physical properties of the **commodity**" (1867: 126); that is, the material uses to which the object can actually be put, the human needs it fulfills. In the exchange of goods on the **capitalist** market, however, exchange value dominates: two **commodities** can be exchanged on the open market because they are always being compared to a third term that functions as their "**universal equivalent**," a function that is eventually taken over by **money**. Exchange value must always be distinguished from use value, because "the exchange relation of **commodities** is characterized precisely by its abstraction from their use-values" (Marx 1867: 127). A good example is gold because its original value was tied to its use value—it is an easily malleable but strong metal that is resistant to corrosion; however, once it was used to create coins and thus to serve as a **universal equivalent**, its value increasingly was bound up with what it represented (**money**) rather than that for which it could be used. In **capital, money** (separated from gold and the gold standard) takes over as **universal equivalent** and facilitates the translation of everything into exchange value; however, **money** in fact hides the real equivalent behind the exchange: **labor**. The more **labor** it takes to produce a product, the greater its value, according to Marx. Marx therefore concludes that "As exchange-values, all **commodities** are merely definite quantities of congealed **labour-time**" (1867: 130).

USURY

Usury refers to the loaning of money in return for the same money with interest, as in banking. Usury abridges Karl Marx's general formula for **capital** (M-C-M or buying a **commodity**-C with **money**-M in order to sell it for more **money**-M). The usurer reduces this formula into its purest form, M-M: "**money** which is worth more **money**, value which is greater than itself" (Marx 1867: 257).

UTOPIA (UTOPIC)

A utopia (which, etymologically means "no place") is an imagined ideal society, though it has sometimes also been applied to actual social experiments. The term comes from Thomas More's 1516 *Utopia,* which imagined a perfect society or, as the subtitle had it, "the Best State of a Republic" and "the Best State of a Public Weal." **Post-modernists** and critical theorists have largely been critical of the effort to imagine a perfect future for our present because they fear that such thinking subscribes to **teleological** principles and therefore imposes a single **grand narrative** on all groups. As a result, **dystopia** (an undesirable imagined community, commonly a frightening future version of our current system) tends to be more commonly associated with critical theory since **dystopic** fiction often functions as a critique of the problems of the present.

Fredric Jameson, however, has consistently argued that we need utopic thinking to undergird effective political activity in the present. He argues that utopic thinking is all the more necessary in our present moment, when so few alternatives to the present system are on offer: "The Utopian form itself is the answer to the universal ideological conviction that no alternative is possible, that there is no alternative to the system" (2005: 232). He argues that disruption is necessary today as a **discursive** strategy and that "Utopia is the form such disruption necessarily takes." As he continues, "it is the very principle of the radical break as such, its possibility, which is reinforced by the Utopian form, which insists that its radical difference is possible and that a break is necessary" (231–32). Utopia for Jameson therefore functions like the **sublime** for Jean-François Lyotard or **dissensus** for Jacques Rancière. It provides us with "a meditation on the impossible, on the unrealizable in its own right" (232); it is "a rattling of the bars and an intense spiritual concentration and preparation for another stage which has not yet arrived" (233). See also **heterotopia**, which Michel Foucault relates to utopia, and **cognitive map**.

In *Lectures on Ideology and Utopia* (1986), Paul Ricoeur engages with Karl Mannheim's *Ideology and Utopia* (1936) and makes the argument that the two terms, ideology and utopia, are intimately connected. Together, they make up a given period's "social" or "cultural imagination, operating in both constructive and destructive ways, as both confirmation and contestation of the present situation" (3). By exploring **ideology** and utopia, we can make sense of our "social imagination," which is, Ricoeur argues, "*constitutive* of social reality" (3).

See also: **Globalization and Global Studies, late capitalism**.

Further reading: Foucault 1986; Mannheim 1936; Jameson 1988, 2005; Ricoeur 1986.

WAR OF MANEUVER AND WAR OF POSITION

See **hegemony**

WHITENESS AS PROPERTY

Cheryl I. Harris influentially makes the argument for **Critical Race Theory** that "Even though the law is neither uniform nor explicit in all instances, in protecting settled expectations based on white privilege, American law has recognized a property interest in whiteness that, although unacknowledged, now forms the background against which legal disputes are framed, argued, and adjudicated" (1993: 1713–14).

This tendency to see whiteness as property has its roots in the early exploitation of both black slaves and Native Americans:

> The hyper-exploitation of Black labor was accomplished by treating Black people themselves as objects of property. **Race** and property were thus conflated by establishing a form of property contingent on **race**—only Blacks were subjugated as slaves and treated as property. Similarly, the conquest, removal, and extermination of Native American life and culture were ratified by conferring and acknowledging the property rights of whites in Native American land. Only white possession and occupation of land was validated and therefore privileged as a basis for property rights. (1716)

In both cases, what occurred is that whiteness was accorded legal status in relation to property rights, thus converting "an aspect of identity into an external object of property, moving whiteness from privileged identity to a vested interest" (1725). That is, whiteness was seen to entail both privilege and property: "Whiteness—the right to white identity as embraced by the law—is property if by property one means all of a person's legal rights" (1726). According to **Critical Race Theory**, this early understanding of whiteness as property has been codified into law and has not been fundamentally challenged but, rather, taken as "an objective fact, although in reality it is an **ideological** proposition imposed through subordination" (1730). As Harris contends, "When the law recognizes, either implicitly or explicitly, the settled expectations of whites built on the privileges and benefits produced by white supremacy, it acknowledges and reinforces a property interest in whiteness that reproduces Black subordination" (1731). What is supported by the law may no longer be slavery but rather an understanding of whiteness as "status property" (1734), "whiteness as reputation" (1734), which influenced a number of law cases across American history (for example, regarding citizenship and voting rights). This situation then persisted even after the *Brown v. Board of Education* (1954) court case that ended state-sponsored segregation, according to Harris:

> White privilege accorded as a legal right was rejected, but de facto white privilege not mandated by law remained unaddressed. In failing to clearly expose the real inequities produced by segregation, the status quo of substantive disadvantage was ratified as an accepted and acceptable base line—a neutral state operating to

the disadvantage of Blacks long after de jure segregation had ceased to do so. In accepting substantial inequality as a neutral base line, a new form of whiteness as property was condoned. Material inequities between Blacks and whites—the product of systematic past and current, formal and informal, mechanisms of racial subordination—became the norm. (1753)

According to Harris, the notion of whiteness as property thus persists into the present, as she illustrates in the examination of recent Affirmative Action and Native American law cases. Beyond specific law cases, there persists a notion of whiteness as status property that transcends any actual class inequality: "Whiteness is an aspect of racial identity surely, but it is much more; it remains a concept based on relations of power, a social construct predicated on white dominance and Black subordination" (1761).

See also: **Matrix of Domination**.

WHITE PRIVILEGE

See **Critical Race Theory**

WORLDING

See **Other and othering**

WRONG

Jean-François Lyotard argues that a "wrong" occurs whenever one attempts to impose the rules of one **genre of discourse** onto another **genre of discourse**. He defines "a wrong" as "a damage [*dommage*] accompanied by the loss of the means to prove the damage" (1988a: 5). One loses the means to prove the damage when one is forced to contest damage done to oneself *within the rules of another's **genre of discourse***. A good example is the exploited **proletariat** worker, whose **wrong** is made invisible by the contract law behind current juridical procedures. The very **distribution of the sensible** in capitalist culture makes **labor** only visible as a **commodity** that can be exchanged on the open market; however, the **wrong** here lies in thinking about **labor** in these terms at all. This **capitalist** way of understanding what can be seen and thought, it has been argued, is designed precisely to exploit the **proletariat** and make invisible the **wrong** done. Lyotard believes that there is no universal measure by which one can administer or proscribe what are ultimately **incommensurable** ways of representing and ordering the world. The term is closely related to his concept of **differend**. Jacques Rancière uses the term in a very similar way, though he argues that he is doing something different than merely following Lyotard's emphasis on language (e.g., **language games** and **phrase regimens**). Rather, he is interested in the wrong that erupts from the clash between a current "**distribution of the sensible**" and that which remains unsayable or undoable within that regime of distribution. Regarding the exploited **proletarian** worker, then, he writes: "The worker who puts forward an argument about the public nature of a 'domestic' wage dispute must demonstrate the world in which his argument counts as an argument and must demonstrate it as such for those who do not have the frame of reference enabling them to see it as one" (2010: 38–39). In other words, for both Lyotard and Rancière, a wrong is, by definition, that which cannot be adjudicated within an extant system of justice. True politics for Rancière results from the effort to establish equality for all, including the excluded, through a reconfiguration of the field of experience, which can then begin to redress such wrongs: "Political argumentation is at one and the same time the demonstration of a possible world in which the argument could count as an argument, one that is addressed by a subject qualified to argue, over an identified object, to an addressee who is required to see the object and to hear the argument that he 'normally' has no reason either to see or to hear" (2010: 39).

See also: **dissensus, aesthetics**.

BIBLIOGRAPHY

Abbott, H. P. (2008) *The Cambridge Introduction to Narrative*, second edition. Cambridge, UK: Cambridge University Press.

Adams, V. J., J. Calahan and M. Hansen (eds) (2015) Special Issue on Historical Poetics, *Modern Language Quarterly* [forthcoming].

Adorno, T. W. (1966) *Negative Dialectics*, translated by E. B. Ashton. New York: Continuum (1995).

——(1970) *Aesthetic Theory*, edited by G. Adorno and R. Tiedemann, translated by R. Hullot-Kentor, Theory and History of Literature 88. Minneapolis: University of Minnesota Press (1997).

Agamben, G. (1993) *The Coming Community*, Theory out of Bounds 1, translated by M. Hardt. Minneapolis: University of Minnesota Press.

——(1998) *Homo Sacer: Sovereign Power and Bare Life*, translated by D. Heller-Roazen. Stanford, CA: Stanford University Press.

——(2005) *State of Exception*, translated by K. Attell. Chicago: University of Chicago Press.

——(2009) *What Is an Apparatus? and Other Essays*, translated by D. Kishik and S. Pedatella. Stanford, CA: Stanford University Press.

——(2011) *The Kingdom and the Glory: For a Theological Genealogy of Economy and Government (Homo Sacer II, 2)*. Stanford, CA: Stanford University Press.

Ahmad, A. (1992) *In Theory: Classes, Nations, Literatures*. London: Verso.

Allen, E. (2003) "Culinary Exhibition: Victorian Wedding Cakes and Royal Spectacle," *Victorian Studies* 45.3: 457–84.

Allen, G. (2000) *Intertextuality*. London and New York: Routledge.

Althusser, L. (2001) *Lenin and Philosophy and Other Essays*, translated by B. Brewster. New York: Monthly Review Press.

Althusser, L. and É. Balibar (1970) *Reading Capital*, translated by B. Brewster. London and New York: Verso (1997).

Anderson, A. (2001) *The Powers of Distance: Cosmopolitanism and the Cultivation of Detachment*. Princeton, NJ: Princeton University Press.

Anderson, B. (1991) *Imagined Communities: Reflections on the Origin and Spread of Nationalism*, revised edition. London: Verso.

Appiah, K. A. (2014) "Making Conversation," in M. Juergensmeyer (ed.) *Thinking Globally: A Global Studies Reader*. Berkeley, CA: University of California Press, pp. 404–8.

Apter, E. and W. Pietz (eds) (1993) *Fetishism as Cultural Discourse*. Ithaca: Cornell University Press.

Archibugi, D. (ed.) (2003) *Debating Cosmopolitics*. London and New York: Verso.

Arendt, H. (1963) *Eichmann in Jerusalem: A Report on the Banality of Evil*. Harmondsworth, UK: Penguin.

Aristotle (c. 345 BCE) *Topics*, translated by W. A. Pickard, in J. Barnes (ed.) *The Complete Works of Aristotle*, volume 1. Princeton, NJ: Princeton University Press.

Armstrong, I. (2000) *The Radical Aesthetic*. Oxford, UK: Blackwell.

Armstrong, T. J. (ed.) (1992) *Michel Foucault Philosopher*, translated by T. J. Armstrong. New York: Routledge.

Ashcroft, B., G. Griffiths and H. Tiffin (2007) *Post-Colonial Studies: The Key Concepts*, second edition. London and New York: Routledge.

Attridge, D., G. Bennington and R. Young (eds) (1987) *Post-Structuralism and the Question of History*. Cambridge, UK: Cambridge University Press.

Austin, J. L. (1962) *How to Do Things with Words*, second edition. Cambridge, MA: Harvard University Press (1975).

Badiou, A. (2001) *Ethics: An Essay on the Understanding of Evil*, translated by P. Hallward. London and New York: Verso.

——(2005a) *Being and Event*, translated by O. Feltham. London: Continuum.

——(2005b) *Handbook of Inaesthetics*, translated by A. Toscano. Stanford, CA: Stanford University Press.

——(2005c) *Metapolitics*, translated by J. Barker. London: Verso.

——(2009a) *Logic of Worlds*, translated by A. Toscano. London and New York, Continuum.

——(2009b) *Theory of the Subject*, translated by B. Bosteels. London and New York: Continuum.

——(2011) *Second Manifesto for Philosophy*, translated by L. Burchill. Cambridge, UK and Malden, MA: Polity Press.

——(2012) *In Praise of Love*, translated by P. Bush. New York: New Press.

Bakhtin, M. M. (1981) *The Dialogic Imagination*, edited by M. Holquist, translated by C. Emerson and M. Holquist. Austin, TX: University of Texas Press.

——(1984a) *Problems of Dostoevsky's Poetics*, edited and translated by C. Emerson, Theory and History of Literature 8. Minneapolis: University of Minnesota Press.

——(1984b) *Rabelais and His World*, translated by H. Iswolsky. Bloomington: Indiana University Press.

——(1986) *Speech Genres and Other Late Essays*, edited by C. Emerson and M. Holquist, translated by V. W. McGee. Austin, TX: University of Texas Press.

——(1990) *Art and Answerability*, edited by M. Holquist and V. Liapunov, translated by V. Liapunov. Austin, TX: University of Texas Press.

Bal, M. (1997) *Narratology: Introduction to the Theory of Narrative*, second edition. Toronto: University of Toronto Press.

Balibar, É. (1990) "The Nation-Form: History and Ideology," *Review (Fernand Braudel Center)* 13.3: 329–61.

Ballantyne, T. (2002) *Orientalism and Race: Aryanism in the British Empire*. New York and Houndmills, UK: Palgrave Macmillan.

Barber, S. M. and D. L. Clark (2002) "Queer Moments," in S. M. Barber and D. L. Clark (eds) *Regarding Sedgwick: Essays on Queer Culture and Critical Theory*. London and New York: Routledge.

Barthes, R. (1967) *Elements of Semiology*, translated by A. Lavers and C. Smith. New York: Hill and Wang, Noonday Press.

——(1972) *Mythologies*, translated by A. Lavers. New York: Noonday Press.

——(1974) *S/Z*, translated by R. Miller. New York: Noonday Press.

——(1977) *Image Music Text*, translated by Stephen Heath. New York: Hill and Wang.

——(1983) *The Fashion System*, translated by M. Ward and R. Howard. Berkeley, CA: University of California Press (1990).

Bartscherer, T. and R. Coover (eds) (2011) *Switching Codes: Thinking through Digital Technology in the Humanities and the Arts*. Chicago: University of Chicago Press.

Bate, J. (1991) *Romantic Ecology: Wordsworth and the Environmental Tradition*. London and New York: Routledge.

Baudrillard, J. (1975) *The Mirror of Production*, translated by M. Poster. St. Louis: Telos Press.

——(1981) *For a Critique of the Political Economy of the Sign*, translated by C. Levin. [New York]: Telos.

——(1988) *America*, translated by C. Turner. London and New York: Verso.

——(1994) *Simulacra and Simulation*, translated by S. F. Glaser. Ann Arbor: University of Michigan Press.

——(1998) *The Consumer Society: Myths and Structures*. London: Sage.

Bell, D. (1974) *The Coming of Post-Industrial Society: A Venture in Social Forecasting*. New York: Basic Books (1999).

Bell, D. A., Jr. (1973) *Race, Racism and American Law*. Boston and Toronto: Little, Brown and Company.

——(1980) "Brown v. Board of Education and the Interest-Convergence Dilemma," in K. Crenshaw, N. Gotanda, G. Peller, and K. Thomas (eds) (1995) *Critical Race Theory: The Key Writings That Formed the Movement*. New York: New Press, pp. 20–29.

Bem, S. L. (1993) *The Lenses of Gender: Transforming the Debate on Sexual Inequality*. New Haven, CT: Yale University Press.

Bender, J. B. (1987) *Imagining the Penitentiary: Fiction and Architecture of Mind in Eighteenth-Century England*. Chicago: University of Chicago Press.

Benjamin, W. (1968) *Illuminations: Essays and Reflections*, edited by H. Arendt, translated by H. Zohn. New York: Schocken Books.

Bennett, L., Jr. (1975) *The Shaping of Black America*. Chicago: Johnson Publishing Company.

Berger, P. L. and S. P. Huntington (eds) (2002) *Many Globalizations: Cultural Diversity in the Contemporary World*. Oxford, UK: Oxford University Press.

Best, S. and S. Marcus (2009) "Surface Reading: An Introduction," *Representations* 108.1: 1–21.

Bhabha, H. K. (1990a) "DissemiNation: Time, Narrative and the Margins of the Modern Nation," in Bhabha (1990b), 291–322.

——(ed.) (1990b) *Nation and Narration*. London and New York: Routledge.

——(1994) *The Location of Culture*. London and New York: Routledge.

——(2005) "Foreword," in F. Fanon, *The Wretched of the Earth*, translated by R. Philcox. New York: Grove Press.

Bogel, F. V. (2013) *New Formalist Criticism: Theory and Practice*. Houndmills, UK and New York: Palgrave Macmillan.

Bordo, M. D., A. M. Taylor, and J. G. Williamson (eds) (2003) *Globalization in Historical Perspective*. Chicago: University of Chicago Press.

Bottomore, T. (1985) *Theories of Modern Capitalism*. London and New York: Routledge.

Bottomore, T., L. Harris, V. G. Kiernan, and R. Miliband (eds) (1983) *A Dictionary of Marxist Thought*. Oxford, UK: Blackwell.

Bourdieu, P. (1977) *Outline of a Theory of Practice*, translated by Richard Nice. Cambridge, UK: Cambridge University Press.

——(1984) *Distinction: A Social Critique of the Judgement of Taste*, translated by Richard Nice. Cambridge, MA: Harvard University Press.

——(1986) "The Forms of Capital," in *Readings in Economic Sociology*, edited by Nicole Woolsey Biggart. Malden, MA and Oxford, UK: Blackwell (2002).

——(1991) *Language and Symbolic Power*, edited by J. B. Thompson, translated by G. Raymond and M. Adamson. Cambridge, MA: Harvard University Press.

——(1992) *The Rules of Art: Genesis and Structure of the Literary Field*, translated by S. Emanuel. Stanford, CA: Stanford University Press.

——(1993) *The Field of Cultural Production*, edited by Randal Johnson. Columbia, NY: Columbia University Press.

——(1996) *The State Nobility: Elite Schools in the Field of Power*, translated by L. C. Clough. Stanford, CA: Stanford University Press.

——(1998) *Practical Reason: On the Theory of Action*. Stanford, CA: Stanford University Press.

Bourdieu, P. and L. J. D. Wacquant (1992) *An Invitation to Reflexive Sociology*. Chicago: University of Chicago Press.

Bowie, M. (1991) *Lacan*. Cambridge, MA: Harvard University Press.

Brassier, R. (2007) *Nihil Unbound: Enlightenment and Extinction*. New York and Houndmills, UK: Palgrave Macmillan.

Breckenridge, C. A. and P. v. d. Veer (eds) (1993) *Orientalism and the Post-colonial Predicament: Perspectives on South Asia*. Philadelphia, PA: University of Pennsylvania Press.

Breckenridge, C. A., H. Bhabha, S. Pollock, and D. Chakrabarty (eds) (2002) *Cosmopolitanism*. Durham: Duke University Press.

Brennan, T. (1990) "The National Longing for Form," in H. K. Bhabha (ed.) *Nation and Narration*. London and New York: Routledge, pp. 44–70.

——(2001) "Cosmopolitanism and Internationalism," *New Left Review* 7: 75–84.

Bronfen, E. (1998) *The Knotted Subject: Hysteria and Its Discontents*. Princeton, NJ: Princeton University Press.

Brooks, C. (1947) *The Well Wrought Urn: Studies in the Structure of Poetry*. New York: Harcourt, Brace & World.

Brooks, C. and R. P. Warren (1938) *Understanding Poetry*, third edition. New York: Holt, Rinehart and Winston (1960).

——(1943) *Understanding Fiction*, second edition. New York: Appleton-Century-Crofts (1959).

Brooks, P. (1985) *Reading for the Plot: Design and Intention in Narrative*. New York: Vintage.

Brown, B. (2001) "Thing Theory," *Critical Inquiry* 28 (Summer): 1–22.

——(2002) *A Sense of Things: The Object Matter of American Literature*. Chicago: University of Chicago Press.

Brown, G. W. and D. Held (eds) (2010) *The Cosmopolitanism Reader*. Cambridge, UK and Malden, MA: Polity Press.

Buchanan, I. and P. MacCormack (eds) (2008) *Deleuze and the Schizoanalysis of Cinema*. London and New York: Continuum.

Buell, L. (1995) *The Environmental Imagination: Thoreau, Nature Writing, and the Formation of American Culture*. Cambridge, MA: Harvard University Press.

Burchell, G., C. Gordon, and P. Miller (eds) (1991) *The Foucault Effect: Studies in Governmentality*. Chicago: University of Chicago Press.

Burdick, A., J. Drucker, P. Lunenfield, T. Presner, and J. Schnapp (2012) *Digital_Humanities*. Cambridge, MA: MIT Press.

Burke, E. (1756) *A Philosophical Enquiry into the Origin of Our Ideas of the Sublime and Beautiful*. London: J. Dodsley (1770).

Butler, J. (1990a) *Gender Trouble: Feminism and the Subversion of Identity*. London and New York: Routledge.

——(1990b) "Performative Acts and Gender Constitution: An Essay in Phenomenology and Feminist Theory," in S.-E. Case (ed.) *Performing Feminisms: Feminist Critical Theory and Theatre*. Baltimore: Johns Hopkins University Press, pp. 270–82.

——(1993) *Bodies that Matter: On the Discursive Limits of "Sex."* London and New York: Routledge.

——(1997) *Excitable Speech: A Politics of the Performative*. New York: Routledge.

——(2000) *Antigone's Claim: Kinship between Life and Death*. New York: Columbia University Press.

Cadava, E., P. Connor, and J.-L. Nancy (eds) (1991) *Who Comes after the Subject?* London and New York: Routledge.

Calhoun, C. J. (ed.) (1992) *Habermas and the Public Sphere*. Cambridge, MA: MIT Press.

Călinescu, M. (1987) *Five Faces of Modernity: Modernism, Avant-Garde, Decadence, Kitsch, Postmodernism*. Durham: Duke University Press.

Castle, T. (1986) *Masquerade and Civilization: The Carnivalesque in Eighteenth-Century English Culture and Fiction*. Stanford, CA: Stanford University Press.

——(1995) *The Female Thermometer: Eighteenth-Century Culture and the Invention of the Uncanny*. New York and Oxford, UK: Oxford University Press.

Chakrabarty, D. (2002) *Habitations of Modernity: Essays in the Wake of Subaltern Studies*. Chicago: University of Chicago Press.

Chatman, S. (1978) *Story and Discourse: Narrative Structure in Fiction and Film*. Ithaca, NY: Cornell University Press.

Cheah, P. and B. Robbins (eds) (1998) *Cosmopolitics: Thinking and Feeling beyond the Nation*. Minneapolis: University of Minnesota Press.

Cixous, H. (1976) "The Laugh of the Medusa," in H. Adams and L. Searle (eds) *Critical Theory Since 1965*. Tallahassee: Florida State University Press (1986), pp. 309–20.

——(1986) *The Newly Born Woman*, Theory and History of Literature 24, translated by C. Clement. Minneapolis: University of Minnesota Press.

Clayton, J. and E. Rothstein (1991) *Influence and Intertextuality in Literary History*. Madison: University of Wisconsin Press.

Codell, J. F. and D. S. Macleod (eds) (1998) *Orientalism Transposed: The Impact of the Colonies on British Culture*. Aldershot, UK: Ashgate.

Cohen, S. and L. M. Shires (1988) *Telling Stories: A Theoretical Analysis of Narrative Fiction*. London and New York: Routledge.

Collins, P. H. (2000) *Black Feminist Thought: Knowledge, Consciousness, and the Politics of Empowerment*, second edition. London and New York: Routledge.

Comte, A. (1848) *A General View of Positivism*, translated by J. H. Bridges. Stanford, CA: Academic Reprints (n.d.).

Cooper, D. E. (ed.) (1992) *A Companion to Aesthetics*. Oxford, UK: Blackwell.

——(1997) *Aesthetics: The Classic Readings*. Oxford, UK: Blackwell.

Cornforth, M. (1971) *Materialism and the Dialectical Method*, fourth revised edition. New York: International Publishers.

Crane, M. T. (2000) *Shakespeare's Brain: Reading with Cognitive Theory*. Princeton: Princeton University Press.

Crenshaw, K. (1991) "Mapping the Margins: Intersectionality, Identity Politics, and Violence against Women of Color," *Stanford Law Review* 43.6: 1241–99.

Crenshaw, K., N. Gotanda, G. Peller, and K. Thomas (eds) (1995) *Critical Race Theory: The Key Writings That Formed the Movement*. New York: New Press.

Cudd, A. E. and R. O. Andreasen (eds) (2005) *Feminist Theory: A Philosophical Anthology*. Oxford, UK and Malden, MA: Blackwell.

Culler, J. (1975) *Structuralist Poetics: Structuralism, Linguistics and the Study of Literature*. Ithaca, NY: Cornell University Press.

——(1981) *The Pursuit of Signs: Semiotics, Literature, Deconstruction*. Ithaca, NY: Cornell University Press.

Dallmayr, F. R. (1996) *Beyond Orientalism: Essays on Cross-Cultural Encounter*. Albany, NY: State University of New York Press.

Darnton, R. (2001) "First Steps Toward a History of Reading," in J. L. Machor and P. Goldstein (eds) *Reception Study: From Literary Theory to Cultural Studies*. London and New York: Routledge.

——(2008) *The Case for Books: Past, Present, and Future*. New York: PublicAffairs.

David-Ménard, M. (1989) *Hysteria from Freud to Lacan: Body and Language in Psychoanalysis*, translated by C. Porter. Ithaca and London: Cornell University Press.

Dean, M. (1999) *Governmentality: Power and Rule in Modern Society*. London: Sage.

de la Durantaye, L. (2009) *Giorgio Agamben: A Critical Introduction*. Stanford, CA: Stanford University Press.

DeLanda, M. (2006) *A New Philosophy of Society: Assemblage Theory and Social Complexity*. New York: Continuum.

de Lauretis, T. (1984) *Alice Doesn't: Feminism, Semiotics, Cinema*. Bloomington: Indiana University Press.

——(1994) *The Practice of Love: Lesbian Sexuality and Perverse Desire*. Bloomington: Indiana University Press.

Deleuze, G. and F. Guattari (1983) *Anti-Oedipus: Capitalism and Schizophrenia*, translated by R. Hurley, M. Seem, and H. R. Lane. Minneapolis: University of Minnesota Press.

——(1987) *A Thousand Plateaus: Capitalism and Schizophrenia*, translated by B. Massumi. Minneapolis: University of Minnesota Press.

Delgado, R. and J. Stefancic (2001) *Critical Race Theory: An Introduction*. New York and London: New York University Press.

De Man, P. (1979) *Allegories of Reading: Figural Language in Rousseau, Nietzsche, Rilke, and Proust*. New Haven, CT and London: Yale University Press.

——(1983) *Blindness and Insight: Essays in the Rhetoric of Contemporary Criticism*, second edition, Theory and History of Literature 7. Minneapolis: University of Minnesota Press.

Derrida, J. (1976) *Of Grammatology*, translated by G. C. Spivak. Baltimore: Johns Hopkins University Press.

——(1978) *Writing and Difference*, translated by A. Bass. Chicago: University of Chicago Press.

——(1980) "The Law of Genre," *Critical Inquiry* 7: 55–81.

——(1981) *Dissemination*, translated by Barbara Johnson. Chicago: University of Chicago Press.

——(1982) *Margins of Philosophy*, translated by A. Bass. Chicago: University of Chicago Press.

——(1986) *Glas*, translated by J. P. Leavey, Jr. and R. Rand. Lincoln, NB and London, UK: University of Nebraska Press.

——(1994) *Specters of Marx: The State of the Debt, the Work of Mourning, and the New International*, translated by P. Kamuf. London and New York: Routledge.

——(1997) *Politics of Friendship*, translated by G. Collins. London and New York: Verso.

——(2000) *Of Hospitality: Anne Dufourmantelle Invites Jacques Derrida to Respond*, translated by R. Bowlby. Stanford, CA: Stanford University Press.

Didi-Huberman, G. (2003) *Invention of Hysteria: Charcot and the Photographic Iconography of the Salpêtrière*. Cambridge, MA: MIT Press.

Dinshaw, C. (1999) *Getting Medieval: Sexualities and Communities, Pre- and Postmodern*. Durham: Duke University Press.

Dollimore, J. (1985) "Introduction: Shakespeare, Cultural Materialism and the New Historicism," in J. Dollimore and A. Sinfield (eds) *Political Shakespeare: New Essays in Cultural Materialism*. Ithaca, NY: Cornell University Press.

Dollimore, J. and A. Sinfield (1985) "Foreword," in *Political Shakespeare: New Essays in Cultural Materialism*, edited by J. Dollimore and A. Sinfield. Ithaca, NY: Cornell University Press.

Drew, J. (1999) "Cultural Composition: Stuart Hall on Ethnicity and the Discursive Turn," in G. A. Olson and L. Worsham (eds) *Race, Rhetoric, and the Postcolonial*. New York: State University of New York Press.

Dreyfus, H. L. and P. Rabinow (1983) *Michel Foucault: Beyond Structuralism and Hermeneutics*. Chicago: University of Chicago Press.

Drucker, J. (2009) *SpecLab: Digital Aesthetics and Projects in Speculative Computing*. Chicago: University of Chicago Press.

During, S. (1998) "Postcolonialism and Globalisation: A Dialectical Relation after All?," *Postcolonial Studies* 1.1: 31–47.

——(2000) "Postcolonialism and Globalisation: Towards a Historicization of Their Inter-Relation," *Cultural Studies* 14: 385–404.

Eagleton, M. (ed.) (1986) *Feminist Literary Theory: A Reader*. Oxford, UK and New York: Basil Blackwell.

Eagleton, T. (1990) *The Ideology of the Aesthetic*. Oxford, UK: Blackwell.

——(1991) *Ideology: An Introduction*. London: Verso.

——(2003) *After Theory*. New York: Basic Books.

Eco, U. (1976) *A Theory of Semiotics*. Bloomington: Indiana University Press.

——(1984) "The Frames of Comic 'Freedom,'" in T. A. Sebeok (ed.) *Carnival!* Approaches to Semiotics 64. Berlin: Mouton Publishers, pp. 1–9.

——(1986) *Semiotics and the Philosophy of Language*. Bloomington: Indiana University Press.

——(2007) *On Ugliness*. New York: Rizzoli.

Edelman, L. (1994) *Homographesis: Essays in Gay Literary and Cultural Theory*. London and New York: Routledge.

——(2004) *No Future: Queer Theory and the Death Drive*. Durham: Duke University Press.

Edgar, A. and P. Sedgwick (2008) *Cultural Theory: The Key Concepts*, second edition. London and New York: Routledge.

Ehlers, N. (2012) *Racial Imperatives: Discipline, Performativity, and Struggles against Subjection*. Bloomington and Indianapolis: Indiana University Press.

Elfenbein, A. (1999) *Romantic Genius: The Prehistory of a Homosexual Role*. New York: Columbia University Press.

Engels, F. (1878) *Anti-Dühring*, in K. Marx and F. Engels, *Collected Works*, volume 25. New York: International Publishers (1987).

——(1883) *Dialectics of Nature*, in K. Marx and F. Engels, *Collected Works*, volume 25. New York: International Publishers (1987).

——(1892) *Socialism: Utopian and Scientific*, translated by E. Aveling. Chicago: Charles H. Kerr (1908).

Eskridge, W. N., Jr. (1999) *Gaylaw: Challenging the Apartheid of the Closet*. Cambridge, MA: Harvard University Press.

Fanon, F. (1963) *The Wretched of the Earth*, translated by Constance Farrington. New York: Grove Press.

——(1967) *Black Skin, White Masks*. New York: Grove Press.

Felluga, D. F. (2006) "Addressed to the NINES: The Victorian Archive and the Disappearance of the Book," *Victorian Studies* 48.2: 305–19.

——(2013) "BRANCHing Out: Victorian Studies and the Digital Humanities," *Critical Quarterly* 55.1: 43–56.

Felman, S. (1983) *The Literary Speech Act: Don Juan with J. L. Austin, or Seduction in Two Languages*, translated by C. Porter. Ithaca, NY: Cornell University Press.

Ferris, I. (1991) *The Achievement of Literary Authority: Gender, History, and the Waverley Novels*. Ithaca, NY: Cornell University Press.

Fink, B. (2007) *Fundamentals of Psychoanalytic Technique: A Lacanian Approach for Practitioners*. New York and London: Norton.

Fish, S. (1980) *Is There a Text in This Class? The Authority of Interpretive Communities*. Cambridge, MA: Harvard University Press.

Foley, D. K. (1986) *Understanding Capital: Marx's Economic Theory*. Cambridge, MA: Harvard University Press.

Foucault, M. (1965) *Madness and Civilization: A History of Insanity in the Age of Reason*. New York: Vintage (1988).

——(1966) *The Order of Things: An Archaeology of the Human Sciences*. London: Tavistock (1970).

——(1971) "The Discourse on Language," in H. Adams and L. Searle (eds), *Critical Theory since 1965*. Tallahassee: University Presses of Florida (1986), pp. 148–62.

——(1972) *The Archaeology of Knowledge and the Discourse on Language*, translated by A. M. S. Smith. New York: Pantheon.

——(1975) *The Birth of the Clinic: An Archaeology of Medical Perception*, translated by A. M. S. Smith. New York: Vintage.

——(1977a) *Discipline and Punish: The Birth of the Prison*, translated by A. Sheridan. New York: Pantheon.

——(1977b) "What Is an Author?" in H. Adams and L. Searle (eds), *Critical Theory since 1965*. Tallahassee: University Presses of Florida (1986), pp. 138–48.

——(1980) *Power/Knowledge: Selected Interviews and Other Writings, 1972–77*, edited by C. Gordon, translated by C. Gordon, L. Marshall, J. Mepham, and K. Soper. New York: Pantheon.

——(1982) "The Subject and Power," in H. L. Dreyfus and P. Rabinow (eds), *Michel Foucault: Beyond Structuralism and Hermeneutics*, 2nd edition. Chicago: University of Chicago Press, pp. 208–26.

——(1986) "Of Other Spaces," *Diacritics* 16.1: 22–27.

——(1990) *The History of Sexuality*, 2 volumes, translated by R. Hurley. New York: Vintage.

——(1991a) "Politics and the Study of Discourse," in G. Burchell, C. Gordon, and P. Miller (eds), *The Foucault Effect: Studies in Governmentality*. Chicago: University of Chicago Press, pp. 53–72.

——(1991b) "Questions of Method," in G. Burchell, C. Gordon, and P. Miller (eds), *The Foucault Effect*, pp. 73–86.

——(1991c) "Governmentality," in G. Burchell, C. Gordon, and P. Miller (eds), *The Foucault Effect*, pp. 87–104.

Freccero, C. (2006) *Queer/Early/Modern*. Durham: Duke University Press.

Freedgood, E. (2006) *The Ideas in Things: Fugitive Meaning in the Victorian Novel*. Chicago: University of Chicago Press.

Freeman, E. (2010) *Time Binds: Queer Temporalities, Queer Histories*. Durham: Duke University Press.

Freud, S. (1900) *The Interpretation of Dreams*, translated by J. Strachey. New York: Anon Books (1965).

——(1912–13) *Totem and Taboo: Some Points of Agreement between the Mental Lives of Savages and Neurotics*, fifth edition, translated by J. Strachey. New York: Norton (1950).

——(1915) "Repression," in *Freud*, vol. 54 of R. M. Hutchins (ed.) *Great Books of the Western World*. Chicago: William Benton (1952), pp. 422–27.

——(1916–17) *Introductory Lectures on Psychoanalysis*, translated by J. Strachey. New York: Norton (1989).

——(1919) "The 'Uncanny,'" in S. L. Gilman (ed.) *Psychological Writings and Letters*. New York: Continuum (1995), pp. 135–53.

——(1920) *Beyond the Pleasure Principle*, translated and edited by J. Strachey. New York and London: Norton (1989).

——(1923) "Ego and the Id," in *Freud*, vol. 54 of R. M. Hutchins (ed.) *Great Books of the Western World*. Chicago: William Benton (1952), pp. 697–717.

——(1929) *Civilization and Its Discontents*, translated by J. Strachey. New York: Norton (2010).

——(1932) "New Introductory Lectures on Psycho-Analysis," in *Freud*, vol. 54 of R. M. Hutchins (ed.) *Great Books of the Western World*, pp. 807–84.

——(1953–74) *The Standard Edition of the Complete Psychological Works of Sigmund Freud*, 24 volumes, translated by J. Strachey. London: Hogarth.

Friedlander, S. (1984) *Reflections of Nazism: An Essay on Kitsch and Death*. New York: Harper & Row.

Gadamer, H.-G. (1960) *Truth and Method*, second revised edition, translated by J. Weinsheimer and D. G. Marshall. New York: Crossroad (1989).

Gaggi, S. (1997) *From Text to Hypertext: Decentering the Subject in Fiction, Film, the Visual Arts, and Electronic Media*. Philadelphia: University of Pennsylvania Press.

Gagnier, R. (1991) *Subjectivities: A History of Self-Representation in Britain, 1832–1920*. Oxford, UK: Oxford University Press.

——(2000) *The Insatiability of Human Wants: Economics and Aesthetics in Market Society*. Chicago: University of Chicago Press.

——(2010) *Individualism, Decadence and Globalization: On the Relationship of Part to Whole, 1859–1920*. Houndmills, UK and New York: Palgrave Macmillan.

Gallop, J. (2011) *The Deaths of the Author: Reading and Writing in Time*. Durham: Duke University Press.

Garcia, T. (2014) *Form and Object: A Treatise on Things*, translated by M. A. Ohm and J. Cogburn. Edinburgh: Edinburgh University Press.

Gates, H. L. (1988) *The Signifying Monkey: A Theory of Afro-American Literary Criticism*. New York and Oxford, UK: Oxford University Press.

Geertz, C. (1973) *The Interpretation of Cultures: Selected Essays*. New York: Basic Books.

Gelpi, B. (1992) *Shelley's Goddess: Maternity, Language, Subjectivity*. Oxford, UK: Oxford University Press.

Genette, G. (1980) *Narrative Discourse: An Essay in Method*, translated by J. E. Lewin. Ithaca, NY: Cornell University Press.

——(1988) *Narrative Discourse Revisited*, translated by J. E. Lewin. Ithaca, NY: Cornell University Press.

Giddens, A. (1973) *The Class Structure of the Advanced Societies*. London: Hutchinson.

Giddens, A. and D. Held (eds) (1982) *Classes, Power and Conflict: Classical and Contemporary Debates*. New York and Houndmills, UK: Palgrave Macmillan.

Gikandi, S. (2001) "Globalization and the Claims of Postcoloniality," *The South Atlantic Quarterly* 100.3: 627–58.

Gilbert, S. M. and S. Gubar (1984) *The Madwoman in the Attic: The Woman Writer and the Nineteenth-Century Literary Imagination*, second edition. New Haven, CT: Yale University Press.

Gilligan, C. and D. A. J. Richards (2008) *The Deepening Darkness: Patriarchy, Resistance, and Democracy's Future*. Cambridge, UK: Cambridge University Press.

Girard, René (1965) *Deceit, Desire, and the Novel: Self and Other in Literary Structure*. Baltimore, MD: Johns Hopkins University Press.

Glotfelty, C. and H. Fromm (eds) (1996) *The Ecocriticism Reader: Landmarks in Literary Ecology*. Athens: University of Georgia Press.

Gold, M. K. (ed.) (2012) *Debates in the Digital Humanities*. Minneapolis: University of Minnesota Press.

Goodbody, A. and K. Rigby (eds) (2011) *Ecocritical Theory: New European Approaches*. Charlottesville: University of Virginia Press.

Graham, G. (1997) *Philosophy of the Arts: An Introduction to Aesthetics*. London: Routledge.

Gramsci, A. (1992) *Prison Notebooks*, 3 volumes, edited by J. A. Buttigieg, translated by J. A. Buttigieg and A. Callari. New York: Columbia University Press.

——(1995) *Further Selections from the Prison Notebooks*, edited and translated by Derek Boothman. Minneapolis: University of Minnesota Press.

——(2000) *The Antonio Gramsci Reader: Selected Writings, 1916–1935*, edited by D. Forgacs. New York: New York University Press.

Grant, I. H. (2008) *Philosophies of Nature after Schelling*. London and New York: Continuum.

Greenblatt, S. (1989) "Towards a Poetics of Culture," in H. A. Veeser (ed.), *The New Historicism*. London and New York: Routledge.

Greimas, A. J. (1976a) "On Anger: A Lexical Semantic Study," in *On Meaning: Selected Writings in Semiotic Theory*, translated by P. J. Perron and F. H. Collins. Minneapolis: University of Minnesota Press, pp. 148–64.

——(1976b) *On Meaning: Selected Writings in Semiotic Theory*, translated by P. J. Perron and F. H. Collins. Minneapolis: University of Minnesota Press.

——(1993) *The Semiotics of Passions: From States of Affairs to States of Feelings*, translated by P. Perron and F. Collins. Minneapolis: University of Minnesota Press.

Grondin, J. (1994) *Introduction to Philosophical Hermeneutics*. New Haven, CT: Yale University Press.

Guha, R. (1988) "On Some Aspects of the Historiography of Colonial India," in R. Guha and G. C. Spivak (eds) *Selected Subaltern Studies*. Oxford, UK: Oxford University Press, pp. 37–44.

Guillory, J. (1993) *Cultural Capital: The Problem of Literary Canon Formation.* Chicago: University of Chicago Press.

Gunn, G. (2013) *Ideas to Die For: The Cosmopolitan Challenge.* London and New York: Routledge.

Habermas, J. (1987) *The Theory of Communicative Action,* 2 vols, translated by T. McCarthy. Boston: Beacon Press.

——(1991) *Moral Consciousness and Communicative Action,* translated by C. Lenhardt and S. W. Nicholsen. Cambridge, MA: MIT Press.

——(1993) *Justification and Application: Remarks on Discourse Ethics,* translated by C. P. Cronin. Cambridge, MA: MIT Press.

——(1999) *The Structural Transformation of the Public Sphere: An Inquiry into a Category of Bourgeois Society,* translated by T. Burger. Cambridge, MA: MIT Press.

Halberstam, J. (2005) *In a Queer Time and Place: Transgender Bodies, Subcultural Lives.* New York: New York University Press.

——(2011) *The Queer Art of Failure.* Durham: Duke University Press.

Hall, D. E. (2004) *Subjectivity.* London and New York: Routledge.

Hall, D. E. and A. Jagose (eds) (2013) *The Routledge Queer Studies Reader.* London and New York: Routledge.

Hall, S. (1986) "Gramsci's Relevance for the Study of Race and Ethnicity," *Journal of Communication Inquiry* 10: 5–27.

Hall, S., D. Hobson, A. Lowe, and P. Willis (eds) (1980) *Culture, Media, Language: Working Papers in Cultural Studies, 1972–79.* London: Hutchinson and Company.

Hallward, P. (2003) *Badiou: A Subject to Truth.* Minneapolis and London: University of Minnesota Press.

Hansen, M. (2000) *Embodying Technesis: Technology beyond Writing.* Ann Arbor: University of Michigan Press.

Harari, J. V. (ed.) (1980) *Textual Strategies: Perspectives in Post-Structuralist Criticism.* London: Methuen.

Hardt, M. and A. Negri (2000) *Empire.* Cambridge, MA: Harvard University Press.

Harman, G. (2010) *Towards Speculative Realism: Essays and Lectures.* Winchester, UK: Zero Books.

——(2011) *Quentin Meillassoux: Philosophy in the Making.* Edinburgh: Edinburgh University Press.

Harraway, D. J. (1991) *Simians, Cyborgs, and Women: The Reinvention of Nature.* New York: Routledge.

Harris, C. I. (1993) "Whiteness as Property," *Harvard Law Review* 106: 1707–91.

Harvey, D. (1989) *The Condition of Postmodernity: An Enquiry into the Origins of Cultural Change.* Oxford, UK: Blackwell.

——(2009) *Cosmopolitanism and the Geographies of Freedom.* New York: Columbia University Press.

Hassan, I. (1987) *The Postmodern Turn: Essays in Postmodern Theory and Culture.* Columbus, OH: Ohio State University Press.

Hayles, N. K. (1999) *How We Became Posthuman: Virtual Bodies in Cybernetics, Literature, and Informatics.* Chicago: University of Chicago Press.

——(2005) *My Mother Was a Computer: Digital Subjects and Literary Texts*. Chicago: University of Chicago Press.

——(2012) *How We Think: Digital Media and Contemporary Technogenesis*. Chicago: University of Chicago Press.

Heath, S. (1977) "Notes on Suture," *Screen* 18.4: 48–76.

Hebdige, D. (1979) *Subculture: The Meaning of Style*. London and New York: Routledge.

Hegel, G. W. F. (1807) *Phenomenology of the Spirit*, translated by A. V. Miller. Oxford, UK: Oxford University Press (1977).

Heidegger, M. (1927) *Being and Time*, translated by J. Macquarrie and E. Robinson. New York: Harper & Row (1962).

Helgerson, R. (1992) *Forms of Nationhood: The Elizabethan Writing of England*. Chicago: University of Chicago Press.

Herman, D. (1997) "Scripts, Sequences, and Stories: Elements of a Postclassical Narratology," *PMLA* 112.5: 1046–59.

Hernadi, P. (1978) *What Is Literature?* Bloomington: Indiana University Press.

——(1981) *What Is Criticism?* Bloomington: Indiana University Press.

Hobsbawn, E. (2008) *On Empire: America, War, and Global Supremacy*. New York and London: New Press.

Hoeveler, D. L. and J. Cass (eds) (2006) *Interrogating Orientalism: Contextual Approaches and Pedagogical Practices*. Columbus, OH: Ohio State University Press.

Hogan, P. C. (2003) *The Mind and Its Stories: Narrative Universals and Human Emotion*. Cambridge, UK: Cambridge University Press.

Holland, E. W. (1999) *Deleuze and Guattari's Anti-Oedipus: Introduction to Schizoanalysis*. London and New York: Routledge.

Holquist, M. (1990) *Dialogism: Bakhtin and his World*. London and New York: Routledge.

Hoogvelt, A. (1997) *Globalization and the Postcolonial World: The New Political Economy of Development*. Baltimore, MD: Johns Hopkins University Press.

Horkheimer, M. (1972) *Critical Theory: Selected Essays*, translated by M. J. O'Connell. New York: Herder and Herder.

Horkheimer, M. and T. W. Adorno (1944) *Dialectic of Enlightenment*, translated by J. Cumming. New York: Continuum (1995).

Hošek, C. and P. Parker (eds) (1985) *Lyric Poetry: Beyond New Criticism*. Ithaca, NY: Cornell University Press.

Husserl, E. (1936) *A Crisis of European Sciences and Transcendental Phenomenology*, translated by D. Carr. Evanston, IL: Northwestern University Press (1970).

——(1999) *The Essential Husserl: Basic Writings in Transcendental Phenomenology*, edited by D. Welton. Bloomington: Indiana University Press.

Hutcheon, L. (1988) *A Poetics of Postmodernism: History, Theory, Fiction*. London and New York: Routledge.

——(1989) *The Politics of Postmodernism*. London and New York: Routledge.

Huyssen, A. (1995) *Twilight Memories: Marking Time in a Culture of Amnesia*. London and New York: Routledge.

Irigaray, L. (1985a) *Speculum of the Other Woman*, translated by G. C. Gill. Ithaca, NY: Cornell University Press.

——(1985b) *This Sex which is Not One*, translated by C. Porter with C. Burke. Ithaca, NY: Cornell University Press.

Iser, W. (1979) "The Repertoire," in H. Adams and L. Searle (eds) *Critical Theory Since 1965*. Tallahassee: Florida State University Press (1986), pp. 360–80.

Jagger, G. (2008) *Judith Butler: Sexual Politics, Social Change and the Power of the Performative*. London and New York: Routledge.

Jagose, A. (2002) *Inconsequence: Lesbian Representation and the Logic of Sexual Sequence*. Ithaca, NY: Cornell University Press.

Jakobson, R. (1960) "Closing Statement: Linguistics and Poetics," in T. A. Sebeok (ed.) *Style in Language*. Cambridge, MA: MIT Press, pp. 350–78.

Jakobson, R. and M. Halle (1956) *Fundamentals of Language*. The Hague: Mouton.

James, J. and T. D. Sharpley-Whiting (eds) (2000) *The Black Feminist Reader*. Oxford, UK and Malden, MA: Blackwell.

Jameson, F. (1971) *Marxism and Form: Twentieth-Century Dialectical Theories of Literature*. Princeton, NJ: Princeton University Press.

——(1972) *The Prison-House of Language: A Critical Account of Structuralism and Russian Formalism*. Princeton: Princeton University Press.

——(1976) "Foreword," in A. Greimas, *On Meaning: Selected Writings in Semiotic Theory*, translated by P. J. Perron and F. H. Collins. Minneapolis: University of Minnesota Press, pp. vi–xxii.

——(1981) *The Political Unconscious: Narrative as a Socially Symbolic Act*. Ithaca, NY: Cornell University Press.

——(1988) "Cognitive Mapping," in C. Nelson and L. Grossberg (eds) *Marxism and the Interpretation of Culture*. Urbana: University of Illinois Press, 1988, pp. 347–57.

——(1991) *Postmodernism, or, the Cultural Logic of Late Capitalism*. Durham: Duke University Press.

——(2005) *Archaeologies of the Future: The Desire Called Utopia and Other Science Fictions*. London and New York: Verso.

Jauss, H. R. (1982) "Literary History as a Challenge to Literary History," in H. Adams and L. Searle (eds) *Critical Theory Since 1965*. Tallahassee: Florida State University Press (1986), pp. 164–83.

Jaworski, A. and N. Coupland (eds) (1999) *The Discourse Reader*. London and New York: Routledge.

Jenks, C. (1991) *The Language of Postmodern Architecture*, sixth edition. London: Academy Editions.

Jockers, M. L. (2013) *Macroanalysis: Digital Methods and Literary History*. Urbana: University of Illinois Press.

Johnson, B. (1987) *A World of Difference*. Baltimore, MD: Johns Hopkins University Press.

Juergensmeyer, M. (ed.) (2014) *Thinking Globally: A Global Studies Reader*. Berkeley, CA: University of California Press.

Kant, I. (1764) *Observations on the Feeling of the Beautiful and the Sublime and Other Writings*, edited by P. Frierson and P. Guyer. Cambridge, UK: Cambridge University Press (2011).

——(1781) *The Critique of Pure Reason*, translated by J. M. D. Meiklejohn, in M. J. Adler (ed.) *Kant*, volume 42 of *Great Books of the Western World*. Chicago: William Benton (1952), pp. ix–250.

——(1788) *The Critique of Practical Reason*, translated by T. K. Abbott, in M. J. Adler (ed.) *Kant*, volume 42 of *Great Books of the Western World*. Chicago: William Benton (1952), pp. 289–361.

——(1790) *The Critique of Judgement*, translated by J. C. Meredith, in M. J. Adler (ed.) *Kant*, volume 42 of *Great Books of the Western World*. Chicago: William Benton (1952), pp. 461–613.

——(1795) *Toward Perpetual Peace: A Philosophical Sketch*, translated by D. L. Colclasure, in P. Kleingeld (ed.), *Toward Perpetual Peace and Other Writings on Politics, Peace, and History*. New Haven, CT: Yale University Press (2006).

Kaplan, E. A. (ed.) (2000) *Feminism and Film*. Oxford, UK: Oxford University Press (2006).

Kaplan, L. J. (2006) *Cultures of Fetishism*. New York and Houndmills, UK: Palgrave Macmillan.

Keller, R. (2011) "The Sociology of Knowledge Approach to Discourse (SKAD)," *Human Studies* 34: 43–65.

Keohane, N. O., M. Z. Rosaldo, and B. C. Gelpi (eds) (1982) *Feminist Theory: A Critique of Ideology*. Chicago: University of Chicago Press.

Kittler, F. A. (1990) *Discourse Networks 1800/1900*, translated by Michael Metteer. Stanford, CA: Stanford University Press.

Kofman, E. and G. Youngs (eds) (2008) *Globalization: Theory and Practice*, third edition. London and New York: Continuum.

Kolakowski, L. (1978) *Main Currents of Marxism: Its Rise, Growth, and Dissolution*, 3 volumes. Oxford, UK: Clarendon Press.

Krishnaswamy, R. (1998) *Effeminism: The Economy of Colonial Desire*. Ann Arbor: University of Michigan Press.

Krishnaswamy, R. and J. C. Hawley (eds) (2008) *The Postcolonial and the Global*. Minneapolis: University of Minnesota Press.

Kristeva, J. (1980) *Desire in Language: A Semiotic Approach to Literature and Art*, edited by L. S. Roudiez, translated by T. Gora, A. Jardine, and L. S. Roudiez. New York: Columbia University Press.

——(1982) *Powers of Horror: An Essay on Abjection*, translated by L. S. Roudiez. New York: Columbia University Press.

——(1984) *Revolution in Poetic Language*, translated by M. Waller. New York: Columbia University Press.

Kuhn, T. S. (1962) *The Structure of Scientific Revolutions*, fourth edition. Chicago: University of Chicago Press (2012).

Kumar, K. (1978) *Prophecy and Progress: The Sociology of Industrial and Post-Industrial Society*. Harmondsworth, UK: Penguin.

Kurtzweil, E. (1980) *The Age of Structuralism: Lévi-Strauss to Foucault*. New York: Columbia University Press.

Lacan, J. (1968) *The Language of the Self: The Function of Language in Psychoanalysis*, translated by A. Wilden. Baltimore, MD: Johns Hopkins University Press.

——(1977) *Écrits: A Selection*, translated by A. Sheridan. New York: Norton.

——(1981) *The Four Fundamental Concepts of Psycho-Analysis*, translated by A. Sheridan, edited by J.-A. Miller. New York and London: Norton.

——(1991) *Freud's Papers on Technique 1953–1954*, The Seminar of Jacques Lacan, Book 1, edited by J.-A. Miller, translated by J. Forrester. New York: Norton.

——(1992) *The Ethics of Psychoanalysis 1959–1960*, The Seminar of Jacques Lacan, Book 7, edited by J.-A. Miller, translated by D. Porter. New York: Norton.

——(1998) *On Feminine Sexuality: The Limits of Love and Knowledge*, translated by Bruce Fink, Book 20 of Encore: The Seminar of Jacques Lacan. New York and London: Norton.

LaCapra, D. (1987) "History and Psychoanalysis," *Critical Inquiry* 13: 222–51.

——(1992) "Representing the Holocaust: Reflections on the Historians' Debate," in S. Friedlander (ed.), *Probing the Limits of Representation*. Cambridge, MA: Harvard University Press, pp. 108–27.

——(1994) *Representing the Holocaust: History, Theory, Trauma*. Ithaca, NY: Cornell University Press.

——(1998) *History and Memory after Auschwitz*. Ithaca, NY: Cornell University Press.

Laclau, E. and C. Mouffe (1985) *Hegemony and Socialist Strategy: Towards a Radical Democratic Politics*. London: Verso.

Lakoff, G. and M. Johnson (1980) *Metaphors We Live By*. Chicago: University of Chicago Press (2003).

Landow, G. P. (1997) *Hypertext 2.0: The Convergence of Contemporary Critical Theory and Technology*. Baltimore, MD: Johns Hopkins University Press.

Laplanche, J. and J.-B. Pontalis (1973) *The Language of Psycho-Analysis*, translated by D. Nicholson-Smith. New York and London: Norton.

Laqueur, T. W. (1990) *Making Sex: Body and Gender from the Greeks to Freud*. Cambridge, MA: Harvard University Press.

——(2003) *Solitary Sex: A Cultural History of Masturbation*. New York: Zone Books.

Latour, B. (1993) *We Have Never Been Modern*, translated by C. Porter. Cambridge, MA: Harvard University Press.

——(1999) *Pandora's Hope: Essays on the Reality of Science Studies*. Cambridge, MA: Harvard University Press.

——(2005) *Reassembling the Social: An Introduction to Actor-Network Theory*. Oxford, UK: Oxford University Press.

Law, J. (2004) *After Method: Mess in Social Science Research*. London and New York: Routledge.

Law, J. and A. Mol (eds) (2002) *Complexities: Social Studies of Knowledge Practices*. Durham: Duke University Press.

Lazarus, N. (ed.) (2004) *The Cambridge Companion to Postcolonial Studies*. Cambridge, UK: Cambridge University Press.

Lechte, J. and S. Newman (2013) *Agamben and the Politics of Human Rights: Statelessness, Images, Violence*. Edinburgh: Edinburgh University Press.

Lefebvre, H. (1968) *Dialectical Materialism*, translated by J. Sturrock. London, UK: Jonathan Cape.

Lentricchia, F. (1980) *After the New Criticism*. Chicago: University of Chicago Press.

Lentricchia, F. and A. DuBois (eds) (2003) *Close Reading: The Reader*. Durham: Duke University Press.

Leverage, P., H. Mancing, R. Schweickert, and J. M. Williams (eds) (2011) *Theory of Mind and Literature*. West Lafayette, IN: Purdue University Press.

Levinas, E. (1991) *Totality and Infinity*. Dordrecht: Kluwer Academic Publishers.

——(1998) *Entre nous: On Thinking-of-the-Other*, translated by M. B. Smith and B. Harshav. New York: Columbia University Press.

——(2003) *Humanism of the Other*, translated by N. Poller. Urbana: University of Illinois Press.

Levine, C. (2006) "Strategic Formalism: Toward a New Method in Cultural Studies," *Victorian Studies* 48.4: 625–57.

Levine, G. L. (ed.) (1994) *Aesthetics and Ideology*. New Brunswick, NJ: Rutgers University Press.

Levinson, M. (2007) "What Is New Formalism?" *PMLA* 122.2: 558–69.

Lévi-Strauss, C. (1963) *Structural Anthropology*, translated by C. Jacobson and B. G. Schoepf. New York: Basic Books.

Librett, J. S. (ed.) (1993) *Of the Sublime: Presence in Question*, translated by J. S. Librett. New York: State University of New York Press.

Liu, A. (1989a) "The Power of Formalism: The New Historicism," *ELH* 56: 721–71.

——(1989b) *Wordsworth: The Sense of History*. Stanford, CA: Stanford University Press.

——(2004) *The Laws of Cool: Knowledge Work and the Culture of Information*. Chicago: University of Chicago Press.

Lockman, Z. (2009) *Contending Visions of the Middle East: The History and Politics of Orientalism*. Cambridge, UK: Cambridge University Press.

Loesberg, J. (2005) *A Return to Aesthetics: Autonomy, Indifference, and Postmodernism*. Stanford, CA: Stanford University Press.

Loizeaux, E. B. and N. Fraistat (eds) (2002) *Reimagining Textuality: Textual Studies in the Late Age of Print*. Madison: University of Wisconsin Press.

Loomba, A. (2005) *Colonialism/Postcolonialism*, second edition. London and New York: Routledge.

Loomba, A., S. Kaul, M. Bunzl, A. Burton, and J. Esty (eds) (2005) *Postcolonial Studies and Beyond*. Durham: Duke University Press.

Luft, S. and S. Overgaard (eds) (2012) *The Routledge Companion to Phenomenology*. London and New York: Routledge.

Lukács, G. (1968) *History and Class Consciousness: Studies in Marxist Dialectics*, translated by R. Livingstone. Cambridge, MA: MIT Press.

——(1977) "Realism in the Balance," translated by R. Taylor, in R. Taylor (ed.), *Aesthetics and Politics*. London: Verso (1980).

Lynch, K. (1960) *The Image of the City*. Cambridge, MA: MIT Press.

Lyotard, J.-F. (1988a) *The Differend: Phrases in Dispute*, translated by G. V. D. Abbeele, *Theory and History of Literature* 46. Minneapolis: University of Minnesota Press.

——(1988b) *Peregrinations: Law, Form, Event*. New York: Columbia University Press.

——(1991) *The Postmodern Condition: A Report on Knowledge*, translated by G. Bennington and B. Massumi, *Theory and History of Literature* 10. Minneapolis: University of Minnesota Press.

——(1993) *Toward the Post-Modern*, edited by R. Harvey and M. S. Roberts. Atlantic Highlands, NJ: Humanities Press.

——(1994) *Lessons on the Analytic of the Sublime*, translated by E. Rottenberg. Stanford, CA: Stanford University Press.

Lyotard, J.-F. and J.-L. Thébaud (1985) *Just Gaming*, translated by W. Godzich, *Theory and History of Literature* 20. Minneapolis: University of Minnesota Press.

Machor, J. L. and P. Goldstein (eds) (2001) *Reception Study: From Literary Theory to Cultural Studies*. London and New York: Routledge.

Malik, K. (1996) *The Meaning of Race: Race, History and Culture in Western Society*. New York: New York University Press.

Mandel, E. (1972) *Marxist Economic Theory*. London: Merlin.

——(1978) *Late Capitalism*, translated by Joris De Bres. London: Verso.

Mannheim, K. (1936) *Ideology and Utopia: An Introduction to the Sociology of Knowledge*, translated by L. Wirth and E. Shils. San Diego, CA: Harcourt, Brace, Jovanovich.

Mannoni, O. (1969) *"Je sais bien, mais quand même ... ,"* Clefs pour l'imaginaire ou l'autre scène. Paris: Éditions du Seuil, pp. 9–33.

Marx, K. (1867) *Capital: A Critique of Political Economy*, vol. 1, translated by B. Fowkes. New York: Penguin (1990).

——(1973) *Grundrisse*, edited and translated by M. Nicolaus. Harmondsworth, UK: Penguin.

Marx, K. and F. Engels (1848) *Manifesto of the Communist Party*, in *Marx*, *Great Books of the Western World*, vol. 50, ed. R. M. Hutchins. Chicago: William Benton (1952), pp. 413–34 .

——(1932) *The German Ideology Part One, with Selections from Parts Two and Three, together with Marx's "Introduction to a Critique of Political Economy."* New York: International Publishers (2001).

——(1962) *Selected Works*, 2 volumes. Moscow: Foreign Languages Publishing House.

Marx, L. (1964) *The Machine in the Garden: Technology and the Pastoral Ideal in America*. Oxford, UK: Oxford University Press.

Masschelein, A. (2011) *The Unconcept: The Freudian Uncanny in Late-Twentieth-Century Theory*. Albany, NY: State University of New York Press.

Mauss, M. (1979) *Sociology and Psychology: Essays*, translated by Ben Brewster. London: Routledge and Kegan Paul.

Maynard, P. and S. Feagin (eds) (1997) *Aesthetics: An Oxford Reader*. Oxford, UK: Oxford University Press.

McCallum, E. L. and M. Tuhkanen (eds) (2011) *Queer Times, Queer Becomings*. Albany, NY: State University of New York Press.

McGann, J. (1983a) *A Critique of Modern Textual Criticism*. Chicago: University of Chicago Press.

——(1983b) *The Romantic Ideology: A Critical Investigation*. Chicago: University of Chicago Press.

——(1985a) *The Beauty of Inflections: Literary Investigations in Historical Method and Theory*. Oxford, UK: Clarendon Press.

——(1985b) *Textual Criticism and Literary Interpretation*. Chicago: University of Chicago Press.

——(2001) *Radiant Textuality: Literature after the World Wide Web*. Houndsmills, UK and New York: Palgrave.

——(2002) "Prologue: Compu[e]ting Editorial Fu[ea]tures," in E. B. Loizeaux and N. Fraistat (eds), *Reimagining Textuality: Textual Studies in the Late Age of Print.* Madison: University of Wisconsin Press.

——(2004) "Marking Texts of Many Dimensions," in S. Schreibman, R. Siemens, and J. Unsworth (eds), *A Companion to Digital Humanities.* Malden, MA and Oxford, UK: Blackwell.

——(2013) "Information Technology and the Troubled Humanities," in M. Terras, J. Nyhan, and E. Vanhoutte (eds), *Defining Digital Humanities: A Reader.* Farnham, UK and Burlington, VT: Ashgate, pp. 49–65.

Meillassoux, Q. (2008) *After Finitude: An Essay on the Necessity of Contingency,* translated by R. Brassier. London: Continuum.

Mellor, A. (2014) "On the Publication of Mary Wollstonecraft's *A Vindication of the Rights of Woman,*" in D. F. Felluga (ed.) *BRANCH: Britain, Representation and Nineteenth-Century History,* Web (http://branchcollective.org – accessed 7 September 2014).

Melville, S. and B. Readings (eds) (1995) *Vision and Textuality.* Durham: Duke University Press.

Merleau-Ponty, M. (2004) *Basic Writings,* edited by Thomas Baldwin. London and New York: Routledge.

Meyer, M. (ed.) (1994) *The Politics and Poetics of Camp.* London and New York: Routledge.

Mies, M. (1986) *Patriarchy and Accumulation on a World Scale: Women in the International Division of Labour.* London: Zed Books.

Mignolo, W. D. (2000) *Local Histories/Global Designs: Coloniality, Subaltern Knowledges, and Border Thinking.* Princeton, NJ: Princeton University Press.

Milgram, S. (1974) *Obedience to Authority: An Experimental View.* New York: Harper Torchbooks.

Miller, D. A. (1981) *Narrative and Its Discontents: Problems of Closure in the Traditional Novel.* Princeton, NJ: Princeton University Press.

——(1988) *The Novel and the Police.* Berkeley, CA: University of California Press.

Miller, J.-A. (1977) "Suture (Elements of the Logic of the Signifier)," *Screen* 18.4: 24–34.

Miller, J. H. (1977) "The Critic as Host," *Critical Inquiry* 3.3: 439–47.

——(1985) *The Linguistic Moment: From Wordsworth to Stevens.* Princeton, NJ: Princeton University Press.

——(1991) *Theory Now and Then.* Durham: Duke University Press.

——(1992) *Illustration.* Cambridge, MA: Harvard University Press.

——(1995) *Topographies.* Stanford, CA: Stanford University Press.

——(1999) *Black Holes.* Stanford, CA: Stanford University Press.

——(2001) *Speech Acts in Literature.* Stanford, CA: Stanford University Press.

Miller, P. and N. Rose (2008) *Governing the Present: Administering Economic, Social and Personal Life.* Cambridge, UK: Polity Press.

Milton, J. (1674) *Paradise Lost,* in M. Y. Hughes (ed.), *Complete Poems and Major Prose.* New York: Macmillan (1957).

Mittelman, J. H. (ed.) (1996) *Globalization: Critical Reflections.* Boulder, CO and London, UK: Lynne Rienner Publishers.

Moghadam, V. M. (ed.) (1996) *Patriarchy and Economic Development: Women's Positions at the end of the Twentieth Century*. Oxford, UK and New York: Clarendon Press.

Mommsen, W. J. (1980) *Theories of Imperialism*, translated by P. S. Falla. Chicago: University of Chicago Press.

Moretti, F. (2005) *Graphs, Maps, Trees: Abstract Models for Literary History*. London and New York: Verso.

——(2013) *Distant Reading*. London and New York: Verso.

Morton, T. (2007) *Ecology without Nature: Rethinking Environmental Aesthetics*. Cambridge, MA: Harvard University Press.

Mouffe, C. (2005) *On the Political*. London and New York: Routledge.

Mulvey, L. (1989) *Visual and Other Pleasures*. Bloomington: Indiana University Press.

Murray, J. H. (2000) *Hamlet on the Holodeck: The Future of Narrative in Cyberspace*. Cambridge, MA: MIT Press.

Nancy, J.-L. (1991) "Introduction," in E. Cadava, P. Connor, and J.-L. Nancy (eds), *Who Comes after the Subject?* London and New York: Routledge.

Nealon, C. (2001) *Foundlings: Lesbian and Gay Historical Emotion before Stonewall*. Durham: Duke University Press.

Negri, A. (2008a) *Empire and Beyond*, translated by E. Emery. Cambridge, UK and Malden, MA: Polity.

——(2008b) *Reflections on Empire*, translated by E. Emery. Cambridge, UK and Malden, MA: Polity.

Nelson, C. and L. Grossberg (eds) (1988) *Marxism and the Interpretation of Culture*. Urbana: University of Illinois Press.

Nkrumah, K. (1965) *Neo-Colonialism: The Last State of Imperialism*, African Writers Series 49. London, Ibadan and Nairobi: Heinemann Educational Books (1968).

Ollman, B. (1993) *Dialectical Investigations*. London and New York: Routledge.

Olson, G. A. and L. Worsham (eds) (1999) *Race, Rhetoric, and the Postcolonial*. New York: State University of New York Press.

Ong, W. J. (1982) *Orality and Literacy: The Technologizing of the Word*. London: Methuen.

Orr, M. (2003) *Intertextuality: Debates and Contexts*. Cambridge, UK and Malden, MA: Polity Press.

Padva, G. and N. Buchweitz (eds) (2014) *Sensational Pleasures in Cinema, Literature and Visual Culture: The Phallic Eye*. New York and Houndmills, UK: Palgrave Macmillan.

Peirce, C. S. (1960) *Collected Papers of Charles Sanders Peirce*, 8 volumes, edited by C. Hartshorne and P. Weiss. Cambridge, MA: Belknap Press.

——(1991) *Peirce on Signs*, edited by James Hoopes. Chapel Hill and London: University of Carolina Press.

Penny, J. (2006) *The World of Perversion: Psychoanalysis and the Impossible Absolute of Desire*. Albany, NY: State University of New York Press.

Pinker, S. (1997) *How the Mind Works*. New York: Norton.

Plotz, J. (2005) "Can the Sofa Speak? A Look at Thing Theory," *Criticism* 47: 109–18.

Pollock, S., H. Bhabha, C. Breckenridge, and D. Chakrabarty (2000) "Cosmopolitanisms," *Public Culture* 12.3: 577–89.

Poulet, G. (1956) *Studies in Human Time*, translated by E. Coleman. New York: Harper & Brothers (1959).

——(1959) *The Interior Distance*, translated by E. Coleman. Ann Arbor: University of Michigan Press (1964).

Pratt, M. L. (1977) *Toward a Speech Act Theory of Literary Discourse*. Bloomington: Indiana University Press.

——(1991) "Arts of the Contact Zone," *Profession* 1991: 33–40.

——(1992) *Imperial Eyes: Travel Writing and Transculturation*. London and New York: Routledge.

Prince, G. (1982) *Narratology: The Form and Functioning of Narrative*. Berlin: Mouton.

——(2003) *A Dictionary of Narratology*, revised edition. Lincoln, NB: University of Nebraska Press.

Propp, V. (1968) *Morphology of the Folktale*, revised second edition, edited by L. A. Wagner, translated by L. Scott. Austin, TX: University of Texas Press.

Radway, J. A. (1997) *The Book-of-the-Month Club, Literary Taste, and Middle-Class Desire*. Chapel Hill: University of North Carolina Press.

Ramsay, S. (2011) *Reading Machines: Toward an Algorithmic Criticism*. Urbana: University of Illinois Press.

Rancière, J. (1999) *Disagreement: Politics and Philosophy*, translated by J. Rose. Minneapolis: University of Minnesota Press.

——(2004) *The Politics of Aesthetics*, translated by G. Rockhill. London: Continuum.

——(2010) *Dissensus: On Politics and Aesthetics*, edited and translated by S. Corcoran. London: Continuum.

Ranke, L. von (1981) *The Secret of World History: Selected Writings on the Art and Science of History*, edited by R. Wines. New York: Fordham University Press.

Ransom, J. C. (1941) *The New Criticism*. Norfolk, CT: New Directions.

Redfield, M. (1996) *Phantom Formations: Aesthetic Ideology and the Bildungsroman*. Ithaca, NY: Cornell University Press.

Rich, A. (1980) "Compulsory Heterosexuality and Lesbian Existence," in *Blood, Bread, and Poetry: Selected Prose, 1979–1985*. New York and London: Norton (1986).

Ricoeur, P. (1970) *Freud and Philosophy: An Essay on Interpretation*, translated by D. Savage. New Haven, CT: Yale University Press.

——(1981) *Hermeneutics and the Human Sciences: Essays on Language, Action and Interpretation*, edited and translated by J. B. Thompson. Cambridge, UK: Cambridge University Press.

——(1984) *Time and Narrative*, volume 1, translated by K. McLaughlin and D. Pellauer. Chicago: University of Chicago Press.

——(1985) *Time and Narrative*, volume 2, translated by K. McLaughlin and D. Pellauer. Chicago: University of Chicago Press.

——(1986) *Lectures on Ideology and Utopia*, edited by G. H. Taylor. New York: Columbia University Press.

——(1988) *Time and Narrative*, volume 3, translated by K. Blamey and D. Pellauer. Chicago: University of Chicago Press.

——(1991) *A Ricoeur Reader: Reflection and Imagination*, edited by M. J. Valdés. Toronto and Buffalo: University of Toronto Press.

——(1992) *Oneself as Another*, translated by K. Blamey. Chicago: University of Chicago Press.

Riffaterre, M. (1978) *Semiotics of Poetry*. Bloomington: Indiana University Press.

——(1990) *Fictional Truth*. Baltimore, MD: Johns Hopkins University Press.

Robbins, B. (1999) *Feeling Global: Internationalism in Distress*. New York and London: New York University Press.

——(2012) *Perpetual War: Cosmopolitanism from the Viewpoint of Violence*. Durham: Duke University Press.

Ronell, A. (1989) *The Telephone Book: Technology—Schizophrenia—Electric Speech*. Lincoln, NB and London: University of Nebraska Press.

——(1994) *Finitude's Score: Essays for the End of the Millenium*. Lincoln, NB and London, UK: University of Nebraska Press.

Rose, N. (1999) *Powers of Freedom: Reframing Political Thought*. Cambridge, UK: Cambridge University Press.

Rosenau, P. M. (ed.) (1992) *Post-Modernism and the Social Sciences: Insights, Inroads, and Intrusions*. Princeton, NJ: Princeton University Press.

Ryan, K. (ed.) (1996) *New Historicism and Cultural Materialism: A Reader*. London: Arnold.

Ryan, M.-L. (1999) *Cyberspace Textuality: Computer Technology and Literary Theory*. Bloomington: Indiana University Press.

——(2001) *Narrative as Virtual Reality: Immersion and Interactivity in Literature and Electronic Media*. Baltimore, MD: Johns Hopkins University Press.

Said, E. W. (1978) *Orientalism*. New York: Vintage.

——(1988) "Foreword," in R. Guha and G. C. Spivak (eds), *Selected Subaltern Studies*. Oxford, UK: Oxford University Press, pp. v–x.

Salecl, R. and S. Žižek (eds) (1996) *Gaze and Voice as Love Objects*. Durham and London: Duke University Press.

Saul, J. M. (2003) *Feminism: Issues and Arguments*. Oxford, UK: Oxford University Press.

Saussure, F. de. (1916) *Course in General Linguistics*, edited by C. Bally and A. Sechehaye, translated by W. Baskin. New York: McGraw-Hill (1966).

Schermerhorn, R. A. (1970) *Comparative Ethnic Relations: A Framework for Theory and Research*. New York: Random House.

Scholte, J. A. (1996) "Beyond the Buzzword: Towards a Critical Theory of Globalization," in E. Kofman and G. Youngs (eds), *Globalization: Theory and Practice*. London: Pinter.

Schreibman, S., R. Siemens, and J. Unsworth (eds) (2004) *A Companion to Digital Humanities*. Malden, MA and Oxford, UK: Blackwell.

Scott, A. (ed.) (1997) *The Limits of Globalization: Cases and Arguments*. London and New York: Routledge.

Scott, H. (2002) "Was There a Time before Race? Capitalist Modernity and the Origins of Racism," in C. Bartolovich and N. Lazarus (eds), *Marxism, Modernity, and Postcolonial Studies*. Cambridge, UK: Cambridge University Press, pp. 167–82.

Searle, J. R. (1969) *Speech Acts: An Essay in the Philosophy of Language.* Cambridge, UK: Cambridge University Press.

——(1979) *Expression and Meaning: Studies in the Theory of Speech Acts.* Cambridge, UK: Cambridge University Press.

Sedgwick, E. K. (1985) *Between Men: English Literature and Male Homosocial Desire.* New York: Columbia University Press.

——(1990) *Epistemology of the Closet.* Berkeley, CA: University of California Press.

——(1994) *Tendencies.* London and New York: Routledge.

——(2003) *Touching Feeling: Affect, Pedagogy, Performativity.* Durham: Duke University Press.

Serres, M. (1987) *Statues.* Paris: François Bourin.

Showalter, E. (ed.) (1985) *The New Feminist Criticism: Essays on Women, Literature, and Theory.* New York: Pantheon Books.

——(1987) *The Female Malady: Women, Madness, and English Culture, 1890–1980.* New York: Penguin.

——(ed.) (1989) *Speaking of Gender.* London and New York: Routledge.

——(1997) *Hystories: Hysterical Epidemics and Modern Culture.* New York: Columbia University Press.

Siewers, A. K. (ed.) (2014) *Re-Imagining Nature: Environmental Humanities and Ecosemiotics.* Lewisburg, PA: Bucknell University Press.

Silverman, H. J. (ed.) (1990) *Postmodernism—Philosophy and the Arts.* London and New York: Routledge.

Silverman, H. J. and G. E. Aylesworth (eds) (1990) *The Textual Sublime: Deconstruction and Its Differences.* New York: State University of New York Press.

Silverman, K. (1983) *The Subject of Semiotics.* Oxford, UK and New York: Oxford University Press.

——(1988) *The Acoustic Mirror: The Female Voice in Psychoanalysis and Cinema.* Bloomington: Indiana University Press.

Slipp, S. (1993) *The Freudian Mystique: Freud, Women, and Feminism.* New York: New York University Press.

Sokolowski, R. (2000) *Introduction to Phenomenology.* Cambridge, UK: Cambridge University Press.

Sontag, S. (1964) *Against Interpretation and Other Essays.* New York: Farrar, Straus and Giroux.

Spivak, G. C. (1985) "The Rani of Sirmur: An Essay in Reading the Archives," *History and Theory* 24.3: 247–72.

——(1987) *In Other Worlds: Essays in Cultural Politics.* New York: Methuen.

——(1988a) "Can the Subaltern Speak?" in C. Nelson and L. Grossberg (eds), *Marxism and the Interpretation of Culture.* Urbana: University of Illinois Press, pp. 271–313.

——(1988b) "Subaltern Studies: Deconstructing Historiography," in R. Guha and G. C. Spivak (eds), *Selected Subaltern Studies.* Oxford, UK: Oxford University Press, pp. 3–32.

Spolsky, E. (1993) *Gaps in Nature: Literary Interpretation and the Modular Mind.* New York: State University of New York Press.

Spolsky, E. and A. Richardson (eds) (2004) *The Work of Fiction: Cognition, Culture, and Complexity.* Aldershot, UK and Burlington, VT: Ashgate.

Stallybrass, P. and A. White (1986) *The Politics and Poetics of Transgression.* Ithaca, NY: Cornell University Press.

Stewart, G. (1990) *Reading Voices: Literature and the Phonotext.* Berkeley, CA: University of California Press.

——(2009) *Novel Violence: A Narratography of Victorian Fiction.* Chicago: University of Chicago Press.

Sturrock, J. (ed.) (1979) *Structuralism and Since: From Lévi-Strauss to Derrida.* Oxford, UK: Oxford University Press.

Suleiman, S. R. and I. Crosman (eds) (1980) *The Reader in the Text: Essays on Audience and Interpretation.* Princeton, NJ: Princeton University Press.

Swarr, A. L. and R. Nagar (eds) (2010) *Critical Transnational Feminist Praxis.* Albany, NY: State University of New York Press.

Tate, A. (1940) "Miss Emily and the Bibliographer," *The American Scholar* 9.4: 449–60.

Terras, M., J. Nyhane, and E. Vanhoutte (2013) *Defining Digital Humanities: A Reader.* Aldershot, UK and Burlington, VT: Ashgate.

Thiele, V. and L. Tredennick (eds) (2013) *New Formalisms and Literary Theory.* Houndmills, UK and New York: Palgrave Macmillan.

Thompson, J. B. (1981) *Critical Hermeneutics: A Study in the Thought of Paul Ricoeur and Jürgen Habermas.* Cambridge, UK: Cambridge University Press.

Tiffin, C. and A. Lawson (eds) (1994) *De-scribing Empire: Post-Colonialism and Textuality.* London and New York: Routledge.

Todorov, T. (1969) *Grammaire du Décaméron,* Approaches to Semiotics 3. The Hague: Mouton.

Tompkins, J. P. (ed.) (1980) *Reader Response Criticism: From Formalism to Post-Structuralism.* Baltimore, MD: Johns Hopkins University Press.

Touraine, A. (1971) *The Post-Industrial Society; Tomorrow's Social History: Classes, Conflicts and Culture in the Programmed Society,* translated by L. F. X. Mayhew. New York: Random House.

Tucker, H. F. (2006) "Tactical Formalism: A Response to Caroline Levine," *Victorian Studies* 49.1: 85–93.

Turner, B. S. (1994) *Orientalism, Postmodernism, and Globalism.* London and New York: Routledge.

Turner, M. (1991) *Reading Minds: The Study of English in the Age of Cognitive Science.* Princeton, NJ: Princeton University Press.

——(1996) *The Literary Mind: The Origins of Thought and Language.* Oxford, UK: Oxford University Press.

Ulmer, G. L. (1994) *Heuretics: The Logic of Invention.* Baltimore, MD: Johns Hopkins University Press.

Vattimo, G. (1988) *The End of Modernity: Nihilism and Hermeneutics in Postmodern Culture,* translated by J. R. Snyder. Cambridge, UK: Polity Press.

Veeser, H. A. (1989) "Introduction," in H. A. Veeser (ed.), *The New Historicism.* London and New York: Routledge.

Virilio, P. (1977) *Speed and Politics: An Essay on Dromology,* translated by M. Polizzotti. Los Angeles: Semiotext(e).

——(1989) *War and Cinema: The Logistics of Perception,* translated by P. Camiller. London and New York: Verso.

——(2008) *Negative Horizon: An Essay in Dromoscopy*, translated by M. Degener. London and New York: Continuum.

——(2010) *The Futurism of the Instant: Stop-Eject*, translated by J. Rose. Cambridge, UK and Malden, MA: Polity Press.

Wacquant, L. (2011) "Habitus as Topic and Tool: Reflections on Becoming a Prizefighter," *Qualitative Research in Psychology* 8: 81–92.

Walby, S. (1986) *Patriarchy at Work*. Cambridge, UK: Polity Press.

——(1990) *Theorising Patriarchy*. Oxford, UK: Blackwell.

Waters, M. (1995) *Globalization*. London and New York: Routledge.

Weber, M. (1921) "The Distribution of Power within the Community: Classes, *Stände*, Parties," translated by D. Waters, T. Waters, and E. Hahnke, *Journal of Classical Sociology* 10.2 (2010): 137–52.

——(1930) *The Protestant Ethic and the Spirit of Capitalism*, translated by T. Parsons. New York: Charles Scribner's Sons, and London: George Allen & Unwin.

Weiskel, T. (1976) *The Romantic Sublime: Studies in the Structure and Psychology of Transcendence*. Baltimore and London: Johns Hopkins University Press (1986).

Wellek, R. and A. Warren (1949) *Theory of Literature*, third revised edition. London, UK: Jonathan Cape (1966).

West, C. (1993) "The New Cultural Politics of Difference," in S. During (ed.), *The Cultural Studies Reader*. London and New York: Routledge, pp. 203–17.

——(1995) "Foreword," in K. Crenshaw, N. Gotanda, G. Peller, and K. Thomas (eds) *Critical Race Theory: The Key Writings That Formed the Movement*. New York: New Press, pp. xi–xii.

——(2001) *Race Matters*. New York: Vintage Books.

White, H. (1973) *Metahistory: The Historical Imagination in Nineteenth-Century Europe*. Baltimore, MD: Johns Hopkins University Press.

——(1978) *Tropics of Discourse: Essays in Cultural Criticism*. Baltimore, MD: Johns Hopkins University Press.

——(1987) *The Content of the Form: Narrative Discourse and Historical Representation*. Baltimore, MD: Johns Hopkins University Press.

——(1992) "Historical Emplotment and the Problems of Truth," in S. Friedlander (ed.), *Probing the Limits of Representation: Nazism and the "Final Solution."* Cambridge, MA: Harvard University Press.

Williams, R. (1958) *Culture and Society: 1780–1950*. New York: Columbia University Press (1983).

——(1961) *The Long Revolution*. London: Chato & Windus.

——(1973) *The Country and the City*. Oxford, UK: Oxford University Press (1975).

——(1977) *Marxism and Literature*. Oxford, UK: Oxford University Press.

——(1983) *Keywords: A Vocabulary of Culture and Society*, revised edition. New York: Oxford University Press.

——(1995) *The Sociology of Culture*. Chicago: University of Chicago Press.

Wilson, J., C. Sandru and S. L. Welsh (eds) (2010) *Rerouting the Postcolonial: New Directions for the New Millennium*. London and New York: Routledge.

Wimsatt, W. K. (1954) *The Verbal Icon: Studies in the Meaning of Poetry*. Lexington, KY: University of Kentucky Press.

Wimsatt, W. K. and M. C. Beardsley (1954) "The Intentional Fallacy," in W. K. Wimsatt, *The Verbal Icon: Studies in the Meaning of Poetry*. Lexington, KY: University of Kentucky, pp. 3–18.

Wittgenstein, L. (1958) *Philosophical Investigations*, second edition, translated by G. E. M. Anscombe. New York: Macmillan.

Wodak, R. (2001) "What CDA is about: A Summary of its History, Important Concepts and its Developments," in R. Wodak and M. Meyer (eds), *Methods of Critical Discourse Analysis*. London: Sage.

Wolfson, S. (1997) *Formal Charges: The Shaping of Poetry in British Romanticism*. Stanford, CA: Stanford University Press.

Wolfson, S. and M. Brown (eds) (2006) *Reading for Form*. Seattle: University of Washington Press.

Wollstonecraft, M. (1792) *A Vindication of the Rights of Woman*, edited by A. K. Mellor and N. Chao. New York: Pearson Longman (2007).

Young, R. E. (ed.) (1981) *Untying the Text: A Post-Structuralist Reader*. London: Routledge and Kegan Paul.

Youngquist, P. (2003) *Monstrosities: Bodies and British Romanticism*. Minneapolis: University of Minnesota Press.

Zimbardo, P. (2007) *The Lucifer Effect: Understanding How Good People Turn Evil*. New York: Random House.

Zinn, H. (1999) *A People's History of the United States: 1492-present*, 20th anniversary edition. New York: HarperCollins.

Žižek, S. (1989) *The Sublime Object of Ideology*. London: Verso.

——(1991a) *For They Know Not What They Do: Enjoyment as a Political Factor*. London: Verso.

——(1991b) *Looking Awry: An Introduction to Jacques Lacan through Popular Culture*. Cambridge, MA: MIT Press.

——(1992a) *Enjoy your Symptom! Jacques Lacan in Hollywood and Out*. London and New York: Routledge.

——(ed.) (1992b) *Everything You Always Wanted to Know about Lacan (but Were Afraid to Ask Hitchcock)*. London: Verso.

——(1993) *Tarrying with the Negative: Kant, Hegel, and the Critique of Ideology*. Durham: Duke University Press.

——(1994) *The Metastases of Enjoyment: Six Essays on Woman and Causality*. London and New York: Verso.

——(1997) *The Plague of Fantasies*. London and New York: Verso.

——(1999) *The Ticklish Subject: The Absent Centre of Political Ontology*. London and New York: Verso.

——(2001) *Did Someone Say Totalitarianism? Five Interventions in the (Mis)Use of a Notion*. London and New York: Verso.

——(2008) *In Defense of Lost Causes*. London and New York: Verso.

——(2012) *Less than Nothing: Hegel and the Shadow of Dialectical Materialism*. London and New York: Verso.

Zunshine, L. (2006) *Why We Read Fiction: Theory of Mind and the Novel*. Columbus: Ohio State University Press.

——(ed.) (2010) *Introduction to Cognitive Cultural Studies*. Baltimore, MD: Johns Hopkins University Press.

Zupančič, A. (2000) *Ethics of the Real: Kant, Lacan*. London and New York: Verso.

INDEX

abject **3–5**, 116, 158, 246–47
Actor-Network Theory (ANT) **5–8**;
  and articulation 19–20; and
  assemblage 14, 21, 24; and
  blackboxing 33–34; and hybridity
  141; and mediators 174–75; quasi-
  objects and quasi-subjects 223; and
  speculative realism 284; and things
  313–14
Adorno, Theodor xvii, 10, 65, 68, 77
aesthetics **8–13**; and abject 4–5;
  aesthetics of existence xv–xvi;
  literarity 167–68; *see also*
  inaesthetic; literarity
Agamben, Giorgio 137; apparatus
  16–17; bare life and *homo sacer*
  24–27; bio-politics and bio-power
  191; coming community 60;
  government 122; nation-state x;
  state of exception 290–92
agency **13–14**, 82, 214, 278, 310; *see
  also* author; subject; text and
  textuality
alienation **15**
Althusser, Louis 196, 242; ideology
  147–51, 172, 243–44, 277, 299;
  Ideological State Apparatuses
  128–29, 143–45, 185;
  interpellation 89, 299
anal-sadistic phase **15**, 41, 180,
  246–47
Anderson, Benedict 186
antagonism **15–16**, 137
Apel, Karl Otto 87
apparatus **16**, 122
archaeology xi, **17–18**, 85, 136–37
arche-writing *see* phonocentrism
Armstrong, Isobel 10, 13, 195

articulation 16, **19–20**
assemblage and Assemblage Theory
  6–7, 14, **20–22**, 24
Aura **22**
Austin, J. L. 213–14, 288–90
author xiv–xv, **22–24**, 82, 310
auto-ethnography *see* contact zone
  and transculturation

Badiou, Alain 28–30, 153–54, 170,
  176–78, 203
Bakhtin, Mikhail 14, 262, 281;
  carnivalesque 39; chronotope 42,
  184; dialogism 77–78, 157; ethics
  203; heteroglossia 132; parody
  209–10; polyphony 222
Balibar, Étienne 186
bare life and *homo sacer* **24–27**, 191,
  291
Barthes, Roland: author 23–24;
  culture 67, 161, 185, 276;
  discourse 86; hermeneutic and
  proiaretic codes 130, 184–85, 262;
  reading 261–62; semiotics 161,
  276; subjectivity 298
base and superstructure **27–28**,
  143–44, 265–66
Bate, Jonathan 96–97
Baudrillard, Jean: kitsch 158–59;
  postmodernism 228–31;
  postmodernity 234–35; simulation
  65, 282–84
being and event **28–30**, 178
Bell, Daniel 161
Benjamin, Walter: aesthetics 9; aura
  22; culture 65; historical
  materialism 134, 136, 184, 223
Bennett, Lerone 257